To Neha,

With respect and admiration,

Sep 25, 2016

Sangkul.

International Criminal Justice Series

Volume 7

Series editors

Gerhard Werle, Berlin, Germany
Lovell Fernandez, Bellville, South Africa
Moritz Vormbaum, Berlin, Germany

Series Information

The *International Criminal Justice Series* aims to create a platform for publications in the whole field of international criminal justice. It, therefore, deals with issues relating, among others, to:

– the work of international criminal courts and tribunals;
– transitional justice approaches in different countries;
– international anti-corruption and anti-money laundering initiatives;
– the history of international criminal law.

The series concentrates on themes pertinent to developing countries. It is peer-reviewed and seeks to publish high-quality works emanating from excellent scholars, in particular from African countries.

Editorial Office

Prof. Dr. Gerhard Werle
Humboldt-Universität zu Berlin
Faculty of Law
Unter den Linden 6,
10099 Berlin, Germany
gerhard.werle@rewi.hu-berlin.de
moritz.vormbaum@rewi.hu-berlin.de

More information about this series at http://www.springer.com/series/13470

Sangkul Kim

A Collective Theory of Genocidal Intent

Sangkul Kim
Law School
Korea University
Seoul
South Korea (Republic of Korea)

ISSN 2352-6718   ISSN 2352-6726 (electronic)
International Criminal Justice Series
ISBN 978-94-6265-122-7   ISBN 978-94-6265-123-4   (eBook)
DOI 10.1007/978-94-6265-123-4

Library of Congress Control Number: 2016934677

Published by T.M.C. ASSER PRESS, The Hague, The Netherlands www.asserpress.nl
Produced and distributed for T.M.C. ASSER PRESS by Springer-Verlag Berlin Heidelberg

Printed on acid-free paper

This Springer imprint is published by Springer Nature
The registered company is Springer Science+Business Media B.V. Dordrecht

To Nayoung

Acknowledgments

This book stems from my doctoral research at Georgetown University Law Center. I deeply thank my dissertation committee members: Pros. David Luban, Julie O'Sullivan, and Neha Jain. My supervisor, Prof. David Luban, has provided me with unwavering support and encouragement for almost 15 years from the days of my master's study. Without him, this book would have never existed.

I thank dean Nan Hunter and director Alexa Freeman for our wonderful S.J.D. program at Georgetown Law. I also remember our former librarian Jill L. Thomson-Riese's kindness.

I am grateful to Profs. Lyou Byung-Hwa, Sang-Hyun Song, Tae Hyun Choi, Ki-Gab Park, Nohyung Park, Pyoungkeun Kang, Joongi Kim and Young Sok Kim for their continuing guidance and invaluable advice.

I thank Morten Bergsmo, Céclile Tournaye, Kil Su Choi, Jaemin Lee, Jong In Bae, Enrique Carnero-Rojo, and David Krivanek for their gentle friendship. Especially, I deeply appreciate my friend Morten's trust in me from the days when we worked together at the Legal Advisory Section of the ICC-OTP. It was an honor that Prof. M. Cherif Bassiouni read my manuscript and provided me with insightful comments. I hereby express my sincere gratitude to him.

It has been a great pleasure to work with members of the T.M.C. Asser Press, especially with my editor Mr. Frank Bakker. I also thank the editors of the International Criminal Justice Series: Profs. Gerhard Werle and Lovell Fernandez, and Dr. Moritz Vormbaum. It is indeed my privilege to publish this book in the series.

I fully trust that Lorenzo Pugliatti will soon recover from his illness and return back to the ICC-OTP. I am also confident that Leena Grover's habilitation will be a groundbreaking work.

I deeply thank my parents, Dong Ung Kim and Young Ja Kim, and my sister, Sung Min Kim, for their enduring love.

My wife, Nayoung Ahn, and my son, Jihoon, have been a source of inspiration, comfort, and happiness. I cannot thank Nayoung and Jihoon enough.

I cherish the memory of September 2004 when my friend, the late Hong-keun Yoo visited The Hague as a member of the Korean delegation to the 3rd ICC-ASP.

And it came to pass, that, when the sun went down, and it was dark, behold a smoking furnace, and a burning lamp that passed between those pieces.

Genesis 15: 17 (KJV)

For my thoughts are not your thoughts, neither are your ways my ways, saith the LORD. For as the heavens are higher than the earth, so are my ways higher than your ways, and my thoughts than your thoughts.

Isaiah 55: 8–9 (KJV)

Because the foolishness of God is wiser than men; and the weakness of God is stronger than men.

1 Corinthians 1: 25 (KJV)

Contents

Chapter 1
Introduction

Contents

They said in their hearts, Let us destroy them together: they have burned up all the syna-
gogues of God in the land. We see not our signs: there is no more any prophet: neither
is there among us any that knoweth how long. O God, how long shall the adversary
reproach? shall the enemy blaspheme thy name for ever? Why withdrawest thou thy hand,
even thy right hand? pluck it out of thy bosom. For God is my King of old, working salva-
tion in the midst of the earth. Thou didst divide the sea by thy strength: thou brakest the
heads of the dragons in the waters. Thou brakest the heads of leviathan in pieces, and gav-
est him to be meat to the people inhabiting the wilderness. Thou didst cleave the fountain
and the flood: thou driedst up mighty rivers. The day is thine, the night also is thine: thou
hast prepared the light and the sun. Thou hast set all the borders of the earth: thou hast
made summer and winter. Remember this, that the enemy hath reproached, O LORD, and
that the foolish people have blasphemed thy name. O deliver not the soul of thy turtledove
unto the multitude of the wicked: forget not the congregation of thy poor for ever. Have
respect unto the covenant: for the dark places of the earth are full of the habitations of
cruelty. O let not the oppressed return ashamed: let the poor and needy praise thy name.
Arise, O God, plead thine own cause: remember how the foolish man reproacheth thee
daily. Forget not the voice of thine enemies: the tumult of those that rise up against thee
increaseth continually.

Psalms 74: 8-23 (KJV).

The psalmist records that the adversaries say in "their hearts" that "let us
destroy them together". This book explores such a collective mindset of perpetrators of genocide. Grasping the essence of genocide as its collective criminality,
this book seeks to develop a collective theory of genocidal intent beyond its individualistic understandings that thus far have governed the relevant discussions
amongst jurists and scholars. Article II of the 1948 Convention on the Prevention
and Punishment of the Crime of Genocide ("Genocide Convention"),[1] the wording

---

[1] Convention on the Prevention and Punishment of the Crime of Genocide, 9 December 1948, 78
U.N.T.S. 277.

© T.M.C. ASSER PRESS and the author 2016
S. Kim, *A Collective Theory of Genocidal Intent*, International Criminal
Justice Series 7, DOI 10.1007/978-94-6265-123-4_1

of which has been adopted *in verbatim* by the statutes of international criminal courts such as the International Criminal Court (hereinafter ICC), International Criminal Tribunal for the Former Yugoslavia (hereinafter ICTY), International Criminal Tribunal for Rwanda (hereinafter ICTR) and Extraordinary Chambers of the Courts of Cambodia (hereinafter ECCC),[2] provides,

Genocide means any of the following acts committed with intent to destroy, in whole or in part, a national, ethnical, racial or religious group, as such:

(a) Killing members of the group;
(b) Causing serious bodily or mental harm to members of the group;
(c) Deliberately inflicting on the group conditions of life calculated to bring about its physical destruction in whole or in part;
(d) Imposing measures intended to prevent births within the group;
(e) Forcibly transferring children of the group to another group.

It is the wording "with intent to destroy" in the chapeau part above that is referred to by such terms as 'genocidal intent', 'special intent', 'specific intent' or '*dolus specialis*'. These terms are generally used interchangeably.[3] Being treated as a unique mental element,[4] it is often said that genocidal intent is the essence of the crime definition of genocide. At the same time, genocidal intent has been the source of confusion and difficulties in applying the definition of the crime of genocide to actual cases. First of all, as to the peculiar *mens rea* of "with intent to destroy"—i.e., genocidal intent—a difficulty arises that, on its face, this mental element appears to be too onerous to accurately characterize the mental state of many perpetrators. Not only the term 'intent' but also the content of this mental element contained in the phrase 'with intent to destroy, in whole or in part, a national, ethnical, racial or religious group, as such' connote something too overwhelming for ordinary people generally used as a tool to commit core international crimes to harbor. At this juncture, a comparison with crimes against humanity and war crimes is instructive. For these two crimes, apart from the

---

[2] Rome Statute of the International Criminal Court, 17 July 1998, 2187 U.N.T.S. 90; Statute of the International Criminal Tribunal for the Former Yugoslavia, 25 May 1993, 32 I.L.M. 1192; Statute of the International Criminal Tribunal for Rwanda, 8 November 1994, 33 I.L.M. 1598; Agreement Between the United Nations and the Royal Government of Cambodia Concerning the Prosecution Under Cambodian Law of Crimes Committed During the Period of Democratic Kampuchea, 6 June 2003, 2329 U.N.T.S. 117.

[3] Amongst these terms, the term 'genocidal intent' will be used to represent the phrase "with intent to destroy" for the purpose of this book.

[4] For the purpose of this book, the term 'mental element', 'subjective element' and '*mens rea*' will be used interchangeably. In addition, the term 'material element', 'objective element' and '*actus reus*' will also be used interchangeably.

mental elements attending the material elements of specific offences,[5] the only mental element required for the Prosecution to prove is 'knowledge' vis-à-vis the objective contextual element of 'a widespread or systematic attack' or 'an armed conflict'.[6] In view of the spectrum of potential perpetrators, from the physical perpetrators at the actual crime scene to the political and/or military leaders masterminding the campaign of atrocities from behind closed doors, requiring this mental element of 'knowledge' of an attack or an armed conflict totally makes sense: it is not legally acceptable to hold a person lacking such knowledge criminally responsible either for a crime against humanity or a war crime. By contrast, from the standpoint of direct perpetrators such as those ordinary Hutu civilians suddenly taking machetes to kill their Tutsi neighbors in Rwanda or foot soldiers carrying the barrels of poisonous gas at Auschwitz, the genocidal intent element as it is phrased in the Genocide Convention and other international instruments might well be something they had never heard of, let alone thought of themselves.[7] In this respect, one might argue that an actual implication of applying the genocidal intent element would be to make it virtually impossible to punish the ordinary Hutu civilians and the German foot soldiers for the crime of genocide. Is genocide a crime only applicable to those actors at the leadership level?

---

[5] Under the ICC law, mental elements corresponding to material elements of a specific offence can be categorized into two groups: (i) general mental elements of 'intent' and/or 'knowledge' as provided in Article 30 of the ICC Statute in respect of material elements of 'conduct', 'consequence' and 'circumstance'; and (ii) special mental elements as specifically provided in the ICC Elements of Crimes pursuant to the second item of para 7 of the General Introduction thereof (stating, "[w]hen required, a particular mental element is listed after the affected conduct, consequence or circumstance".). Report of the Preparatory Comm'n for the Int'l Criminal Court, Finalized Draft Text of the Elements of Crimes, Article 6, U.N. Doc. PCNICC/2000/1/Add.2, 2 November 2000 [hereinafter ICC Elements of Crimes or Elements of Crimes]. Some examples falling into the group (ii) are: "The perpetrator knew, or should have known, that the person or persons were under the age of 18 years". (Article 6(e) Genocide by forcibly transferring children); "The perpetrator knew or should have known that such person or persons were under the age of 15 years". (Article 8(2)(b)(xxvi) War crime of using, conscripting or enlisting children); "The perpetrator knew that the conduct could result in death or serious personal injury". (Article 8(2)(b)(vii)-1 War crime of improper use of a flag or truce); "The perpetrator knew of the prohibited nature of such use". (Article 8(2)(b)(vii)-3 War crime of improper use of a flag, insignia or uniform of the United Nations).

[6] Note that, in the case of the ICC law, intent can also constitute the mental element for the contextual element of crimes against humanity, as seen from the Elements of Crimes that states, "[t]he perpetrator know that the conduct was part of or *intended* the conduct to be part of a widespread or systematic attack against a civilian population". (emphasis added). Note also, however, that the crime definition in the ICC Statute itself refers only to the knowledge. *See* the phrase "with knowledge of the attack" in the chapeau of Article 7(1) of the ICC Statute.

[7] Such was the defense that Karadžić presented on the issue of physical perpetrators' genocidal intent. *See* Prosecutor v. Karadžić, Transcript, 11 June 2012, at 28594 (During the Rule 98*bis* hearing, Karadžić states, "[t]he repenting perpetrators who admitted to the killings of prisoners of war confirmed that the thought never crossed their minds of exterminating Muslims as a group".). *See also* Chap. 4, footnotes 243 and 244 *infra* and accompanying text.

In the first judgment convicting the accused of the crime of genocide (as an
aider and abettor) rendered by the ICTY, the Appeals Chamber in *Krstić* observes,

> Genocide is one of the worst crimes known to humankind, and its gravity is reflected in
> the stringent requirement of specific intent. Convictions for genocide can be entered only
> where that intent has been unequivocally established.[8]

It is not exaggerating to say that the legitimacy of convicting a person of genocide, which has been commonly considered the 'crime of crimes',[9] depends upon
an establishment of a sole legal element—i.e., the element of genocidal intent.[10]
What is emphasized by the ICTY Appeals Chamber in *Krstić* as quoted above is
that this element should be "strictly construed"[11] because it signals the unparal-
leled gravity and blameworthiness of the 'crime of crimes'.[12] In the same vein, it
has been generally understood that the concept of genocidal intent exists right in
the center of the legal definition of the crime of genocide, characterizing the nature
of the crime itself as a 'crime of *mens rea*'.[13] At the same time, though often

---

[8] Prosecutor v. Krstić, Appeals Judgment, 19 April 2004, para 134. See also, *Ibid.*, para 37 ("The
gravity of genocide is reflected in the stringent requirements which must be satisfied before this
conviction is imposed. These requirements – the demanding proof of specific intent and the
showing that the group was targeted for destruction in its entirety or in substantial part – guard
against a danger that convictions for this crime will be imposed lightly".).

[9] The expression "crime of crimes" was first used by Raphael Lemkin who coined the term
'genocide'. Lemkin 1948, p. 70 ("Indeed, genocide must be treated as the most heinous of all
crimes. It is the crime of crimes, one that not only shocks our conscience but affects deeply the
best interests of mankind".). Mr. Bakuramusta representing Rwanda also used the term "crime
of crimes" during a U.N. Security Council meeting discussing the establishment of the ICTR.
U.N. Doc. S/PV.3453, 8 November 1994, at 15. *See also* Prosecutor v. Musema, Trial Judgment,
27 January 2000, para 981 ("crime of crimes"); Dunér 2004, p. 221 ("the worst of all crimes");
D'Amato 2000, p. 121 ("the world's most heinous crime").

[10] *See, e.g.,* Prosecutor v. Krstić, Appeals Judgment, 19 April 2004, para 32 ("In determining
that genocide occurred at Srebrenica, the cardinal question is whether the intent to commit genocide existed".).

[11] Article 22(2) of the ICC Statute is applicable not only to genocide but also to other crimes
under the statute. It provides, "[t]he definition of a crime shall be strictly construed and shall not
be extended by analogy. In case of ambiguity, the definition shall be interpreted in favour of the
person being investigated, prosecuted or convicted".

[12] *See* Prosecutor v. Krstić, Appeals Judgment, 19 April 2004, para 36 ("Among the grievous
crimes this Tribunal has the duty to punish, the crime of genocide is singled out for special con-
demnation and opprobrium".).

[13] During the seventh meeting of the Ad Hoc Committee on Genocide in 1948, a representative
of France emphasized on the importance of taking note of the intention behind the physical acts
in order to determine whether the crime of genocide had been committed. It is noteworthy that he
made this point in connection with the involvement of a State. Intention in this context should be
viewed as a bigger concept than that of an individual. UNESC Ad Hoc Committee on Genocide:
Summary Record of the Seventh Meeting, at 8–9, UN Doc. E/AC.25/SR.7, 12 April 1948 ("One
element remained – the status of the author of the crime. Genocide could be committed by an
individual or by a group of individuals not connected with the State or without the intervention
of the State. It could also be committed at the instance and with the complicity of the State. In
that case the State itself could be considered guilty of the crime. [...] The crime committed by the
Nazis and Fascists had been committed by the State itself. Genocide [...] was dangerous precisely

overlooked in relevant academic discussions on the subject of genocidal intent, substantive legal thinking about selecting a mode of liability for the purpose of charging a person with the crime of genocide also hinges upon the way we interpret the concept of genocidal intent. Unfortunately, this concept is very elusive and there are differing approaches to interpreting it.[14] Moreover, the strong emphasis placed on the subjective aspect of the crime in the case of genocide by its own definition conflicts significantly with the common reality of core international crimes—i.e., an extensive context or scale of the criminal state of affairs. Within this context or scale, we can find every *objective* factual feature of mass atrocities such as perpetrators from all ranks, victims, specific criminal conducts, their consequences, system of persecution, plan or policy and material resources involved. As to the crime of genocide, however, it has been largely agreed that it is not primarily the *objective* fact such as conduct, consequence and/or circumstance that decide whether this particular international crime has been committed. Instead, at least in theory, it is said that a *subjective* state of mind of a person or a group of persons plays a pivotal role in determining whether genocide has taken place.

The primary issue behind all interpretative approaches to the 'intent to destroy' element proposed thus far is the conceptual scope of this *mens rea*. Some suggest that the scope should be restrictively circumscribed to the internal volition of an individual, while others say it can be extended to some degree by means of cognitive knowledge. The former position is generally referred to as the purpose-based approach and the latter the knowledge-based approach. Many scholars talk about the *intensity* or *degree* of intent. They also refer to such concepts of 'purpose/desire/aim (direct intent/*dolus directus* /*dolus directus in the first degree*)', 'knowledge (indirect intent/*dolus indirectus*/*dolus directus* in the second degree/oblique intent)', and 'recklessness (conditional intent/*dolus eventualis*)'.[15] More precisely, however, the hidden

---

Footnote 13 (continued)

because it was a crime committed with the complicity of the State, or made possible as a result of the default of a State. That was a determining factor".). *See* U.N. GAOR, 6th Comm., 3d Sess., 73d mtg. at 93, U.N. Doc. A/C.6/SR.73, 13 October 1948 (The Yugoslavian representative states, "the main characteristic of genocide lay in the intent to attack a group. That particular characteristic should be brought out, as in it lay the difference between an ordinary crime and genocide".).

[14] *See* Chap. 2 *infra*.

[15] For more detailed explanation on these distinct forms of intent, *see* Chap. 2, footnote 6 *infra*. For the two differing meanings of the term 'conditional intent', *see* Fletcher 2000, p. 454 (in German, the term 'conditional intent' means *dolus eventualis*; in English it means "an intent to commit a harm if a certain condition is fulfilled".). For national criminal law which accepts two kinds of intent—i.e., *dolus directus* in the first degree and *dolus eventualis*, skipping the *dolus directus* in the second degree, *see* Csúri 2011, p. 368; Tellenbach 2011, pp. 391–392; Rinceanu 2011, p. 425. As to Romania, note that it appears the author mistakenly explains that "the intellectual element dominates" in the cases of direct intent (*dolus directus*). See *Ibid*. For national jurisdictions where the term 'indirect intent' conceptually encompasses *dolus eventualis*: Paramonova 2011, p. 438. Carl-Friedrich Stuckenberg criticizes the pervasive use of national criminal law terminology (such as *dolus directus* in the first degree, *dolus directus* in the second degree, and *dolus eventualis*) in the field of international criminal law, *see* Stuckenberg 2014, pp. 316–317.

agenda is the conceptual *scope* of intent in a sense that, according to the size of that scope, the concept of 'intent to destroy' covers a varying range of perpetrators. That is to say, if the scope is broad, many can be convicted as *principals* of the crime of genocide. If it is narrow, of course, only a small portion of them can. For others outside the applicable range of the genocidal intent element, only accessorial liability remains as an option. In this way, the theme of genocidal intent closely connects to locating the dividing line between principal liability and accessorial liability. In particular, though hardly discussed in a serious manner by scholars and practitioners, it is noteworthy that the knowledge-based approach to interpreting genocidal intent makes it possible to impute *principal liability* to a broad range of persons especially from mid- or low-ranks through the concept of genocidal intent *per se*, without needing to resort to any mode of liability theory such as joint criminal enterprise (hereinafter also referred to as 'JCE'). We will closely look into the purpose-based approach and the knowledge-based approach to genocidal intent in Chap. 2 hereunder. I hope to show that a peculiar structural mechanism of the crime definition of genocide renders the genocidal intent element a quasi-mode of liability theory directly determining who is a principal and who is an accomplice. In this sense, genocide is a "composite crime"[16] in which the logic of crime and the logic of mode of liability coexist.[17]

In short, thus far, genocidal intent has been generally regarded as a *mens rea* reflecting an individual inner state of mind. In this respect, however, there is a problem which concerns the primary reference point of inferring individual genocidal intent at the ICTY and the ICTR: international judges there infer individualistic genocidal intent mainly from the general context of atrocious campaigns. Maneuvering the ambiguous dividing line between substantive law and evidence law, judges "squeeze ambiguous fact patterns into" the notion of individualistic genocidal intent.[18] In this context, suspects charged with the crime of genocide have complained that 'you infer my intent from act of others'.[19]

The main reason for all these confusions lie in the conflicts and discrepancies between the *individualistic* manner in which the crime definition of genocide is literally provided and the essentially *collective* nature of genocide. Under the principle of individual criminal responsibility which has dominated the field of international criminal law for decades, the law of genocide has developed in a lopsided manner, significantly leaning toward individualistic scrutiny of its key features, while ostensibly marginalizing the *intrinsically* collective characteristic of the crime of

---

[16] Lemkin 1947, p. 150.

[17] For more discussion, *see* Sect. 4.2.1 *infra*.

[18] Greenawalt 1999, p. 2281 (1999) ("[t]he danger of adhering to a specific intent standard in such situations is not merely that culpable perpetrators will escape liability for genocide, but perhaps more ominously that the evidentiary problems will compel courts to squeeze ambiguous fact patterns into the specific intent paradigm".).

[19] For more discussion, *see* Sect. 4.1.2 *infra*.

genocide. Yet, if something is called 'intrinsic', it is not easy to really deny it. That is precisely the case of the inherently collective nature of the crime of genocide, which has silently and covertly governed the relevant case law of the *ad hoc* tribunals.[20]

In this book, I employ two terms representing this intrinsic character of genocide: 'collective genocide' and 'collective genocidal intent'. In so doing, my analysis starts from an observation that the crime definition of genocide has a two-layered structure just like crimes against humanity and war crimes: 'conduct level' and 'context level'.[21] On the basis of this two-layered structural scheme, this book casts doubt on the characterization of genocide as a 'crime of *mens rea*'. In other words, my focus will be on the *objective* aspects of the crime of genocide in terms of both the collective intention and the collective conduct. In this manner, my theory tries to treat obesity of the genocidal intent element, pulling out its content from the realm of subjectivity to that of objectivity. I believe that, till now, the concept of genocidal intent has been elusive, as its face and body have been swollen up. Thus, in order to see clearly the shape of genocidal intent, it is necessary to provide it with obesity treatment. In this respect, it is noteworthy that Claus Kress observes:

> [...] [T]he way forward may lie in taking account of the fact that genocide, for all practical purposes, is a systemic crime. If a collective level of genocidal activity must normally be distinguished from the level of the individual genocidal conduct, it is worth asking whether the construction of the word 'intent' should not be construed accordingly.[22]

In this book, I will demonstrate that, within the relevant case law of international criminal courts, the collectivist intuition of genocide has prevailed over the individualistic account of genocidal intent, albeit in an implicit and covert manner. On this basis, I will stress the importance of the objective features of genocide reflected in the substantiality requirement and the peculiar logic of criminal enterprise inherently existing within the notion of genocide.

For this purpose, this book begins with a critique of prior individualistic approaches to interpreting genocidal intent in Chap. 2. I provide the overview of both the purpose-based theory and its knowledge-based counterpart. Then, I engage in a critical reconsideration of the knowledge-based approach that has increasingly gained support particularly from commentators. There are two themes under which I criticize the knowledge-based account of genocidal intent.

First, I cast a doubt on the most critical legal consequence of applying the knowledge-based approach—i.e., convicting subordinate actors of genocide *as principals* (as opposed to accessories). At the outset of my critical account, I show the awkward and counterintuitive result of applying the knowledge-based theory with a hypothetical of a conscience-stricken militia leader: the "insomniac

---

[20] *See e.g.* the title of Sect. 3.2 *infra*: "Who Are You?: The Hidden Concept of 'Collective Genocide' Governing the Case Law".

[21] *See* Sect. 3.1 *infra*.

[22] Kress 2005, pp. 572–573.

commander". Then, the actual legal effect of attaching principal liability to subordinate actors will be critically assessed in comparison with 'joint criminal enterprise' and 'perpetration by means'. Ultimately, I ask whether there still remains a legal space of the aiding and abetting liability in the case of applying the knowledge-based theory to the notion of genocidal intent. What I argue is that the knowledge-based understanding of genocidal intent risks shaking the basic legal foundation of differentiating principals and accomplices.

Second, applying a conceptual framework of *mens rea* that I draw from a survey of literatures of comparative criminal law, I discuss the conceptual superiority of the notion of 'direct intent/purpose' over 'indirect intent/knowledge' in terms of being a reference point of 'destruction of a group'. This position will be developed in view of the fact that the 'destruction of a group' is conceptually incompatible with the notion of 'unwanted (or uninterested) but only permitted side effect' that, by definition, always accompanies the *mens rea* of 'indirect intent/knowledge'. Instead, it will be shown that the *mens rea* of 'direct intent/purpose' which is, by definition, always to be directed toward the 'desired main effect' better fits in with 'destruction of a group' than does 'indirect intent/knowledge'.

Before engaging in this discussion based on the distinction between 'side-effect' and 'main-effect'. an analysis of the concept of 'special intent' will be performed, in which I criticize the mistaken understanding of the purpose-based genocidal intent involving the notion of *intensity* of volition. I also explain that the correct account of the purpose-based theory should employ the notion of 'desire in a broad sense' that is conceptually compatible with both the positive emotions and the negative emotions.

This chapter, however, will not conclude that the purpose-based approach is the right path to the proper understanding of the notion of genocidal intent. Rather, in the Section 5 entitled "Complications and Frustrations", I characterize the individualistic notion of genocidal intent reflected in the relevant case law of the ICTY and the ICTR as something complicated, elusive and even paradoxical. This characterization results from the evidentiary practice of the *ad hoc* tribunals in finding the individualistic genocidal intent. That is, while they claim to espouse the purpose-based notion of genocidal intent doctrinally, it is the knowledge-based factual analysis that appears to guide the relevant evidentiary examinations, due to the tribunals' heavy reliance upon the general context of genocidal campaigns for the purpose of inferring individualistic genocidal intent. Since this discrepancy between the doctrinal side and the evidentiary side of the individualistic concept of genocidal intent is too colossal, I conclude this chapter by emphasizing that it is necessary to see the notion of genocidal intent from a different standpoint than the individualistic perspective. Accordingly, I employ the collectivist approach to guide and direct subsequent discussions contained in Chaps. 3 and 4.

In Chap. 3, my analysis begins with expounding the two-layered structure of genocide—i.e., the 'conduct level' and the 'context level'. Throughout this chapter, I place an emphasis on the importance of the 'context level' for the purpose of individual prosecution of the crime of genocide. I demonstrate that, in the relevant case law of the *ad hoc* tribunals, a finding of the 'context level' as genocidal precedes the legal consideration of personal conduct and individual genocidal intent at the 'conduct level'. For the purpose of indicating such genocidal context, I employ the term 'collective genocide'. By reference to the acquittal decision in the *Jelisić* case of the ICTY, I also show that the existence of 'collective genocide' at the 'context level' is a quasi-legal requirement of the crime of genocide.

Then, providing an overview of the historical development of the substantiality requirement as an interpretation of the term 'in part' in the definition of genocide, I argue that the destructive consequence of a substantial part of a group at the 'context level' constitutes the essence of the crime of genocide. In doing so, I acknowledge the existence and importance of the objective contextual element of genocide. This line of argument constitutes a part of the obesity treatment of genocidal intent in that the notion of 'destruction' is identified as a crucial objective element of the crime of genocide.

Subsequently, I discuss the problematic decision from the ICC Pre-Trial Chamber in *Al Bashir* in which 'concrete threat' is regarded as a legal requirement in relation to the objective contextual element of genocide. Arguing against this position, I point out that the Chamber neglects to give due consideration to the substantiality requirement that carries with it the notion of 'concrete threat'. In this respect, I argue that the 'concrete threat' requirement is redundant. However, I admit the usefulness of 'concrete threat' as a proof of 'collective genocide' when it is difficult to determine whether a given situation satisfies the substantiality requirement.

In the end, I conclude the chapter by explaining the degraded importance of individualistic notions of genocidal intent at the 'conduct level', which results from the pivotal role played by the concept of 'collective genocide' at the 'context level' for the purpose of prosecuting the crime of genocide.

The Chap. 4 constitutes the final part of this book, and this chapter scrutinizes the notion of collective genocidal intent, which I argue is the most essential element of the crime of genocide, together with the 'collective genocide'. I grasp each of these key notions of genocide as an objective element existing outside an individual state of mind, which challenges the validity of the famous nickname of genocide—i.e., the 'crime of *mens rea*'.

Quoting the *Krstić* Trial Judgment which states that genocidal intent "must be discernible in the criminal act itself, apart from the intent of particular perpetrators[,]" I demonstrate that collective genocidal intent has been a necessary condition of finding individual genocidal intent in the relevant international case law. In this respect, I point out that the reasoning of the International Commission of Inquiry's report on Darfur (hereinafter Darfur Report)[23] which, within the same overall context of violence, acknowledges the possibility of individual genocidal intent (and thereby the possibility of an individual crime of genocide) while rejecting the existence of collective genocidal intent, is mistaken.

---

[23] International Commission of Inquiry on Darfur, Established Pursuant to Resolution 1564 (2004), Report to the United Nations Secretary–General, 25 January 2005.

Then, I address the final consideration of my collectivist account of genocide by comparing the conceptual structure of genocide with that of joint criminal enterprise. The purpose of this section is to project the crime of genocide itself as a criminal enterprise. There are two sets of corresponding notions that provide a conceptual framework of this analogy: (i) the parallel between 'collective genocidal intent' (objective element of genocide) and 'common purpose/plan' (objective element of JCE) on the one hand; and (ii) the parallel between 'individual genocidal intent' (subjective element of genocide) and 'shared intent' (subjective element of JCE) on the other. I will show that the close interaction of these four notions suggests an existence of an inherent logic of JCE within the crime of genocide itself.

Drawing upon the relevant case law, I then demonstrate that the logic of JCE within genocide tends to water down the individual genocidal intent element by attaching evidentiary significance to such objective aspects of individual actors' action, contribution and rank. I argue that this result is similar to the actual operation of JCE at the *ad hoc* tribunals: an individual *mens rea* is presumed based upon a participant's contribution and rank under the guise of the 'shared intent' element of JCE. The more a case is solid in terms of its objective factual basis (e.g., the accused's essential contribution; complete *de facto* control over physical perpetrators; or the highest rank and position of authority possessed by him), the stronger the force to presume individual *mens rea*.

Lastly, I argue that, due to the inherent logic of JCE within genocide, it is not possible to attribute principal liability to the low-level actors. I demonstrate that physical perpetrators' genocidal intent at the 'conduct level' cannot be a legitimate legal requirement of genocide. Instead, I argue that the logic of JCE within genocide operates in a way that constitutes only one crime of genocide in a given situation, but not two or more: in the same manner as the 'common purpose/plan' shared by JCE members and acts performed by non-JCE members completes one JCE liability, collective genocidal intent at the 'context level' plus underlying acts at the 'conduct level' constitutes one crime of genocide. I also point out the top-down verticality of genocidal intent which tends to locate the crime of genocide closer to a leadership crime.

References

Csúri A (2011) Subjective aspects of the offence in Hungary. In: Sieber U, Forster S, Jarvers K (eds) National criminal law in a comparative legal context, vol 3.1. Duncker & Humblot, Berlin, pp 365–376

D'Amato A (2000) On genocide. Intl L Stud Ser US Naval War Col 75:119–130

Dunér D (2004) What can be done about historical atrocities? the Armenian case. The Intl J Human Rights 8:217–233

Fletcher GP (2000) Rethinking criminal law. Oxford University Press, Oxford

Greenawalt AKA (1999) Rethinking genocidal intent: the case for a knowledge-based interpretation. Colum Law Rev 99:2259–2294

Kress C (2005) The Darfur report and genocidal intent. J Intl Crim Justice 3:562–578

Lemkin R (1948) Genocide as a crime under international law. UN Bull 4:70–71

Lemkin R (1947) Genocide as a crime under international law. American J Intl Law 41:145–151

Paramonova S (2011) Subjective aspects of the offence in Russia. In: Sieber U, Forster S, Jarvers K (eds) National criminal law in a comparative legal context, vol 3.1. Duncker & Humblot, Berlin, pp 436–452

Rinceanu J (2011) Subjective aspects of the offence in Romania. In: Sieber U, Forster S, Jarvers K (eds) National criminal law in a comparative legal context, vol 3.1. Duncker & Humblot, Berlin, pp 421–435

Stuckenberg CF (2014) Problems of 'subjective imputation' in domestic and international criminal law. J Intl Crim Justice 12:311–323

Tellenbach S (2011) Subjective aspects of the offence in Iran. In: Sieber U, Forster S, Jarvers K (eds) National criminal law in a comparative legal context, vol 3.1. Duncker & Humblot, Berlin, pp 389–404

Chapter 2
A Critique of Individualistic Approaches to Genocidal Intent

Abstract In this chapter, my discussion begins with a critique of individualistic approaches to interpreting the genocidal intent element. I criticize the knowledge-based approach mainly in view of its legal implications of attaching principal liability to subordinate actors. I ask whether there still remains room for aiding and abetting liability of genocide in the territory of the knowledge-based theory. In the context of a systematic genocidal campaign, there should be only a few who lacks knowledge of such overall context of violence, which factually overlaps with the destructive consequences to a significant extent. Therefore, in terms of the crime of genocide, the applicable scope of the knowledge standard is almost limitless. What I argue is that the knowledge-based understanding of genocidal intent risks shaking the basic legal foundation of differentiating principals and accessories. In the next section, I criticize the mistaken understanding of the purpose-based approach to genocidal intent involving the notion of intensity of volition, surrounding the term 'special intent'. This criticism is based on the conceptual distinction between 'general intent' and 'special intent'. I also explain that the correct account of the purpose-based theory should employ the notion of 'desire in a broad sense' that is conceptually compatible not only with positive emotions but also with negative emotions. Then, my second challenge to the knowledge-based analysis relies heavily on the distinctive feature of the two *mens rea* concepts of 'direct intent/purposely' and 'indirect intent/knowingly'. I understood that the former is always directed toward 'desired main effect', while the latter, by definition, corresponds to 'unwanted or uninterested side-effect'. I then demonstrated that 'destruction of a group' should always be perceived as a 'main effect' desired by an actor. Yet, the actual practice of the *ad hoc* tribunals where genocidal intent has been primarily inferred from the overall context of genocidal campaigns kept me from proclaiming the victory of the purpose-based theory over its knowledge-based counterpart. How can you infer my mind primarily from the general context which is geographically and temporally far exceeds my personal realm? In this context, I put the title of the last section of the analysis of individualistic approaches to genocidal intent as 'Complications and Frustrations'. These observations urged me to depart from the individualistic analysis.

© T.M.C. ASSER PRESS and the author 2016

S. Kim, *A Collective Theory of Genocidal Intent*, International Criminal Justice Series 7, DOI 10.1007/978-94-6265-123-4_2

Keywords Purpose-based approach · Knowledge-based approach · Principal liability · Accessory liability · Special intent · Direct intent/purposely · Indirect intent/knowingly

Contents

2.1 The Traditional Individualistic Understanding of Genocidal Intent: Its Pure Subjectivity

The modern international criminal law that developed in the aftermath of the World War II is based on the principle of 'individual responsibility'—as opposed to 'collective responsibility'—as proclaimed by the International Military Tribunal at Nuremberg as follows: "Crimes against international law are committed by men, not by abstract entities, and only by punishing individuals who commit such crimes can the provisions of international law be enforced".[1] The enthusiasm to punish individuals rather than groups or any other entities for the commission of core international crimes has been upheld and maintained by subsequent international criminal courts. As a consequence, the ICC Statute ultimately provides that "[t]he Court shall have jurisdiction over natural persons pursuant to this Statute. A person who commits a crime within the jurisdiction of the Court shall be individually responsible and liable for punishment in accordance with this Statute".[2] From this perspective, it is natural to understand the genocidal intent element pursuant to an *individualistic* approach, which has been the pervasive view shared by both scholars and practitioners in the field thus far. Although this book tries to propose and expound the concept of collective genocidal intent, as opposed to its individualistic counterpart, it is necessary to explore the traditional individualistic concepts of genocidal intent for a better construction of the collectivist theory. Thus, drawing on the relevant case law and scholarly literature, this chapter seeks to provide an overview and critique of the individualistic approach to interpreting genocidal intent.

The prior individualistic approaches can largely be classified into two categories: the 'purpose-based approach' and the 'knowledge-based approach'. Although proponents of each of these two approaches have divergent understandings of genocidal intent, they do concur that the genocidal intent element is a *mens rea,* with no necessary connection to the *actus reus.* Hence, the concept of genocidal intent as grasped by them is purely of a subjective nature involving only the inner state of mind of an individual perpetrator of genocide. Both of the purpose-based and the knowledge-based theories define the individualistic genocidal intent element one way or another, and thereby propose a standard for distinguishing principals from accessories.[3] An observation made by the Office of the Prosecutor of the ICTY in the *Jelisić* case and the *Krstić* case well summarizes the individualistic approach to genocidal intent, encompassing both the purpose-based and the knowledge-based approaches. In its Pre-Trial Briefs, the Prosecution submits that

---

[1] The Trial of Major War Criminals: Proceedings of the International Military Tribunal Sitting at Nuremberg Germany, Part 22, at 447, *as cited by* Prosecutor v. Tadić, Decision on the Defence Motion for Interlocutory Appeal on Jurisdiction, 2 October 1995, para 128. *See also* Prosecutor v. Tadić, Appeals Judgment, 15 July 1999, para 186 ("The basic assumption must be that in international law as much as in national systems, the foundation of criminal responsibility is the principle of personal culpability: nobody may be held criminally responsible for acts or transactions in which he has not personally engaged or in some other way participated (*nulla poena sine culpa*)".). For a brief discussion on the unsuccessful USSR proposal, submitted during the drafting negotiations of the Genocide Convention, to criminalizing organizations that commit or incite genocide, see Bush 2009, p. 1227. Through a meticulous examination of unpublished documents, Jonathan A. Bush shows in this article, *inter alia*, that, jurists at Nuremberg were of the view that criminal charges against organizations (in particular, corporations) were legally permissible, though not actually adopted.

[2] ICC Statute, Article 25(1)–(2).

[3] This aspect indeed guides my discussion contained in Sect. 2.4 *infra. See* Kress 2006, p. 495 ("The precise construction of the word 'intent' [i.e., genocidal intent] and the resulting delineation between principal and accessory participation in the case of genocide [...]".).

the accused committed genocide with the requisite genocidal intent if (i) "he consciously desired the acts to result in the destruction, in whole or in part, of the group, as such"; (ii) "he knew his acts were destroying, in whole or in part, the group, as such"; or (iii) "he knew that the likely consequence of his acts would be to destroy, in whole or in part, the group, as such".[4] Thus, the Prosecution is of the view that either the purpose-based genocidal intent (category (i)) or the knowledge-based genocidal intent (categories (ii) and (iii)) can legally fulfill the 'intent to destroy' element.[5] Regardless of whether they (categories (i) through (iii)) are equivalent to such domestic legal concepts as *dolus directus* (*dolus directus* in the first degree; direct intent; purposely)', *dolus indirectus* (*dolus directus* in the second degree; indirect intent; oblique intent; knowingly)', or *dolus eventualis*' (advertent recklessness; recklessness; conditional intent) respectively,[6] it is evident

---

[4] Prosecutor v. Jelisić and Češić, Prosecutor's Pre-Trial Brief, 19 November 1998, para 3.1. *See also* Prosecutor v. Jelisić, Trial Judgment, 14 December 1999, para 85 (according to the Trial Judgment, the Prosecution in this case did plead the knowledge-based notion of genocidal intent.); Prosecutor v. Krstić, Prosecutor's Pre-Trial Brief pursuant to Rule 65 ter (E) (i), 25 February 2000, para 90; Prosecutor v. Sikirica et al., Prosecutor's Second Revised Pre-Trial Brief, 13 October 2000, para 141.

[5] Note that during the oral argument before the *Jelisić* Appeals Chamber, the Prosecution clarified that the category (iii) standard of *dolus eventualis*/recklessnes' is only applicable to aiding and abetting genocide. Prosecutor v. Jelisić, Appeals Judgment, 5 July 2001, p. 16, footnote 77.

[6] Thomas Weigend explains these three forms of the Continental notion of intent employing the following terms: "intention (*Absicht*)", "knowledge (*Wissentlichkeit*)" and "conditional intent (*bedingter Vorsatz*)". Weigend 2011, p. 261. While Weigend identifies *dolus indirectus* with 'knowledge', George Fletcher however is of a different view when he states that "Continental [criminal] statutes have no comparable form" of 'knowingly' as provided in the Model Penal Code. Fletcher 2000, pp. 442–443. It seems that Fletcher was more concerned with the interaction of the volition and the cognition within the Continental notion of *dolus indirectus*. Concerning the first two categories of intent—i.e., *dolus directus* and *dolus indirectus*—, there is not much conceptual difference between the Continental tradition and the Anglo-American tradition. *See e.g.*, Taylor 2004, p. 106 ("there are three alternative forms of intention in German law: intention in the narrow 'purpose' sense, certain knowledge and *dolus eventualis*. The first two forms will be broadly familiar to an English-speaking audience and do not require a great deal of explanation".). Taylor's article thus focuses on explaining the German notion of *dolus eventualis* for English-speaking audience. Throughout this chapter, I will cite *mens rea* concepts of many national jurisdictions, which will suggest such similarity between the Continental tradition and the Anglo-American tradition. For an international case law in which *dolus eventualis* is identified with 'advertent recklessness', see Prosecutor v. Tadić, Appeals Judgment, 15 July 1999, para 220; Prosecutor v. Bemba, Decision Pursuant to Article 61(7)(a) and (b) of the Rome Statute on the Charges of the Prosecutor Against Jean-Pierre Bemba Gombo, 15 June 2009, para 357. See also, *Ibid.* at 121, footnote 447 (citing many international judgments, states that "[t]he concept of subjective or advertent recklessness known in common law systems is generally treated as equivalent to the notion of *dolus eventualis* in the continental law systems".). Note however that, while the Continental notion of *dolus eventualis* places emphasis on the perpetrator's *subjective* attitude toward the risk—such as 'being indifferent to the result', 'reconciling himself to the result'. or 'accepting the result', the Anglo-American concept of (advertent) recklessness pays more attention to the *objective* probability of the risk. For a more explanation, *see* Fletcher 2000, pp. 444–449 (observing that the closest analogue to *dolus eventualis* in the Anglo-American system is the Model Penal Code provision on 'purposeful conduct' as to attendant circumstances.).

that all these *mens rea* are of an *individualistic* nature as clearly indicated by the phrases "*he* consciously desired" and "*he* knew". Hence, according to the individualistic approach, *individual* genocidal intent of the accused—i.e., *his own* genocidal inner state of mind—is a requisite for establishing the accused's criminal liability. Genocidal intent, then, always resides *within* the mind.[7] In the same way, the Trial Chambers of the ICTR state that genocidal intent is "characterized by a *psychological nexus* between the physical result and the mental state of the perpetrator".[8] Consequently, the individualistic approach declares that the genocidal intent element "should be met *individually*"[9] by showing that the accused "*personally possessed* […] the specific intent to commit the crime at the time he did so".[10]

These are the main features of the individualistic approach to genocidal intent agreed with by both the purpose-based and the knowledge-based approaches. But, as to the question of the *content* of genocidal intent, their answers diverge. While the purpose-based approach stresses the volitional aspect of genocidal intent, the knowledge-based approach claims that cognitive knowledge is sufficient to satisfy the genocidal intent element. The latter view has been voiced more recently, coinciding with the inception of active international criminal prosecutions at the ICTY and the ICTR. Before proceeding further, let us examine these two approaches. In what follows, I explain the two approaches and criticize the knowledge-based approach.

---

[7] In the *Krstić* Trial Judgment, however, genocidal intent first resides *outside* the mind. This *external* genocidal intent is afterwards to be imputed to the accused through his 'sharing' thereof. Such 'sharing' was established from the point when Krstić was aware of the "widespread and systematic killings [of military-aged men in Srebrenica] and became clearly involved in their perpetration[.]" Prosecutor v. Krstić, Trial Judgment, 2 August 2001, para 633. For more discussion, *see* Sect. 4.2.2.2 *infra*. Note that the theme of this book—i.e., the notion of collective genocidal intent—conceptually exists *outside* the mind as an *external* element. Some commentators use the term 'external elements' in explaining the *actus reus*. See e.g., Duff 1990, p. 7. For more discussion, *see* Sects. 4.1.1 and 4.1.2 *infra*.

[8] Prosecutor v. Rutaganda, Trial Judgment, 6 December 1999, para 60; Prosecutor v. Musema, Trial Judgment, 27 January 2000, para 166. (emphasis added). In this respect, the jurisprudence of the ICTR on genocidal intent is said to accommodate a 'descriptive' nature of the concept of intent (as opposed to a 'normative' or 'moral' nature). See Tadros 2007, p. 214 ("[…] the concept of intention is a purely descriptive concept: it is a concept that describes the psychology of an agent. It is not, as some have claimed, a moral concept".). For an opposing view that places a significant emphasis on the normative characteristic of intention, *see* Duff 2013, pp. 155–177 (referring to intention as a "thick normative concept", Duff argues that "intention is not, and should not be, a purely descriptive concept".). For a mixed approach, *see* Maljević 2011, p. 353 (with regard to the Criminal Code of Bosnia and Herzegovina, some commentators are of the view that the law understands 'intent' as a notion of a psychological-normative nature.).

[9] Mettraux 2006, p. 263. (emphasis added).

[10] Prosecutor v. Rutaganda, Appeals Judgment, 26 May 2003, para 525. (emphasis added).

2.2 An Overview of the Purpose-Based Approach

It is generally said that the traditional purpose-based approach to interpreting genocidal intent places a significant emphasis on its *volitional* aspect.[11] It is commonly believed that this approach originated in *Akayesu* at the ICTR. Genocidal intent ("intent to destroy"), generally connoting the purpose-based notion, has been referred to by international judges and commentators as '*dolus specialis*', 'special intent', 'specific intent', 'specific genocidal intent', 'particular intent',[12] 'particular state of mind', 'exterminatory intent'[13] and so forth. Although the relevant international case law has never used phrases such as the 'purpose-based approach' or 'purpose-based genocidal intent',[14] commentators are, in general, of the view that the case law of the ICTR and the ICTY follows the purpose-based

---

[11] Unless otherwise specified, the conception of 'volition', for the purpose of this book, indicates an attitude towards a *result* and/or *consequence* of a conduct, which should be distinguished from the concept of 'volition' in the sense that it prompts or induces bodily movements/actions. For the former usage of the term 'volition', *see* Csúri 2011, p. 366 ("[In Hungarian criminal law,] [t]he volitional/emotional side [of intent] [...] describes the perpetrator's attitude towards the consequence of his act".). For the latter usage of the term 'volition', *see* Moore 2009, p. 101 (pointing out that a bodily movement is caused by a volition); Jain 2011, p. 378 (explaining that in Indian criminal law, intent, volition and motive are distinct concepts, and volition "indicates the desire that impels the bodily motion that constitutes a conscious act".). For an understating of 'volition' that encompasses both the former and the latter usages, *see* Rinceanu 2011, p. 424 (under Romanian criminal law, "[t]he volitional element (*factorul volitiv*) is that element of the intent that comprises the possibility of the freedom to perform the physical action that is required to accomplish the pursued purpose. In other words, the volitional element is the psycho-physical capacity [...] of the offender for self-determination and control of his activities. The volition/will is the aptitude that impels the physical activity of the offender. The volitional element must be aimed at the result of the offense or the commission of the conduct. [...] The volition activates the physical causality of the act. The volitional element is generally missing [...] where there is a lack of capacity for self-determination and self control".). For the meaning of the notion of 'volition' generally understood in the field of international criminal law, *see* Clark 2008, p. 219, footnote.42 (observing that, in the context of the ICC Pre-Trial Chamber's interpretation of Article 30 ("Mental Elements") of the ICC Statute, the concept of 'volition' is used [...] in the sense of an "attitude towards the result [or consequence], not as it is sometimes used in the common law to describe the voluntariness of an act (as opposed to acting, say, in a state of automatism)".). In this connection, note that George Fletcher points out a difficulty in distinguishing the notions of 'volition' and 'desire'. *See* Fletcher 2000, p. 450.

[12] Study of the Question of the Prevention and Punishment of the Crime of Genocide, Study Prepared by Mr. Nicodeme Ruhashyankiko, Special Rapporteur, UN Doc. E/CN.4/Sub.2/416 (1978), paras 96 and 99.

[13] Prosecutor v. Jelisić, Trial Judgment, 14 December 1999, para 83.

[14] Instead of the term 'purpose-based approach', the ICC Pre-Trial Chamber in *Al Bashir* uses the term "traditional approach". Prosecutor v. Al Bashir, Decision on the Prosecution's Application for a Warrant of Arrest against Omar Hassan Ahmed Al Bashir, 4 March 2009, p. 49, footnote 154.

approach.[15] For instance, while explicitly rejecting the knowledge-based concept of genocidal intent, the ICTY Trial Chamber in *Blagojević and Jokić* straightforwardly upholds the purpose-based approach by stating,

> It is not sufficient that the perpetrator simply knew that the underlying crime would *inevitably* or *likely* result in the destruction of the group. The destruction, in whole or in part, must be the *aim* of the underlying crime(s).[16]

I think this observation is quite insightful because it contains all the key notions representing the three competing *mens rea*: 'direct intent/purposely' ("aim"), 'indirect intent/knowingly' ("inevitably ... result in"), and *'dolus eventualis/recklessness'* ("likely result in").[17] This explanation of the essential characteristic of "intent to destroy"—i.e., 'aim' that signifies the *mens rea* classification of 'direct intent/purposely'—is in line with the landmark statement of the purpose-based notion of genocidal intent made by the ICTR Trial Chamber in *Akayesu* as follows:

> Genocide is distinct from other crimes inasmuch as it embodies a special intent or *dolus specialis*. Special intent of a crime is the specific intention, required as a constitutive element of the crime, which demands that the perpetrator *clearly seeks to produce the act* charged. Thus, the special intent in the crime of genocide lies in 'the intent to destroy, in whole or in part, a national, ethnical, racial or religious group, as such'.[18]

At this juncture, it is important to note that the purpose-based concept of genocidal intent ("clearly seek to produce") is closely related to the concept of *'dolus specialis/special intent/specific intent'*. Yet, in the context of the scholarly discussions of the purpose-based nature of genocidal intent centering around the notion of 'strong/intensive volition', the adjective *'specialis/special/specific'* has been the source of all the confusions that will be explicated in subsection 2.5.1 below. The *Akayesu* Trial Chamber further explains the 'special intent' by saying,

> Special intent is a well-known criminal law concept in the Roman–continental legal systems. It is required as a constituent element of certain offences and demands that the perpetrator have the *clear intent* to cause the offence charged. According to this meaning,

---

[15] *See* Kress 2006, pp. 492–493 ("[a]fter an initial period of some uncertainty, the jurisprudence of ICTR and ICTY now seem to concur in the view that a perpetrator of the crime of genocide must act with the aim, goal, purpose or desire to destroy part of a protected group"); Sliedregt 2007, p. 193 ("the formula used by the [ICTY and the ICTR] insists on a purpose-based interpretation of genocidal intent [...]"); Vest 2007, p. 794 ("The interpretation of genocidal intent by the ad hoc Tribunals is not absolutely consistent but nevertheless reveals a clear preference for a purpose-based reading [...]".); Marchuk 2014, p. 137 ("The jurisprudential line of interpretation [of genocidal intent] is also purpose-oriented".). Note that the ICC Pre-Trial Chamber in *Al Bashir* also endorses the purpose-based approach primarily based on the literal interpretation of the ICC Statute and the Elements of Crimes. Prosecutor v. Al Bashir, Decision on the Prosecution's Application for a Warrant of Arrest against Omar Hassan Ahmed Al Bashir, 4 March 2009, p. 49, footnote 154.

[16] Prosecutor v. Blagojević and Jokić, Trial Judgment, 17 January 2005, para 656.

[17] It was also the case with the relevant view the ICTY Office of the Prosecutor. *See* footnote 4 *supra* and accompanying text.

[18] Prosecutor v. Akayesu, Trial Judgment, 2 September 1998, para 498. (emphasis added).

special intent is the key element of an intentional offence, which offence is characterized by a psychological relationship between the physical result and the mental state of the perpetrator.[19]

> With regard to the crime of genocide, the offender is culpable only when he has committed one of the offences charged under Article 2(2) of the Statute with the *clear intent* to destroy, in whole or in part, a particular group. The offender is culpable because he knew or should have known that the act committed would destroy, in whole or in part, a group.[20]

In explaining the meaning of 'special intent' which encompasses the concept of 'genocidal intent', it is conspicuous that the Chamber keeps using the word "clear"—i.e., "*clearly* seeks to produce", "*clear* intent to cause", and "*clear* intent to destroy". In this connection, one might ask what the term 'clear intent' really means. Is there a legal distinction between 'clear intent', 'ambiguous or unclear intent', and, simply, 'intent'?[21]

On the ICTY side, probably the most often cited purpose-based definition of genocidal intent is found in the Appeals Judgment in the *Jelisić* case, which states, "[t]he specific intent [of genocide] requires that the perpetrator, by one of the prohibited acts enumerated in Article 4 of the Statute [providing genocide], *seeks to achieve the destruction*, in whole or in part, of a national, ethnical, racial or religious group, as such".[22] Similarly, subsequent case law from the *ad hoc* tribunals uses phrases such as "clearly intended the result charged",[23] "ulterior purpose to destroy",[24] or "surplus of intent"[25] in explaining the concept of genocidal intent.

---

[19] *Ibid.* para 518. (emphasis added). Quoting the same paragraph from *Akayesu*, however, Claus Kress stresses the evasive nature of the concept of '*dolus specialis*/special intent' as follows: "This statement quite considerably underestimates the complexity of the matter. Neither the 'Roman–continental systems' nor the legal family of the common law can be relied upon for a clear cut and uniform concept of *dolus specialis* ('*dol special*', '*special intent*', '*Absicht*'/'*erweiterter Vorsatz*', '*dolo especifico*', '*oogmerk op*', '*amesos dolos/skopos*' etc.) as meaning aim, goal, purpose or desire. It is thus highly improbable whether a valid comparative law argument could be developed in support of the assertion put forward in *Akayesu*. But apart from this, the definition of genocide does not use any of those terms, but simply the word 'intent' which leaves the necessary room to have due regard to genocide's specific interplay between individual and collective acts". Kress 2006, p. 494.

[20] Prosecutor v. Akayesu, Trial Judgment, 2 September 1998, para 520. (emphasis added). For a discussion concerning the phrase "knew or should have known", *see* Sect. 4.1.3 *infra*.

[21] The *Jelisić* Trial Chamber is of the view that the fact that the accused killed Muslim victims "arbitrary" tends to disprove the existence of the "clear intent to destroy a group". *See* Prosecutor v. Jelisić, Trial Judgment, 14 December 1999, para 108.

[22] Prosecutor v. Jelisić, Appeals Judgment, 5 July 2001, para 46. For subsequent judgments that appear to endorse the expression "seeks to achieve the destruction", *see e.g.*, Prosecutor v. Sikirica et al., Judgement on Defence Motions to Acquit, 3 September 2001, p. 27, footnote 165; Prosecutor v. Stakić, Trial Judgment, 31 July 2003, p. 147, footnote 1100; Prosecutor v. Krstić, Appeals Judgment, 19 April 2004, p. 72, footnote 363; Prosecutor v. Blagojević and Jokić, Trial Judgment, 17 January 2005, para 656.

[23] Prosecutor v. Rutaganda, Trial Judgment, 6 December 1999, para 58.

[24] *Ibid.* para 59.

[25] Prosecutor v. Stakić, Trial Judgment, 31 July 2003, para 520.

Apparently following the phrase used by the ICTY Prosecution ("consciously desired"),[26] the Darfur Report states that "an aggravated criminal intention or *dolus specialis* [...] implies that the perpetrator *consciously desired* the prohibited acts he committed to result in the destruction, in whole or in part, of the group as such [...]".[27] The phrase "consciously desired" also sounds similar to the language of "conscious object" found in the definition of "purposely" in the Model Penal Code.[28] The *Jelisić* Trial Judgment further provides a good example of the purpose-based interpretation of genocidal intent when it acquits the accused because his acts "are not the physical expression[s] of an *affirmed resolve to destroy* in whole or in part a group as such".[29] The crux of the purpose-based approach has been summarized by Kai Ambos when he says, "[i]n sum, the case-law's approach is predicated on the understanding, as originally suggested by *Akayesu*, that 'intent to destroy' means a special or specific intent which, in essence, expresses the

---

[26] Note that the phrase "consciously desired" was previously used by the ICTY Prosecution in *Jelisić* case and *Krstić* case. *See* footnote 4 *supra* and accompanying text.

[27] International Commission of Inquiry on Darfur, Established Pursuant to Resolution 1564 (2004), Report to the United Nations Secretary–General, 25 January 2005, para 491. The phrase "consciously desired" represents the volitional level, as understood by the Darfur Commission, required by the concept of genocidal intent. The report also mentions the cognitive level of genocidal intent by stating that "[the perpetrator] knew that his acts would destroy in whole or in part, the group as such". *Ibid.* It seems there is only one additional instrument in which the term 'aggravated criminal intent' is used in relation to genocide: Prosecutor v. Karadžić and Mladić, Review of the Indictments pursuant to Rule 61 of the Rules of Procedure and Evidence, 11 July 1996, para 92 ("[...] genocide requires that acts be perpetrated against a group with an *aggravated criminal intent*, namely, that of destroying the group in whole or in part".). For a view that characterizes the term 'aggravated criminal intent' as being 'less precise' in explaining the notion of genocidal intent, *see* Ambos 2014, pp. 21–22.

[28] American Law Institute, Model Penal Code § 2.02(2)(a) (defining four levels of culpability: purposely, knowingly, recklessly and negligently. Among these four levels, 'purposely' contains the strongest volitional element when it is defined that "[a] person acts purposely with respect to a material element of an offense when: (i) if the element involves the nature of his conduct or a result thereof, it is his *conscious object* to engage in conduct of that nature or to cause such a result [...]"). Note also that American Law Institute, Model Penal Code §1.13(12) states, "'intentionally' or 'with intent' means 'purposely'". On the basis of the phrase "conscious object", Kai Ambos observes that the Model Penal Code defines the "purposely" standard "in a cognitive sense". *See* Ambos 2009, p. 843. The phrase "conscious object" should however be understood as indicating the required level of volition vis-à-vis a consequence of an action. In my view, the reason why the drafters of the Model Penal Code avoided using such terms as 'desire' or 'wish' is that they were concerned about the emotional connotation attached thereto. Having a consequence as a "conscious object" is irrelevant to an actor's positive emotion (e.g., enthusiasm or want) or negative emotion (e.g., regret, sorrow or repugnance) of an actor. Rather, it has more to do with a rational choice or decision. For more discussion on this point, *see* Sect. 2.5.2 *infra*.

[29] Prosecutor v. Jelisić, Trial Judgment, 14 December 1999, para 107. (emphasis added).

volitional element in its most intensive form and is purpose-based".[30] It seems to me that it is mainly the nuance of emotion, enthusiasm, eagerness and intensity that conceptually accompanies the purpose-based notion of genocidal intent. It is therefore generally thought by the proponents of the purpose-based analysis that genocidal intent must connote something *intense*. In the subsection 2.5.1 below, I will argue against this line of understanding. At any rate, according to the purpose-based approach, genocidal intent is regarded as an element which is very difficult to prove.[31] It was in this context that the knowledge-based approach was proposed as an alternative interpretative method of the concept of genocidal intent.

2.3 An Overview of the Knowledge-Based Approach

The knowledge-based approach leads to the lightening of the burden of proving the genocidal intent element by introducing a theory that places an emphasis on the cognitive aspect of intention (as opposed to the volitional aspect stressed by the purpose-based approach). This approach claims that, while the purpose-based notion of genocidal intent is to be applied to high-level actors, 'knowledge' should be considered sufficient to constitute the genocidal intent element, at least for

---

[30] Ambos 2009, p. 838; Ambos 2014, p. 24. (emphasis added). *See also* Schabas 2009, p. 363 ("genocide requires the prosecution to establish the highest level of specific intent".); Schomburg and Peterson 2007, p. 129 ("[…] genocide thus requires an extraordinarily high standard with regard to the *mens rea* (subjective element), often referred to as a *surplus* of intent"); Fournet 2007, p. 61 ("an extremely high standard of proof regarding the mental element in the sense that a very specific intent to destroy the group […]"); Szonert-Binienda 2012, p. 699 ("the proof of specific intent, which is the highest standard of proof to be met"); Kelly 2011, p. 435 ("[t]he higher threshold for the *mens rea* element on charges of genocide requires a showing of specific intent to commit the crime".); Turns 2007, p. 426 ("that very high level of specific intent"); Nersessian 2006, p. 98 ("[…] genocide—a narrowly-defined offense that covers limited acts committed with the highest degree of specific intent"); Saul 2001, pp. 508–509 ("[t]he requisite criminal intention for genocide is clearly a higher level of intention than for ordinary crimes".). As opposed to the general understanding of the case law approach that places an emphasis on the strong degree of volition, there is a differing view. Zahar and Sluiter suggest that what the Trial Chamber in *Akayesu* meant was to exclude recklessness from the scope of genocidal intent. *See* Zahar and Sluiter 2007, p. 163. *See also* Cassese 2008, p. 137 ("This intent amounts to *dolus specialis*; that is, to an aggravated criminal intention, […] It logically follows that other categories of mental element are excluded: recklessness (or *dolus eventualis*) and gross negligence".). Kai Ambos considers this view as "critical but misleading". Ambos 2014, p. 23, footnote 152.

[31] Prosecutor v. Akayesu, Trial Judgment, 2 September 1998, para 523 ("On the issue of determining the offender's specific intent, the Chamber considers that intent is a mental factor which is difficult, even impossible, to determine".). Numerous subsequent case law and commentators have approvingly cited this sentence.

mid- or low-level participants of genocidal atrocities.[32] What it really means is that, by a showing of 'knowledge', a court can convict a mid- or low-level actor of genocide as a *principal* (as opposed to an accessory).[33] In this sense, the knowledge-based approach to genocidal intent is considered to be a good example of an expansion of definitions of crimes that casts serious doubts on international criminal law's faithfulness to the fundamental principles of personal culpability, legality, and fair labeling, as illustrated by Darryl Robinson as follows:

> Despite [international criminal law's] claim of exemplary adherence to these fundamental principles, recent scholarship has questioned this adherence in specific areas, most notably the doctrine of 'joint criminal enterprise'. [...] [S]erious issues about [international criminal law's] compliance with its fundamental principles may also be found in many other doctrines, including sweeping modes of liability, *expanding definitions of crimes*, and reticence towards defences.[34]

One can assume that the advent of the knowledge-based approach is a product of the 'expand it' movement within ICL. This movement played a crucial role at the beginning of the operations of the ICTY and the ICTR by making ICL workable through the application of the "victim-focused teleological reasoning"[35] that was prevalent in the area of human rights law and humanitarian law.[36] As summarized by Robinson,[37] in view of the subsequent development of the scholarly approaches such as (i) a 'restrict it' approach that criticizes the 'expand it' movement from the standpoint of the basic criminal law principles of legality, culpability, and fair labeling;[38] and (ii) an 'international' approach that in turn criticizes

---

[32] In the same vein, a commentator explains the knowledge-based approach as follows: "Normally, the participants of such collective operations can be roughly divided into two categories: a small number of string-pullers and masterminds behind the genocidal plot on the one hand, and on the other a much larger number of interchangeable 'foot soldiers', henchmen and followers who contribute to the execution of the plan. Of these two types of perpetrators, the argument [of the knowledge-based approach] runs, only the leading figures need to act purposefully, whereas with regard to the others, a certain degree of knowledge is sufficient". Tams et al. 2014, p. 141.
It seems, however, that, among the proponents of the knowledge-based approach, Claus Kress and Hans Vest do not differentiate leadership-level actors and mid- or low-level participants in applying the knowledge-based approach. *See* Kress 2005; Vest 2007.

[33] For a similar view, *see* Bantekas 2010, p. 48 ("The school of thought in support of the so-called 'knowledge-based' doctrine argues that mid-level and lower-ranking executioners that are merely aware of the ultimate object of a genocidal campaign should be deemed liable *as principals* to genocide".). (emphasis added).

[34] Robinson 2008, p. 927. (emphasis added).

[35] *Ibid.* at 929.

[36] See generally, *Ibid.*; Robinson 2013; Sliedregt 2012a, p. 1186 ("[Cassese] believed that the rudimentary character of international criminal law allowed for progress and a certain flexibility with regard to the principle of legality".), citing Cassese 2008, p. 32, footnote 1.

[37] Robinson 2013, pp. 127–129.

[38] *See e.g.*, Ambos 2007, pp. 173–174 (discussing the conflict between the JCE doctrine and the principle of culpability).

the 'restrict it' approach emphasizing the difference between ICL and domestic criminal law,[39] it would be accurate to conclude that the knowledge-based approach appeared in the midst of an overall trend of interpreting "the rules on genocide [...] in such a manner as to give them their maximum legal effects"[40] pursuant to the 'expand it' approach.

Though Alexander Greenawalt's 1999 article is generally considered the leading authority of the proposal of the knowledge-based approach,[41] already in 1993, M. Cherif Bassiouni advanced a knowledge-based concept of genocidal intent applicable to *executors* of underlying acts. It is to be noted that Bassiouni's distinction between high-level decision makers and subordinate actors in applying the knowledge-based approach has been followed by its subsequent proponents. In his "proposed text" of 'Article 19: Genocide' in the International Law Commission's 1991 Draft Code of Crimes Against the Peace and Security of Mankind, Bassiouni observes:

> 3. Intent to commit Genocide, as defined above, can be proven by objective legal stand-ards with respect to decision makers and commanders. With respect to executants, *knowl-edge* of the nature of the act based on an objective reasonable standard shall constitute intent.[42]

In 1995, knowledge as a *mens rea* of genocide for subordinate actors was also suggested during the Ad Hoc Committee meetings for the establishment of the International Criminal Court:

> There was a further suggestion to clarify the intent requirement for the crime of genocide by distinguishing between a specific intent requirement for the responsible decision makers or planners and a general-intent or *knowledge requirement for the actual perpetrators of geno-cidal acts*. Some delegations felt that it might be useful to elaborate on various aspects of the intent requirement without amending the Convention, including the intent required for the various categories of responsible individuals, and to clarify the meaning of the phrase "intent to destroy", as well as the threshold to be set in terms of the scale of the offence or the num-ber of victims.[43]

---

[39] *See generally* Luban 2010. For a critical overview of the 'restrict it' approach, *see* Osiel 2009, p. 118 *et seq.* For a proposal for independent criminology, penology, and victimology of interna-tional criminal law, *see* Drumbl 2005.

[40] International Commission of Inquiry on Darfur, Established Pursuant to Resolution 1564 (2004), Report to the United Nations Secretary–General, 25 January 2005, para 494.

[41] Greenawalt 1999.

[42] Bassiouni 1993, pp. 235–236. (emphasis added). In relation to "decision makers and com-manders", Bassiouni is here proposing a quite radical genocidal intent theory which replaces a traditional purpose-based genocidal intent with a "particular objective pattern of conduct". *Ibid.* at 234. It seems Bassiouni's observation in this respect was insightful in that the *ad hoc* tribunals subsequently developed the relevant jurisprudence on the theme of genocidal intent placing a sig-nificant evidentiary emphasis on the 'objective pattern of conduct' feature.

[43] U.N. G.A. Rep. of the Ad Hoc Comm. on the Establishment of the Int'l Criminal Court, para 62, U.N. Doc. A/50/22, GAOR, 50th Sess., Supp. No. 22, 6 September 1995. (emphasis added). *See also* Options Paper on "Applicable Law" by Canada, Ad Hoc Committee on the Establishment of an International Criminal Court, August 14–25, 1995, at 5–6 ("A third option is to include the relevant provisions of international conventions in the Statute (as in Option 2)

In 1996, M. Cherif Bassiouni and Peter Manikas further suggested,

> This means that: (a) policymakers and others at any level of decisionmaking must have the requisite specific intent to "destroy in whole or in part" the protected group by the means described in the Article; and (b) those who execute the policy must intend to commit the acts enumerated in the Article, and also have intent, *knowledge*, or reasonable belief that they are acting in furtherance of the policy to "destroy in whole or in part the protected group".[44]

At this point, it is worth noting that all these initial proposals of the knowledge-based approach to interpreting genocidal intent already came up with a differentiated *mens rea* scheme for decision makers, planners and commanders on the one hand, and for physical executors at the low-level on the other. Such a special concern for subordinate actors' genocidal responsibility has also been reflected in an observation of the International Law Commission (hereinafter ILC) in its 1996 report as follows:

> The definition of the crime of genocide would be equally applicable to any individual who committed one of the prohibited acts with the necessary intent. The extent of knowledge of the details of a plan or a policy to carry out the crime of genocide would vary depending on the position of the perpetrator in the governmental hierarchy or the military command structure. This does not mean that a *subordinate* who actually carries out the plan or policy cannot be held responsible for the crime of genocide simply because he did not possess the same degree of information concerning the overall plan or policy as his superiors. The definition of the crime of genocide *requires* a degree of knowledge of the ultimate objective of the criminal conduct rather than knowledge of every detail of a comprehensive plan or policy of genocide. A *subordinate* is presumed to *know* the intentions of his superiors when he receives orders to commit the prohibited acts against individuals who belong to a particular group. He cannot escape responsibility if he carries out the orders to commit the destructive acts against victims who are selected because of their membership in a particular group by claiming that he was not privy to all the aspects of the comprehensive genocidal plan or policy. [...] For example, a soldier who is ordered to

---

Footnote 43 (continued)

but, rather than modify the definitions (as in Option 2), elaborate the meaning of specific elements for the purpose of the Statute. [...] Ambiguity or uncertainty of meaning of the phrase "with intent to destroy" in Article 2 of the Convention on the Prevention and Punishment of the Crime of Genocide, for example, could be resolved by defining its meaning for the purposes of the Statute (e.g. "with intent to destroy" could be defined to include both an intention to destroy and knowledge that destruction is a likely consequence of one's acts)".). In my view, given that the knowledge/foresight of a *likelihood* of causing a consequence is the cognitive level required for '*dolus eventualis*/recklessness' (as opposed to the cognitive level of 'knowledge/foresight of virtual/practical certainty' for 'indirect intent/knowingly'), this opinion of the Canadian delegations seems rather excessive as it signifies a possibility of 'reckless genocide'.

[44] Bassiouni and Manikas 1996, p. 529. (emphasis added). This proposal must be read in conjunction with the following elaboration: "The Genocide Convention [...] requires that the perpetrator act with 'specific intent'. The distinction between 'general intent' and 'specific intent' exists in the world's major criminal justice systems. In the criminal justice systems of continental Europe, the Roman law concept of '*dolus*' is similar to 'specific intent'. It is *dolus* that must be established, requiring a showing that the actor either specifically sought to produce a particular result or knew that his conduct was part of an overall plan or practice designed to eliminate in whole or in part a certain group of people. It is this element of specific intent which distinguishes genocide from crimes against humanity, war crimes, and common crimes". *Ibid.* at 527.

go from house to house and kill only persons who are members of a particular group cannot be unaware of the irrelevance of the identity of the victims and the significance of their membership in a particular group.[45]

In this paragraph, the ILC is trying to construct a *mens rea* framework based on the knowledge of subordinate actors of a genocidal campaign. For those low-level participants, the purpose-based genocidal intent is plainly excluded by the ILC. By stating that "the definition of the crime of genocide *requires* a degree of knowledge", the ILC gives a status of an 'element of the crime' to the *mens rea* of knowledge at least in relation to physical perpetrators of underlying acts. In this regard, this observation sounds radical. The cited paragraphs above, from Bassiouni to the ILC, reflect the long-standing apprehension that a strict interpretation of the genocidal intent element would provide room for mid- or low-level actors to flee from punishment. This was demonstrated by a concern expressed by the USSR delegation during the drafting negotiations of the Genocide Convention as follows:

> The perpetrators of acts of genocide would in certain cases be able to claim that they were not in fact guilty of genocide, having had not intent to destroy a given group, either wholly or partially; they might likewise assert that they had simply carried out superior orders and that they had been unable to do otherwise.[46]

In 1999, a scholarly article offered an articulated proposal for the knowledge-based approach. Alexander Greenawalt's landmark article on the knowledge-based approach to interpreting genocidal intent has gained much support from scholars in the field. "Drawing upon a more traditional understanding of intent",[47] Greenawalt argues, "in defined situations, *principal culpability* for genocide should extend to those who may personally lack a specific genocidal purpose, but who commit genocidal acts while understanding the *consequences* of their actions".[48] Despite the conditional phrase of "in defined situations" (which has not been specifically substantiated in the article), this is certainly a bold statement, especially because it implies a significant expansion of the scope of principal culpability of the 'crime of crimes'.[49] Thus, Greenawalt proposes an interpretative

---

[45] Report of the International Law Commission on the Work of Its Forty-Eight Session, May 6-July 26, 1996, at 45, U.N. Doc. A/51/10. (emphasis added).

[46] U.N. GAOR, 6th Comm., 3d Sess., 73d mtg. at 96, U.N. Doc. A/C.6/SR.73, Oct. 13, 1948. Karadžić during his trial at the ICTY actually made an observation in which he reported the accounts of his subordinates who physically committed killings at Srebrenica that they did not have genocidal intent. For more discussion on this argument made by Karadžić, *see* Chap. 4, footnotes 243 and 244 *infra* and accompanying text.

[47] Greenawalt 1999, pp. 2264–2265.

[48] *Ibid.* at 2259 (1999) (emphasis added). Though a text almost verbatim in language appears in the body of the article (pp. 2264–2265), I cite here a text from the 'abstract' because the key word "principal culpability" is omitted in the body.

[49] *See* Prosecutor v. Kayishema and Ruzindana, Appeals Judgment, 1 June 2001, para 367 (opining that, while the description of genocide as a 'crime of crimes' in the trial judgment should be understood to express a general appreciation, there is no hierarchy among the core international crimes provided in the Statute.).

approach that renders it possible to punish subordinate actors as principals if they "knew that the goal or manifest effect of the genocidal campaign was the destruction of the group in whole or in part".[50] In short, the most significant implication of this proposal lies in the fact that, through the knowledge of the destructive result, mid- or low-level actors, regardless of their position or rank, can be convicted as *principals* of the crime of genocide without a need to resort to any expansive liability doctrines.[51]

In view of the wide conceptual scope of intent in both the Continental and the Anglo-American legal traditions and the ambiguous and confusing understanding of it during the drafting negotiations of the Genocide Convention, Greenawalt concludes that the drafting history mandates neither the purpose-based approach nor the knowledge-based approach.[52] Greenawalt further understands that the 'intent' under the ICC Statute "embraces a relatively broad understanding of intent analogous to the Model Penal Code definition of 'knowledge'".[53] In this respect, it appears that the notion of 'knowledge' when Greenawalt speaks of the 'knowledge of the destructive consequence' falls into the concept of 'indirect intent/knowingly' as the *mens rea* of knowledge in the Model Penal Code adopts the 'practical certainty' standard.[54] In any event, it should be remembered that Greenawalt's knowledge-based approach is premised on the notion that the perpetrator knows the *result or consequence of destruction*. In this respect, Greenawalt further observes,

> [The knowledge-based] approach emphasizes the *destructive result* of genocidal acts instead of the specific reasons that move particular individuals to perform such acts. It addresses the related problems of subordinate actors and ambiguous goals by unhinging the question of genocidal liability from that of the perpetrator's particular motive or desires with regard to the group as a whole.[55]

Currently, many commentators follow the knowledge-based approach. Among them, Hans Vest also maintains that the 'practical certainty' standard should be applied to his version of the knowledge-based approach. In particular, he claims

---

[50] Greenawalt 1999, p. 2288 ("In cases where a perpetrator is otherwise liable for a genocidal act, the requirement of genocidal intent should be satisfied if the perpetrator acted in furtherance of a campaign targeting members of a protected group and knew that the goal or manifest effect of the campaign was the destruction of the group in whole or in part".).

[51] *Ibid.* at 2288 (1999) (note the phrase "without relying on an expansive liability framework"). The difficulty in attributing individual responsibility in a mass criminality tends to entice legislators and legal theorists into expanding the scope of the (i) concept of intention, and/or (ii) the doctrines of modes of liability. For instance, Thomas Weigend explains that, in resolving the problem of attribution in relation to the crimes committed during the World War II and also the crimes of the German Democratic Republic decades later, the German courts and scholars have produced a satisfactory result by cautiously expanding both the traditional modes of liability and the notion of intent. Weigend 2014, p. 255.

[52] Greenawalt 1999, p. 2266.

[53] *Ibid.* at 2269 (1999).

[54] American Law Institute, Model Penal Code, § 2.02(2)(b) (1962). For more discussion on the cognitive standards of *mens rea* including the 'practical certainty' standard, *see* Sect. 2.5 *infra*.

[55] Greenawalt 1999, p. 2288. (emphasis added).

that "the knowledge-based standard of genocidal intent is established when the perpetrator's knowledge of the *consequences* of the overall conduct reaches the level of practical certainty".[56] One implication of this position is that '*dolus eventualis*/recklessness' is not sufficient to constitute the genocidal intent element. Thus, in view of (i) the characterization of a subordinate actor's knowledge as being directed at the destructive consequence, and (ii) the proposal of the practical certainty standard that signifies the *mens rea* of 'indirect intent/knowingly', Vest's version of the knowledge-based approach appears to be largely in line with that of Greenawalt. This already reduced notion of genocidal intent (from a purpose-based concept equivalent to 'direct intent/purposely' to 'indirect intent/knowingly' that accompanies a foresight of a consequence to a practical certainty) was even further degraded to the level of '*dolus eventualis*/recklessness' when Claus Kress proposed that: "individual genocidal intent requires (a) knowledge of a collective attack directed to the destruction of at least part of a protected group, and (b) *dolus eventualis* as regards the occurrence of such destruction".[57] Kai Ambos advances yet another proposal for a knowledge-based approach according to which the notion of knowledge means a low-level actor's "knowledge that his acts are part of an overall genocidal context or campaign".[58] The scheme of knowledge in relation to an act forming part of an objective context reminds us of the parallel requirement in the ICC's definition of crimes against humanity that "[t]he perpetrator knew that the conduct was part of [...] a widespread or systematic attack against a civilian population".[59] More specifically, it appears that Ambos' view on this point is at least partly influenced by the 'structural congruity' between genocide and crimes against

---

[56] Vest 2007, p. 793. (emphasis added). It is important to note that Hans Vest rightly places a significant emphasis on the collective dimension of genocide, which, he considers, conceptually reshapes the genocidal intent element into an "extended subjective element [that] refers to the overall context of the collective action (in German *Gesamttat*) combining the efforts of different perpetrators and accomplices". *Ibid.* at 784.

[57] Kress 2005, p. 577. Otto Triffterer seems to be of the same view when he observes that "*[d]olus eventualis* [...] is sufficient to [...] have [...] the particular 'intent to destroy [...]'". Triffterer 2001, p. 399. According to Claus Kress, Alicia Gil Gil is also of the same opinion. Kress summarizes her view by saying that "[a]ccording to her, the individual perpetrator of genocide must, first, know of the existence of a genocidal campaign and secondly, act with at least *dolus eventualis* as regards the occurrence of the destructive result". Kress 2005, p. 567. Already in 1985, Leo Kuper also advanced a similar proposal of genocidal intent via *dolus eventualis*. He seemed to consider that genocidal intent might take on either the form of 'indirect intent/ knowingly' or '*dolus eventualis*/recklessness'. Kuper 1985, p. 12 ("I will assume that intent is established if the foreseeable consequences of an act are, or seem likely to be, the destruction of a group".). For a critical view on introducing *dolus eventualis* into the reading of genocidal intent, *see* Ambos 2014, p. 31 ("[...] a lower mental standard, for example *dolus eventualis* or even recklessness, cannot be admitted, since it would radically change the character of the genocide offence in terms of its wrongfulness and speciality vis-à-vis crimes against humanity".).

[58] Ambos 2009, p. 858. *See also* Ambos 2014, p. 31.

[59] ICC Element of Crimes provides a common subjective contextual element for all offences of crimes against humanity as follows: "The perpetrator knew that the conduct was part of [...] a widespread or systematic attack against a civilian population".

humanity.[60] In the end, he concludes that "[t]he combination of the structure- and knowledge-based approaches suggested here calls for a knowledge-based reading of the 'intent to destroy' requirement in the case of low-level perpetrators with regard to *the genocidal context as the object of reference of the intent to destroy*".[61]

What then is the reason behind proposing the knowledge-based approach to genocidal intent? Although Greenawalt shared the enduring concern that obedient executors at the low-level might "escape liability for genocide" by exploiting the strict standard of the purpose-based notion of genocidal intent,[62] the main reason that seemed to urge him to propose the knowledge-based approach lie in the ICTR's troublesome practice of *presuming* genocidal intent while doctrinally upholding the strict purpose-based notion of genocidal intent. Greenawalt critically quotes the *Akayesu* Trial Chamber's observation that "it is possible to deduce the genocidal intent inherent in a particular act charged from the general context of the perpetration of other culpable acts systematically directed against that same group, whether these acts were committed by the same offender or by others".[63] Apparently, Greenawalt was troubled by the practice of seemingly presuming the genocidal intent element proclaimed as the gist of the 'crime of crimes' "largely by virtue of the fact that a perpetrator participates in a genocidal campaign".[64] Inferring individual *mens rea* from a genocidal campaign, a context of violence or an overall circumstance of such an extensive temporal and geographical scope as the atrocities in Rwanda is certainly a questionable practice.[65]

---

[60] *See* Ambos 2014, p. 30 ("[…] all this means that a simple, low-level *génocidaire* as well as a perpetrator of a crime against humanity must (only) act with knowledge of the respective context required by both crimes".). The term 'structural congruity' was introduced by Claus Kress when he argued that "[…] the construction of individual genocidal intent in accordance with the knowledge-based approach would bring the definitions of genocide and crimes against humanity into *structural congruity*, to the extent that both definitions apply to the participation of individual perpetrators in a *systemic* act".). (emphasis in original). Kress 2005, p. 575 (2005).

[61] Ambos 2014, p. 31. For more discussion on Ambos's "genocidal context as the object of reference of the intent to destroy", *see* Sect. 2.4.2 *infra*.

[62] Greenawalt 1999, p. 2281.

[63] *Ibid.* at 2282. The practice of inferring genocidal intent from "other culpable acts systematically directed against the same group" is repeatedly endorsed by the Appeals Chamber of the *ad hoc* tribunals. *See e.g.*, Prosecutor v. Krstić, Appeals Judgment, 19 April 2004, para 33 ("The genocidal intent may be inferred, among other facts, from evidence of "other culpable acts systematically directed against the same group".); Prosecutor v. Gacumbitsi, Appeals Judgment, 7 July 2006, para 44 ("In the Appeals Chamber's view, it is appropriate and consistent with the Tribunal's jurisprudence to consider, in determining whether the Appellant meant to target a sufficiently substantial part of the Tutsi population to amount to genocide, that the Appellant's actions took place within the context of other culpable acts systematically directed against the Tutsi population. The Trial Chamber's findings discussed above clearly establish that the Appellant was an active participant in those culpable acts".). For more discussion on the *ad hoc* tribunals' practice of inferring individual genocidal intent from 'acts of others'. *see* Sect. 4.1.2 *infra*.

[64] Greenawalt 1999, p. 2282.

[65] The Appeals Chamber of the ICTY, for instance, has taken a cautious approach in finding an individual *mens rea* by inference. Accordingly, the Chamber is of the view that "that inference must be the only reasonable inference available on the evidence". Prosecutor v. Krstić, Appeals Judgment, 19 April 2004, para 41, and sources cited therein.

In the end, Greenawalt expressed his doubt by stating that the ICTR's practice of presuming individual genocidal intent "begs the question as to whether the specific intent standard does any work at the individual level".[66] In this context, it is noteworthy that a wanted or unwanted effect of the knowledge-based approach is that it tends to justify such practices of inferring individual genocidal intent from the overall context and circumstances because it is exactly the *mens rea* of knowledge that normally attends the *actus reus* of 'circumstance'.[67] In this manner, courts are free from the accusation of "squeez[ing] ambiguous fact patterns into the specific intent paradigm" because the paradigm itself has been broadened by virtue of the knowledge-based notion of genocidal intent.[68] In this respect, would it be an overstatement if one claims that the knowledge-based approach is an example of extending a crime definition itself in order to legitimize a doubtful practice? This question seems to be in line with an observation that "the issue of subordinates not personally sharing the destructive purpose of the high-level authors of the genocidal plot does not necessarily call for lowering the intent requirements to mere knowledge".[69] In the following section, I will elaborate on the problematic aspects of the knowledge-based approach in more detail.

2.4 Rethinking the Knowledge-Based Approach (I): Some Observations

2.4.1 A Hypothetical: An Insomniac Commander

"Sleep no more! Macbeth does murder sleep,"

– William Shakespeare, Macbeth act 2, sc. 2, lines 39–40.

On the basis of the overview of the purpose-based and the knowledge-based approaches that I provided in the previous sections, let us think about a hypothetical that reads as follows:

An old woman approached a militia commander with a contract offer to destroy a protected group. The militia commander accepted the contract. He acted in

---

[66] Greenawalt 1999, p. 2282.

[67] *See* ICC Statute, Article 30(3) ("[…] 'knowledge' means awareness that a circumstance exists […]".); American Law Institute, Model Penal Code, § 2.02(2)(b) ("A person acts knowingly with respect to a material element of an offense when: (i) if the element involves the nature of […] the attendant circumstances, he is aware […] that such circumstances exist[.]"). Similarly, Otto Triffterer observes, "[w]e can prove by circumstantial evidence what the perpetrator was aware of and of which facts he had knowledge". Triffterer 2001, p. 405.

[68] Greenawalt 1999, p. 2281 ("[t]he danger of adhering to a specific intent standard in such situations is not merely that culpable perpetrators will escape liability for genocide, but perhaps more ominously that the evidentiary problems will compel courts to squeeze ambiguous fact patterns into the specific intent paradigm".).

[69] Tams et al. 2014, p. 147.

accordance with the detailed terms of the contract, and, after all, one third of the members of the group were killed by his subordinates. While the relevant facts satisfy all the material elements of genocide, the commander himself did not desire the destruction of the group at all. Rather, he was very concerned about the destructive consequence of the deadly operations meticulously planned and performed by his militia unit. The commander even wanted to hit the old woman when she said to him, "I have a clear intent to destroy the group". However, he stayed calm because she offered an enormous amount of money. Throughout the genocidal campaign, each time he carefully drafted, reviewed and signed on killing orders, he expressed a deep regret at the overall context of violence reported to him on a daily basis. He often suffered from insomnia because of his revulsion for what he was doing, which gave him extra time to refine the killing plan throughout the night. The prosecutor charged him with genocide. Now as a judge, would you convict him of genocide?

In terms of the question of genocidal intent, the proponents of the prior purpose-based approach that places an emphasis on the intensity of volition would claim that the commander is not guilty of genocide as a principal, because his mental state has not reached the level of volitional element in its most intensive form. On the other hand, the expected answer from the camp of the knowledge-based approach is twofold. First, if the theory does not differentiate among high-, mid-, and low-level actors, the commander would certainly be convicted of genocide as a principal (together with his subordinates) on the basis of his knowledge (of the destructive consequences, the context of genocidal campaign and/or the old woman's genocidal intent). Second, if the theory treats the high-ranking actors differently from subordinate actors (applying the purpose-based theory to the former, and the knowledge-based theory to the latter), an awkward result ensues: while the insomniac commander would be acquitted of genocide as a principal due to the fact that his state of mind did not reach the level of volition in its most intensive form, his subordinates would be convicted of genocide as principals for their knowledge. Can you accept this answer from the proponents of the knowledge-based theory? In what follows, let us critically consider what underlies this counterintuitive result.

2.4.2 Consequence or Context? On Valid Objects of Knowledge

Kai Ambos claims that the knowledge-based approach requires a showing of low-level perpetrators' knowledge of "the genocidal context as the object of reference of the intent to destroy".[70] As we will see in this subsection, when he argues for this position, he does not accept the destructive consequence as a valid object of knowledge. In this context, it should be noted that Ambos's version of knowledge-based approach is, at least theoretically, different from other scholars like Alexander

---

[70] Ambos 2014, p. 31.

Greenawalt, Hans Vest or Claus Kress in that his concept of knowledge is directed at the *overall context* of violence that falls into the *actus reus* of 'circumstance' (as opposed to destructive consequence that corresponds to the *actus reus* of 'consequence'). Although 'knowledge of an overall context' also forms part of Kress's version of the knowledge-based approach (together with *dolus eventualis* vis-à-vis the destructive consequences), that of Ambos seems to involves the knowledge of an overall context *only*.[71] On this issue, Ambos observes:

> As to the ultimate destruction of the group, the low-level perpetrator can, by definition, have no knowledge thereof but may only wish or desire this result, since it is *a future event*. In any case, his attitude towards this ultimate consequence is not decisive for the required intent to destroy.[72]

His contention that the 'context' should be the *only* reference point of subordinate actors' knowledge is also explained:

> [A] simple, low-level *génocidaire* as well as a perpetrator of a crime against humanity must (only) act with knowledge of the respective context required by both crimes. [...] The context serves in both cases as the object of reference of the perpetrator's knowledge, in other words, the knowledge needs not to be directed at the ultimate destruction of the group *in the future*, but only at the overall genocidal context. Indeed, the ultimate destruction of the group is only *a future expectation* which as such cannot be known, but only hoped for or desired.[73]

In my view, however, there is no problem in relating the knowledge-based genocidal intent to the destruction of a group *in the future*. That is because, within the *mens rea* framework of 'indirect intent/oblique intent/knowingly', the 'knowledge' is directed at a result or consequence *in the future* by taking the conceptual form of 'foresight'.[74] Thus, there seems to be no grounds to exclude the destruction of a group (destructive consequence) from the pool of valid objects of knowledge by reason of its *timing*.[75] Furthermore, given the considerable extent of factual

---

[71] Note that I use the adverb 'only' with caution. Without specifying particular reasons, Ambos also mentions 'masterminds' genocidal intent' and 'possibility of destruction' as an object of knowledge. *See* Chap. 2, footnotes 132, 133 and 137 *infra* and accompanying text.

[72] Ambos 2009, p. 858. (emphasis added).

[73] Ambos 2014, p. 30. (emphasis added). See also *Ibid.* at 32

[74] For more about Ambos's understanding of the notions of 'knowledge' and 'foresight/foreseeability' (in the context of discussing the JCE III doctrine), *see* Ambos 2007, pp. 174–175. Though my conceptual framework of intention is based on the notion of 'foresight' (cognitive side of intention), Ambos expresses a seemingly directly opposite view as follows: "In fact, knowledge is a standard for intent crimes (*see* ICC Statute, Article 30), while foreseeability belongs to the theories of recklessness and negligence". *Ibid.* at 175.

[75] Although Gabriel Hallevy's opinion is apparently similar to that of Ambos, it actually supports my position. In line with Ambos, Hallevy is of the view that 'cognition/knowledge' can only relate to occurrences in the past and present, but not in the future. However, he conceptually distinguishes 'the occurrence in the future' and 'the possibility of the occurrence in the future'. Since Hallevy classifies the latter as an event *in the present*, he concludes that 'the *possibility* of a result/consequence to occur in the future' can be an object of 'cognition/knowledge'. Hallevy 2014, pp. 37–38. In this context, it seems that recognizing the notion of '*foresight* of a result/consequence' as a form of 'cognition/knowledge' would make the relevant analysis simpler and easier.

overlap between the 'destructive consequence' and the 'overall genocidal context/campaign'. it appears that accepting only the genocidal context as an object of knowledge (while excluding the destructive consequence) is not persuasive. Indeed, the genocidal context/campaign itself includes a process of destruction in which numerous small destructions are being produced.[76] Let us consider a case of high-level actors. In *Krstić*, the ICTY Trial Chamber draws its conclusion on the question of the accused's genocidal intent on the basis of the accused's knowledge of the destructive consequence as follows:

> Having already played a key role in the forcible transfer of the Muslim women, children and elderly out of Serb-held territory, General Krstić undeniably *was aware of the fatal impact* that the killing of the men would have on the ability of the Bosnian Muslim community of Srebrenica to survive, as such. General Krstić thus participated in the genocidal acts of "killing members of the group" under Article 4(2)(a) with the intent to destroy a part of the group.[77]
>
> In the present case, General Krstić participated in a joint criminal enterprise to kill the military-aged Bosnian Muslim men of Srebrenica with the *awareness that such killings would lead to the annihilation* of the entire Bosnian Muslim community at Srebrenica. His intent to kill the men thus amounts to a genocidal intent to destroy the group in part.[78]

The object of knowledge in both paragraphs above is the destructive consequence that conceptually exists *in the future* to which the standard of the 'foresight to a virtual/practical certainty' is applicable.[79] Put otherwise, national criminal law theories on the *mens rea* of 'indirect intent/knowingly'. in particular, the distinction between the 'desired main effect' and 'permitted side-effect' should be considered to be applicable to the relevant discussions of the notion of the knowledge-based genocidal intent, because such phrases as "fatal impact" and "would lead to the annihilation" connote an expected occurrence *in the future*.[80] In the same vein,

---

[76] In this respect, consider Bruno Latour's observation: "Actors [are] simultaneously held by the context and holding it in place, while the context [is] at once what makes actors behave and what is being made in turn". Latour 2005, p. 169, *as cited in* Osiel 2009, p. 3, footnote 11.

[77] Prosecutor v. Krstić, Trial Judgment, 2 August 2001, para 634. (emphasis added).

[78] *Ibid.* para 644. (emphasis added).

[79] I again emphasize that, in relation to both the Trial Judgment and the Appeals Judgment in *Krstić*, the notion of 'destruction' should be understood as a *future event*. That is because, in terms of definition of the crime of genocide, while grasping the 'group in whole' as the 'Bosnian Muslims'. the Trial and Appeals Chambers in *Krstić* define the 'Bosnian Muslims in Srebrenica' as the 'group in part'/'substantial part'. That is to say, *the past or present event* of killing the Bosnian Muslim men of military age in Srebrenica does not form part of the 'destruction' per se. It only serves as evidence of the *future* destruction of the Bosnian Muslims in Srebrenica. In this sense, despite the fact that both the Trial and Appeals Chambers in *Krstić* are of the view that it is the '*physical* destruction of the Bosnian Muslims in Srebrenica' that constitutes the crime of genocide in this case, I believe that '*biological* destruction of the Bosnian Muslims in Srebrenica' that is foreseen *in the future* is a more precise notion for the *Krstić* case. Thus, in my view, depending on the way you define the 'group in part'/'substantial part'. the nature of destruction in a given case may vary between 'physical destruction' and 'biological destruction'. For more discussion, *see* Chaps. 3, footnotes 116 and 214 *infra* and Chap. 4, footnote 32 *infra*.

[80] For the distinction between 'desired main effect' and 'permitted side effect'. *see* Sects. 2.5.2.2 through 2.5.2.4 *infra*.

when the *Blagojević and Jokić* Trial Chamber explicitly rejects the knowledge-based approach, the knowledge is about the destructive consequence foreseen in the future.

> It is not sufficient that the perpetrator simply knew that the underlying crime would *inevitably* or *likely* result in the destruction of the group. The destruction, in whole or in part, must be the *aim* of the underlying crime(s).[81]

For the reasons specified thus far, I believe that the claim that the genocidal context/campaign is the only objective reference point of the knowledge for the purpose of applying the knowledge-based approach is hard to justify.[82]

2.4.3 Why Principals? A Comparison with Joint Criminal Enterprise and Perpetration by Means

As I said earlier, the most significant legal effect of the knowledge-based approach is to classify the subordinate actors as principals of genocide. With respect to the question of distinguishing principals and accessories concerning the crime of genocide, the Trial Chamber in *Stakić* observes:

> [I]n most cases, the principal perpetrator of genocide are those who devise the genocidal plan at the highest level and take the major steps to put it into effect. The principal perpetrator is the one who fulfils "a key co-ordinating role" and whose "participation is of an extremely significant nature and at the leadership level".[83]

Arguing for the knowledge-based approach vis-à-vis low-level participants in a genocidal campaign, Kai Ambos seems to maintain that they should be convicted "as principals", because they are the "direct executors of the genocidal plan".[84] This view is considered to be a product of applying the 'objective approach' to distinguishing principals and accessories used in Germany.[85] On the other hand, however, he is also of the view that those subordinate actors are "only secondary participants, thus more precisely aides and assistants" because they "were not involved in designing [the genocidal] plan but are [...] only used as mere

---

[81] Prosecutor v. Blagojević and Jokić, Trial Judgment, 17 January 2005, para 656.

[82] My discussion on the question of valid object of knowledge will continue: *see* Chap. 2, footnotes 126 through 140 *infra* and accompanying text.

[83] Prosecutor v. Stakić, Decision on Rule 98 *bis* Motion for Judgment of Acquittal, 31 October 2002, para 50. *See also* Prosecutor v. Krstić, Trial Judgment, 2 August 2001, para 642; Prosecutor v. Blagojević and Jokić, Trial Judgment, 17 January 2005, para 776.

[84] Ambos 2009, p. 847.

[85] For a brief overview of the three German approaches to distinguishing principals and accessories—i.e., the subjective approach, the objective approach, and the Roxin's control theory (Tatherrschaft), *see* Fletcher 2011, pp. 189–190. For an overview of the various standards applied at the *ad hoc* international criminal tribunals in distinguishing principals and accessories, *see* Ambos 2013, pp. 134–135.

instruments to implement it".[86] This observation sounds contradictory to the previous claim that low-level actors should be punished "as principals". Classifying the low-level actors in a genocidal campaign as 'secondary participants', 'aides and assistants', or 'mere instrument' reflects the 'subjective approach' or the 'control theory' to distinguishing principals and accessories. Thus, it is confusing that Ambos seems to apply all three differing approaches at once. As far as the distinction between principal liability and accessory liability is concerned, the knowledge-based approach gets things in a muddle. In this regard, the knowledge-based approach reminds us of the JCE doctrine, which is widely criticized for its overly broad scope of application of the principal liability, mockingly reflected in the joke that JCE stands for 'just convict everybody'.[87] Even JCE, however, is better situated in this respect than the knowledge-based approach, in that its principal culpability scheme is at least based on the 'shared intent' or the 'intent to further the common purpose'.[88] Accordingly, the purpose-based notion of intention is an essential feature of JCE: it renders the doctrine a 'commission' liability; thus, classifying the members of JCE as 'principals' (as opposed to 'accessories'). In this respect, the Appeals Chamber in *Ojdanić* observes,

> The Prosecution's approach is correct to the extent that, *insofar as a participant shares the purpose* of the joint criminal enterprise (as he or she must do) *as opposed to merely knowing about it*, he or she cannot be regarded as a mere aider and abettor to the crime which is contemplated. The Appeals Chamber therefore regards joint criminal enterprise as a form of "commission" pursuant to Article 7(1) of the Statute.[89]

Thus, in my view, JCE is more faithful to the principle of fair labeling and the rights of the accused than the knowledge-based approach in that (i) it requires a purpose-based intention ('shared intent' or 'intent to further the common

---

[86] Ambos 2009, p. 847. *See also* Ambos 2014, p. 29 ("these low-level perpetrators are, albeit carrying out the underlying genocidal acts with their own hands, in terms of their overall contribution to the genocidal campaign, [to be regarded as] only secondary participants—more precisely, aiders or assistants [...] only used as a mere instruments [...]".).

[87] *See e.g.*, Ohlin 2007, pp. 85–88.

[88] See also, albeit in a slightly different context, Jens David Ohlin's criticism of Article 25(3)(d) of the Rome Statute for its uniform treatment of 'people who share the group intent' (Article 25(3)(d)(i)) and 'people who do not share the group intent' (Article 25(3)(d)(ii)). Ohlin 2011, p. 746. For an overview of JCE, *see* Haan 2005.

[89] Prosecutor v. Milutinović et al., Decision on Dragoljub Ojdanić's Motion Challenging Jurisdiction – Joint Criminal Enterprise, 21 May 2003, para 20. (emphasis added). Note that, emphasizing the importance of a differentiated treatment between principals and accessories, Jens David Ohlin advances an interesting proposal to specify the JCE liability by splitting it into two separate modes of liability of 'co-perpetrating a joint criminal enterprise' (requiring the *intent* to further the criminal purpose of the group endeavor); and "aiding and abetting a joint criminal enterprise" (requiring the *knowledge* of the group's efforts). This proposal draws upon the *Kvočka* Trial Judgment and the *Stakić* Trial Judgment. Ohlin 2011, pp. 714–715 and 745–746. *See also* Ambos 2007, pp. 169–171 (arguing that JCE III constitutes only a form of aiding and abetting the JCE, whilst it is only JCE I that can be regarded as 'commission' or 'co-perpetration'.). In England and Wales, aiding and abetting a conspiracy is feasible as conspiracy itself is an offence. Cryer 2014, p. 279.

purpose'); and (ii) it sets a boundary of the applicable scope (the commission liability is to be applied to its members only). To the contrary, it is troubling to note that the knowledge-based approach to genocidal intent lacks any such self-restrictive measures. The applicable scope is almost limitless under the name of 'subordinate actors'; and 'knowledge' is sufficient to classify a person as a principal of genocide. Furthermore, such 'knowledge' is subject to an almost automatic presumption provided that a low-level actor was present within an overall genocidal context or campaign performing the *actus reus* of underlying acts. In this manner, it appears that, as far as the issue of principal liability is concerned, the knowledge-based approach introduces a worse version of JCE to the crime definition of genocide through the genocidal intent element.

To sum up: although hardly discussed in a serious manner by commentators,[90] the main legal effect of applying the knowledge-based approach is to facilitate the punishment of subordinate actors *as principals* (as opposed to accessories) by virtue of an extended definition of genocidal intent *itself*. Consequently, through the knowledge-based approach, a court can attach principal liability to them without resorting to an expansive mode of criminal responsibility (e.g., JCE)[91] or to the practice of circumventing the purpose-based notion of genocidal intent through the 'evidentiary backdoor'.[92] It is therefore like planting a very convenient principal liability theory within the crime definition of genocide itself, which might marginalize the utility of Article 25(3) of the ICC Statute.

It is true that Raphael Lemkin was concerned about the possibility of subordinate actors escaping criminal responsibility of genocide by invoking "the plea of superior orders".[93] But it is hard to imagine that he envisaged a sweeping principal

---

[90] Examples of some commentators who take note of the implication of the knowledge-based approach in this respect are: Jørgensen 2001, p. 293; Bantekas 2010, pp. 48 and 209; Tams et al. 2014, p. 145.

[91] Greenawalt 1999, p. 2288 ("[The knowledge-based approach] addresses the related problems of subordinate actors and ambiguous goals by unhinging the question of genocidal liability from that of the perpetrator's particular motive or desire with regard to the group as a whole. And in the particular case of subordinate perpetrators, it does so *without relying on an expansive liability framework* [...]".) (emphasis added).

[92] Kress 2005, pp. 571–572 ("[...] formulat[ing] the rigid purpose-based approach to genocidal intent in the abstract and then circumvent this very standard through the evidential backdoor. [...] In his analysis of the *Akayesu* judgment, Greenawalt had already identified the danger that the purpose-based approach to genocidal intent 'will compel courts to squeeze ambiguous fact patterns into the specific intent paradigm'".). *See also* Kress 2006, p. 494; Wilt 2006, p. 242 ("In the absence of complete confessions, prosecutors will have a hard job in inferring 'special intent' from the conduct in question, however heinous it may be. And courts will face the awkward choice between acquittals and 'squeezing ambiguous fact patterns into the specific intent paradigm', as Greenawalt has put it succinctly".); Haren 2006, pp. 223–224.

[93] Lemkin 2008, 93 ("An international multilateral treaty should provide for the introduction, not only in the constitution but also in the criminal code of each country, of provisions protecting minority groups from oppression because of their nationhood, religion, or race. Each criminal code should have provisions inflicting penalties for genocide practices. In order to prevent the invocation of the plea of superior orders, the liability of persons who *order* genocide practices, as well as persons who *execute* such orders, should be provided expressly by the criminal codes of

liability scheme such as the knowledge-based approach. Indeed, the most troubling implication of applying the knowledge-based interpretation of genocidal intent is that it is not clear why mid- or low-level actors should be labeled principals (as opposed to accessories).[94] Wouldn't convicting them of genocide as an accessory be enough?[95] In this respect, one might argue that the proponents of the knowledge-based approach were worrying about sentencing in the sense that it is only the principals to whom grievous penalties are to be imposed. But it cannot be a reason to classify the subordinate actors as principals. That is because, contrary to most of the countries in the Continental tradition in which the criminal code itself provides for a lenient punishment for accessories (in comparison with that of

---

Footnote 93 (continued)

the respective countries".). Lemkin's concern however is now almost obsolete by virtue of Article 33 of the ICC Statute that permits the invocation of the superior order doctrine only when the order is "not manifestly unlawful". Article 33(2) proclaims that orders to commit genocide are always "manifestly unlawful". That is to say, under the ICC law, the superior order doctrine is not applicable to genocide.

[94] Similarly, *see* May 2010, p. 126 ("My view is that Greenawalt supplies too meager an intent requirement for such an important crime as genocide".). *See also* Mettraux 2005, pp. 214–215 (indicating that, in view of the status of genocide as being "located at the top of the hierarchy of international crimes", one should be cautious not to succumb to the temptation to extend the scope of its application.).

[95] *See e.g.*, Jørgensen 2001, p. 313. Jørgensen's position is that "knowledge of the genocidal plan" can only constitute the 'complicity in genocide' which is still an extremely serious offence. She observes, "it is submitted that culpability for genocide should not extend to those who merely have knowledge of the genocidal plan, with the exception of those accused of complicity. A better approach is to make the knowledge the first stage of inferring special intent. If special intent cannot be inferred then the accused should be found guilty of complicity in genocide which, despite being regarded as a secondary crime, is nevertheless an extremely serious one". Moreover, denying the inherent hierarchy within Article 25(3)(a)–(d) of the ICC Statute, Judge Christine van den Wyngaert observes that "[i]n fact, I fail to see an inherent difference in blameworthiness between 'aiding and abetting' and 'committing' a crime". Prosecutor v. Ngudjolo, Concurring Opinion of Judge Christine van den Wyngaert, 18 December 2012, para 24. In particular, given the 'purposes' standard of *mens rea* required by Article 25(3)(c), she is of the view that it is doubtful whether the ICC would ever follow the *ad hoc* tribunals' sentencing practice of imposing a reduced sentence for 'aiding and abetting'. *Ibid.* para 25. It should however be noted that, in addressing the distinction between principal and accessory liability, Judge van den Wyngaert seems to follow the objective approach. She explains that "[u]nder Article 25(3)(a), only persons who have committed a crime together can be held responsible. The essence of committing a crime is bringing about its material elements. Only those individuals whose acts made a direct contribution to bringing about the material elements can thus be said to have jointly perpetrated the crime". *Ibid.* para 44. Ultimately, taking the example of the Charles Taylor trial at the Special Court for Sierra Leone in which the accused has been sentenced to 50 years imprisonment on the basis of 'aiding and abetting', Judge van den Wyngaert observes that 'masterminds' and 'intellectual authors' of core international crimes are not necessarily labeled 'principals'. *Ibid.* paras 26 and 29. She concludes by stating that "[t]he interpretation of Article 25(3) thus needs to move away from preserving a misguided assumption that accessories are inherently less blameworthy than principals and that the blameworthiness of political and military leaders can therefore only be fully captured by treating them as principals". *Ibid.* para 70.

principals), there is, as Judge Adrian Fulford in *Lubanga* rightly points out,[96] no such legal scheme of mandatory sentencing adjustment both at the *ad hoc* tribunals and the ICC. Thus, at the international criminal courts, there is no reason to label the subordinate actors principals for the purpose of securing a severe sentence. Regardless of whether a person is convicted as a principal or an accessory, the courts have a full discretion in terms of sentencing.

It is acknowledged that, in ordinary scenarios in domestic criminal jurisdictions, accessories do not carry out the *actus reus* themselves. Hence, this domestic scheme of accessory liability is not directly applicable to genocide because, in most cases, subordinate actors prosecuted for the crime of genocide would be the ones who himself performed the *actus reus* of the crime. Labeling such persons accessories would certainly sound awkward to the ears of domestic criminal lawyers, in particular' those from the Anglo-American tradition where 'principals' are those who most immediately perform the relevant conducts provided in the crime definition.[97] Conversely, the peculiar structure of genocide combining the subordinate-level *actus reus* and the leadership-level *mens rea* also causes a conceptual difficulty in labeling them principals due to their obvious lack of the purpose-based genocidal intent.[98] In this respect, one might describe the knowledge-based approach as harsh in a sense that it attaches principal liability to obedient executors too easily. As I see it, this dilemma results from the peculiar structure of the crime definition of genocide in which the core *mens rea* of 'intent to destroy a group' is placed at the 'context level'.[99] What this idiosyncratic conceptual

---

[96] In the context of challenging the control theory of co-perpetration adopted by the ICC Pre-Trial Chamber and the Majority of the Trial Chamber in *Lubanga*, Judge Adrian Fulford observes as follows: "Whilst it might have been of assistance to 'rank' the various modes of liability if, for instance, sentencing was strictly determined by the specific provision on which an individual's conviction is based, considerations of this kind do not apply at the ICC. [...] Under the German legal system, the sentencing range is determined by the mode of liability under which an individual is convicted, and it is therefore necessary to draw clear distinctions between principals on the one hand and accessories on the other. As set out above, these considerations do not apply at the ICC, where sentencing is not restricted in this way, and this example of differences that exist is of significance in this context". Prosecutor v. Lubanga, Separate Opinion of Judge Adrian Fulford, 14 March 2012, paras 9 and 11. On the other hand, while acknowledging that "the legal classifications [under Article 25(3)] have no apparent bearing on punishment[,]" George Fletcher still maintains that "[l]et us hope the [international] courts will read the statute in the conceptual system expressed in the history of the German *Dogmatik*, which distinguishes rigorously between the punishment of perpetrators and accessories [...]". Fletcher 2011, p. 190. For an examination of the competing views between the majority and the separate opinion of Judge Fulford in *Lubanga, see* Vest 2014.

[97] Smith 1991, pp. 27–28; Sliedregt 2012a, p. 1183; Jain 2013, p. 838.

[98] In the same vein, Kai Ambos observes that "the acts of the subordinate and the thoughts of the superiors complement each other". Ambos 2014, p. 30. *See also* Kress 2006, p. 496. Note, however, that, when Kress mentions "an *actus reus* list formulated from the perspective of the subordinate level with what is typically a leadership standard of *mens rea*", he is not discussing the structure of the genocide definition, but criticizing the purpose-based approach.

[99] The two-layered structure of the crime of genocide composed of the 'conduct level' and the 'context level' will form the main theme of Chap. 3 *infra*.

structure suggests is a personification of the genocidal context (through the collective genocidal intent at the 'context level') which perpetrates the crime of genocide *by means of* subordinate actors.[100] In this sense, one might argue that the crime definition of genocide incorporates within itself the liability doctrine of 'perpetration by means' (also known as 'indirect perpetration' or 'perpetrator behind the perpetrator').[101] That is exactly the third alternative mode of 'perpetration' provided in Article 25(3)(a), which reads: "[…] [c]ommits […] a crime […] through another person, regardless of whether that other person is criminally responsible". As seen from the phrase "regardless of whether that other person is criminally responsible", the criminal liability of a physical perpetrator who is used as a means or an instrument in this context is simply irrelevant to that of a real perpetrator behind him. In my view, this conceptual framework is also directly applicable to the crime definition of genocide where the personified genocidal context, viewed as a real perpetrator, decides everything under the authority of a collective genocidal intent

---

[100] The notion of 'collective genocidal intent' at the 'context level' forms part of the main theme of Chap. 4 *infra*. It is not unusual to see that international judges use the verb 'occur' in referring to genocide, rather than 'commit'. The idea that genocide 'occurs' seems to (remotely) support my argument of the personified genocidal context. Most importantly, *see* Prosecutor v. Karemera et al., Decision on Prosecutor's Interlocutory Appeal of Decision on Judicial Notice, 16 June 2006, paras 34–36. *See also* Prosecutor v. Krstić, Appeals Judgment, 19 April 2004, para 32 ("In determining that genocide occurred at Srebrenica, the cardinal question is whether the intent to commit genocide existed".); *Ibid.* para 34 ("[…] a finding that genocide has occurred may be entered".).

[101] ICC Statute, Article 25(3)(a), the third mode of perpetration. For an overview of this mode of liability, see Jessberger and Geneuss 2008; Olásolo and Cepeda 2004, p. 489 *et seq.*; Osiel 2009, p. 91 *et seq. See also* Fletcher 2000, p. 639 ("Virtually all legal systems, it should be noted, recognize the institution of perpetration by means. The Model Penal Code provides that an actor is guilty of an offense if, with the requisite state of mind, he 'causes an innocent or irresponsible person to engage in the [proscribed] conduct'. The German code says simply that the perpetrator is anyone who commits the offense himself or 'through another'. Other legal systems recognize the doctrine as implicit in the concept of perpetration".). In order to precisely grasp the theory of the 'perpetrator behind the perpetrator', a historical development of the doctrine of 'indirect perpetration' is of help. When the notion of indirect perpetrator was first invented by German theorists in 19th century, it meant perpetrator behind a mere tool who did not have the requisite intent for the offence. After the Fall of Berlin Wall, the German Court of Justice extended the notion of indirect perpetration so as to encompass the perpetrator behind the perpetrator who also had the requisite intent for the offence. Weigend 2014, pp. 258–260. Note that, through the phrase "regardless of whether that other person is criminally responsible", Article 25(3)(a) of the ICC Statute provides both prongs of 'perpetration by means': (i) perpetration by innocent means (perpetrator behind the innocent agent); and (ii) perpetration by guilty means (perpetrator behind the perpetrator). With regard to the latter, in the Anglo-American tradition where it is generally thought that "a person cannot act through a voluntary act of a third party", such notion of the 'perpetrator behind the perpetrator' is inconceivable. Accordingly, the perpetrator behind the closed door orchestrating another perpetrator's criminal act would be considered aider or abettor. Yet, the ultimate outcome is not that much different from that of the German theory of 'perpetrator behind the perpetrator' as the person behind the closed door is to be treated as a 'perpetrator' pursuant to the 'equivalency theory' and 'conspiracy theory'. For more detailed explanation, *see* Cryer 2014, pp. 270–272.

that exclusively belongs to itself.[102] In this scenario, it is not unreasonable to regard low-level perpetrators as morally and legally equivalent to accessories in spite of the fact that they personally committed the *actus reus*. It thus follows that the crime of genocide is conceptually located on the verge of the leadership crime.[103] In this respect, in terms of the question of distinguishing principals and accessories, the 'subjective approach' or the 'control theory' is suitable to be applied to the crime of genocide. In the *Stashchynsky* case in Germany, the accused, an agent of the KGB, who committed two political assassinations, was convicted as an accessory following the 'subjective approach'[104]; and George

---

[102] For more discussion, *see* Sect. 4.2.2.5 *infra*. Consider the following observations made by the ICC Trial Chamber in *Lubanga*: In the context of discussing the 'control theory' as a mode of liability falling into the second alternative of Article 25(3)(a) ("commits such a crime [...] jointly with others"), the Majority of the Chamber states that "[n]one of the [co-perpetrators] exercises, individually, control over the crime as a shoe but, instead, the control over the crime falls in the hands of a collective as such". Prosecutor v. Lubanga, Judgment Pursuant to Article 74 of the Statute, 14 March 2012, para 994. *See also* Prosecutor v. Krstić, Appeals Judgment, 19 April 2004, para 34 ("The inference that a particular atrocity was motivated by genocidal intent may be drawn, moreover, even where the individuals to whom the intent is attributable are not precisely identified".).

[103] For more discussion, *see* Sect. 4.2.3 *infra*. *See also* Prosecutor v. Stakić, Decision on Rule 98 *bis* Motion for Judgment of Acquittal, 31 October 2002, paras 50–51 (characterizing the principal perpetrators of genocide as "those who devise the genocidal plan at the highest level and take the major steps to put it into effect" and "who willfully assume a key co-ordinating role and whose participation is of an extremely significant nature and at the leadership level".).

[104] Fletcher 2000, pp. 657–659. For a criticism of the *Stashchynsky* case regarding it as an extreme form of subjective approach and even solipsism, *see* Ohlin 2014, p. 334. Ohlin paraphrases the subjective approach applied to the *Stashchynsky* case as follows: "the defendants could not be principals because they did not view themselves as primary actors and they thought of themselves as supporting others". It is noteworthy that Ohlin argues against this extreme form of subjective approach by saying: "This extreme theory is problematic, not because it is subjective, but because it conflates motive with intention. [*Stashchynsky* did not] have particularly strong personal motives for performing the killing, though [he] performed [his] killings purposely, and [his] lack of a strong personal motive should not disqualify them from being principals even under a subjective theory". In my view, it would be conceptually more precise if we challenge the extreme theory without employing the elusive notion of motive. I think the concept of 'desire in a broad sense' that I will explain in Sect. 2.5.2.4. *infra* enables us to solve the problem *within* the notion of intention, in particular, 'direct intent/purposely'. Currently, another *Stashchynsky* case is not possible in Germany. Demonstrating the historical prevalence of the subjective approach in Germany, Thomas Weigend explains that it was only in 1975 when the German legislature amended the Penal Code (providing 'whoever commits the offence himself or through another person shall be punished as a perpetrator') that "courts found themselves constrained to abandon the extreme subjectivism in distinguishing between perpetrators and accessories". He further notes that, when the East German border guards were prosecuted for shooting fugitives after the Fall of Berlin Wall, the German Federal Court of Justice "did not even consider the possibility that these soldiers might only be aiders and abettors [...]". Weigend 2014, pp. 257–258. At present, for the purpose of distinguishing principals and accessories, the German Federal Court of Justice uses the 'overall evaluation' test, taking into account both objective and subjective factors, which grants much discretion to trial courts. *Ibid.* at 258. In contrast, it is to be noted that, historically, the Anglo-American tradition has follows the "objective theory of perpetration" which regards only those who perform the *actus reus* of an offence as principals. Ohlin 2014, p. 327.

Fletcher has observed that even Palestinian suicide bombers should be classified also as an accessory pursuant to the 'control theory'.[105] Labeling subordinate actors of genocide accessories should thus be considered within a reasonable boundary particularly if we follow the 'subjective approach' or the 'control theory'.[106] Put otherwise, the peculiar structure of the crime of genocide keeps compelling such an understanding despite the obvious seriousness of performing *actus reus* with Zyklon B at Auschwitz, machetes in Rwanda and guns at Srebrenica. In this connection, even discussing the subordinate actors' genocidal intent sounds too farfetched because of their being conceptually sidelined, as is the case with their equivalents in the theory of 'perpetration by means'. It is not exaggerating to say that low-level actors in both genocide and 'perpetration by means' are mere instruments who are always 'replaceable'. Concerning both the notions of 'perpetration by means' and 'genocide', law has already expressed its near-indifference to subordinate actors' culpability including their *mens rea*: explicitly in relation to the former (through the phrase 'regardless of whether that other person is criminally responsible'), and implicitly to the latter (through the peculiar structure of genocide currently stipulated in its definition, giving the principal status only to the personified genocidal context).[107] Consequently, labeling low-level actors principals of genocide is hardly justifiable.

2.4.4 Why Knowledge? A Comparison with Aiding and Abetting Genocide

In this subsection, let us consider the problem of attaching principal liability to physical perpetrators of genocide pursuant to the knowledge-based approach by comparison with 'aiding and abetting genocide'. After a period of confusing and inconsistent jurisprudence, now it is settled law for both the ICTY and the ICTR

---

[105] Fletcher 2011, pp. 189–190.

[106] It is to be noted, however, that the 'control theory' was an objective answer to the subjective approach. Ohlin 2014, p. 331 (observing that ICC's functional control theory defines its mental elements requirement "in a notoriously lax way", which "is predictable because the Control Theory is designed as a functional objective apporoach, which inevitably means that it deemphasizes the mental elements and places far less emphasis on them compared to a subjective approach to imputation".). Citing George Fletcher, Ohlin also characterizes the 'functional control theory' as a "functional variant of an objective theory with a mixture of subjective and objective elements". *Ibid.* at 337.

[107] Note that, as Chaps. 3 and 4 *infra* will demonstrate, I am not denying the individual criminal responsibility of committing the crime of genocide. What is connoted by the term 'personified genocidal context' is a proposition that collective intention is not a mere accumulation of individual intentions. Mark Osiel states that "[…] mass atrocity's far-reaching scope often lies beyond anyone's complete control or contemplation". Osiel 2009, p. xi. Osiel also cites John Lachs, an "influential Holocaust scholar", who observes that "[i]t is difficult to accept that often there is no person and no group that planned or caused it all[.]" *Ibid.* at 26, citing Lachs 1981, p. 58. For more discussion, *see* Sect. 4.2.2.5 *infra*.

that the required *mens rea* standard for 'aiding and abetting genocide' is knowledge, not purpose-based genocidal intent.[108] Accordingly, the ICTY Trial Chamber in *Blagojević and Jokić* states, "[a]n individual may be held responsible for aiding and abetting genocide if it is shown that he assisted in the commission of the crime in the knowledge of the principal perpetrator's specific intent".[109] Given, however, that there are views that even accessories to genocide must possess purpose-based genocidal intent,[110] imputing principal liability for genocide to obedient executors who only possessed 'knowledge' is certainly a bold approach. In other words, since the mental element required for 'aiding and abetting genocide' is generally thought to be 'knowledge'. the knowledge-based approach's legal effect of attaching principal liability on the basis of the same *mens rea* standard as aiding and abetting sounds quite dubious. The fact that subordinate actors addressed by the knowledge-based approach in most cases are the ones who carried out the *actus reus* of underlying acts of genocide might be the only argument that appears to offset such a doubt. But, what makes our discussion in this respect even more difficult is that, except for the underlying act of "genocide by killing",[111] the dividing line between 'performing the *actus reus*' and 'performing aiding and abetting' is difficult to draw in relation to all other underlying acts. For instance, how would you distinguish those who perform the *actus reus* of 'deliberately inflicting conditions of life calculated to bring about physical destruction' (ICC Statute, Article 6(c)) and others who merely aided or abetted such infliction? Since the act pattern of inflicting such conditions of life covers a very broad scope,[112] the *actus reus* of this underlying act is almost impossible to spell out. Furthermore, the scope of conduct that potentially falls into the underlying act of 'causing serious bodily or mental harm' (ICC Statute, Article 6(b)) is even wider

---

[108] *See* Prosecutor v. Krstić, Appeals Judgment, 19 April 2004, para 140 (knowledge of the "principal perpetrator's genocidal intent"); Prosecutor v. Ntakirutimana, Appeals Judgment, 13 December 2004, para 501 (knowledge of the "principal perpetrator's genocidal intent"). *See also* Prosecutor v. Seromba, Appeals Judgement, 12 March 2008, para 56 ([…] in cases of crimes requiring specific intent, such as genocide, it is not necessary to prove that the aider and abettor shared the *mens rea* of the principal, but that he must have known of the principal perpetrator's specific intent".); Werle 2009, p. 184. For an overview of the relevant case law on *mens rea* of 'aiding and abetting genocide'. see Sliedregt 2009, pp. 169–171.

[109] Prosecutor v. Blagojević and Jokić, Trial Judgment, 17 January 2005, para 782.

[110] *See* Mettraux 2005, pp. 212–215 (opposing the knowledge standard for accessory liability of genocide, not to mention principal liability); Mysliwiec 2009, pp. 405–412 (as to accessory liability of genocide, advocating the application of the purpose standard, instead of knowledge).

[111] ICC Statute, Article 6(a); ICC Elements of Crimes, Article 6(a) is entitled "Genocide by killing".

[112] *See e.g.*, Prosecutor v. Kayishema and Ruzindana, Trial Judgment, 21 May 1999, paras 115–6 ("[…] this concept […] include[s] circumstances which will lead to a slow death, for example, lack of proper housing, clothing, hygiene and medical care or excessive work or physical exertion[,] […] methods of destruction which do not immediately lead to the death of members of the group [such as] rape, the starving of a people, reducing required medical services below a minimum, and withholding sufficient living accommodation […]".).

in compass: "acts of torture, inhumane or degrading treatment, sexual violence including rape, interrogations combined with beatings, threats of death, and harm that damages health or causes disfigurement or serious injury to members of the targeted […] group. The harm inflicted need not be permanent and irremediable […]".[113] If the Prosecution accuses a number of persons of 'genocide by forcibly transferring children' (ICC Statute, Article 6(e)), how would judges distinguish the ones who carried out the *actus reus* and others who just aided and assisted the crime? Should only the bus drivers be considered the ones who performed the *actus reus*?[114] In these dubious situations, the application of the knowledge-based approach risks shaking the basic legal foundation of differentiating principals and accessories. More specifically, keeping the same *mens rea* threshold for both the principal and accessory liabilities in relation to an offence whose *actus reus* is not clearly distinguishable is destined to seriously undermine the principle of fair labeling and ultimately the rights of the accused.[115] Such an undesirable result was well-phrased by Jens David Ohlin, albeit in a different context, as follows: "The culpability of lower participants is inflated and implicitly, the culpability of higher participants is deflated simply by virtue of their inclusion in the same category as those at the bottom of the culpability ladder".[116] Thus, worrisome implications of applying the knowledge-based approach not only involves the inflating effect vis-à-vis the culpability of subordinate actors (directly through the application of the knowledge-based approach) but also the deflating effect vis-à-vis that of high-ranking decision makers and commanders (indirectly through the extended scope of principal liability resulted from the application of the knowledge-based approach). Consequently, the upshot of the knowledge-based theory is significantly detrimental to the overall trend of the jurisprudence of international criminal courts towards the normative approach (as opposed to the naturalistic approach

---

[113] Prosecutor v. Brđanin, Trial Judgment, 1 September 2004, para 690. It seems this wide scope of potential acts falling into the concept of genocide is not inconsistent with Raphael Lemkin's original thought. For instance, the first potential act of genocide ever referred to by Lemkin was the "confiscation of property". He observed that, if the confiscations were conducted against individuals for the sole reason of their being members of a group, those acts should constitute the crime of genocide. Lemkin 2008, p. 79.

[114] *See* Prosecutor v. Rutaganda, Trial Judgment, 6 December 1999, para 53 (holding that this underlying act is "aimed at sanctioning not only any direct act of forcible physical transfer, but also any acts of threats or trauma which would lead to the forcible transfer of children from one group to another group".). For a scholarly view that is developed on the basis of clear distinction between genocidal acts and non-genocidal acts, *see* Cupido 2014, pp. 34–35 ("The judicial practice to partially infer genocidal intent from the commission of non-genocidal acts should therefore be looked upon critically".).

[115] As regards the growing importance of the principle of fair labeling in international criminal law, *see* Sliedregt 2012a, pp. 1182–1183 ("Increasingly, value is attached to fair labeling requiring that liability be branded in a way that it fairly represents the nature and magnitude of the law-breaking. […] Fair labeling accounts for the advance of the normative approach to criminal participation and the desire to adhere to the distinction between those who are culpable as principals and those who are culpable as accessories".).

[116] Ohlin 2011, p. 752.

adopted by Anglo-American system) to the principal-accessory distinction, which reflects the spirit of 'fair labeling'—i.e., the "desire to bolster the principal-status" in comparison with that of accessories to international crimes.[117] Furthermore, as I have sketched out at the beginning of this section,[118] the proposal of applying the purpose-based standard to the leadership actors (while applying the knowledge-based theory to subordinate actors) leads to a result that seems to completely ignore the common sense, not to mention the principle of fair labeling—i.e., acquitting the leadership actor, whilst convicting subordinate actors as principals.

It should be further noted that the aiding and abetting provision of the ICC Statute (Article 25(3)(c)) adds another troubling dimension: the phrase "[f]or the *purpose* of facilitating the commission of [...] a crime" signifies a stricter *mens rea* standard than 'knowledge'.[119] That is to say, if we follow the knowledge-based approach within the legal framework of the ICC, convicting a person as an aider and abettor of genocide pursuant to Article 25(3)(c) would require even a stronger mental element than that required for the principal liability of genocide pursuant to the knowledge-based notion of genocidal intent.[120] Furthermore, if the Court ever follows the relevant view of William Schabas, a legal effect even more awkward might ensue. That is to say, since Schabas regards the concept of 'purpose' in

---

[117] *See* Sliedregt 2012a, pp. 1184–1185. For an overview of the normative approach and the naturalistic approach to criminal participation, *see* Sliedregt 2012b, pp. 71–73. As regards the 'overall trend', think of (i) the *ad hoc* tribunal's case law attaching the commission/principal liability to JCE which was originally treated as a form of accessorial liability in its origin—viz. Anglo-American law; and (ii) the move from the unitary codification of modes of liability (e.g., Article 7(1) of the ICTY Statute) to its more differentiated counterpart (Article 25(3) of the ICC Statute).

[118] *See* Sect. 2.4.1 *supra*.

[119] Ambos 2013, pp. 165–166 ("it is clear that purpose generally implies a specific subjective requirement which goes, in its volitional dimension, beyond mere knowledge".). *See also* Ambos 2008, p. 757 ("The formula [of "for the purpose of facilitating"], therefore, ignores the [...] jurisprudence of the ICTY and ICTR, since this jurisprudence holds that the aider and abettor must only know that his or her acts will assist the principal in the commission of an offence. [...] In conclusion, the formulation confirms the general assessment that subparagraph (c) provides for a relatively low objective but relatively high subjective threshold (in any case higher than the ordinary *mens rea* requirement according to article 30)".); Eser 2002, p. 801. For a differing view, *see* Cassel 2007, pp. 310–315 (arguing that the 'purpose' as provided in Article 25(3)(c) needs not be "exclusive or primary". That is, a 'secondary purpose' covering a *knowing* contribution suffices to satisfy the purpose test of aiding and abetting under Article 25(3)(c) of the ICC Statute.). For an overview of the requirement of a secondary actor's intention under the law of complicity, *see* Kadish 1985, pp. 346–349.

[120] From the prosecutorial strategy point of view, the prosecutor might circumvent the *mens rea* standard under Article 25(3)(c) (which is stricter than 'knowledge') by instead invoking the 'common purpose' liability pursuant to Article 25(3)(d) in respect of which "the knowledge of the intention of the group" is provided for as one of the two alternative mental elements. For a relevant discussion, *see* Ohlin 2010, p. 197, footnote 23.

Article 25(3)(c) as something that "amount[s] to a form of specific intent",[121] one might even assert that while a genocidal principal is, following the knowledge-based approach, only required to possess 'knowledge', an aider or abettor must have the 'specific intent' in accordance with the interpretation of the term 'purpose' in Article 25(3)(c). Clearly, this would be an absurd outcome.

At this juncture, a point made by Kai Ambos is noteworthy:

> It is important to note that this higher subjective threshold [of 'purpose' provided in Article 25(3)(c)] only applies to the relation between the contribution and the execution of the crime ('facilitation'). With regard to additional *mens rea* requirements, for example, the 'intent to destroy' in Article 6, it suffices for the assistant to be aware of the perpetrator's special intent, but he need not himself possess this intent.[122]

This observation provides a clarification of the valid object of 'purpose' provided in Article 25(3)(c). As the language reads literally ("[f]or the purpose of *facilitating* the commission"), that 'purpose' must be directed at the act of 'facilitation'.[123] Thus, under this legal framework in conjunction with the knowledge-based approach, a subordinate actor who only has the knowledge of a high-level actor's purpose-based genocidal intent is to be labeled a principal (pursuant to the knowledge-based approach), while another person who possesses the same knowledge of the high-level actor's purpose-based genocidal intent ("it suffices for the assistant to be aware of the perpetrator's special intent") and has the purpose to 'facilitate' (not the purpose to 'destroy') is to be convicted as an aider or abettor. Isn't it an odd result? At this juncture, one might respond that the subordinate actor who is labeled a principal should have carried out the *actus reus* of underlying acts and, thus, should not be considered parallel with the second person who only aided or assisted the commission of the crime. As I have already said, however, the difficulty in distinguishing 'performing the *actus reus*' and 'performing aiding and abetting' particularly in relation to the four underlying acts of genocide other than 'genocide by killing' renders such an argument unconvincing.

---

[121] Schabas 2010, pp. 435–436. Since the concept of 'specific intent' has a number of varying definitions, it is unfortunate that Schabas uses the term here. (For those varying definitions, *see* Chap. 2, footnote 222 *infra*). It is considered that Schabas here uses the term 'specific intent' in the sense of 'ulterior intent'. Since 'ulterior intent' should accompany 'desire' (in particular the notion of 'desire in a broad sense' that I will explicate in Sect. 2.5.2.4 *infra*) that forms the definitional basis of 'direct intent/purposely', Schabas' view is considered to be agreeable. I think that Schabas' observation on the 'purpose' requirement under Article 25(3)(c) of the ICC Statute is consistent with what Sanford Kadish explains the intentionality of aider and abettor as follows: "[w]hether the mode of involvement in another's criminal act is influence or assistance, the law of complicity generally requires that the secondary actor act intentionally; that is, he must act with the intention of influencing or assisting the primary actor to engage in the conduct constituting the crime". Kadish 1985, p. 346.

[122] Ambos 2013, p. 166.

[123] *See* Simester and Sullivan 2010, p. 220 (In England and Wales, "[i]t is the assistance or the encouragement, not the ultimate crime, that must be intended by [a secondary party]".).

A related observation made by the ICC itself states,

> In this regard, the literal interpretation of the definition of the crime of genocide in article 6 of the [ICC] Statute and in the Elements of Crimes makes clear that only those who act with the requisite genocidal intent can be principals to such a crime pursuant to article 25(3)(a) of the Statute. Those others, who are only aware of the genocidal nature of the campaign, but do not share the genocidal intent, can only be held liable as accessories [...].[124]

This position is meaningless if one applies the knowledge-based approach because, in so doing, the distinction between the "requisite genocidal intent" and the awareness "of the genocidal nature of the campaign" is negated. We must seriously question whether the knowledge-based approach acknowledges the distinction between 'principal' and 'accessory' in the crime of genocide. That is to say, the knowledge-based theory urges us to doubt that, within a given territory of individual criminal liability of genocide as a whole, whether there still remains any space for the genocidal accessory liability to survive. That is because, owing to the knowledge-based approach, the terrain of principal liability of genocide has been excessively expanded.[125]

Furthermore, another feature of the knowledge-based approach that exacerbates the problem is that the knowledge-based approach has failed to specify the valid object of knowledge,[126] which results in an even broader scope of the principal liability scheme. That is, not only the 'knowledge of the destructive consequences' originally proposed by Greenawalt, but also the 'knowledge of the masterminds' genocidal intent' and 'knowledge of an overall genocidal context/campaign' are recognized as a potential objective reference point of 'knowledge' (for the purpose of applying the 'knowledge-based approach') by the International Law Commission and other commentators as follows:

- a subordinate's "knowledge of the nature of the act based on an objective reasonable standard";[127]
- a subordinate's knowledge that "the ultimate purpose of such a campaign is to destroy";[128]

---

[124] Prosecutor v. Al Bashir, Decision on the Prosecution's Application for a Warrant of Arrest against Omar Hassan Ahmed Al Bashir, 4 March 2009, p. 49, footnote 154.

[125] In this regard, note what James G. Stewart observes: "complicity is the remainder of responsibility by participation left over once perpetration is subtracted. [...] the meaning we attach to [complicity] is inexorably bound up in our definition of perpetration [...]". Stewart 2014, p. 536.

[126] The discussion of the valid object of knowledge here is a continuation of the similar consideration contained in Sect. 2.4.2 *supra*.

[127] Bassiouni 1993, p. 236.

[128] Prosecutor v. Al Bashir, Decision on the Prosecution's Application for a Warrant of Arrest against Omar Hassan Ahmed Al Bashir, 4 March 2009, p. 49, footnote 154.

- a subordinate's "knowledge of the ultimate objective of the criminal conduct rather than knowledge of every detail of a comprehensive plan or policy of genocide";[129]
- a subordinate's knowledge of "the ultimate object of a genocidal campaign";[130]
- a subordinate's knowledge of "the [genocidal] intentions of his superiors";[131]
- a subordinate's knowledge of "the genocidal intent of the main perpetrators";[132]
- a subordinate's knowledge of the fact "that the masterminds of the genocidal campaign are acting with a genocidal intent construed in the narrow sense";[133]
- a subordinate's knowledge of "the destructive effect of this criminal conduct on the group itself";[134]
- a subordinate's knowledge of "the destructive consequences";[135]
- a subordinate's "knowledge of the consequences of the overall conduct";[136]
- a subordinate's knowledge of "the possibility of the destruction";[137]
- a subordinate's knowledge of "the goal or manifest effect of the campaign was the destruction of the group in whole or in part";[138]
- a subordinate's knowledge of the overall genocidal context;[139]
- a subordinate's knowledge of a collective attack directed to the destruction of at least part of a protected group;[140]

---

[129] Report of the International Law Commission on the Work of Its Forty-Eight Session, May 6-July 26, 1996, at 45, U.N. Doc. A/51/10. ("This does not mean that a subordinate who actually carries out the plan or policy cannot be held responsible for the crime of genocide simply because he did not possess the same degree of information concerning the overall plan or policy as his superiors. The definition of the crime of genocide requires a degree of knowledge of the ultimate objective of the criminal conduct rather than knowledge of every detail of a comprehensive plan or policy of genocide".).

[130] Bantekas 2010, p. 48.

[131] *Ibid.* ("A subordinate is presumed to know the intentions of his superiors when he receives orders to commit the prohibited acts against individuals who belong to a particular group".).

[132] Ambos 2010, p. 159.

[133] Ambos 2009, p. 847.

[134] Report of the International Law Commission on the Work of Its Forty-Eight Session, May 6-July 26, 1996, at 45, U.N. Doc. A/51/10.

[135] Greenawalt 1999, p. 2259.

[136] Vest 2007, p. 793. Note that Hans Vest adds that a subordinate actor's knowledge should reach "the level of practical certainty". The 'practical certainty' standard representing the cognitive side of intent surely points at the concept of 'indirect intent/oblique intent/knowingly'.

[137] Ambos 2010, p. 159. Note that the 'possibility/likely/probability' standard (corresponding to '*dolus eventualis*/recklessness') representing the cognitive side of intent is a lower standard than that of 'practical certainty' (corresponding to 'indirect intent/oblique intent/knowingly'). Accordingly, recognizing "the possibility of destruction" as an object of knowledge for the purpose of the knowledge-based interpretation of genocidal intent is considered a bold statement because its close connection to the concept of 'reckless genocide'.

[138] Greenawalt 1999, p. 2288.

[139] Ambos 2009, pp. 848–849 and 858.

[140] Kress 2005, p. 577.

In this regard, one might say that the knowledge-based approach not only lowers the standard of genocidal intent from 'purpose' to 'knowledge', but the scope of this already lowered *mens rea* of 'knowledge' is broad and imprecisely specified. A comparison of the knowledge-based approach and 'aiding and abetting genocide' made us doubt whether this well-established mode of liability at both international and national levels—i.e., 'aiding and abetting genocide'—is still applicable in the territory of the knowledge-based approach. For, as we have seen, anyone satisfying the *mens rea* for aiding and abetting will almost inevitably qualify as a principal under the knowledge-based approach.

2.4.5 Just an Aiding and Abetting Theory? A Wake-Up Call from the Popović et al. Case

Contrary to the pairing suggested by proponents of the knowledge-based approach—i.e., 'purpose-based genocidal intent required for high-level actors' and 'knowledge-based genocidal intent for mid- or low-level actors', judges might well, in practice, be inclined to decide the opposite way. In other words, it is very likely that they would be reluctant to label a subordinate actor a principal of genocide unless it is clearly shown that he personally had the purpose-based genocidal intent.[141] It is especially so in view of the extraordinary gravity of the crime of genocide. In a sense, it is natural to expect such response from the judges, because doing otherwise would (as I said earlier)[142] result in a complete nonsense—i.e., acquittals (as principals) for high-level actors and conviction (as principals) for subordinate actors.

One such example in which international judges decided in a way contrary to the knowledge-based theory is the *Popović* et al. case at the ICTY in which the Trial Chamber, following the purpose-based approach, refused to convict a low-ranking military officer, Drago Nikolić, of genocide proper. Instead, he was found guilty of 'aiding and abetting genocide' on the basis of his knowledge-based *mens rea*. As to other two defendants, Ljubiša Beara and Vujadin Popović, who were high-ranking military officers, we can find traces of their purpose-based genocidal intent discussed by the Trial Chamber mainly in relation to their knowledge, acts, contribution, utterances and rank.[143] On the other hand, the Trial Chamber amply

---

[141] In this respect, it is to be noted that the manner in which the purpose-based individual genocidal intent is to be found by international judges in practice might betray the doctrinal meaning outwardly proclaimed by them. In Sect. 4.2 *infra*, I will demonstrate that, contrary to general expectations, the purpose-based individual genocidal intent has been grasped in an objective manner, in particular, at the ICTY. As to the 'reluctance' of judges that I mentioned, Ilias Bantekas also observed that "[t]he ICTY has generally been reluctant to convict lower-ranking personnel of genocide, despite the large number of victims in particular cases". Bantekas 2010, p. 209.

[142] *See* Sect. 2.4.1 *supra*.

[143] For a more detailed discussion on Ljubiša Beara's individual genocidal intent, *see* Sect. 4.2.2.2 *infra*.

acknowledges Nikolić's knowledge of 'superior officers' genocidal intent', 'destructive consequences', and 'overall genocidal context/campaign'. The Chamber affirms Nikolić's knowledge of (i) the "details of the plan" to murder the able-bodied men in Srebrenica[144]; (ii) the "composition of the victims: soldiers and civilians, men, boys and elderly"[145]; (iii) the scale, scope and the systematic and organized manner of the killing operation[146]; (iv) the "sheer determination that every detained Bosnian Muslim male would be killed, including the incident when Popović enjoined the soldiers at an execution site to shoot a young boy"[147]; (v) his superiors' (Beara and Popović) genocidal intent[148]; and of (vi) the overall genocidal campaign.[149] While clearly recognizing the relevant knowledge possessed by Nikolić, who was a "2nd Lieutenant, the lowest rank of officer",[150] the Trial Chamber declined to follow the knowledge-based approach by convicting Nikolić as a principal. Instead, it treated such knowledge only as a proof of *mens rea* required for the mode of liability of 'aiding and abetting' under Article 7(1) of the ICTY Statute. In this respect, the Chamber observes,

> The central issue, however, is whether those actions, combined with his knowledge of the genocidal intent of others, considered in the totality of the evidence, are sufficient to satisfy the Trial Chamber beyond reasonable doubt that Nikolić *not only knew of the intent but that he shared it*. In reaching this determination the Trial Chamber recalls that "[t]he gravity of genocide is reflected in the stringent requirements which must be satisfied before this conviction is imposed". In this context, "the demanding proof of specific intent" is one of the safeguards to ensure that convictions for this crime will not be imposed lightly.[151]

In the end, on the basis of his knowledge of other participants' genocidal intent,[152] the Chamber held that Nikolić is guilty of aiding and abetting

---

[144] Prosecutor v. Popović et al., Trial Judgment, 10 June 2010, para 1404.

[145] *Ibid.*

[146] *Ibid.* para 1405.

[147] *Ibid.*

[148] *Ibid.* para 1406 ("His knowledge of the genocidal nature of the plan can also be inferred from his close association and interaction with Beara and Popović, whom the Trial Chamber has found harbored genocidal intent".).

[149] *Ibid.* para 1407 ("[…] Nikolić knew that this was a massive killing operation being carried out with a genocidal intent".).

[150] *Ibid.* para 1412. Despite the importance of the position occupied by Nikolić—i.e., the Chief of Security in the Zvornik Brigade, a post usually reserved for the rank of Major or higher, the Trial Chamber is of the view that, "in the context of an operation directed by Beara and Popović, Nikolić would have little authority of his own". *Ibid. See also* Prosecutor v. Popović et al., Appeals Judgment, 30 January 2015, para 515.

[151] Prosecutor v. Popović et al., Trial Judgment, 10 June 2010, para 1408. (emphasis added).

[152] *Ibid.* para 1017 ("With respect to specific-intent crimes such as genocide and persecution, [an aider or abettor] needs to know that the person or persons in the joint criminal enterprise possessed the genocidal or discriminatory intent".). Note that the Appeals Chamber in the Special Tribunal for Lebanon also follows this approach. Prosecutor v. Ayyash, Interlocutory Decision on the Applicable Law: Terrorism, Conspiracy, Homicide, Perpetration, Cumulative Charging, 16 February 2011, p. 119, footnote 343.

genocide.[153] While the knowledge-based approach proposes the formula of 'the lower the rank, the lower the *mens rea*', the Nikolić example appears to suggest the opposite. In this respect, since the knowledge-based approach does not differ from the purpose-based approach vis-à-vis high-level actors, the Nikolić example compels us to question what is the knowledge-based approach for. In other words, it is doubtful whether the knowledge-based analysis serves any purpose. What the knowledge-based approach ostensibly asserts in relation to low-level participants—i.e., applying the reduced *mens rea* of knowledge—sounds plausible, provided that a lower-level liability is to be attributed to them. Yet, it would be odd to apply a reduced *mens rea* to a lower-level participant, while ascribing the same level of liability as high-level actors. It is especially so if the relevant offence is the 'crime of crimes'. Isn't the Nikolić example a wake-up call? Isn't the knowledge-based approach just a speculative armchair argument? At this juncture, the following observation deserves quotation:

> Knowledge of criminal activity, by itself, is rarely morally significant. Many individuals may be aware of criminal activity but they are not complicit in the conspiracy just because they receive advance knowledge of it. Indeed, when the crime in question is a crime against humanity or a war crime, the whole community may be aware of the activity. [...] [M]ere knowledge of criminal activity, with no significant contribution with the intention of furthering the common enterprise, should yield the lowest level of liability.[154]

Now, let us examine the individualistic approaches to genocidal intent from a deeper theoretical perspective in the next section, which also serves the purpose of verifying the theoretical soundness of the knowledge-based approach.

2.5 Rethinking the Knowledge-Based Approach (II): A Purpose-Based Theory of Individualistic Genocidal Intent

In the previous section, I have addressed the inadequacy of the knowledge-based approach from a *macro* perspective by analogy of other legal doctrines. By so doing, I have demonstrated that the knowledge-based analysis fails to differentiate the roles of principal and accessory and leads to counterintuitive results. In this section, I provide another critical analysis of the knowledge-based theory from a *micro* perspective by drawing upon the definitional difference between 'direct intent/purposely' (conceptually connected *only* with the 'desired main effect') and

---

[153] Prosecutor v. Popović et al., Trial Judgment, 10 June 2010, para 1415. More precisely, it was (i) the limited scope of Nikolić's participation/contribution to the Srebrenica massacre; and (ii) his low-level rank that kept the Trial Chamber from labeling him a principal of genocide. Note that both of these factual aspects were of an objective nature. For a more detailed discussion on Nikolić's genocidal liability, *see* Sect. 4.2.2.2 *infra*.

[154] Ohlin 2007, pp. 79–80.

'indirect intent/knowingly' (conceptually connected *only* with the 'unwanted (or uninterested) but permitted side-effect'). In the course of this study, I argue that genocidal intent should take the form of 'direct intent/purposely' only, because the 'destruction of a group' can only constitute the 'desired main effect' (as opposed to the 'unwanted (or uninterested) but permitted side-effect'). That is to say, it is nonsensical to envisage the 'destruction of a group' as a 'side-effect' that is doctrinally characterized as something 'unwanted (or uninterested) but permitted' by the notion of 'indirect intent/knowingly'. Yet, what I do in this section is not necessarily supporting the prior purpose-based approach. Rather, I will try to develop a more refined purpose-based theory of individualistic genocidal intent. Thus, I begin this section by arguing that purpose-based theorists sometimes go astray, in two related ways. First, they define genocidal purpose in terms of the *intensity* of the perpetrator's desire to destroy a group; more generally, they often build into their conception of desire a kind of emotional commitment. Second, they doctrinally connect this requirement of special intensity or emotion with the notion of special (or specific) intent, *dolus specialis*. In what follows, I argue that both these ideas are mistaken. If, however, we take care to avoid these confusions, the purpose-based theory of individual genocidal intent works far better than the knowledge based-account.

For the purpose of this section, it is to be kept in mind that my arguments are based upon a conceptual framework of 'intention', which has been drawn from comparative studies performed by commentators.[155] The scheme that I want to propose is to be described as follows:

	Volitional element	Cognitive element
Dolus directus/Direct intent/*Dolus directus* in the first degree/purposely	Desire in a broad sense[156]	Either one of the cognitive elements below
Dolus indirectus /Indirect intent/ /*Dolus directus* in the second degree/Oblique intent/ Knowingly	Consciously permit (encompassing 'accept/reconcile oneself to/indifferent to')	Foresight of a consequence to a virtual/practical certainty
Dolus eventualis/(Advertent) Recklessness	Consciously permit (encompassing 'accept/reconcile oneself to/indifferent to')	Foresight of a consequence as being probable/likely/possible

2.5.1 'Special Intent': A Matter of Intensity/Degree, or of Object?

The purpose of this subsection 2.5.1 is to critically examine the way to grasp the purpose-based concept of genocidal intent, in particular, taking into account the

---

[155] Most significantly, Sieber et al. (eds) 2011; Heller and Dubber (eds) 2011.

[156] For the definition of this notion, *see* Sect. 2.5.2.4 *infra*.

emphasis placed upon the *intensity/degree* of volition. My ultimate conclusion to be drawn from the whole discussion throughout this Sect. 2.5 is that the purpose-based understanding of genocidal intent is doctrinally preferable to the knowledge-based theory. The main reason for that conclusion is to be explained in the next subsection 2.5.2 in connection with the distinction between the notions of 'main/desired effect' as an object of 'direct intent/purposely' and 'side-effect' as an object of 'indirect intent/knowingly'. For the purpose of this subsection, what I am arguing is that the manner in which the purpose-based genocidal intent is currently understood by paying attention to the *degree or intensity* of volition, under the slogan of '*dolus specialis*/special intent/specific intent' is inappropriate. Instead, I will demonstrate that the legal significance of '*dolus specialis*/special intent/specific intent' lies in the *object* of volition—i.e., the result/consequence of an action desired by an actor. Thus, as will be discussed in this subsection, in a sense that an individual state of mind is directed towards a result/consequence, there is no reason to conceive the genocidal intent dressed with the notion of '*dolus specialis*/special intent/specific intent' in a different manner than the ordinary domestic *mens rea* concepts.

As reflected in the expression "volitional element in its most *intensive* form",[157] the notion of purpose-based genocidal intent has been generally viewed as a subjective element that significantly connotes an *emotional* aspect of an individual inner state of mind.[158] If we follow this logic, in which the essential feature of '*dolus specialis*/special intent/specific intent' is its *intensity*,[159] we might ask the following questions: Is it really possible to legally differentiate 'volition in its most intensive form' from 'volition in its moderate form'? If yes, what is the benefit of drawing such a distinction? Does it make sense to acquit a suspect of genocide because he only possessed 'volition to destroy in its moderate form' falling short of 'volition to destroy in its most intensive form'? As seen from the fact that a prominent commentator characterizes the national law concepts of '*dolus specialis*/special intent/specific intent' as 'enigmatic',[160] a review of the relevant domestic criminal law does not provide a clear explanation of what these concepts

---

[157] Ambos 2009, p. 838.

[158] *See e.g.*, Vest 2007, p. 796 ("The [purpose-based genocidal intent], with its rather emotional connotation, is open to a very subjective evaluation of evidence".).

[159] I think the notion of emotion tends to connote intensity, as John Finnis states that "'feelings' and 'emotions' have some unwelcome connotations of conscious experience and intensity". Finnis 2011, p. 176.

[160] Schabas 2001, p. 49 ("But it would probably be preferable to eschew importation of enigmatic concepts like *dolus specialis* or "specific intent" from national systems of criminal law. They seem valuable only to the extent that they recall what can in any case be gleaned from the plain words of the definition of the international crime of genocide. The *Sikirica* Trial Chamber accused the Prosecutor of unnecessarily complicating matters by introducing a debate about theories of intent, noting that the matter should be resolved with reference to the text of the provision[.]"). *See also* Cécile Tournaye's comments on the view of the *Sikirica* Trial Chamber which denies a need to consider the theories of intent from national criminal law. Tournaye 2003, p. 450.

really mean.[161] But we can obtain a clue from some national jurisdictions, including Australia, Iran and France, that, while 'general intent' attends the act/conduct element of offences, the notion of 'special intent' concerns the *result or consequence* element.[162] I choose these three because commentators on their law make the distinction between 'general intent' and 'special intent' especially clear. In Australia, 'general intent' and 'special intent' are distinguished in that "the former refers to conduct, and the latter refers to the result or consequence element".[163] Likewise, under Iranian criminal law, "[while] general intent refers to an act, special intent refers to a result".[164] Bearing this in mind, for the purpose of clarifying the key characteristic of the 'enigmatic' notion of '*dolus specialis*/special intent/ specific intent', we might briefly look into the French notion of *dol spécial*—the original term that represented the genocidal intent element in *Akayesu*, the first genocide conviction ever rendered by an international court.[165]

In French criminal law, there are two kinds of intention: 'general intent' (*dol général*) and 'special intent' (*dol spécial*).[166] The 'general intent' is composed of "desire" and "awareness".[167] For the purpose of 'general intent', "desire" means simply a 'desire to commit an act' and does not concern the criminal *result* of that act (e.g., death of a person).[168] Under the French doctrine, since voluntariness of taking an *action* is sufficient to show the existence of the "desire", there is little practical value for judges to discuss the "desire" component vis-à-vis the notion of 'general intent'.[169] Likewise, the "awareness" component of 'general intent' is usually presumed as it "simply requires the accused to be aware that they are breaking the law".[170] On the other hand, under French criminal law, 'special

---

[161] Not only the distinction between the terms (in particular, 'general intent' and 'specific (special) intent') is far from clear throughout the legal systems, but also there exists a widespread confusion about the relevant terminology. *See e.g.*, Hall 1960, pp. 141–145.

[162] Cumes 2011, p. 327; Tellenbach 2011, p. 392.

[163] Cumes 2011, p. 327.

[164] Tellenbach 2011, p. 392. Compare the cases of Australia and Iran with slightly different distinction in Indian criminal law: *see* Jain 2011, p. 378 (while general intent never go beyond the *actus reus* of an offence, specific intent goes beyond thereof.).

[165] *See* Aptel 2002, p. 277 (note a rather laconic view expressed by the author: "[t]he concept of *dolus specialis* corresponds to the French legal concept of *dol spécial*. It is used in certain civil law countries, although its definition is often disputed".).

[166] Elliott 2001, p. 66.

[167] *Ibid.* at 66.

[168] *Ibid.* at 67.

[169] Bell et al. 1998, p. 225. Note, however, that I will argue in the subsequent subsections that, as far as it concerns the *result or consequence* element, the notion of 'desire' is crucial in understanding the true nature of genocidal intent. Thus, for the purpose of my argument, while the notion of 'desire' concerning the act/conduct element plays no role, 'desire' vis-à-vis the result/consequence element is important.

[170] Elliott 2001, p. 66; Bell et al. 1998, p. 225 ("Since there is a presumption that all citizens know the law, this element [of awareness] plays little practical part in the findings of criminal liability […]").

intent' (*dol spécial*) means "the determined will on the side of the perpetrator to achieve the *result* prohibited by law".[171] Thus, a French commentator says, "[a]s a general rule, all crimes defined to require the commission of a result need special intention".[172] French criminal law, therefore, does not hesitate to use the term 'special intent' *for ordinary domestic crimes*, as long as a 'result' is provided in the respective crime definitions.[173] Such crimes include, *inter alia*, (i) the offence of murder (special intent to cause death)[174]; (ii) the offence of theft (special intent to permanently appropriate an object that belongs to another person)[175]; (iii) the offence of non-fatal battery against a person (special intent to injure)[176]; (iv) the offence of providing intelligence information to a foreign power (special intent to incite hostilities or acts of aggression against France)[177]; and (v) the offence of possessing information concerning national defence (special intent to handing it over to a foreign power).[178] So, the principal feature of the French notion of 'special intent' involves a 'result' as an *object* of intent, rather than its *intensity*.[179] Consequently, we may conclude that, at least seen from the French perspective, the concept of genocidal intent as accompanied by the term 'special intent' primarily has to do with the 'destruction' or 'destructive result' as an object of intent.

---

[171] Badar 2013, p. 162. (emphasis added).

[172] Elliott 2001, p. 70. In relation to the Nuremberg Trials (particularly citing the Krupp case before the Nuremberg Military Tribunals under the Control Council Law No. 10), Johan D. van der Vyver conceptually concatenates (i) 'general intent' and 'conduct crime' on the one hand; and (ii) 'special intent' and 'result crime' on the other. *See* Vyver 2004, pp. 69–70. For more discussion on the distinction between 'conduct crime' and 'result crime'. *see* Kim 2011, pp. 214–216. For a view that regards genocide as a 'result crime'. *see* Vest 2007, p. 784. I will further discuss the feature of genocide being a 'result crime' in Sect. 3.3.3 *infra*.

[173] I deliberately use the term 'a result' instead of 'a result element'. because only the former encompasses both (a) the result provided in a crime definition as an *actus reus*, and therefore required to be materialized; and (b) the result that only forms part of a *mens rea*, and thus not required to be materialized. Among the five offences mentioned as examples of the 'special intent' offences, only the item (i) 'offence of murder' falls into the category (a). All others from the item (ii) 'offence of theft' to the item (v) 'offence of possessing information concerning national defence' are to be included in the category (b).

[174] Elliott 2001, p. 69; Badar 2013, p. 162.

[175] Badar 2013, p. 163.

[176] Elliott 2001, p. 69.

[177] *Ibid.* at 70; Badar 2013, p. 163.

[178] Bell et al. 1998, p. 225; Badar 2013, p. 163.

[179] In this context, I think it is not important if the 'result' is required to be materialized as an *actus reus* of an offence or not. As to the crime of genocide, it is generally said that destruction is a component of *mens rea* and, thus, not required to be materialized. *See e.g.,* Heine and Vest 2000, p. 186 ("in the case of the crime of genocide, "destroy" is not part of the *actus reus* but refers only to the specific intent".). In this sense, Mohamed Badar is, doctrinally speaking, mistaken when he says 'destruction' as a result element. *See* Badar 2013, p. 426. It should be noted, however, that the recent development in the jurisprudence of genocide has rendered a 'substantial destruction of a group' a quasi-*actus reus* of genocide. In this regard, Badar's observation is to some extent understandable. For more discussion, *see* Sect. 3.3.3 *infra*.

In this respect, Claus Kress rightly points out that "[...] the French distinction between *dol général* and *dol spécial* does not refer to the intensity but to the object of the intent. While the concept of *dol général* refers to the perpetrator's consciousness to act in contravention of a rule of criminal law, the concept of *dol spécial* refers to the occurrence of a specific result".[180] In short, I think that the French notion of 'special intent' (*dol spécial*), together with the similar interpretation of the term in Australia and Iran, provides us with an illuminating insight to comprehend the concepts of '*dolus specialis*/special intent/specific intent' representing the phrase "with intent to destroy": it is not the *intensity* of intent, but the *object* that matters—i.e., the 'destruction' or 'destructive result'. In the same vein, Nehemiah Robinson, a prominent early commentator of the Genocide Convention, plainly observes that "[t]he main characteristic of [g]enocide is its *object*: the act must be directed toward the *destruction* of a group".[181] All these considerations make it apparent that it is misleading to understand the concepts of '*dolus specialis*/special intent/specific intent' from the perspective of the 'intensity/degree' of *mens rea*.[182]

Indeed, the *Jelisić* Appeals Chamber gives us reason to doubt that the relevant international case law on the purpose-based approach adopts the 'intensity/degree' analysis of genocidal intent. Although the pertinent portion of the Appeals Judgment is not crystal clear,[183] we can still precisely grasp the position of the Appeals Chamber because it concurs with the opinion of the Defence.[184] Fortunately, the Appeals Judgment records the tenet of the Defence's view that '*dolus specialis*/special intent/specific intent' does "not refer to the *degree* of the requisite intent [...]".[185] So, the notion of genocidal intent conceived by the *Jelisić* Appeals Chamber should be distinguished from the purpose-based genocidal intent analysis emphasizing 'intensity/degree'. In this context, however, it is important to note that the *Jelisić* Appeals Chamber's understanding of genocidal intent is also distinct from the knowledge-based analysis of genocidal intent. Rather, what the Chamber considers '*dolus specialis*/special intent/specific intent' is simply "whether destruction of a

---

[180] Kress 2005, pp. 567–568. Kress states this for the purpose of making a case for the knowledge-based approach to genocidal intent. Thus, the immediately following argument says, "[t]here is, accordingly, no conceptual problem in also characterizing the knowledge-based definition of individual genocidal intent as a form of *dol spécial* because such knowledge would refer specifically to the occurrence of the destructive result and not just to the illegality of the conduct". For a differing view that regards *dol spécial* as a *mens rea* of a stronger volitional character than *dol général*, *see* Badar and Marchuk 2013, p. 28.

[181] Robinson 1960, p. 58. (emphasis added).

[182] For a different view, *see* Vest 2007, p. 790, footnote 28 ("[t]he argumentation developed here is based on the assumption that genocidal intent to destroy a protected group is referring to the requested standard of the intensity of that intent".).

[183] *See* Prosecutor v. Jelisić, Appeals Judgment, 5 July 2001, paras 41–52.

[184] *Ibid.* para 52 ("Accordingly, the Appeals Chamber agrees with the respondent and holds that prosecution's challenge to the Trial Chamber's finding on this issue is not well founded, being based on a misunderstanding of the [Trial] Judgement".).

[185] *Ibid.* para 43. (emphasis added).

group was intended".[186] This is consistent with the insight drawn from the study of the French notion of 'special intent' above: it is not the intensity of intent, but the object thereof that matters—i.e., the 'destruction' or 'destructive result'.

I believe, at this juncture, the agitated attitude of some commentators towards the notion of genocidal intent as a *mens rea* filled with *Sturm und Drang* needs to be toned down. Of course, the extraordinary content of genocidal intent—i.e., 'to destroy a protected group as such in whole or in part'—is heavy and gruesome. As far as the psychological mechanism is concerned, however, genocidal intent operates in the same way as *mens rea* for ordinary domestic crimes. How can it be different? Regardless of their significance and immensity, all the objects touched by guilty minds are to be processed in the same psychological manner—namely, as objects. Both the 'offence against a petty property' and the 'offence against God' have the same intentional structure: both are guilty minds directed towards *a particular result/consequence*—'damaging petty property' on the one hand, and 'disobeying God' on the other. In this sense, compared with the phrase "volitional element in its most intensive form", the manner in which Claus Kress epitomizes the gist of the purpose-based approach appears to be closer to what should be meant by the purpose-based notion of genocidal intent: "[p]ursuant to the 'purpose-based approach'. the individual perpetrator [...] must act with the '*conscious desire*' to contribute to the group's (partial) destruction".[187] Kai Ambos also calls into question the intensity/degree connotation of the term 'special intent' as follows:

> To be sure, genocide requires a general 'intent to destroy'. not a 'special' or 'specific' intent in the sense of a '*dolus specialis*'. While the 'intent to destroy' may be understood as an ulterior intent in the sense of the double intent structure of genocide explained at the beginning of this paper, it is quite another matter to give this requirement a purpose-based meaning by reading into the offence definition the qualifier 'special' or 'specific'. Even if this qualifier were part of the offence definition, *it does not necessarily refer to the degree or intensity of the intent*; instead it may also be interpreted, as opposed to 'general' intent, in the sense of the double intent structure, i.e. it would merely clarify that the 'special' intent to destroy must be distinguished from the 'general' intent referring to the underlying acts.[188]

---

[186] *Ibid.* para 51 ("Read in context, the question with which the [Trial] Judgement was concerned in referring to *dolus specialis* was whether destruction of a group was intended. The Appeals Chamber finds that the Trial Chamber only used the Latin phrase [*dolus specialis*] to express specific intent as defined above".). In this context, the phrase "as defined above" indicates paras 45–46 where the Appeals Chamber states, "[t]he Appeals Chamber will use the term "specific intent" to describe the intent to destroy in whole or in part, a national, ethnical, racial or religious group, as such. [...] The specific intent requires that the perpetrator, by one of the prohibited acts enumerated in Article 4 of the Statute, seeks to achieve the destruction, in whole or in part, of a national, ethnical, racial or religious group, as such". To sum up, in my view, the Appeals Chamber interprets '*dolus specialis*/special intent/specific intent' as *dolus directus* (direct intent/purposely), nothing more, nothing less.

[187] Kress 2009, p. 305, footnote 30. (emphasis added). Note that, concerning the cited sentence, I understand the term 'desire' broadly as will be discussed in Sect. 2.5.2.4 *infra*.

[188] Ambos 2009, pp. 844–845. (emphasis added). In the context of the Continental tradition, Ambos is rightly of the view that "specific intent corresponds to *dolus directus* of first degree, that is, it emphasizes the volitive element of the *dolus*". Ambos 2014, p. 21. For a similar view, *see* Heine and Vest 2000, p. 185.

In this paragraph, Ambos casts doubt on giving a special meaning to the term '*dolus specialis*/special intent/specific intent'. Instead, he suggests that this term might merely indicate a structure of 'general intent' (concerning the underlying acts) and 'special intent' (concerning the destruction of a group).[189] In the same vein, Nina Jørgensen states,

> Genocide has also been described as requiring an 'aggravated' intent or a 'surplus' of intent because in addition to proving the criminal intent accompanying the underlying acts, such as killings, it must be proved that the perpetrator also intended to destroy, in whole or in part, a protected group.[190]

William Schabas also joins observing,

> But for 'killing' to constitute the crime of genocide, it must be accompanied by the 'intent to destroy, in whole or in part, a national, ethnical, racial or religious group as such'. This presumably is all that is meant by the *dolus specialis*, or the special intent, or the specific intent, of the crime of genocide. Importation of enigmatic concepts like *dolus specialis* or 'specific intent' from national systems of criminal law may have unduly complicated matters.[191]

Let me summarize my argument up until this point. The feature of intensity of volition is not the main characteristic of genocidal intent represented by the term '*dolus specialis*/special intent/specific intent'. Instead, the notion '*dolus specialis*/special intent/specific intent' only means that an individual state of mind is directed towards a result/consequence of an action. Genocidal intent can be characterized as *special and specific* because it only concerns the *special and specific result/consequence of 'destruction of a group'*. The adjective 'special' or 'specific', in this context, is apt to be misleading and deceptive. In a similar vein, regarding

---

[189] Note that, apparently, the use of the term 'general intent' in this quoted paragraph is not consistent with the distinction between the notions of 'general intent' and 'special intent' in Australia, Iran, and France. That is because some of the underlying acts of genocide themselves require 'result/consequence'—e.g., 'killing' or 'causing serious bodily or mental harm'. I think, however, from a macro-collective perspective, Ambos's use of the terms 'general intent' and 'special intent' is acceptable. In other words, seen from the macro-collective perspective, underlying acts of genocide can be considered being equivalent to 'engaging in a conduct/act'. whilst the destruction of a group is tantamount to the 'result/consequence' of such conduct/act. The way I see it, there are two sets of act-result combination in the crime of genocide: one at the 'conduct level' ('immediate act – immediate result' involving an underlying act) and another at the 'context level' ('collective genocidal act – destruction of a group' involving collective act). The distinction between the 'conduct level' and the 'context level' forms the foundation of the whole discussion contained in Chap. 3 *infra*.

[190] Jørgensen 2011, p. 254. Note that, concerning the meaning of the term 'surplus of intent', Kai Ambos explains the meaning of 'surplus' in connection with the notion of 'extended mental element' when he observes that "[i]t has been said that a specific intent offence requires performance of the *actus reus*, but in association with an intent or purpose that goes beyond the mere performance of the act, that is, a surplus of, or ulterior intent […]". Ambos 2014, p. 21.

[191] Schabas 2002, p. 148. Otto Triffterer opines that the notion of '*dolus specialis*/special intent/specific intent' is highly elusive in both the Continental and the Anglo-American traditions. *See* Triffterer 2001, p. 404.

the common law notion of 'specific intent' in the sense of an intent to commit a further offence, Glanville Williams observes,

> The adjective "specific" seems to be somewhat pointless, for the intent is no more specific than any other intent required in criminal law. The most it can mean is that the intent is specifically referred to in the indictment. There is no substantive difference between an intent specifically mentioned and one implied in the name of the crime.[192]

In this connection, let me briefly talk about the case of Raphael Lemkin. In the chapter entitled 'Genocide' where he coined the term 'genocide', he did not use the terms such as 'special intent' or 'specific intent'. Actually, Lemkin hardly used the word 'intent' or 'intention'. The only reference to the word 'intent' is in a footnote which mentions "Hitler's oft-repeated intention to exterminate the Jewish people in Europe".[193] Three years later in 1947, Lemkin indeed used the term 'specific criminal intent' when he advised on UN member states' national legislation criminalizing genocide as follows: "The main task [in enacting such national legislation] will be to redraft existing provisions into criminal law formulae based upon the specific criminal intent to destroy entire human groups".[194] Given the context, however, it seems the adjective 'specific' in this sentence is employed for general usage. Moreover, in another occasion, Lemkin used the term 'criminal intent' rather than 'specific criminal intent'.[195] As far as the relevant legal doctrine is concerned, the genocidal intent element is not special as a *mens rea*: it should be just identified as one of the three ordinary *mens rea* classifications as generally understood by national criminal law, which is the subject of next subsection.

2.5.2 Genocidal Intent as 'Direct Intent/Purposely'

As demonstrated in the previous subsection, while it is mistaken to understand the notion of 'special intent/specific intent/*dolus specialis*' with the lens of intensity of volition, volition still remains as a useful reference point to clarify the notion of genocidal intent. That is, on the national jurisdictions' side, both the Continental tradition and the Anglo-American tradition largely agree that the *mens rea* of 'direct intent/*dolus directus*/ *dolus directus* in the first degree/purposely' is the one

---

[192] Williams 1961, p. 49.

[193] Lemkin 2008, p. 89, footnote 45.

[194] Lemkin 1947, pp. 150–151.

[195] *Ibid.* at 147 ("All these actions are subordinated to the criminal intent to destroy or to cripple permanently a human group".).

that requires the highest volitional element.[196] In this subsection, I will advance an argument that the genocidal intent element should be understood as taking the form of 'direct intent/*dolus directus*/*dolus directus* in the first degree/purposely' for reasons that (i) the result/consequence of the 'destruction of a group' can only be a 'main/desired effect' (as opposed to a 'side-effect') of an action; and that (ii) only the highest volitional level of 'desire' corresponding to 'direct intent/*dolus directus*/*dolus directus* in the first degree/purposely' can accommodate the result/consequence of the 'destruction of a group'.

2.5.2.1 The Three-Level Hierarchy of *Mens Rea*

In this context, it is important to note that the 'degree of volition' should be understood in relation to the hierarchy of *mens rea* covering (i) 'direct intent (*dolus directus*; *dolus directus* in the first degree; purposely)', (ii) 'indirect intent (*dolus indirectus*; *dolus directus* in the second degree; oblique intent; knowingly)', and (iii) '*dolus eventualis* (advertent recklessness; recklessness)'.[197] Thus, the notion

---

[196] Triffterer 2001, pp. 405–406 (stating that the term *Absicht* has been chosen for the notion of genocidal intent in German-speaking countries, the author observes that "*Absicht* in the sense of Civil Law theory needs a low intellectual threshold, but an extremely strong volitive element".); Badar 2013, p. 137 (citing Triffterer, states, "*Absicht* or *dolus directus* of the first degree requires a low intellectual threshold, but an extremely high volitional element".). Badar indeed regards genocidal intent as requiring proof of *dolus directus* in the first degree on the part of the accused. *Ibid*. 301–302. *See also* Blomsma 2012, p. 63 ("*Dolus directus* is characterized by a very strong volitional element. The actor shoots at the victim with a firearm because he intends to, he *wants* to kill him".); Ohlin 2013a, p. 104 ("Acting with purpose (*dolus directus*) involves the highest form of volition, i.e. a desire to bring about a particular state of affairs into being. Acting with knowledge (*dolus indirectus*) also involves a volitional component because the actor brings about a state of affairs that is practically certain to obtain, even though that state of affair is not his or her purpose for acting".). For a differing view that points out the cognitive sense of 'Absicht', *see* Ambos 2009, p. 844 (casting doubt on the purpose-based interpretation of 'intent to destroy'. states, "[i]n legal terminology even the German term '*Absicht*'. which in ordinary language possesses a clear volitional tendency, is not invariably understood in a purpose-based sense".).

[197] The *Lubanga* Pre-Trial Chamber shares the same understanding. *See* Prosecutor v. Lubanga, Decision on the Confirmation of Charges, 29 January 2007, paras 351–352 (recognizing the volitional element within each of these three *mens rea*). *See also* Prosecutor v. Bemba, Decision Pursuant to Article 61(7)(a) and (b) of the Rome Statute on the Charges of the Prosecutor Against Jean-Pierre Bemba Gombo, 15 June 2009, paras 357–360 ("[t]he Chamber stresses that the terms "intent" and "knowledge" as referred to in Article 30(2) and (3) of the [ICC] Statute reflect the concept of *dolus*, which requires the existence of a volitional as well as a cognitive element. As explained previously, *dolus* can take one of three forms depending on the strength of the volitional element vis-à-vis the cognitive element – namely, (1) *dolus directus in the first degree* or direct intent, (2) *dolus directus in the second degree* – also known as oblique intention, and (3) *dolus eventualis* – commonly referred to as subjective or advertent recklessness".). For a succinct but well-presented overview of the Continental scheme of *mens rea* covering '*dolus directus* in the first degree', '*dolus directus* in the second degree', and '*dolus eventualis*', *see Ibid*. For a historical overview of the German concept of intention, *see* Taylor 2004, pp. 102–108. For a detailed explanation of the Continental scheme of *mens rea*, *see* Blomsma 2012, pp. 59–134; Badar 2013, pp. 130–171.

of 'degree of volition' has *only* two levels corresponding to each level of *mens rea* within this hierarchy: The highest volitional level of 'desire' (corresponding to 'direct intent/purposely') is followed by the next volitional level of 'consciously permitting' (corresponding to both 'indirect intent/knowingly' and *dolus eventualis*/recklessness').[198] That is to say, 'degree of volition' is a notion external to *each* level of *mens rea*. What I mean is that it is misleading to conceive the 'degree of volition' *internally*—i.e., *within each* of the three levels of *mens rea*. For instance, if the mental states of each of one hundred criminal suspects from various backgrounds fall into the *mens rea* classification of 'direct intent/purposely', those one hundred mental states are legally of the same degree. That is to say, there is no differentiation based on degree *within* the subjective element of 'direct intent/purposely' itself. In this regard, John Finnis, placing the notion of *free choice* at the center of the consideration of moral responsibility,[199] explains the 'direct intent/purposely' as "[c]hoosing to (try to) bring about X, in the sense that if X does not result, one's choice and efforts have failed. In this sense, there is no question of being 'more' or 'less' willing; either one is choosing ('willing') X or one is not".[200] Thus, the notion of 'direct intent/purposely' is "not in itself a matter of degree".[201] In sum, while there is no room for the standard of 'degree of volition'

---

[198] *See* the chart on page 51 *supra*. I draw this two-level framework of 'volition' mainly based on a review of materials discussing the notion of intention from both domestic and comparative perspectives. For materials in the latter category, *see e.g.*, Sieber et al. (eds) 2011; Heller and Dubber (eds) 2011.

[199] Finnis 2011, p. 149 (emphasis added) (to Finnis, the term 'choice' means an "adoption of a proposal, viz. a proposal for action (or omission) in order to bring about a state of affairs either as an end in itself or as means to some such end".).

[200] *Ibid.* at 146. In this respect, note that, when George Fletcher discusses the difference between a 'strong sense of desiring' and a 'weak sense of desiring', he explains that "[a] bank teller who opens a safe at gunpoint desires (in a weak sense) to save his life, but does not desire (in the strong sense) to turn over the money to the thief. [...] Whether we say that the teller desires to open the safe [...] depends on whether we use these terms in their strong sense or weak sense". Fletcher 2000, p. 450. Here, it seems that either applying the 'test of failure' or conceptually separating the 'weak sense of desiring' from the notion of *dolus directus* would clarify the matter. First, applying the 'test of failure' to the hypothetical situation: if turning over the money does not result, it is obvious that the teller's choice or effort has not failed. Thus, the teller does not intend (in the sense of *dolus directus*) to turn over the money. Second, it is evident from the fact that the teller desires to transfer the money only in a weak sense of 'desiring'. His 'actual intention/specific intention/purpose/goal/want/desire in the strong sense' is to save his life. Put otherwise, turning over the money should be classified only as a side-effect. Consequently, the teller does not intend (in the sense of *dolus directus*) to turn over the money. Conceptually speaking, it is only the *dolus indirectus* that might be still considered. This example, however, seems to be a bit inappropriate in that the situation is rather closer to the legal notion of 'duress' than 'intent'. The 'test of failure' and the notion of 'side-effect' accompanying the notion of *dolus indirectus* will be discussed further throughout this subsection. For the 'test of failure', *see* Sect. 2.5.2.4 *infra*.

[201] Finnis 2011, p. 146. Compare this with the opinion of the Canadian Supreme Court in *Lewis* concerning 'motive' which states, "each case will turn on its own unique set of circumstances. The issue of motive is always a matter of degree". *See* Lewis v. The Queen, [1979] 2 S.C.R. 821 at 822, 47 C.C.C. (2d) 24, at http://scc-csc.lexum.com/scc-csc/scc-csc/en/item/2635/index. do. Accessed 23 December 2015.

to vary *within* each notion of *mens rea* ('internal degree' denied), the distinction between 'direct intent/purposely', 'indirect intent/knowingly' and *'dolus eventualis*/recklessness' is basically a matter of such degree ('external degree' affirmed).[202] (Although 'indirect intent/knowingly' and *'dolus eventualis*/recklessness' share the same volitional element of 'consciously permitting', they are to be distinguished by differing cognitive elements: 'foresight of a consequence to a virtual/practical certainty' for 'indirect intent/knowingly' and 'foresight of a consequence as being probable/likely/possible' for *'dolus eventualis*/recklessness'.). Accordingly, since the 'internal degree' is denied, defining the 'direct intent/purposely' per se with such a phrase as 'most intensive' should be avoided: because it misleadingly connotes that there is something like 'most intensive', 'a bit less most intensive', 'strongly intensive', 'moderately intensive', or 'weakly intensive' direct intent/purposely. The danger of employing the *internal* degree of volition in understanding the concept of 'direct intent/purposely' has been aptly warned against by John Finnis when he observed,

> The fact is that the emotional dispositions or attitudes which enable us to speak of *degrees* of willingness and unwillingness do not control, and are often scarcely or in no way correlated with, the choices one makes. One's enthusiasm, one's reluctance, one's repugnance, and so forth, are not the ground of one's choice.[203]

Compare this with Payam Akhavan's opinion as follows:

> The term *dolus specialis* refers to the *degree* rather than *scope* of intent. By way of comparison, *dolus generalis* requires that the perpetrator 'means to cause' a certain consequence 'or is aware that it will occur in the ordinary course of events', whereas special intent requires that the perpetrator 'clearly intended the result', signifying 'a psychological nexus between the physical result and the mental state of the perpetrator'. The ICTR Appeals Chamber has not elaborated on this qualitative hierarchy of intent, merely indicating that the perpetrator 'seeks' to destroy a group by means of the enumerated acts.[204]

---

[202] *See e.g.*, Silverman 2011, p. 494 ("[a]lthough eschewing the word "intent", the Model Penal Code recognizes three levels of mental fault that imply some degree of intention on the part of the actor: purpose, knowledge, and recklessness".); Petrig 2011, p. 457 ("[u]nder Swiss criminal law three types of intent are distinguished. These are based on the quality and intensity of the intellectual and volitional component of intent as well as their combination: first degree *dolus directus*, second degree *dolus directus*, and *dolus eventualis*".); Maljević 2011, p. 352 ("The Criminal Code [of Bosnia and Herzegovina] differentiates between two types of intent: direct intent (*direktni umišljaj*) and indirect intent (*eventualni umišljaj*). The two types of intent are differentiated according to the intensity with which the intellectual and volitional elements of culpability are realised. [...] A perpetrator acts with direct intent when he was aware of his deed and wanted its perpetration. So defined, direct intent represents the highest level or the most serious form of culpability in which both the intellectual and the volitional element are present in their highest intensity".). As to the 'intellectual' element of 'direct intent', only a minimum level of cognition may still constitute the 'direct intent/purposely' insofar as it comes together with the highest level of volition—i.e., 'desire'.

[203] Finnis 2011, p. 147. (emphasis added).

[204] Akhavan 2005, pp. 992–993. (emphasis in original).

In addition to differing on what distinguishes the notions of 'special intent' and 'general intent',[205] it appears that Akhavan and I each have a different understanding of the phrase 'degree of volition' or 'degree of intent' in connection with the notion of genocidal intent. While my understanding of the volitional 'degree' of *dolus specialis* must correspond to one of the three levels of *mens rea*,[206] he seems to assume an additional *level* which is stronger than '*dolus directus* (*dolus directus* in the first degree; direct intent; purposely)'.[207] That is because Akhavan classifies the 'direct intent/purposely' ("means to cause a certain consequence") as "*dolus generalis*".[208] In other words, as to the *mens rea* category of 'means to cause a certain consequence' (Article 30 of the ICC Statute), I think it should be regarded as 'direct intent/purposely', which reflects the highest volitional aspect of 'desire' directed at a 'desired main effect'. How can you "means to cause" something without *desiring* it?[209] In contrast, by classifying 'means to cause a certain consequence' as "*dolus generalis*", Akhavan seems to place the notion of "*dolus specialis*" outside the three-level hierarchy of *mens rea*. Assuming that the concept of *dolus specialis* (as he interprets it, 'clearly intending the result') is something 'qualitatively' higher or stronger than what he calls the *dolus generalis*,[210] I might observe that he

---

[205] For a discussion on the distinction between 'special intent' and 'general intent', *see* Sect. 2.5.1 *supra*.

[206] As said earlier, they are: (i) '*dolus directus* (*dolus directus* in the first degree; direct intent; purposely)', (ii) '*dolus indirectus* (*dolus directus* in the second degree; indirect intent; oblique intent; knowingly)', and (iii) '*dolus eventualis* (advertent recklessness; recklessness)'.

[207] For a similar position, *see e.g.*, Prosecutor v. Stakić, Trial Judgment, 31 July 2003, para 520 ("[Genocide] is, in fact characterized and distinguished by a 'surplus' of intent. [...] The *level* of this intent is the *dolus specialis* or 'specific intent', terms that can be used interchangeably".). (emphasis added).

[208] Although I am not sure exactly how Akhavan defines the term '*dolus generalis*', it seems evident that his understanding of the term is different from mine in that he relates '*dolus generalis*' to the 'result/consequence' element. As I explained in Sect. 2.5.1 *supra*, it is '*dolus specialis*' that should be directed toward the 'result/consequence' element, while '*dolus generalis*' concerns the 'act/conduct' element.

[209] This notion of 'desire' encompasses both the positive emotions and negative emotions. Thus, you can, for instance, desire something either with enthusiasm (positive emotion) or repugnance (negative emotion). 'Desire' in this sense connotes 'reason/rationality' rather than 'emotion'. I will call 'desire' in this sense 'desire in a broad sense' in Sect. 2.5.2.4 *infra*.

[210] In a similar vein, the *Kupreškić* et al. Trial Chamber understands that the *mens rea* threshold for genocide is higher than that for persecution as follows: "As set forth above, the *mens rea* requirement for persecution is higher than for ordinary crimes against humanity, although lower than for genocide. [...] Thus, it can be said that, from the viewpoint of *mens rea*, genocide is an extreme and most inhuman form of persecution. To put it differently, when persecution escalates to the extreme form of willful and deliberate acts designed to destroy a group or part of a group, it can be held that such persecution amounts to genocide". Prosecutor v. Kupreškić et al., Trial Judgment, 14 January 2000, para 636. Note that it seems the International Court of Justice endorses the view of the *Kupreškić* et al. Trial Chamber. *See* Application of Convention on Prevention and Punishment of Crime of Genocide (Bosn. & Herz. v. Serb. & Montenegro), 2007 I.C.J. 91, para 188 (26 February). In my view, however, it is not the degree or level ("higher"/"lower") of *mens rea*, but its content that differentiate genocidal intent from persecutory intent.

presumes a four-level-hierarchy of *mens rea* in understanding the concept of genocidal intent dressed with *dolus specialis*. I do not believe it is legally meaningful to differentiate between 'intent' ('means to cause a certain result') and 'clear intent' ('clearly means to cause a certain result'). Let me explain further.

It is needless to say that the distinction between *dolus directus* (*dolus directus* in the first degree; direct intent; purposely)' and '*dolus indirectus* (*dolus directus* in the second degree; indirect intent; oblique intent; knowingly)' has been extensively discussed throughout the Continental tradition and the Anglo-American tradition.[211] There is, however, hardly any discussion of the supposed concept of 'clear intent'. This concept is outside the scope of ordinary discussion on intent in the domestic law context by leading theorists. For instance, H.L.A. Hart distinguishes 'bare intentions', 'intentional actions' and 'further intentions'.[212] In his schema, there is no room for another kind of intention called 'clear intent'. Calling it the 'core notion' or 'central notion', R.A. Duff also places the *dolus directus* (purpose) at the top of the hierarchy of *mens rea*.[213] He articulates,

> There is, courts and commentators seem to agree, a *central notion* of 'actual' (or 'specific') intention or 'purpose': but they differ on whether that notion need be defined at all; and on whether, if it needs defining, it should be defined in terms of 'desire' (or 'want'), or of 'decision', or of acting 'in order' to bring a result about. That *core notion* may also include consequences that are 'inseparable' from the agent's end – though it is not clear what it is for a consequence to be thus 'inseparable'. There is also, many would say, a broader notion of intention which encompasses consequences of whose occurrence the agent is 'almost certain' or 'has no substantial doubt'. But while it is clear since *Moloney* that the law does not count as intended consequences which are foreseen only as likely or probable, it is not clear whether the law takes foresight of a morally certain consequence to amount to a 'specific intent'.[214]

---

[211] *See e.g.*, Duff 1990, p. 73 ("the perennial issue of the relation between intention and foresight".). For a view that stresses the similarity between *mens rea* concepts in the Continental tradition and the Anglo-American tradition, especially with respect of the notion of 'indirect intent'. *see* Bantekas 2010, pp. 40–41. For a differing usage of the term 'indirect intent' at the *ad hoc* international criminal tribunals, *see* Cassese et al. 2013, pp. 48–49 (contrary to domestic criminal law, the *ad hoc* tribunals abandon the 'virtual certainty'/'practical certainty' standard of 'indirect intent'. which results in equating the meanings of 'indirect intent' and 'recklessness'/'*dolus eventualis*' following the lower standard of 'probability'/'likeliness'.).

[212] Hart 2008, p. 117 *et seq.*

[213] For the purpose of indicating the 'intention in action' (equivalent to *dolus directus*), Duff uses such terms as 'actual intention'. 'specific intention'. and 'purpose'. *See* Duff 1990, pp. 21, 27, 37, 40 and 74. Note also that Duff, in other occasions, uses the term 'specific intent' in a different sense: indicating the *mens rea* equivalent to H.L.A. Hart's 'further intent'. (See *Ibid.* at 18–19). For the conceptual scope of 'specific intent'. *see* Chap. 2, footnote 222 *infra*.

[214] Duff 1990, p. 27. (emphasis added). See also *Ibid.* at 43 ("I shall focus initially on intended action (intending a result), rather than on intentional action (bringing a result about intentionally), since these notions are distinct: intended agency [equivalent to *dolus directus* (purposely)] reveals the core meaning of the concept of intention; the idea of intentional agency [equivalent to *dolus indirectus* (oblique intent; knowingly)] involves an extension of that core notion".). Duff explains *dolus directus* as follows: (i) "The agent wants (or desires) that result"; (ii) "She believes that what she does might bring that result about"; (iii) "She acts as she does because of that want and that belief"; and (iv) "What she does causes that result". (See *Ibid.* at 66). In his view, intention (equivalent to *dolus directus*) is "best defined" without referring to such notions of desires or wants. Instead, he prefers the phrase "in order to". (See *Ibid.* at 72–73).

In this paragraph, Duff is discussing the three kinds of intention: (i) a "core notion" of intention, (ii) a "broader notion of intention" accompanying the cognitive standard of 'certainty/virtual certainty/practical certainty/moral certainty', and (iii) another "broader notion of intention" accompanying the cognitive standard of 'probability/likeliness/possibility'. First, the "core notion" of intention connotes 'desire',[215] 'want', 'decision', or acting 'in order to' bring about a result, and called 'actual intention', 'specific intention', or 'purpose'. This "core notion" of intention, thus, means the 'direct intent/*dolus directus*/*dolus directus* in the first degree/purposely'. Second, the "broader notion of intention" defined by the standard of foresight to a 'certainty/virtual certainty/practical certainty/moral certainty' of a consequence falls into the notion of 'indirect intent/*dolus indirectus*/*dolus directus* in the second degree/oblique intent/knowingly'. Third, another "broader notion of intention" attending a foresight of a 'probable/likely/possible' consequence equals '*dolus eventualis*/(advertent) recklessness'. Hence, introducing a *mens rea* such as *dolus specialis* outside this framework generally shared by both the Continental and the Anglo-American systems would only confuse the whole discussion on the issue of genocidal intent. The genocidal intent element dressed with 'special intent/specific intent/*dolus specialis*' should be conceived as one of the three forms of *mens rea*. In our journey to the conclusion that genocidal intent should be regarded as 'direct intent/purposely', in the next sub-subsection, let us explore why it cannot take the form of 'indirect intent/knowingly' which is exactly the *mens rea* classification that represents the genocidal intent element in the knowledge-based analysis.

2.5.2.2 Destruction as an 'Unwanted (or Uninterested) but Permitted Side-Effect'?

Employing the term 'motive', the *Akayesu* Trial Chamber states that the destruction of a group itself ought to form part of a reason for action as an ulterior motive as follows:

> The perpetration of the act charged therefore extends beyond its actual commission, for example, the murder of a particular individual, for the realization of an *ulterior motive*, which is to destroy, in whole or in part, the group of which the individual is just one element.[216]

In like manner, there are scholars who appear to understand genocidal intent as something equivalent to 'ulterior intent'. For example, Kai Ambos categorizes the

---

[215] For the importance of 'desire' in defining 'intention' in both the Continental tradition and the Anglo-American tradition, *see* Fletcher 2000, p. 440 ("In German and Soviet law, it is generally assumed that an actor intends a result only if he desires to bring about that result. There is considerable support for an analogous account of intending in the common law".).

[216] Prosecutor v. Akayesu, Trial Judgment, 2 September 1998, para 522. *See also* Prosecutor v. Jelisić, Trial Judgment, 14 December 1999, para 108 ("The Trial Chamber therefore concludes that it has not been proved beyond all reasonable doubt that the accused was *motivated by* the *dolus specialis* of the crime of genocide".). (emphasis added).

'intent to destroy' as 'ulterior intent' in the sense that it indicates something beyond the *actus reus* of the offence definition.[217] In this sense, the notion of 'ulterior intent' can be identified with the Anglo-American notion of 'specific intent' (in the sense of H.L.A. Hart's 'further intention').[218] Pointing at the genocidal intent element, the ICC Pre-Trial Chamber in *Al Bashir* also specifically employed the term 'ulterior intent'.[219] The Cambridge Dictionary defines the word 'ulterior' as "(of a reason) hidden or secret".[220] This notion of 'ulterior intent' is the closest legal term to the concept of 'motive' as both share the character of hiddenness.[221] In terms of a reason or motive for an action, you don't hide something unless you really want (to do) something. So, if your reason or motive for an action is characterized or called as 'ulterior', it indicates that what you secretly want cannot be an 'unwanted (or uninterested) but permitted side-effect'. Instead, it must be the 'desired main effect' of your ulterior motive or intent. The term 'ulterior intent' is generally used in respect of the category of crimes that require an intent to produce a consequence beyond the *actus reus* required by the definition of the crime in question—e.g., the intent to commit an additional felony in the course of a burglary.[222] This feature of requiring an intent to cause a result beyond the *actus reus* also seems to fit in with the crime definition of genocide because it is generally

---

[217] Ambos 2009, pp. 835–836 and 849. *See also* Ambos 2010, p. 159. For a view expressing a preference for the term 'ulterior intent' in indicating the genocidal intent element (citing Ambos), *see* Tams et al. 2014, p. 132.

[218] *See e.g.*, George Fletcher identifies the 'specific intent' (in the sense of the intent to realize a particular objective, excluding undesired side-effects) with the term 'ulterior intent' (as in the offense of burglary: the intent to commit a felony). Fletcher 2000, pp. 453–454. For more explanation, *see* Chap. 2, footnote 222 *infra* and accompanying text.

[219] Prosecutor v. Al Bashir, Decision on the Prosecution's Application for a Warrant of Arrest against Omar Hassan Ahmed Al Bashir, 4 March 2009, p. 49, footnote 154.

[220] Cambridge Dictionaries Online at dictionary.cambridge.org.

[221] Williams 1961, p. 48 ("Motive is ulterior intention – the intention with which an intentional act is done. Intention, when distinguished from motive, relates to the means, motive to the end".).

[222] Although burglary is generally said to be a 'specific intent' crime, I think the term 'ulterior intent' is preferable to the term 'specific intent'. That is because the term 'specific intent' covers not only the case of 'ulterior intent' (e.g., the intent to commit a further offence in burglary), but also other species of intent. Richard Card lists them as follows: (i) "the intention which must be proved to secure a conviction for a particular offence for which intention is the only state of mind specified in relation to an element"; (ii) "a direct intention" (as distinct from an 'oblique intention'); (iii) "a further intention" (i.e., 'ulterior intention'); and (iv) "a state of mind, required for particular offences only, in relation to which the defendant may successfully plead its absence by relying on evidence of voluntary intoxication". Card 2006, p. 101; Ormerod 2011, p. 136. *See also* Fletcher 2000, p. 453 (explaining that the term 'specific intent' can mean: (i) "a well-defined, particular intent (e.g., an intent to deprive the owner permanently of his property)" (i.e., 'ulterior intention'); (ii) "an intent to realize a particular objective (if the intent is specific in this sense, undesired side-effects are not included)" (i.e., 'direct intention'); or (iii) "an intent that affects the "species or degree" of a crime and therefore may be negated by a claim of intoxication".).

said that the destruction of a group is not required to be materialized.[223] That is to say, apparently, the main feature of the concept of 'ulterior intent' is precisely the one shared by that of 'intent to destroy', in that 'ulterior intent' crimes "specify, as part of the *mens rea*, an intent to do something that is not part of the *actus reus*".[224] Indeed, the United States Code on genocide expressly specifies that genocidal intent is a 'specific intent' by providing, "with the *specific intent to destroy, in whole or in substantial part*, a national, ethnic, racial, or religious group as such".[225] Against this theoretical background, how relevant is the notion of 'ulterior intent' to our ongoing discussion of genocidal intent in connection with the distinction between 'direct intent/purposely' and 'indirect intent/knowingly'? Let us refer to George Fletcher:

> Though legal systems may differ on this point, there is good reason to believe that in the patterns of manifest and subjective liability, the "intent" required is a genuine intent—as we understand that word in ordinary English. Take larceny as an example. It is hard to imagine "an intent permanently to deprive the owner of his property" unless that were *the goal rather than a side-effect* of the actor's conduct. All inchoate offenses arguably require a narrowly defined intent to consummate the ultimate offense. This is most clearly true about crimes defined as "assault with intent to rape or murder". It is also true about burglary and the intent to commit a felony after entry. It is also true about criminal attempts, though some writers have reservations. Legal systems typically employ some term to indicate that what is required in these cases is not simply an "intention" the way the term is ordinarily understood. Anglo-American lawyers are wont to refer to a "specific intent"—in one of the many acceptations of that term. The Model Penal Code's definition of "purposeful" commission covers these cases. German lawyers distinguish between Vorsatz (intention) and Absicht (purpose or aim) and use the latter term to refer to the intent requirement in larceny, fraud and various forms of inchoate offenses.[226]

Fletcher's discussion in this paragraph centers around the distinction between the 'desired main effect' and the 'permitted side-effect' when he uses the phrase "the goal rather than a side-effect". Sharing the fundamental feature of 'desired main effect', Fletcher uses all the following terms interchangeably: "genuine intent", "goal", "a narrowly defined intent", "not simply an intention", "specific intent", "purposeful", and "Absicht (purpose or aim)". In this context, the 'ulterior intent' feature of the genocidal intent element suggests that the purpose-based understanding of genocidal intent, at least theoretically, prevails over its knowledge-based counterpart. Put otherwise, genocidal intent as an ulterior intent cannot

---

[223] *See* e.g., Badar 2008, p. 499 ("Another difficulty appears in applying the rule of '*mens rea* coverage' to particular crimes which require a proof of 'special intent' [...]. In such types of offences, this 'ulterior intent' has no material element to cover, since the actual destruction of a group is not an ingredient element of the offence".). Note, however, that I will argue that the actual destruction of at least a substantial part of a group is legally required. *See* Sect. 3.3 *infra*.

[224] *See* Simester and Sullivan 2010, pp. 138–139. *See also* Horder 1996, pp. 154–155 (taking an example of "wounding with intent to do grievous bodily harm is an ulterior intent crime because the *mens rea* (the intent to do grievous bodily harm) goes 'beyond' the *actus reus* (the wounding)").

[225] 18 U.S.C. § 1091 (2006). (emphasis added).

[226] Fletcher 2000, pp. 443–444. (emphasis added).

be directed towards a 'permitted side-effect'. Instead, genocidal intent as an ulterior intent requires that destruction of a group should be the 'desired main effect' of an actor's conduct. Thus, it is only the notion of 'direct intent/purposely' (at the exclusion of 'indirect intent/knowingly') that can conceptually accommodate the view that identifies the genocidal intent element with the notion of 'ulterior intent'.[227] That is to say, a combination of 'indirect intent/knowingly' and the 'ulterior intent' feature of genocidal intent is not feasible. The destruction of a group must be a purpose itself, and cannot just be accompanied as a 'permitted side-effect' of what the actor purposely intended.

Leaving the argument based on the analogy between genocidal intent and 'ulterior intent' behind, let us move one step closer to the problem of 'destruction of a group' being a 'side-effect'. Drawing on national criminal law concepts of 'knowledge' represented by such terms as 'indirect intent', *'dolus indirectus'*, *'dolus directus* in the second degree', 'oblique intent', or 'knowingly',[228] I would paraphrase the knowledge-based approach proposed by commentators as follows: *foreseeing* the destruction of a group as a virtually/practically certain 'side-effect' of conduct that itself pursues another 'desired main effect' (cognitive element) + *consciously permitting* that foreseen destruction (volitional element) = individual genocidal intent. Although Greenawalt and most of other commentators who proposed the knowledge-based approach did not explicitly mention any such distinction between the notions of 'side-effect' (as accompanied by *mens rea* variously labeled 'indirect intent/*dolus indirectus/dolus directus* in the second degree/oblique intent/knowingly') and 'desired main effect' (as accompanied by *mens rea* variously labeled 'direct intent/*dolus directus/dolus directus* in the first degree/purposely'),[229] I think this distinction is the key to unravelling the confusion and misconception that has plagued the whole discussion of the concept of genocidal intent. Let me explain further.

---

[227] In a similar vein, Car-Friedrich Stuckenberg explains that "[i]n German law [...] many offences contain an ulterior intent formulated as *Absicht* [...]". Stuckenberg 2014, p. 318. At the same time, Stuckenberg further makes it clear that the current terminology of *Absicht* means 'purpose'. *Ibid.*

[228] *See e.g.* Blomsma and Roef 2015, p. 106 ("Indirect intent exists when the actor knows his conduct will almost certainly bring about consequences that he does not desire or primarily aim at. It deals with side effects that the actor knows are almost certain to occur".). Blomsma and Roef further explain the notion of 'side-effect' as follows: "the result known or believed to be a condition of the achievement of the purpose is considered to be intended, even when it is not desired". *Ibid.* at 107.

[229] Greenawalt, however, takes note of the proper definition of 'indirect intent/oblique intent/ knowingly' when he states, "[a]ccording to the traditional common law-doctrine, criminal perpetrators intended the consequences of their actions if they knew to a practical certainty what the consequences of those actions would be, regardless of whether or not they deliberately sought to realize those consequences". Greenawalt 1999, p. 2266. The following quotation also seems to suggest that Greenawalt had in mind the distinction between 'desired main effect' and 'permitted side-effect': "However, to the extent that victims already are singled out on the basis of their group membership, the requirement that broader group destruction be a desired rather than foreseen consequence may be overly strict". *Ibid.* at 2287–88. It is also to be noted that, in the context of discussing the concept of intent from a comparative law perspective, Carl-Friedrich Stuckenberg observes that "[w]hile the concept of 'purpose' or *animus*, which points to the *direct or main*

Despite an almost complete absence of any serious consideration of the knowledge-based concept of genocidal intent in conjunction with the notion of 'side-
effect', Hans Vest's summary of Greenawalt's knowledge-based proposal deserves
our attention:

> Greenawalt's proposal has been extensively quoted as it seems to be eventually the most
> elaborated alternative interpretation with regard to the character and intensity of genocidal
> intent. It has already been mentioned that knowledge that a certain conduct will lead not
> only to the *intended consequence* but also inevitably to *another result* constitutes a special
> form of genocidal intent. As there is absolutely no uncertainty left, the desire of a perpe-
> trator that such consequence may not occur becomes completely irrelevant. Taking a cer-
> tain consequence for granted should be seen as a particular form of desiring this
> consequence in the sense of intention or purposefulness. This knowledge-based variant of
> genocidal intent may be called *indirect o[r] oblique intent*.[230]

Seen from the perspective of the *mens rea* framework that I proposed at the outset of this section,[231] I would say that the quoted paragraph is mixing up volitional
aspects and cognitive aspects of *mens rea*. At any rate, in this paragraph, the terms
"intended consequence" and "another result" are important to note in that the former signifies 'direct intent/purposely' and the latter 'indirect intent/oblique intent/
knowingly'.[232] Throughout this Sect. 2.5, I use the term 'desired main effect' for
what Vest called the "intended consequence" and 'permitted side-effect' for
"another result" that the actor knows will inevitably happen but still permits it
even though it is not the 'desired main effect'. What is meant by Vest's summary
of the knowledge-based approach is that (i) the *mens rea* of the knowledge-based
genocidal intent reflects the notion of 'indirect intent/oblique intent/knowingly'
that, by definition, only concerns a side-effect (of another main effect)[233]; and,
thus, (ii) the 'destruction of a group' as a side-effect is compatible with the notion
of genocidal intent: the genocidal intent element is to be met when the actor knew
that his conduct will *inevitably* lead to the side-effect of the 'destruction of a
group'. The problem in this understanding is that the concept of 'side-effect' is, by
definition, something that provides an actor with a 'reason against' (conceptually

---

Footnote 229 (continued)

effects of a deliberate action, is fairly easy to grasp – even small children know to defend themselves with 'I didn't mean it' – and largely beyond dispute, the most serious definitional problems
concern the *side effects* of an action and the requisite delimitation of the notion of intent or intention to the bottom, that is, where the nether region of intent end and where the respective lesser
form of culpability begins [...]". Carl-Stuckenberg 2014, p. 313. (emphasis in original).

[230] Vest 2007, p. 793. (emphasis added).

[231] *See* the chart on page 51 *supra*.

[232] In the cited paragraph, the term "consequence" that subsequently follows the phrase "another
result" in three occasions corresponds to "another result"—i.e., 'permitted side-effect': note the
term "consequence" as used in the phrases "such consequence may not occur ..."; "Taking a certain consequence for granted ..."; and "a particular form of desiring this consequence ...".

[233] For one of the rare discussions distinguishing the 'desired main effect' and 'permitted side-
effect' in connection with genocidal intent, *see* Vyver 1999, p. 307 ("*dolus indirectus*, in which
event certain (secondary) consequence in addition to those desired by the perpetrator of the act were
foreseen by the perpetrator as a certainty, and although the perpetrator did not desire those secondary consequences he/she nevertheless committed the act and those consequences did set in".).

encompassing both 'unwanted'[234] and 'uninterested') engaging in his act.[235] Put otherwise, applying the notion of 'indirect intent/oblique intent/knowingly' to a genocide case means: despite such a cognitive realization that 'destruction of a group' as an unwanted or uninterested side-effect to happen to a virtual/practical certainty,[236] the actor still volitionally permits it *in order to* achieve the 'desired main effect' (which is distinct from the 'destruction of a group' as a side-effect). In this way, the crucial and decisive feature of 'destruction of a group' is marginalized through the application of the knowledge-based approach. In this respect, is it an overstatement to says that the knowledge-based theory completely change the essential characteristic of the crime of genocide by detaching it from the notion of 'destruction of a group'? Under the conceptual framework of 'indirect intent/ oblique intent/knowingly', the 'destruction of a group' is only to be 'consciously permitted' by an actor. It is never 'desired' by him, because it can't be.

That is to say, the distinguishing feature of 'direct intent/purposely' and 'indirect intent/oblique intent/knowingly' is the *volitional* aspect of each *mens rea*— i.e., 'desiring' for the former and 'consciously permitting' for the latter.[237] The 'desired main effect' can only be triggered by the volitional level of 'desiring' that exclusively belongs to 'direct intent/purposely'. Contrastingly, the *cognitive* aspect is not adequate to function as a distinguishing feature between 'direct intent/purposely' and 'indirect intent/knowingly'. That is because, as the chart that I put at the beginning of this section shows, the same cognitive standard of the 'foresight of a consequence to a virtual/practical certainty' is applicable to both 'direct intent/purposely' and 'indirect intent/knowingly'. In both the Continental tradition and the Anglo-American tradition, 'indirect intent/oblique intent/knowingly' is certainly considered as a form of intention. For instance, let me repeat the typical textbook example. For the purpose of receiving an inheritance, a person who killed his wife by exploding an airplane, with 100 other passengers also aboard, is legally considered as *intentionally* killing those other passengers even if he did not want any of them to die (or was simply indifferent to their fate). Notwithstanding his uneasiness for the *unwanted or uninterested* fate of all those passengers at his fingertips, his knowledge to a virtual/practical certainty of their

---

[234] I take the term "unwanted" from Glanville Williams' account of 'indirect intent/knowingly'. *See* Chap. 2, footnote 241 *infra* and accompanying text. I use the term "unwanted" in a broad sense: it means that the foreseen 'side-effect' is simply not part of things that an actor actively want. Thus, the term 'unwanted' does not necessarily connote an actor's opposition for the 'side-effect' to occur. In other words, a foreseen 'side-effect' to which an actor is merely indifferent can still fall into the notion of 'unwanted'. For a literature in which the term 'unwanted side-effect' is used in the same sense, *see* e.g., Blomsma and Roef 2015, p. 108. For clarification, throughout this subsection, I use the term 'unwanted or uninterested' instead of 'unwanted'.

[235] For more discussion on the meaning of "reason against", *see* Chap. 2, footnote 245 *infra* and accompanying text.

[236] For the precise meaning and connotation of the phrase 'virtual certainty', *see* Norrie 2002, p. 50 ("[…] 'virtual certainty' is a kind of certainty (the only kind in fact that ever exists) and not a kind of high probability or chance".).

[237] *See* the chart on page 51 *supra*.

deaths (and his conscious permission thereof) suffices to constitute an intention (more specifically, 'indirect intent/oblique intent/knowingly'). In this respect, the knowledge-based approach puts the 'destruction of a group' into the same fact pattern of this '100 people on board' whose deaths are just an *unwanted (or uninterested) side-effect* caused by an actor who had in mind another desired main effect. The distinction between 'desired main effect' and 'unwanted (or uninterested) but permitted side-effect' is all the more important for Greenawalt's version of the knowledge-based approach in which the object of knowledge is a result/consequence of an act—i.e., the destruction of a group.[238]

In short, the ultimate difficulty caused by the application of the knowledge-based approach (conceptually reflecting the 'indirect intent/oblique intent/knowingly') to the crime of genocide is the cognitive dissonance between the 'destruction of a group' and 'unwanted/uninterested but permitted side-effect'. The term of 'side-effect' always connotes the concept of 'despite'. I take medicine for my health *despite* its side-effect of drowsiness that I don't want (or I don't really care about). I bomb Hiroshima to end the World War II *despite* its side-effect of killing innocent civilians that I don't want (or I don't really care about). Thus, what is really meant by me is to take medicine *for my health*; and to bomb Hiroshima *to end the World War II*. The side-effects of my actions are just a secondary consideration (or, in some cases, non-consideration). In line of this reasoning, what the knowledge-based approach tries to do is to put the 'destruction of a group' in this conceptual paradigm of 'despite': I engage in action despite its side-effect of destroying a group. In this context, the 'destruction of a group' only forms part of my secondary consideration (or non-consideration). The 'desired main effect' of ending the World War II tends to excuse the side-effect of killing innocent civilians in Hiroshima. Is there any 'desired main effect' that tends to excuse the side-effect of destroying a group or committing genocide? Isn't committing genocide the last thing in the world to fall into the category of 'side-effect' of something primarily pursued? Given the boundless evilness of human mind which knows no end,[239] switching the stage of discussion from the individualistic level to the collective level would clarify the matter, whilst, in that case, we leave the realm of *mens rea*. The factual circumstances of genocidal campaigns involving a State or State-like entity putting all its resources toward the purpose of destroying a protected group is certainly in discordance with the notion of destruction being a 'side-effect'.[240] In what follows, I will further address this problem from a theoretical and conceptual perspective.

---

[238] Strictly speaking, within the crime definition of genocide, 'destruction' is not an *actus reus* of 'consequence', but a component of *mens rea*. Yet, in view of the development of the relevant case law in which a destruction of a substantial part of a group is always required to be shown, regarding the destruction of a group as a result or consequence is not incorrect. For more discussion on the legal character of 'destruction', *see* Sect. 3.3 *infra*.

[239] Jeremiah 17:9 (KJV: "The heart is deceitful above all things, and desperately wicked: who can know it?")

[240] Strictly speaking, this sentence may not fit with other observations in this Sect. 2.5.2.2. That is to say, all other discussions are made from an *individualistic* perspective, whilst this sentence connotes the *collective* genocidal intent that is the main theme of Chap. 4 *infra*.

As to the distinction between 'direct intent/purposely' and 'indirect intent/ knowingly', Glanville Williams observes,

> Direct intention is where the consequence is what you are aiming at. Oblique intention ['indirect intent/knowingly'] is something you see clearly, but out of the corner of your eye. The consequence is (figuratively speaking) not *in the straight line of your purpose*, but a side-effect that you accept as an inevitable or "certain" accompaniment of your direct intent (desire-intent). There are *twin consequences* of the act, x and y; the doer *wants* x, and is prepared to accept its *unwanted* twin y. Oblique intent is, in other words, a kind of knowledge or realization.[241]

In this paragraph, the phrase "twin consequences" is very helpful: despite being brought into the world at the same time, one being 'wanted' (as a 'desired main effect') and another 'unwanted or uninterested' (as a 'permitted side-effect').[242] Article 25 of the Criminal Code of the Russian Federation is an example in which this paradigm of 'wanted' vis-à-vis 'direct intent/purposely' versus 'unwanted' vis-à-vis 'indirect intent/knowingly' is clearly provided in national criminal law.[243] Article 25 of the Criminal Code of Russian Federation, entitled "Crime Committed Intentionally" provides,

> An act committed with direct intent or indirect intent shall be deemed to be a crime committed intentionally.

> A crime shall be deemed to be committed with direct intent if the person was aware of the social danger of his actions (omissions), foresaw the possibility or inevitability of socially dangerous consequences ensuing from them, and *wished for these consequences to ensue*.

> A crime shall be committed with indirect intent if the person was aware of the social danger of his actions (omissions), foresaw the possibility of socially dangerous consequences ensuing, and *did not wish them*, but consciously permitted these consequences, or was indifferent to them.

There are also traces which show this distinction between the *wanted or desired* main effect and the *unwanted (or uninterested) but permitted* side-effect is also recognized by international criminal law when the ICC Pre-Trial Chamber in *Bemba* refers to the notion of "*undesired* proscribed consequence" in explaining the '*dolus directus* in the second degree'.[244] While it is conceptually feasible for the wanted

---

[241] Williams 1987, pp. 420–421. (emphasis added).

[242] For a doubtful view that a 'side-effect' might sometimes be wanted, *see* Duff 1990, p. 74 ("The [extended] paradigm [of intent] distinguishes an action's intended effects, which an agent acts in order to bring about, from its foreseen side-effects, which she expects and *might want*, but does not act in order to bring about".). (emphasis added).

[243] Article 25, Criminal Code of the Russian Federation (*Ugolovnij Kodeks Rossijskoj Federacii*), as translated and cited in Paramonova 2011, p. 438. (emphasis added). Given the phrase "or was indifferent to them", it seems the Russian version of 'indirect intent' also covers *dolus eventualis*.

[244] Prosecutor v. Bemba, Decision Pursuant to Article 61(7)(a) and (b) of the Rome Statute on the Charges of the Prosecutor Against Jean-Pierre Bemba Gombo, 15 June 2009, paras 358–389 (emphasis in original). The ICC Pre-Trial Chamber in *Bemba* is of the view that the standard to distinguish '*dolus directus* in the first degree' and '*dolus directus* in the second degree' is 'desire'. In particular, the Chamber explains the latter as an "awareness that his or her acts or omission "will" cause the *undesired* proscribed consequence".

baby ('desired main effect') to be born without the unwanted baby ('permitted side-effect'), the reverse is not possible. That is, the unwanted baby ('permitted side-effect') can only be born together with a twin brother ('desired main effect'): the latter always being the first-born child. In a similar vein, Antony Duff states,

> There are thus three categories of foreseen effect of my action: intended effects, which provide my *reasons for* action; expected side-effects which provides *reasons against* the action; and expected side-effects which, since they provide *no reason either for or against* the action, are irrelevant to it. I bring the first two kinds of effect about intentionally, since I am properly held responsible for them: but I do not bring the third kind of effect about intentionally; such effects should not figure in descriptions of my intentional actions, since I am not properly held responsible for them.[245]

If 'destruction of a group' is something 'wanted' or something providing you with a 'reason for' an action, your state of mind should be classified as 'direct intent/purposely'. Putting 'destruction of a group' into the paradigm of 'indirect intent/knowingly' makes the destruction something 'unwanted (or uninterested)' or something providing you with a 'reason against' your action. That is to say, it is counterintuitive to see that, theoretically speaking, what the knowledge-based notion of genocidal intent presumes is the fact that 'destruction of a group' is an *unwanted or uninterested* (but permitted) side-effect, which provides an actor with a 'reason against' an action. Isn't the 'destruction of a group' being a 'reason for' action the minimum culpability requirement for genocidal liability? Doesn't the rationale behind requiring a showing of an accessory's knowledge of high-ranking actors' genocidal intent for the liability of aiding and abetting genocide consist in checking whether the accessory's mental state was in line with that of principals, together directed toward the destruction of a group? Is it too much to require a more active and positive level of *mens rea* for principal liability beyond that involving 'unwanted (or uninterested) but only permitted side-effect'? Is the knowledge-based theory really applicable to actual cases of genocide? Would you convict a person of genocide as a principal when the destruction of Jews, Tutsis and Bosnian Muslims was actually something unwanted by him? In the insomniac commander hypothetical, did the commander want the destruction of a group? (Didn't he in fact mourn the tragedy?) How do you define the notion 'want'? What is the *mens rea* classification that fits with the state of mind of the commander? Is it 'direct intent/purposely'? Or, 'indirect intent/knowingly'? In order to answer this question, the following study is necessary.

2.5.2.3 Destruction as a 'Desired Main Effect' on the 'Straight Line of Your Purpose'

In addition to the dichotomy of 'desired main effect' and 'permitted side-effect' as a distinguishing feature between 'direct intent/purposely' and 'indirect intent/

---

[245] Duff 1990, p. 79. (emphasis added). *See also Ibid.* at 82 ("I bring about intentionally those foreseen side-effects which are relevant to my actions as providing reasons against them; it is for these side-effects that I am properly held responsible".).

knowingly', the phrase "[is or is not] on the straight line of your purpose" in the above quoted paragraph from Glanville Williams points at another crucial criterion to discern these two *mens rea* classifications.[246] That is to say, 'direct intent/purposely' concerns only the 'desired main effect' which is always 'on the straight line of your purpose'. If a consequence/effect is not 'on the straight line of your purpose', it can only constitute the 'permitted side-effect' which is an object of 'indirect intent/knowingly'. What the phrase '[is or is not] on the straight line of your purpose' signifies is twofold: the first implication (paying attention to the term 'purpose') is that the 'test of failure' (to be explained below) distinguishes the 'desired main effect' ('direct intent/purposely') and the 'permitted side-effect' ('indirect intent/knowingly') as the former always forms a 'reason *for* action' as briefly discussed above; and, the second implication (paying attention to the term 'line') acknowledges that not only the ultimate consequence/effect but also intermediate consequences/effects are to be encompassed by the notion of 'direct intent/purposely'. Let us have a closer look at each of these two aspects.

First, the phrase "[is or is not] on the straight line of your purpose" signifies that the 'desired main effect' (pursued by 'direct intent/purposely') always forms part of a *reason for* action because it constitutes at least a part of your *purpose*. On the other hand, the 'permitted side-effect' that is not "on the straight line of your purpose" does not constitute any such *reason* because it is irrelevant to your *purpose*. In this regard, Antony Duff clarifies,

> An intended effect provides at least a part of her *reason for* action; its non-occurrence entails at least the partial *failure* of her action: a foreseen side-effect forms no part of her reason for action; its occurrence or non-occurrence is irrelevant to the success or failure of her action.[247]

Duff here relates a 'reason for action' to the 'test of failure' expressing the idea that, without a reason, there is no success or failure. He employs the 'test of failure' in verifying whether an individual state of mind falls into the category of 'direct intent/purposely'.[248] More specifically, we can distinguish the 'desired main effect' (direct intent/purposely) and the 'permitted side-effect' (indirect intent/knowingly) by applying the 'test of failure'.[249] If a non-occurrence of what you foresee as 'virtually/practically/morally certain' or as 'probable/likely/possible' is conceived as a *failure* in your eyes, what you foresee should be categorized

---

[246] Similarly, Jeremy Bentham uses the metaphor of "the links in the chain of causes by which the person was determined to do the act". *See* Flannery 1995, p. 378 (1995).

[247] Duff 1990, p. 74. (emphasis added).

[248] Even before Antony Duff, John Finnis also made a similar observation. *See* Chap. 2, footnote 200 *supra* and accompanying text.

[249] Antony Duff explains, "We can draw the distinction between intended effects and foreseen side-effects by the 'test of failure'. If my action does not produce an expected effect, will it have been a failure? If so, that effect is one which I acted with the intention of bringing about [thereby 'direct intent/purposely' becomes applicable to me]; if not, it is merely a foreseen side-effect of my action [thereby 'indirect intent/knowingly' becomes applicable to me]". *See* Duff 1990, pp. 60–63.

as a 'desired main effect'. And, your mental state at such an occasion is to be legally characterized as 'direct intent/purposely', but not 'indirect intent/knowingly'. Contrastingly, if an occurrence or non-occurrence of an object of your foresight of 'a virtual/practical/moral certainty' or of 'a probability/likeliness/possibility' is neither a success nor a failure to you, it cannot constitute a 'desired main effect'. It thus follows that the *mens rea* of 'direct intent/purposely' is not applicable to you in that occasion, but only the possibility of applying 'indirect intent/knowingly' remains. The 'direct intent/purposely' concept to be tested in this manner does not have internal degrees; you just either have it (when the test result is 'you failed') or not (when the test result is 'you did not fail').[250] Accordingly, there is no such distinction as 'clear direct intent/purposely' and 'ordinary direct intent/purposely'.

Second, the phrase "[is or is not] on the straight line of your purpose" signifies that there are multiple spots where "your purpose" can sit because "your purpose" might be linear.[251] In other words, "your purpose" can sit either at the end of the line or somewhere in the middle.[252] Thus, not only the ultimate object of your purpose (at the end of the line), but also an *intermediate* object of your purpose (somewhere in the middle) still forms a part of your reason for action, and subsequently to be characterized as a 'desired main effect'.[253] In this respect, Itzhak Kugler states,

---

[250] Similarly, proposing a distinction between 'purposive intentions' (corresponding to 'direct intent/purposely') and 'non-purposive intentions' (corresponding to 'indirect intent/knowingly'), Jack W. Meiland suggests the two tests to distinguish the two concepts: (i) the test of 'trying'; and (ii) the test of 'deciding not to doing (changing your mind)'. That is, (i) if you can say 'I tried to bring it about', you had the 'purposive intention'; and (ii) if you could say 'I decided not to bring it about (I changed my mind about bringing it about)', you had the 'purposive intention'. For more explanation, *see* Meiland 1970, pp. 9–11. For a close similarity between Jeremy Bentham's distinction between direct and oblique intentions and Jack W. Meiland's distinction between purposive and non-purposive intentions, *see* Zaibert 1998, p. 473.

[251] In the same vein, Hans Vest uses the phrase "a (endless and diverging) continuum of means-to-end-relations" concerning the genocidal intent element. *See* Vest 2007, pp. 793–794.

[252] An old example in which the destruction of a group is clearly described as an intermediate consequence/effect of a genocidal campaign is an indictment of the U.S. Military Tribunal under Control Council Law No. 10 in the Subsequent Nuremberg Proceedings. The relevant part of the indictment, albeit concerning the charge of crimes against humanity, reads: "The acts, conduct, plans and enterprise charged in para 1 of this Count were carried out as part of a systematic program of genocide, aimed at the destruction of foreign nations and ethnic groups, in part by murderous extermination, and in part by elimination and suppression of national characteristics. The object of this program was to strengthen the German nation and the so-called 'Aryan' race at the expense of such other nations and groups [...]". United States v. Ulrich Greifelt et al. ('RuSHA Case'), Case No. 8, Indictment, at 5 (1947–1948), available at http://www.loc.gov/rr/frd/Military_Law/pdf/NT_Indictments.pdf. Accessed 23 December 2015.

[253] *See e.g.*, Paramonova 2011, p. 439 ("The volitional content of the intent refers to either wishing the ensuing of socially dangerous consequences [...]. The wish is characterized as striving for certain results which appear as a final goal, or as an intermediate stage of the conduct, or as a means for achieving these goals".). Greg Taylor points out that "[a]fter all, as is sometimes said, an actor's final goal (getting rich, enjoying life more) is, generally speaking, unlikely to be punishable in itself". Taylor 2004, p. 106.

The consequence need not be desired as an end in itself; it may be desired as *a means to* another end. For example, if a person causes the death of his relative in order to receive an inheritance, he is considered, from the perspective of the law, to act with intent to cause his death, although for him the death is only desired as *a means to* a further end (to receive the inheritance), so that he may be convicted of an offence conditioned upon an intention to cause death.[254]

In connection with this paragraph, note also the following observation from Jeroen Blomsma:

It is irrelevant whether the actor wished for or in fact mourns the consequence. For example, he might mourn the consequence of death because he killed an innocent person, but *want it anyway* to cover up his crime. The death is *the means to* further the end of covering up the crime. Not primarily desired goals that are understood *as necessary means for* the end-goal qualify as *dolus directus* as well.[255]

An actor's purpose that sits in the middle of the 'straight line of his purpose' (as opposed to 'sitting at the end of the line') is described by both of these two commentators as something *desired* as a "means to" a further end. Indeed, the phrase 'an end or a means to a further end' is a set phrase frequently used by scholars in relation to the notion of 'direct intent/purposely'.[256] And since the "means" *sitting on the line* should be classified as a 'desired main effect', the relevant state of mind of the actor is to be characterized as 'direct intent/purposely'.

Let us then apply the 'test of failure' and the 'test of the straight line of your purpose', to the hypothetical of insomniac commander. First, it is obvious that the non-occurrence of the destruction of the group should have been perceived by him as a failure. That is because the commander cannot receive the enormous amount of money that the old woman promised without first achieving the destruction. We can, therefore, safely conclude that his mental state is to be classified as 'direct intent/purposely'. Second, for the commander, the destruction of a group was just a means to a further end of being wealthy and affluent. However, the test of 'straight line of purpose' says that the destruction of a group being an intermediate object of his purpose does not keep a court from applying the *mens rea* of 'direct intent/purposely' to him.[257] Thus, both tests indicate that the insomniac commander's state of mind should be interpreted as 'direct intent/purposely'. But he expressed deep regrets, and even suffered from insomnia. In this respect, isn't it too harsh to say that his mental state fits in with the highest volitional level of 'desire' (corresponding to 'direct intent/purposely')? That's the subject of the next sub-subsection.

---

[254] Kugler 2002, p. 4. (emphasis added). *See also* Kugler 2011, p. 362 ("[...] it is not necessary for the actor to desire the result as an end in itself. Intention is established even if the actor only needs the result to occur as a means to another end".).

[255] Blomsma 2012, p. 67. (emphasis added).

[256] *See e.g.,* Finnis 2011, pp. 142 and 176 ("whether as its end or as a means to that end"); Hart 2008, p. 122.

[257] *See* Bassiouni and Manikas 1996, p. 529 (in the context of 'ethnic cleansing' in the Former Yugoslavia, observing that the atrocities "would still constitute genocide even if the ultimate goal, or motive, was expulsion".).

2.5.2.4 The Notion of 'Desire in a Broad Sense'

Explaining the *mens rea* of 'direct intent/purposely', Itzhak Kugler observes,

> [S]ome scholars [...] suggest that we should define 'intention' without using the notion of *desire or wish* because sometimes when we act in order to achieve a certain result which is only needed by us as a means to another end, we may be very sorry that we have to cause that result. If a person causes the death of his dog in order to put it out of its pain, he may be very sad when he is acting. In this case we say that he intends to kill the dog, since he acts in order to kill it, in spite of the fact that he is very sorry that he must cause the death of the dog. The fact that in these kinds of cases the actor is sad and sorry has led some scholars to suggest that we cannot say that in such cases there is a *desire or wish* that the result [...] ensue. And this, in turn, has led them to claim that intention should not be defined in terms of *desire or wish.*[258]

So, there is a view that says that this 'direct intent/purposely' "should not be defined in terms of desire or wish" in view of the fact that the actor might be sad, sorry or even mourns the result that he himself is bringing about. In this context, it is important to note that the notion 'desire or wish' as used in this quoted paragraph connotes a positive *emotional* attitude (e.g., want, will, eagerness or enthusiasm), while excluding its negative counterparts (e.g., reluctance, sorrow or repugnance). At this juncture, a crucial question in understanding a clear distinction between 'direct intent/purposely' and 'indirect intent/knowingly' emerges: how do you define the concept of 'desire' as the volitional element of 'direct intent/purposely'? It is to be remembered that, in the *mens rea* framework that I proposed in the beginning of this section,[259] it is the volitional element of 'desire' (that exclusively belongs to 'direct intent/purposely') that distinguishes 'direct intent/purposely' and 'indirect intent/knowingly' (because they might share the same cognitive element of 'foresight of a consequence to a virtual/practical certainty'). In this regard, pay attention to the term 'desire' in the following quotation from David Ormerod. Does the term have the same meaning as 'desire' used in the quoted paragraph from Kugler?

> Everyone agrees that a person intends to cause a result if he acts with the *purpose* of doing so. If D has resolved to kill V and he fires a loaded gun at him with the *object* of doing so, he intends to kill. It is immaterial that he is aware that he is a poor shot, that V is nearly out of range, and that his chances of success are small. It is sufficient that killing is his *object* or *purpose*, that he *wants* to kill, that he acts *in order to* kill. Note that the focus is on D's *purpose*, not his *desire* or *wish* as to the consequences. D can intend by having a result as his *purpose* without *desiring* it, as where D gives V a lethal injection to put him out of his pain, but wishes he did not have to.[260]

In this paragraph, the notion of "desire" directed towards the consequence of an action is used as opposed to those concepts of "purpose", "object", "want", and "in order to". They all signify a pro-attitude toward a consequence. In the context of this paragraph, the "desire" and 'purpose/object/want/in order to' are, however, differentiated in that the former connotes a pro-attitude based on 'emotion' and the

---

[258] Kugler 2002, p. 4 (2002). (emphasis added).

[259] *See* the chart on page 51 *supra*.

[260] Ormerod 2011, pp. 106–107. (emphasis added).

latter a pro-attitude based on 'reason'. In the quoted paragraph above from Kugler, the term 'desire' also connotes 'emotion', rather than 'reason'. While the desire as an *emotion* cannot accompany any negative emotions such as regrets, 'purpose/object/want/in order to' as being a *reason* can.[261] So, you may have a 'purpose/object/want/in order to' with regrets, reluctance, sorrow or repugnance, as was the case in the hypothetical of the insomniac commander. In this context, you are free to replace the 'purpose/object/want/in order to' with such terms as 'desire' because both share the common character of being a pro-attitude. What is important is not the term used, but the content. To the extent that a term of a pro-attitude contains a content of 'reason' or 'rationality' (as opposed to 'emotion'), that term is free to accompany any negative emotions such as regrets, reluctance, sorrow or repugnance. In this respect, John Finnis observes that "one can choose and intend to do what is utterly repugnant to one's dominant feelings. —that is the important reality (or the most important of the realities) which [English] judges recall when they state, at large, that *one can intend what one does not desire*".[262] The oft-cited phrase "most unwillingly but yet intentionally"[263] also signifies the same. Citing John Austin's account saying "intended consequences not always desired", George Fletcher further clarifies:

> Yet an influential analysis beginning with John Austin in the nineteenth century holds that intending should be considered apart from the issue of desiring. It would follow that acting intentionally consists merely in "having" certain cognitive states, such as the foresight of consequences and the knowledge of what one is doing. The Model Penal Code offers a definition of acting "purposely" that minimizes the importance of the desires, wishes, or wants of the actor. The critical facts in deciding whether someone purposely commits an offense are his "conscious object" [vis-à-vis the results of his conduct].[264]

---

[261] In a different context of discerning '*dolus directus* in the first degree' and '*dolus directus* in the second degree', Mohamed Elewa Badar opines that, '*dolus directus* in the second degree' can 'regret'. Badar 2013, p. 424.

[262] Finnis 2011, p. 174–175 (emphasis added) (describing the contrasting views of English judges and the legal academics on the meaning of intention: judges distinguish intention and desire; legal academics assert that "to intend a consequence is to desire it".). For national criminal codes which explicitly contain a negative description of 'not desiring' in their definition of intent (particularly, indirect intent and *dolus eventualis*), *see* the italicized phrases as follows: Article 19(1) of the Romanian Criminal Code ("An act is committed with intent when the offender: […] (b) foresees the result of his action and, *even though he does not intend it*, accepts the possibility of its consequences".); Article 18 of the Uruguayan Criminal Code ("[…] An action is considered intentional when the result coincides with the intention […]. A result *which was not wanted* but which was foreseen is considered intentional. […]"). (all English translations from Sieber et al. (eds) 2011, pp. 423, 438 and 473 respectively).

[263] *See* the quoted text from *Lynch* case (1976) before the Court of Appeal of England and Wales in Duff 1990, p. 19. In *Lynch*, the accused was found to be guilty of aiding and abetting murder on the basis of his intentional act of reluctantly driving a member of IRA to the killing site under duress. Thus, strictly speaking the intent in this context is an intent concerning the conduct of aiding/abetting as such. See *Ibid.* at 24 (comparing with cases involving a direct attack on a victim in which the attacker's "intent will have been the same as his desire and motive", the author says, "[i]n the more problematic kind of case, the jury may need to be told that 'a man may intend to achieve a certain result whilst at the same time not desiring it to come about'".).

[264] Fletcher 2000, pp. 440–441.

What is indicated by all these discussions is that the notion of 'direct intent/
purposely' should be defined in terms of 'reason' or 'rationality' because 'emotion'
is irrelevant. In this regard, distinguishing 'sense (a) of desire' (desire based on
reason/rationality) and 'sense (b) of desire' (desire based on emotion), John Finnis
observes,

> The [English] judges [as opposed to English legal academics] are right insofar as 'inten-
> tion', 'intend', and 'with intent' unequivocally belong with sense (a) of 'desire'; these
> terms refer to what is *freely chosen* just insofar as it is *chosen* as an intelligent and ration-
> ally appealing option, desirable in sense (a), whether it is also desired in sense (b) *or not*.
> [...] The conception of intention used in moral and legal reasoning, properly understood,
> is tightly linked to sense (a) of 'desire' precisely because it is tightly linked to the moral
> significance of *choice*.[265]

Thus, choice being the decisive content of intention renders the notion of intention free from emotion. We make choices sometimes happily, and at other times
painfully. And, by making a choice, we intend something. To sum up, when it is
said that "intention should not be defined in terms of desire [...]",[266] the term
"desire" means a 'desire as an *emotion*'. Put differently, there is no problem to
define intention in terms of desire as far as the concept of desire is a 'desire as a
reason'. But we should be cautious at this point that the purpose of this conceptual
analysis is just not to exclude the desire with negative emotions such as regrets,
reluctance, sorrow or repugnance from the realm of 'direct intent/purposely'. That
is, both the 'desire with positive emotions' and 'desire with negative emotions' can
constitute 'direct intent/purposely'. Thus, the notion of 'direct intent/purposely' is
capable of accompanying all the concepts of 'desire as a reason', 'desire with positive emotions', 'desire with negative emotions' and 'desire with neither the positive nor the negative emotions'. When they say "intention should not be defined in
terms of desire", what they are concerned with is that they just do not want to be
deceived by negative emotions. They know that the notion of 'direct intent/pur-
posely' is broad enough to encompass the actor's regrets, reluctance, sorrow or
repugnance. In this respect, I think it is preferable to use the notions of 'desire in a
broad sense' and 'desire in a narrow sense' in explaining the 'direct intent/pur-
posely',[267] rather than the combination of 'desire as an emotion' and 'desire as a
reason'.[268] Let us keep in mind that 'direct intent/purposely' should be defined in

---

[265] Finnis 2011, pp. 175–176. (emphasis in original). In this respect, it is noteworthy that, for
the purpose of clarifying the definition of 'intention', especially in reference to the concept of
'desire', John Finnis emphasizes the distinction between 'intelligible/rational factors' and 'factors contributed by feeling, sense and imagination'. It appears that the former concerns the
'desire based on reason', and the latter 'desire based on emotion'. *Ibid.*

[266] *See* Chap. 2, footnote 258 *supra* and accompanying text.

[267] For a similar observation in which 'want in a broad sense' and 'want in a narrow sense' are
differentiated, *see* Kugler 2002, pp. 4–5.

[268] Alternatively, provided that there is a general consensus on the term that can represent the
volitional element of 'direct intent/purposely', simply stop using the term 'desire' would be
another option.

terms of 'desire in a broad sense' that covers both the positive emotions and the negative emotions. In this connection, Otto Triffterer seems to suggest something similar:

> The international jurisprudence establishes quite often that the perpetrator acted with the specific, special intent "to destroy" and that he in fact was aiming at such destruction. But it nowhere expressly states that this particular intent needs an extremely strong will as an indispensable element and, therefore, has to be denied, if this *intensity on the emotional side* is lacking. […] [A] premeditated, well founded, and calculated behavior is much more dangerous for the protected values than a foolish execution of a strong will, by which the perpetrator knows what he wants to achieve, but does not have the intellectual capacity to choose the most effective means to get there.[269]

I believe one of the most significant causes of the pervasive confusion and difficulty that troubled the relevant discussions on genocidal intent thus far is that commentators have failed to catch the notion of 'desire in a broad sense'. A careful conceptual scrutiny of such crucial distinctions as 'desired main effect versus permitted side-effect' and 'desire in a broad sense versus desire in a narrow sense' has hardly been performed. This heedlessness has permitted the issue of 'degree/intensity of volition' to occupy the center of whole discussions on the notion of genocidal intent under such vain slogans as '*dolus specialis*/special intent/specific intent' and 'purpose-based approach versus knowledge-based approach'. In a very rare example in which the notion of 'permitted side-effect' is mentioned, we still notice conceptual confusions as follows:

> Does it, in substance, really make a difference for the punishability of genocide, whether someone is *aiming with all his will* to achieve such a destruction "in whole or in part," of the "group, as such"? Should it not be sufficient that he commits a genocidal act just with an ordinary intent "to destroy," meaning that he accepts that his act *ought to* or *most probably might* have this *additional consequence*? Who kills a group or part of it by a massacre for sadistic motives, but knowing that he may eliminate the group by the act, and who merely agrees to this *additional consequence*, does he not fulfil the minimum requirements for genocidal intent? Should he not be responsible for committing genocide in the same way as a person acting exactly in the same way and with the same knowledge, but motivated by his hate against this group and therefore aiming to achieve the *additional result* with all his emotional will?[270]

Applying the *mens rea* framework that I proposed at the beginning of this section,[271] it seems the legal concepts used in this paragraph connote *mens rea* classifications as follows: (i) "ought to": the cognitive standard of the 'foresight of a virtual/practical certainty' vis-à-vis 'indirect intent/knowingly'; (ii) "most probably might": the cognitive standard of the 'foresight of a high probability' vis-à-vis

---

[269] Triffterer 2001, pp. 405–406. (emphasis added). Likewise, Hans Vest observes, "[i]nterestingly, the case law of the ad hoc Tribunals seems never to have underlined the emotional engagement and strength of the perpetrator's intent to destroy the protected group except in the *Jelisić* Judgments". Vest 2007, p. 796.

[270] Triffterer 2001, pp. 404–405. (emphasis added). Hans Vest also briefly mentions the notion of "side-effect" in his article on genocidal intent. *See* Vest 2007, pp. 788–789.

[271] *See* the chart on page 51 *supra*.

'*dolus eventualis*/recklessness'; and (iii) "additional consequence": the permitted side-effect as the object of 'indirect intent/knowingly'. Given that Triffterer conceptually relates 'aiming to' to 'additional result' and so forth, the quoted paragraph sounds confusing. Talks on the theme of genocidal intent always return back to 'degree/intensity of volition', which is unfortunate. The phrase "aiming with all his will" tends to be delusive as it suggests that there exists something like "aiming with his moderate will". In a real life, surely, such distinction can be made. But, in the law of *mens rea*, there is no such distinction. If you aim, it is legally irrelevant whether you aimed something with all your will or with just some portion of your will. Insofar as you 'desired' something based on a reason and rationality, the law characterizes your mental state as 'direct intent/purposely'. The weighty content of genocidal intent as contained in the phrase 'to destroy a group, in whole or in part, as such' cannot affect the law of *mens rea* insofar as that content is to be wrapped by an individual state of mind. The theory of *mens rea* does not discriminate between a weighty content and a light content. If the genocidal intent element wants to receive a special treatment, it must give up being a *mens rea*.

To sum up, genocidal intent as a *mens rea* is a 'direct intent/purposely' directed to the 'desired main effect' of the destruction of a group.[272] Non-occurrence of 'destruction of a group' should be conceived as a *failure* to the actor (the test of failure), and the destruction must be on the straight line of your purpose being the ultimate end or an intermediate end for a further end (the test of the straight line of your purpose). A person can possess genocidal intent with such negative emotions of regret, sorrow or repugnance, because the volitional element of 'desire' for 'direct intent/purposely' is to be defined as 'desire in a broad sense'. In other words, the genocidal intent element understood in this manner on the basis of a rational choice and decision is to be legally established regardless of the emotion, be it of a positive or a negative nature, of an actor. The insomniac commander's mental state, therefore, should be classified as 'direct intent/purposely': In addition to passing the two tests of 'test of failure' and 'test of the straight line of your purpose', he had the 'desire in a broad sense' which is the volitional element of 'direct intent/purposely' despite his regret and sorrow.

2.6 Complications and Frustrations: Individualistic Genocidal Intent at the *Ad Hoc* Tribunals

In this section, we will look into the relevant case law of the *ad hoc* tribunals. The purpose of this section is to demonstrate how complex and counterintuitive the relevant analysis of the genocidal intent element in the jurisprudence of the tribunals

---

[272] For the same view, *see* Blomsma and Roef 2015, p. 108; Vyver 1999, p. 308. In this respect, also consider the relevant national jurisprudence, such as Hungary where "in cases when the statutory offense definition contains a particular purpose, like financial advantage or premeditation […], the crime can only be committed with *dolus directus*. The reason behind this is that setting a specific goal cannot be just accepted but must be desired by the offender". Csúri 2011, p. 368.

is. The analysis in Chaps. 3 and 4 surrounding the notions of 'collective genocide' and collective genocidal intent is to be performed against the backdrop of this section in which the complications and frustrations concerning the doctrinal and evidentiary aspects of genocidal intent are to be further revealed. It should be kept in mind that the discussion of the *ad hoc* tribunals' practice in relation to the genocidal intent element contained in this section reflects the mostly one-layered perspective of the case law vis-à-vis the crime of genocide in general and genocidal intent in particular. Contrastingly, the analysis contained in Chaps. 3 and 4 starts from establishing the two-layered structure of genocide—i.e., the 'conduct level' and the 'context level'.

2.6.1 The Akayesu Paradox: Applying the Knowledge-Based Theory to the Purpose-Based Concept of Genocidal Intent?

The claim that the judges of the ICTY and the ICTR issuing decisions on the crime of genocide almost universally support the purpose-based approach tells only a part of the whole story. While it is evident that they appear to espouse the purpose-based notion of genocidal intent *in theory*, the extent to which the knowledge-based approach is implicitly applied *in practice* is so enormous that the doctrinally proclaimed purpose-based definition of genocidal intent has become 'the emperor's new clothes'. Everybody is perplexed, but they still chant. 'The emperor's new clothes' has been predicted and forewarned by commentators by way of such expressions as 'squeezing facts' and 'evidential backdoor'.[273] Most notably, although the *Akayesu* Trial Judgment has been cited by almost all the commentators who explain the purpose-based approach as the leading authority, a careful reading of the judgment surely embarrasses us. It is not uncommon to spot the self-contradictory statements in international decisions dealing with genocide. They often say something like, "[the Trial Chamber's] sole task is to assess the individual criminal responsibility of the accused […]. [T]he seriousness of the charges brought against the accused makes it all the more necessary to examine scrupulously and meticulously all the inculpatory and exonerating evidence, in the context of a fair trial and in full res[p]ect of all the rights of the Accused".[274] Their treatment of facts adduced on the charge of genocide, however, often betrays such

---

[273] *See* Greenawalt 1999, p. 2281 ("[t]he danger of adhering to a specific intent standard in such situations is not merely that culpable perpetrators will escape liability for genocide, but perhaps more ominously that the evidentiary problems will compel courts to squeeze ambiguous fact patterns into the specific intent paradigm".); Kress 2005, p. 571 ([case law is] "formulat[ing] the rigid purpose-based approach to genocidal intent in the abstract and then circumvent this very standard through the evidential backdoor".).

[274] Prosecutor v. Akayesu, Trial Judgment, 2 September 1998, para 129.

a self-declared legal duty to examine the evidence in a strict manner, which is evident from the following paragraphs from *Akayesu*:

> The Chamber is of the opinion that it is possible to infer the genocidal intention that presided over the commission of a particular act, *inter alia*, from all acts or utterances of the accused, or from the *general context* in which other culpable acts were perpetrated systematically against the same group, *regardless of whether such other acts were committed by the same perpetrator or even by other perpetrators.*[275]
>
> Owing to the very high number of atrocities committed against the Tutsi, their widespread nature not only in the commune of Taba, but also throughout Rwanda, and to the fact that the victims were systematically and deliberately selected because they belonged to the Tutsi group, with persons belonging to other groups being excluded, the Chamber is able to infer, beyond reasonable doubt, the *genocidal intent of the accused* in the commission of the above-mentioned crimes.[276]

The core message of these two paragraphs is that one can prove the purpose-based individualistic genocidal intent through non-individualistic overall facts. Unfortunately, the conceptual gap between the purely individualistic purpose-based *mens rea* and the circumstantial facts of a collective nature has largely been overlooked and ignored. It is, however, certainly an overstatement that the accused's personal 'desire in a broad sense' is to be inferred mostly from the contextual circumstances.[277] In this respect, Nina Jørgensen rightly asks, "[i]t may be questioned whether this truly satisfies the [purpose-based] specific intent requirement or is only sufficient to prove knowledge of the genocidal plan".[278]

The two paragraphs cited above can be regarded as a summary of a more detailed discussion on the issue of *collective* genocidal intent in the preceding part of the judgment, from paras 112 to 129, entitled "Genocide in Rwanda in 1994?". There, the *Akayesu* Trial Chamber considers the collective genocidal intent under such expressions as "the intention of the perpetrators of these killings"[279]; "the resolve of the perpetrators of these massacres"[280]; and "an intention to wipe out the Tutsi group in its entirety".[281] For the purpose of the Chamber's analysis contained in paras 112 through 129, the collective genocidal intent represented by these phrases is certainly treated as being distinct from the individual genocidal intent of the accused. Thus, in the final paragraph of the section "Genocide in Rwanda in 1994?", the Chamber says,

> [...] the Chamber holds that the fact that genocide was indeed committed in Rwanda in 1994 and more particularly in Taba, cannot influence it in its decisions in the present case.

---

[275] *Ibid.* para 728. (emphasis added).

[276] *Ibid.* para 730. (emphasis added).

[277] For the notion of 'desire in a broad sense', *see* Sect. 2.5.2.4 *supra*.

[278] Jørgensen 2001, p. 298. Furthermore, note that Jørgensen is of the view that "the concept of genocide was elaborated against the background of a genocidal scheme that was meticulously documented with the result that it was not difficult to prove the intent of the Nazi leaders". *Ibid.*

[279] Prosecutor v. Akayesu, Trial Judgment, 2 September 1998, para 118.

[280] *Ibid.* para 119.

[281] *Ibid.* para 121.

Its sole task is to assess *the individual criminal responsibility of the accused* for the crimes with which he is charged, the burden of proof being on the Prosecutor.[282]

Unfortunately, however, this proclamation of the Chamber turns out to be empty because the decision on the accused's individual genocidal intent (paras 727–730) is made mainly on the basis of the evidence already considered to find the 'collective genocide' and 'collective genocidal intent' (paras 112–129).[283] In other words, the evidence supporting individual genocidal intent and collective genocidal intent overlap so much that one might assert that the accused's individual genocidal intent is just an imputed collective genocidal intent which can be inferred from the overall context of atrocities without any significant evidential considerations about the individual state of mind of the accused.[284] In this regard, it appears that, in practice, individual genocidal intent of the accused is established on the basis of his *presumed knowledge* of the overall context of the massacres.[285] That is because, in spite of the absence of any reference to the accused's knowledge of the overall context in the *Akayesu* Trial Judgment, there is no possible legal nexus between the context of massacres and his individual genocidal intent except for that knowledge. In this regard, one might say that a significant portion of the Chamber's reasoning on Akayesu's individual genocidal intent drawing from the context of atrocities is actually applying a version of the knowledge-based approach to genocidal intent. Given that the concept of genocidal intent theoretically understood by the Chamber appears to be in line with the purpose-based definition of genocidal intent,[286] rather than its knowledge-based counterpart, such a covert application of the knowledge-based approach looks puzzling. In this respect, Hans Vest observes,

> Interestingly, the case law of the *ad hoc* tribunals seems never to have underlined the emotional engagement and strength of the perpetrator's intent to destroy the protected group except in the *Jelisić* judgments. Probably feeling that risk, the evidence held to be decisive by the courts has actually always been inferred from the knowledge-based acts of the accused.[287]

---

[282] *Ibid.* para 129. (emphasis added).

[283] The notions of 'collective genocide' and 'collective genocidal intent' will be the main themes of Chaps. 3 and 4 *infra* respectively.

[284] In *Akayesu*, in addition to his conviction on the charge of genocide proper (count 1), the Trial Chamber finds the accused guilty of 'direct and public incitement to commit genocide' (count 2) based on his speeches, on several occasions, "calling, more or less explicitly, for the commission of genocide". *See* Prosecutor v. Akayesu, Trial Judgment, 2 September 1998, paras 672–675 and 729. This seems to be the only individualistic evidence considered vis-à-vis the genocidal intent of the accused.

[285] Prosecutor v. Akayesu, Trial Judgment, 2 September 1998, paras 727–730.

[286] *Ibid.* para 498 (stating, "[g]enocide is distinct from other crimes inasmuch as it embodies a special intent or *dolus specialis*. Special intent of a crime is the specific intention, required as a constitutive element of the crime, which demands that the perpetrator clearly seeks to produce the act charged".).

[287] Vest 2007, p. 796.

As will be explicated in more detail in the next subsection 2.6.2, the purpose-based approach has become nominal as its doctrinal proclaimer—i.e., the case law of the ICTY and the ICTR—betrayed itself by taking a self-contradictory path of proving the doctrinally purpose-based genocidal intent mainly through the circumstantial facts surrounding the overall context. Since it is 'cognition' rather than 'volition' that is more apt to attend the *actus reus* of 'circumstance', it seems that the knowledge-based approach, in practice, prevails over the purpose-based approach at the ICTY and the ICTR. Let us continue our examination on this point of actual proof of the genocidal intent element in more detail in the following subsection.

2.6.2 Case Law Claiming the Purpose-Based Approach Doctrinally, but Denying It Evidentially?

The *Krstić* Appeals Chamber reverses the Trial Chamber's conviction of genocide stating,

> As has been demonstrated, all that the evidence can establish is that Krstić was aware of the intent to commit genocide on the part of some members of the VRS Main Staff, and with that knowledge, he did nothing to prevent the use of Drina Corps personnel and resources to facilitate those killings. *This knowledge on his part alone cannot support an inference of genocidal intent.*[288]

This paragraph appears to be a strong vindication of the purpose-based approach. An individual person's inner state of mind—i.e., his *mens rea* in criminal law terms—generally manifests itself in two forms: words and deeds. So judges usually infer the accused's *mens rea* from his individual words and deeds. This principle has also been applied to genocidal intent, and it is not uncommon to see such observations made by international judges placing an emphasis on individual 'words and deeds'.[289] The relevant case law, however, does not stop there. For the purpose of inferring individual genocidal intent, international judges almost universally add another point of reference which can be represented by such phrases as 'a context of violence' or 'surrounding circumstances of massacres'. In criminal law, inferring *mens rea* indeed involves the consideration of the relevant context.[290] That context, however, is closely connected to the actor and

---

[288] Prosecutor v. Krstić, Appeals Judgment, 19 April 2004, para 134. (emphasis added).

[289] *See e.g.*, Prosecutor v. Kayishema and Ruzindana, Trial Judgment, 21 May 1999, paras 527 and 541. *See also* Sect. 4.1.2 *infra*, text accompanying the notes 77–84.

[290] *See e.g.*, Shapira-Ettinger 2007, pp. 2580–2581 ("The physical, observable act can be proven by direct evidence, but only circumstantial evidence can be offered to prove a mental event".). See also *Ibid.* at 2582 ("The only difference between what happens internally and other external facts is the inherent inaccessibility of the internal facts. Thus, proof of a mental state is never direct because it is not observable by anyone other than the person experiencing it".).

his action.[291] Thus, Duff states that "[w]e discover her intentions by locating this particular action within a broader pattern of actions and reactions; by relating it to an end [...], and by relating that to its own wider context".[292] The attention is primarily given to a "particular action" and the "wider context" that belongs to or surrounds the action. Yet, the context and surrounding circumstances from which international judges infer genocidal intent far exceeds such individualistic boundaries of a specific actor and his action. Moreover, the pattern of judicial analysis of genocidal intent carried out by international judges reveals that the probative importance of this category of 'circumstantial' evidence is so colossal as to almost obviate the first two reference points of 'words and deeds'. The prevalence of this phenomenon of heavy reliance on contextual/circumstantial evidence signifies damaging implications for the individualistic approach to genocidal intent in general, and for the purpose-based approach in particular. That is, despite this phenomenon, as Article 30 of the ICC Statute shows, there is still room for the knowledge-based concept of genocidal intent to survive, as 'knowledge' is the sole subjective element applicable to the 'circumstantial' facts.[293] In the same vein, Otto Triffterer observes,

> [Genocidal] intent can be – and has been proven – on the international level regularly by circumstantial evidence and in none of the decisions the emotional part of "Absicht" [identical to 'dolus directus in the first degree' in the Continental tradition or 'purposely' in the Model Penal Code] has been expressly mentioned. But this part of the particular intent would be necessary if "Absicht" is required and is very difficult to prove. *We can prove by circumstantial evidence what the perpetrator was aware of and of which facts he had knowledge.*[294]

---

[291] In this respect, the *Bagilishema* Trial Chamber's observation deserves quotation: "Thus evidence of the context of the alleged culpable acts may help the Chamber to determine the intention of the Accused, especially where the intention of a person is not clear from what that person says or does. The Chamber notes, however, that the use of context to determine the intent of an accused must be counterbalanced with the actual conduct of the Accused. The Chamber is of the opinion that the Accused's intent should be determined, above all, from his words and deeds, and should be evident from patterns of purposeful action". Prosecutor v. Bagilishema, Trial Judgment, 7 June 2001, para 63.

[292] Duff 1990, pp. 131–132. Duff makes the cited observation in discussing the *Hyam* case in England. He further emphasizes the importance of an actor's 'words and deeds' in inferring an individual *mens rea* by stating, "[t]hat wider context includes, of course, her own beliefs, desires and responses. But these are themselves shown, or could in principle be discerned, in her actions: in what she does, in what she says (or would say), and in how she responds or would respond to what happens". *Ibid.*

[293] The ICTY Appeals Chamber in *Krstić* closely relates 'knowledge' (in particular, 'constructive knowledge') to circumstantial evidence. Prosecutor v. Krstić, Appeals Judgment, 19 April 2004, para 81 ("The Trial Chamber's reliance upon language such as 'must have known' is indicative of the nature of the case against Krstić being one based upon circumstantial evidence".). In a similar vein, William Schabas observes as follows: "Adoption of a 'purpose–based' approach, which dwells on intent, results in a focus on individual offenders and their own personal motives. A 'knowledge–based' approach, on the other hand, directs the inquiry towards the plan or policy of a State or similar group, and highlights the collective dimension of the crime of genocide". Schabas 2009, p. 242.

[294] Triffterer 2001, p. 405 (emphasis added). Yet, contrary to Triffterer, I do not think that the "emotional part" is necessary to constitute the mental element of '*Absicht/dolus directus* in the first degree/purposely'. For more discussion, *see* Sect. 2.5.2.4 *supra*.

Yet, *doctrinally speaking*, the overwhelming probative significance attached to the 'context' is likely to cripple the purpose-based notion of genocidal intent because volitional aspect of *mens rea* is barely in sync with the *actus reus* of circumstance.[295] It is 'words and deeds' from which individual volition is to be inferred far more comfortably. It is to be, however, noted that I said "doctrinally speaking". What I mean is that, *practically speaking*, since context/circumstance of genocide significantly overlaps with destructive consequences in actual genocidal campaigns,[296] there is still room for the purpose-based theory to survive (in that the destructive consequence forms the 'desired main effect').

In this connection, let me sketch out some instances in which judges seem to infer the purpose-based genocidal intent from words and deeds, in particular, from words. The priority of words over deeds in this context is due to the fact that the usual suspects in international criminal proceedings are mostly political and military leaders of high ranks who rarely commit the underlying acts of genocide themselves. First, the Appeals Chamber in the *Karadžić* case admits the possibility of genocidal intent of Karadžić and other JCE members on the basis of their utterances.[297] Such evidence includes (i) "in meetings with Karadžić, it had been decided that one third of Muslims would be killed, one third would be converted to the Orthodox religion and a third will leave on their own and thus all Muslims would disappear from Bosnia"[298]; (ii) Karadžić's alleged statement that "his goal was to get rid of the enemies in our house, the Croats and Muslims, and not to be in the same state with them [anymore] and that if war started in Bosnia, Muslims would disappear and be annihilated".[299]; (iii) the Commander Mladić's alleged statement that "my concern is to have them vanish completely"[300]; and (iv) the

---

[295] For a similar view, *see* Haren 2006, pp. 223–224 ("Although circumstantial evidence certainly is a helpful tool to prove that the perpetrator was aware and had knowledge of the fact that he acted in the furtherance of a genocidal campaign, it, however, is much more difficult to prove by circumstantial evidence that the perpetrator also had a strong will, i.e., he had a conscious desire to destroy a protected group. Consequently, one cannot avoid the impression that when the *Akayesu* Trial Chamber posed a broad evidentiary standard, it circumvented the purposeful standard by introducing the knowledge standard through the evidentiary backdoor. This behavior indeed could be an indication for the purposeful standard to be reconsidered".). Note however that, contrary to the mental element framework under Article 30 of the ICC Statute, the *mens rea* of 'purposely' is applicable to 'circumstance' under the Model Penal Code. *See* American Law Institute, Model Penal Code, § 2.02 (2)(a)(ii) ("A person acts purposely with respect to a material element of an offense when: [...] (ii) if the element involves the attendant circumstances, he is aware of the existence of such circumstances or he believes or hopes that they exist".).

[296] In respect of this overlap, *see also* Sect. 2.4.2 *supra*.

[297] Prosecutor v. Karadžić, Rule 98 *bis* Appeals Judgement, 11 July 2013, paras 97–101.

[298] *Ibid.* para 97 (also note that at the hearing before the Appeals Chamber, "Karadžić's legal advisor accepted that, taken at its highest, this statement could constitute evidence of genocidal intent".). It seems that, in the relevant case law, decisions made during meetings are regarded as something equivalent to utterances.

[299] *Ibid.* para 98.

[300] *Ibid.*

President of Serbia, Slobodan Milosević's statement that "Momcilo Krajišnik, President of the Bosnian-Serb Assembly, wished to kill off all the [Muslims and Croats]".[301] Second, the *Tolimir* Trial Chamber's finding of individual genocidal intent of the accused is partly based on the evidence of the use of derogatory and dehumanizing language on the part of the accused and his colleagues.[302] Given that subordinate soldiers would interpret such use of derogatory language as a green light to behave in the same way, the Chamber concludes that "the Accused encouraged the use of derogatory terms so as to provoke ethnic hatred among members of the Bosnian Serb Forces and an attitude that Bosnian Muslims were human beings of a lesser value, with a view to eradicate this particular group of the population from the Eastern BiH".[303]

These facts of utterances are indeed compatible with the purpose-based notion of genocidal intent. As considered previously mainly in respect of the jurisprudence of the *Akayesu* case, despite the common understanding that the origin of the purpose-based approach is international case law, an actual review of evidence set out therein reveals that there exists a significant discrepancy between the purposed-based definition of genocidal intent and the evidence in support thereof. In broad terms, the most significant reason for this discrepancy is the *excessive reliance placed on 'overall context'* by international judges in proving the purpose-based genocidal intent. Despite the caveat always heralded by the judges that they are *inferring* the *mens rea* of genocidal intent from those circumstances, the gap between such circumstantial evidence and the purpose-based definition of a purely subjective nature is considerable. In this regard, it is not surprising to see that individual defendants habitually complain, 'they infer my intent from the acts of others'.[304]

---

[301] *Ibid.*

[302] Prosecutor v. Tolimir, Trial Judgment, 12 December 2012, para 1172. The relevant case law often mentions derogatory language in relation to members of a group targeted. It is to be noted, however, that the probative value of such utterances needs to be assessed cautiously, in particular, in the context of collective violence. Such was the case in *Krstić* where the Appeals Chamber gave no evidentiary weight to the accused's use of derogatory language towards the Bosnian Muslims, because "this type of charged language is commonplace amongst military personnel during war". Prosecutor v. Krstić, Appeals Judgment, 19 April 2004, para 130. Similarly, in *Popović* et al., both the Trial and Appeals Chamber are of the view that evidence of Popović's use of derogatory language ("balija") did not form part of the decisive factor in finding the accused's genocidal intent. Prosecutor v. Popović et al., Appeals Judgment, 30 January 2015, para 470. The same applies to another defendant Drago Nikolić in *Popović* et al.: Regarding his use of derogatory language, the Trial Chamber observes "there is nothing to suggest [that] this was [something] other than a reflection of an unacceptable but common practice". In this respect, it is to be noted that the Trial Chamber takes into account the culture of the VRS in which the use of such derogatory language was commonplace. Prosecutor v. Popović et al., Trial Judgment, 10 June 2010, para 1399. See also *Ibid.* para 1312; On the other hand, *Tolimir* Trial Chamber indeed draws the accused's genocidal intent partly on the basis of his use of derogatory languages against the Bosnian Muslim group. Prosecutor v. Tolimir, Trial Judgment, 12 December 2012, paras 1168–69.

[303] Prosecutor v. Tolimir, Trial Judgment, 12 December 2012, para 1169.

[304] For a more detailed discussion, *see* Sect. 4.1.2 *infra*.

I think that an example of the most obvious and, perhaps, the strongest evidence demonstrating the existence of the purpose-based notion of genocidal intent can be found in the *Tolimir* Trial Judgment of the ICTY[305]: a written report prepared by the accused in which he proposed to another high-level actor that "we could force Muslims to surrender sooner if we *destroyed* groups of Muslim refugees fleeing from the direction of Stublic, Radava, and Brloska Planina and that the *best way to destroy* them would be *by using chemical weapons or aerosol grenades or bombs*".[306] While characterizing this report as an expression of the accused's "complete lack of humanity and utter contempt of human life", the Prosecution asserts that, from this document in which the accused's ruthless attitude towards women and children fleeing from their homes in Žepa is demonstrated, the "Trial Chamber can reasonably infer" his even harsher stance against the able-bodied men in Srebrenica.[307] Consequently, the Chamber observes that, "[t]aking into consideration the context in which the Accused sent this report and its meaning, [...] the only reasonable inference to be drawn by the Majority is that this document manifests the Accused's *determination* to destroy the Bosnian Muslim population".[308] It is important to note in this context, however, that this strong evidence only forms part of the facts on the basis of which the Chamber drew a conclusion that the accused "possessed genocidal intent".[309] In other words, the proof of the *overall context of violence* surrounding the accused's individual participation in and contribution to 'JCE to Murder' and 'JCE to Forcibly Remove' are the key factual platform to find the accused's individual genocidal intent. Moreover, the Chamber's emphasis on the accused's knowledge of the "large-scale criminal operations on the ground" and of the "genocidal intentions of the JCE members" signals a trace of the application of the knowledge-based concept of genocidal intent.[310] Despite the existence of such strong evidence of the accused's purpose-based genocidal intent as his written report proposing the use of chemical weapons etc., it looks as if the *Tolimir* Trial Chamber exclaims that 'without context, there is no genocidal intent'.

---

[305] As to the concept of genocidal intent, the *Tolimir* Trial Chamber does not make any clear observation. Yet, the Trial Chamber cites the paragraph 498 of the *Akayesu* Trial Judgment in which the representative expression of the purpose-based approach—i.e., "clearly seek to produce"—is found. Thus, it appears that the Trial Chamber in *Tolimir* follows the purpose-based approach. *See* Prosecutor v. Tolimir, Trial Judgment, 12 December 2012, p. 328, footnote 3117 and accompanying text.

[306] Prosecutor v. Tolimir, Trial Judgment, 12 December 2012, para 1170. (emphasis added).

[307] *Ibid.* para 1170.

[308] *Ibid.* para 1171. The term 'only reasonable inference' originates in the principle that "when the Prosecution relies upon proof of the state of mind of an accused by inference, that inference must be the only reasonable inference available on the evidence". Prosecutor v. Vasiljević, Appeals Judgment, 25 February 2004, para 120; Prosecutor v. Krstić, Appeals Judgment, 19 April 2004, para 41; Prosecutor v. Popović et al., Appeals Judgment, 30 January 2015, para 517.

[309] Prosecutor v. Tolimir, Trial Judgment, 12 December 2012, para 1172.

[310] *Ibid.*

In like manner, it might be rather awkward for advocates of the purpose-based approach to see that an unambiguous finding of the purpose-based genocidal intent in the *Popović* et al. Trial Judgment (para 1179) serves only a supplementary role in finding Popović's genocidal intent. The para 1179 reads,

> Popović was not a marginal participant in the JCE to Murder. The evidence shows that he was entrenched in several aspects of the operation, and that *he participated with resolve*. He was ubiquitous in the Zvornik area, present at all but one of the major killing sites. His own words at the outset of the operation, telling Momir Nikolić that *"all the balija have to be killed"* […] are also evidence of his genocidal intent. Even after thousands had been executed and the large-scale killing was complete, *Popović remained determined*—he arrived at the Standard Barracks to arrange for the murder of the injured Bosnian Muslim men held at the hospital facilities there. The evidence supports the finding that *Popović aimed to spare no one amongst the Bosnian Muslims within his reach, not even a young boy.*[311]

The factual findings such as "he participated with resolve", "all the balija have to be killed", "Popović remained determined", and "Popović aimed to spare no one amongst the Bosnian Muslims within his reach, not even a young boy" appear to be clear findings of the purpose-based genocidal intent in that they manifests his 'conscious desire'. Yet, this paragraph is subordinate to the next paragraph in which the Trial Chamber sets forth the factors most "decisive" to the finding of Popović's individual genocidal intent. They are: (i) "the scale of the atrocities committed"[312]; (ii) "[t]he systematic, exclusive targeting of Bosnian Muslims"[313]; (iii) Popović's "vigorous participation in […] the organization of large-scale murders"[314]; and (iv) "the repetition by Popović of destructive and discriminatory acts".[315] It seems that these factors do not demonstrate the accused's state of mind, in particular, his 'desire in a broad sense' in a direct manner. Rather, they tend to concern the context of the genocidal campaign in which the accused participated. In short, in view of the *Tolimir* example and the *Popović* example, one might even postulate that the genocidal intent element is not supposed to be fully met by the purpose-based genocidal intent alone. Is it really so? Why do the Trial Chambers keep discussing the circumstantial evidence even after noticing proof of the purpose-based genocidal intent?[316]

2.6.3 *From Individualistic Intent to Collective Intent*

To sum up, in practice, the inherent dilemma of the purpose-based approach is its conceptual incompatibility with the prevalent and almost universal

---

[311] Prosecutor v. Popović et al., Trial Judgment, 10 June 2010, para 1179. (emphasis added). Note that "balija" is a term to call Bosnian Muslims in a derogatory way.

[312] *Ibid.* para 1180.

[313] *Ibid.*

[314] *Ibid.*

[315] *Ibid.*

[316] *See also* Chap. 4, footnote 41 *infra*.

evidentiary practice of international trials dealing with genocide—i.e., the practice of *heavy and substantial* reliance on 'overall context' in finding the genocidal intent element. While the case law claims the purpose-based definition of genocidal intent doctrinally, it seems to deny it evidentiary. With regard to the genocidal intent element, it is indeed troubling to keep noticing the discrepancy between the theories and actual practices. The theoretical debate on the purpose-based and the knowledge-based understandings of genocidal intent seems to touch upon only a marginal aspect of the crime of genocide. In the *mens rea* framework on which I have relied,[317] it is the 'destructive consequence' that conceptually connects all those volitional elements and cognitive elements: did you have a 'desire in a broad sense' directed toward the 'destructive consequence'?; did you consciously permit the happening of the 'destructive consequence' in your mind?; did you have foresight of the 'destructive consequence' to a virtual/practice certainty? However, are you really sure that these are the valid questions? How do you define the 'destructive consequence'? Can you really distinguish the 'destructive consequence' with 'destructive or genocidal context/circumstance'? At this point, it is worthwhile to quote the following text from Carl-Friedrich Stuckenberg:

> The real issue are not whether conscious risk-taking forms part of *dolus* or not, or can be attributed to somebody's will or not, but whether acting despite the awareness of a small, medium-sized or substantial risk that a certain prohibited result will occur, or willful blindness thereof, deserve punishment for a particular crime under international law. This is a normative decision about blameworthiness and not a question what *dolus* 'is'. [...] Purpose and awareness are not necessarily more blameworthy than reckless disregard which does not even take into consideration the effects one's action might have on other people. International criminal law theory, whether dealing with customary law or the Rome Statute, should therefore, in the interest of intellectual candour and methodological progress, address the critical value judgments openly and not hide them in a maze of confused terms and get caught in the traps of conceptualism. This is a lesson that can be learned from domestic laws.[318]

Because genocide is unique in that it has a character of criminal enterprise in which such major substantive notions of criminal law—i.e., conduct, consequence and circumstance—are all intermingled, we should be cautious in engaging in doctrinal discourse in relation to the crime of genocide.[319] Moreover, the fact that various conducts, consequences and circumstances all together constitute the content of genocidal intent further exacerbates the problem. Put otherwise, the concept of genocidal intent suffers from obesity: it has too much content within itself to be adequately perceived by the individualistic notion of genocidal intent. That is why

---

[317] *See* the chart on page 51 *supra*.

[318] Stuckenberg 2014, p. 317.

[319] As to the issue of 'genocide as a criminal enterprise', *see* Sect. 4.2 *infra*.

we see such complaints from the suspects of genocide that 'you infer my intent from the acts of others'.[320] Isn't it a time to let genocidal intent take some diet pills? By the way, do we really need genocidal intent?[321]

For a more precise understanding of genocidal intent, it is necessary to see this difficult notion from a different standpoint than the individualistic perspective. What is the essential quality of genocide? Philosopher Brook Jenkins Sadler says that singing duet, dancing tango and genocide are "intrinsically cooperative".[322] I think this remark does elucidate something we lawyers have too easily taken for granted in the midst of colorful substantive doctrines surrounding the catchphrase of individual criminal responsibility. In this connection, Emanuela Fronza was right when she pointed out that it is the feature of genocide being a "macro-criminal phenomenon" that caused the "major interpretative problems" related to genocidal intent.[323] George Fletcher also precisely points out:

> My point is to demonstrate that our conventional, liberal, individualistic ways of thinking about criminal liability simply do not account for the sentiments that actually shape the operative contours of international criminal law. The mind of the law may speak in the language of liberal individualism, but its heart lies in the disfavored ideas of collective action and collective guilty.[324]

Accordingly, in the following two chapters (Chaps. 3 and 4), I employ the collectivist approach to grasp what it really means the cryptic term 'genocidal intent'. In doing so, my attention is to be not only given to the genocidal intent element but also to the inner conceptual structure of the crime definition of genocide. Hence, I begin my discussion in Chap. 3 by looking into the two-layered structure of the crime of genocide—i.e., the 'conduct level' and the 'context level'.

---

[320] For more discussion on this complaints, *see* Sect. 4.1.2 *infra*.

[321] Consider the following observation: "Strictly speaking, there is no 'subjective imputation' because all imputation, by its very nature, is objective. Subjective or mental elements are relevant only as indicators of the objective degree of a person's law-abidingness or lack thereof". Stuckenberg 2014, p. 311.

[322] Sadler 2006, p. 127. In a similar vein, Jens David Ohlin observes: "Since fundamentally collective acts, like genocide, are only possible with deep collaboration among its members, a purely individualist account fails to explain the group-level dynamics among the individual members. Genocide is a case in point – it isn't just the aggregate of many individuals committing isolated acts of murder. [...] Without mutual collaboration, the Rwandan genocide would never have occurred". Ohlin 2013b, footnote 24 through 26 and accompanying text.

[323] Fronza 1999, p. 127.

[324] Fletcher 2002, pp. 1525–1526.

References

Akhavan P (2005) The crime of genocide in the ICTR jurisprudence. J Intl Crim Justice 3:989–1006

Ambos K (2007) Joint criminal enterprise and command responsibility. J Intl Crim Justice 5:159–183

Ambos K (2008) Article 25: individual criminal responsibility. In: Triffterer O (ed) Commentary on the Rome Statute of the International Criminal Court: observers' notes, article by article, 2nd edn. C.H. Beck oHG, München, pp 743–770

Ambos K (2009) What does "intent to destroy" in genocide mean? Intl Rev Red Cross 91:833–858

Ambos K (2010) Criminologically explained reality of genocide, structure of the offence and the "intent to destroy" requirement. In: Smeulers A (ed) Collective violence and international criminal justice: an interdisciplinary approach. Intersentia, Cambridge, pp 153–174

Ambos K (2013) Treatise on international criminal law, vol I: foundations and general part. Oxford University Press, Oxford

Ambos K (2014) Treatise on international criminal law, vol II: the crimes and sentencing. Oxford University Press, Oxford

Aptel C (2002) The intent to commit genocide in the case law of the International Criminal Tribunal for Rwanda. Crim Law Forum 13:273–291 (2002)

Badar ME (2008) The mental element in the Rome Statute of the International Criminal Court: A commentary from a comparative criminal law perspective. Crim Law Forum 19:473–518

Badar ME (2013) The concept of mens rea in international criminal law: the case for a unified approach. Hart Publishing, Oxford

Badar ME, Marchuk I (2013) A Comparative study of the principles governing criminal responsibility in the major legal systems of the world (England, United States, Germany, France, Denmark, Russia, China, and Islamic legal tradition). Crim Law Forum 24:1–49

Bantekas I (2010) International criminal law, 4th edn. Hart Publishing, Oxford

Bassiouni MC (1993) Article 19: genocide. In: Bssiouni MC (ed) Commentaries on the International Law Commission's 1991 draft code of crimes against the peace and security of mankind. Nouvelles Études Pénales 11:233–236

Bassiouni MC, Manikas P (1996) The law of the international criminal tribunal for the former Yugoslavia. Transnational Publishers, New York

Bell J, Boyron S, Whittaker S (1998) Principles of French law. Oxford University Press, Oxford

Blomsma J (2012) Mens rea and defences in European criminal law. Intersentia, Cambridge

Blomsma J, Roef D (2015) Forms and aspects of mens rea. In: Keiler J, Roef D (eds) Comparative concepts of criminal law. Intersentia, Oxford, pp 103–132

Bush JA (2009) The prehistory of corporations and conspiracy in international criminal law: what Nuremberg really said. Colum Law Rev 109:1094–1262

Card R (2006) Card, Cross and Jones criminal law, 17th edn. Oxford University Press, Oxford

Cassel D (2007) Corporate aiding and abetting of human rights violations: confusion in the courts. Northwestern Univ J Intl Hum Rts 6:304–326

Cassese A (2008) International criminal law, 2nd edn. Oxford University Press, Oxford

Cassese A, Gaeta P, Baig L, Fan M, Gosnell C, Whiting A (2013) Cassese's international criminal law. Oxford University Press, Oxford

Clark RS (2008) Elements of crimes in early confirmation decisions of pre-trial chambers of the international criminal court. New Zealand Y B Intl Law 6:209–238

Cupido M (2014) The contextual embedding of genocide: a casuistic analysis of the interplay between law and facts. Melbourne J Intl Law 15:1–36

Cryer R (2014) Imputation and complicity in common law states: a (partial) view from England and Wales. J Intl Crim Justice 12:267–281

Csúri A (2011) Subjective aspects of the offence in Hungary. In: Sieber U, Forster S, Jarvers K (eds) National criminal law in a comparative legal context, vol 3.1. Duncker & Humblot, Berlin, pp 365–376

Cumes G (2011) Subjective aspects of the offence in Australia. In: Sieber U, Forster S, Jarvers K (eds) National criminal law in a comparative legal context, vol 3.1. Duncker & Humblot, Berlin, pp 321–349

Drumbl Mark A (2005) Collective violence and individual punishment: the criminality of mass atrocity. Northwestern U Law Rev 99:539–610

Duff RA (1990) Intention, agency and criminal liability: philosophy of action and the criminal law. Basil Blackwell, Oxford

Duff RA (2013) Intention revisited. In: Baker D, Horder J (eds) The sanctity of life and the criminal law: the legacy of Glanville Williams. Cambridge University Press, Cambridge, pp 148–177

Elliott C (2001) French criminal law. Willan Publishing, Cullompton

Eser A (2002) Individual criminal responsibility. In: Cassese A, Gaeta P, Jones JRWD (eds) The Rome Statute of the International Criminal Court: a commentary, vol I. Oxford University Press, Oxford, pp 767–822

Finnis K (2011) Intention and identity: collected essays, vol II. Oxford University Press, Oxford

Flannery KLSJ (1995) Natural law mens rea versus the Benthamite tradition. Am J Juris 40:377–400

Fletcher GP (2000) Rethinking criminal law. Oxford University Press, Oxford

Fletcher GP (2002) The storrs lectures: liberals and romantics at war: the problem of collective guilt. Yale Law J 111:1499–1573

Fletcher GP (2011) New court, old dogmatic. J Intl Crim Justice 9:179–190

Fournet C (2007) The crime of destruction and the law of genocide. Ashgate Publishing Ltd, Hampshire

Fronza E (1999) Genocide in the Rome Statute. In: Lattanzi F, Schabas W (eds) Essays on the Rome Statute of the International Criminal Court. Il Sirente, Ripa Fagnano Alto, pp 105–138

Greenawalt AKA (1999) Rethinking genocidal intent: the case for a knowledge-based interpretation. Colum Law Rev 99:2259–2294

Haan V (2005) The development of the concept of joint criminal enterprise at the international criminal tribunal for the former Yugoslavia. Intl Crim Law Rev 5:167–201

Hall J (1960) General principles of criminal law, 2nd edn. Bobbs-Merrill, Indianapolis

Hallevy G (2014) Liability for crimes involving artificial intelligence systems. Springer, Heidelberg

Hart HLA (2008) Punishment and responsibility, 2nd edn. Oxford University Press, Oxford

Heine G, Vest H (2000) Murder/wilful killing. In: McDonald GK, Swaak-Goldman O (eds) Substantive and procedural aspects of international criminal law: the experience of international and national courts, vol I. Kluwer Law International, The Hague, pp 175–196

Heller KJ, Dubber MD (eds) (2011) The handbook of comparative criminal law. Stanford University Press, Stanford

Horder J (1996) Crimes of ulterior intent. In: Simester AP, Smith ATH (eds) Harm and culpability. Clarendon Press, Oxford, pp 153–168

Jain N (2011) Subjective aspects of the offence in India. In: Sieber U, Forster S, Jarvers K (eds) National criminal law in a comparative legal context, vol 3.1. Duncker & Humblot, Berlin, pp 377–388

Jain N (2013) Individual responsibility for mass atrocity: in search of a concept of perpetration. Am J Comp Law 61:831–872

Jessberger F, Geneuss J (2008) On the application of a theory of indirect perpetration in Al Bashir: German doctrine in the Hague? J Intl Crim Justice 6:853–869

Jørgensen N (2001) The definition of genocide: joining the dots in the light of recent practice. Intl Crim Law Rev 1:285–313

Jørgensen N (2011) Complicity in genocide and the duality of responsibility. In: Swart B, Zahar A, Sluiter G (eds) The legacy of the International Criminal Tribunal for the Former Yugoslavia. Oxford University Press, Oxford, pp 247–274

Kadish S (1985) Complicity, cause and blame: a study in the interpretation of doctrine. California Law Rev 73:323–410

Kelly MJ (2011) Ending corporate impunity for genocide: the case against China's state-owned petroleum company in Sudan. Oregon Law Rev 90:413–448

Kim S (2011) The anatomy of the means of proof digest. In: Bergsmo M (ed) Active complementarity: legal information transfer, pp 197–221

Kress C (2005) The Darfur report and genocidal intent. J Intl Crim Justice 3:562–578

Kress C (2006) The crime of genocide under international law. Intl Crim Law Rev 6:461–502

Kress C (2009) The crime of genocide and contextual elements: a comment on the ICC Pre-Trial Chamber's decision in the Al Bashir case. J Intl Crim Justice 7:297–306

Kugler I (2002) Direct and oblique intention in the criminal law: an inquiry into degrees of blameworthiness. Ashgate, Aldershot

Kugler I (2011) Israel. In: Heller KJ, Dubber MD (eds) The handbook of comparative criminal law. Stanford University Press, Stanford

Kuper L (1985) The prevention of genocide. Yale University Press, New Haven

Lemkin R (1947) Genocide as a crime under international law. American J Intl Law 41:145–151

Lemkin R (2008) Axis rule in occupied Europe: laws of occupation, analysis of government, proposals for redress, 2nd edn. The Law Book Exchange Ltd, Clark

Luban D (2010) Fairness to rightness: jurisdiction, legality, and the legitimacy of international criminal law. In: Besson S, Tasioulas J (eds) The philosophy of international law. Oxford University Press, Oxford, pp 569–588

Lachs J (1981) Responsibility and the individual in modern society. Harvester Press, Brighton

Latour B (2005) Reassembling the social. Oxford University Press, Oxford

Maljević A (2011) Subjective aspects of the offence in Bosnia and Herzegovina. In: Sieber U, Forster S, Jarvers K (eds) National criminal law in a comparative legal context, vol 3.1. Duncker & Humblot, Berlin, pp 350–364

Marchuk I (2014) The fundamental concept of crime in international criminal law: a comparative law analysis. Springer, Heidelberg

May L (2010) Genocide: a normative account. Cambridge University Press, Cambridge

Meiland JW (1970) The nature of intention. Mathuen & Co., London

Mettraux G (2006) International crimes and the ad hoc tribunals. Oxford University Press, Oxford

Moore M (2009) Causation and responsibility: an essay in law, morals and metaphysics. Oxford University Press, Oxford

Mysliwiec P (2009) Accomplice to genocide liability: the case for a purpose mens rea standard. Chicago J Intl Law 10:389–413

Nersessian DL (2006) Whoops, i committed genocide! the anatomy of constructive liability of serious international crimes. Fletcher F World Aff 30:81–106

Norrie A (2002) Crime, reason and history: a critical introduction to criminal law, 2nd edn. Cambridge University Press, Cambridge

Ohlin JD (2007) Three conceptual problems with the doctrine of joint criminal enterprise. J Intl Crim Justice 5:69–90

Ohlin JD (2010) The torture lawyer. Harv Int'l Law J 51:193–256

Ohlin JD (2011) Joint intentions to commit international crimes. Chicago J Intl Law 11:693–753

Ohlin JD (2013a) Targeting and the concept of intent. Michigan J Intl Law 35:79–130

Ohlin JD (2013b) The one or the many. Cornell legal studies research paper, no 13–88

Ohlin JD (2014) Searching for the hinterman: in praise of subjective theories of imputation. J Intl Crim Justice 12:325–343

Olásolo H, Cepeda AP (2004) The notion of control of the crime and its application by the ICTY in the Stakić case. Intl Crim Law Rev 4:475–526

Ormerod D (2011) Smith and Hogan's criminal law, 13th edn. Oxford University Press, Oxford

Osiel M (2009) Making sense of mass atrocity. Cambridge University Press, Cambridge

Paramonova S (2011) Subjective aspects of the offence in Switzerland. In: Sieber U, Forster S, Jarvers K (eds) National criminal law in a comparative legal context, vol 3.1. Duncker & Humblot, Berlin, pp 436–452

Petrig A (2011) Subjective aspects of the offence in Switzerland. In: Sieber U, Forster S, Jarvers K (eds) National criminal law in a comparative legal context, vol 3.1. Duncker & Humblot, Berlin, pp 453–470

Rinceanu J (2011) Subjective aspects of the offence in Romania. In: Sieber U, Forster S, Jarvers K (eds) National criminal law in a comparative legal context, vol 3.1. Duncker & Humblot, Berlin, pp 421–435

Robinson D (2008) The identity crisis of international criminal law. Leiden J Intl Law 21:925–963

Robinson D (2013) A cosmopolitan liberal account of international criminal law. Leiden J Intl Law 26:127–153

Robinson N (1960) The genocide convention: a commentary. Institute of Jewish Affairs, New York

Sadler BJ (2006) Shared intentions and shared responsibility. In: French PA, Wettstein HK (eds) Shared intentions and collective responsibility. Midwest Stud. Phil. 30:115–144

Saul B (2001) Was the conflict in east timor 'genocide' and why does it matter? Melb J Intl Law 2:477–522

Schabas W (2001) Was genocide committed in Bosnia and Herzegovina? First judgments of the International Criminal Tribunal for the Former Yugoslavia. Fordham Intl Law J 25:23–53

Schabas W (2002) Developments in the law of genocide. Yearb Intl Humanitarian Law 5:131–166

Schabas W (2009) Genocide in international law: the crime of crimes, 2nd edn. Cambridge University Press, Cambridge

Schabas W (2010) The International Criminal Court: a commentary on the Rome Statute. Oxford University Press, Oxford

Schomburg W, Peterson I (2007) Genuine consent to sexual violence under international criminal law. Am J Intl Law 101:121–140

Shapira-Ettinger K (2007) The conundrum of mental states: substantive rules and evidence combined. Cardozo Law Rev 28:2577–2596

Sieber U, Forster S, Jarvers K (eds) (2011) National criminal law in a comparative legal context, vol 3.1. Duncker & Humblot, Berlin

Silverman E (2011) Subjective aspects of the offence in USA. In: Sieber U, Forster S, Jarvers K (eds) National criminal law in a comparative legal context, vol 3.1. Duncker & Humblot, Berlin, pp 492–515

Simester AP, Sullivan GR (2010) Simester and Sullivan's criminal law: theory and doctrine, 4th edn. Hart Publishing, Oxford

Smith KJM (1991) A modern treatise on the law of criminal complicity. Oxford University Press, Oxford

Stewart JG (2014) Complicity. In: Dubber MD, Hornle T (eds) The oxford handbook of criminal law. Oxford University Press, Oxford, pp 534–559

Stuckenberg CF (2014) Problems of 'subjective imputation' in domestic and international criminal law. J Intl Crim Justice 12:311–323

Szonert-Binienda M (2012) Was Katyn a genocide? Case W Reserve J Intl Law 44:633–718

Tadros V (2007) Criminal responsibility. Oxford University Press, Oxford

Tams CJ, Berster L, Schiffbauer B (2014) Convention on the prevention and punishment of the crime of genocide: commentary. C.H. Beck oHG, München

Taylor G (2004) Concepts of intention in German criminal law. Oxford J Legal Stud 24:99–127

Tellenbach S (2011) Subjective aspects of the offence in Iran. In: Sieber U, Forster S, Jarvers K (eds) National criminal law in a comparative legal context, vol 3.1. Duncker & Humblot, Berlin, pp 389–404

Tournaye C (2003) Genocidal intent before the ICTY. Intl Comp Law Q 52:447–462

Triffterer O (2001) Genocide, its particular intent to destroy in whole or in part the group as such. Leiden J Intl Law 14:399–408

Turns D (2007) Application of the convention on the prevention and punishment of the crime of genocide. Melb J Int'l Law 8:398–427@@@

van Haren MK (2006) The report of the international commission of inquiry on Darfur & geno-
    cidal intent—a critical analysis. Netherlands Intl Law Rev 53:205–245
van Sliedregt E (2007) Joint criminal enterprise as a pathway to convicting individuals for geno-
    cide. J Intl Crim Justice 5:184–207
van Sliedregt E (2009) Complicity to commit genocide. In: Gaeta P (ed) The UN genocide con-
    vention: a commentary. Oxford University Press, Oxford, pp 162–192
van Sliedregt E (2012a) The curious case of international criminal liability. J Intl Crim Justice
    10:1171–1188
van Sliedregt E (2012b) Individual criminal responsibility in international law. Oxford University
    Press, Oxford
Vest H (2007) A structure-based concept of genocidal intent. J Intl Crim Justice 5:781–797
Vest H (2014) Problems of participation—unitarian, differentiated approach or something else? J
    Intl Crim Justice 12:295–309
van der Vyver JD (1999) Prosecution and punishment of the crime of genocide. Fordham Intl
    Law J 23:286–356
van der Vyver JD (2004) The International Criminal Court and the concept of mens rea in inter-
    national criminal law. Univ Miami Int'l Comp Law Rev 12:57–149
Weigend T (2011) Germany. In: Heller KJ, Dubber MD (eds) The handbook of comparative
    criminal law. Stanford University Press, Stanford, pp 252–287
Weigend T (2014) Problems of attribution in international criminal law: a German perspective. J
    Intl Crim Justice 12:253–266
Werle G (2009) Principles of international criminal law. T.M.C. Asser Press, The Hague
Williams G (1961) Criminal law: the general part, 2nd edn. Steven & Sons, London
Williams G (1987) Oblique intention. Cambridge Law J 46:417–438
van der Wilt HG (2006) Genocide, complicity in genocide and international v. domestic jurisdic-
    tion: reflection on the van Anraat case. J Intl Crim Justice 4:239–257
Zahar A, Sluiter G (2007) International criminal law: a critical introduction. Oxford University
    Press, Oxford
Zaibert LA (1998) Intentionality, voluntariness, and culpability: a historical-philosophical analy-
    sis. Buffalo Crim Law Rev 1:459–500

Chapter 3
Collective Genocide, Contextual Element and Substantiality

Abstract Newly equipped with a lens of collectivist perspective, in this chapter, my analysis begins with expounding the two-layered structure of genocide—that is, the 'conduct level' and the 'context level'. Throughout this chapter, I place an emphasis on the importance of the 'context level' for the purpose of individual prosecution of the crime of genocide. I demonstrate that, in the relevant case law of the *ad hoc* tribunals, a finding of the 'context level' as genocidal always precedes the legal consideration of personal conduct and individual genocidal intent at the 'conduct level'. For the purpose of indicating such genocidal context, I employ the term 'collective genocide'. By reference to the relevant case law of the *ad hoc* tribunals, I also show that the existence of 'collective genocide' at the 'context level' is a quasi-legal requirement of the crime of genocide. Then, providing an overview of the historical development of the substantiality requirement as an interpretation of the term 'in part' in the definition of genocide, I argue that the destructive consequence of a substantial part of a group at the 'context level' constitutes an essence of the crime of genocide. In doing so, I show the existence and importance of the objective contextual element of genocide. This line of argument constitutes a part of obesity treatment of genocidal intent in that the notion of 'destruction' is identified as a crucial objective element of the crime of genocide. Subsequently, I discuss the problematic decision from the ICC Pre-Trial Chamber in *Al Bashir* in which 'concrete threat' was regarded as a legal requirement in relation to the objective contextual element of genocide. Arguing against this position, I point out that the Chamber neglected to give due consideration to the substantiality requirement that inherently carries with it the notion of 'concrete threat'. In this respect, I argue that the 'concrete threat' requirement is redundant. However, I demonstrate the usefulness of 'concrete threat' as a proof of 'collective genocide' when it is difficult to determine whether a given situation satisfies the substantiality requirement. In the end, I conclude this chapter by explaining the degraded importance of individualistic notion of genocidal intent at the 'conduct level', which results from the pivotal role played by the concept of 'collective genocide' at the 'context level' for the purpose of prosecuting the crime of genocide.

© T.M.C. ASSER PRESS and the author 2016

S. Kim, *A Collective Theory of Genocidal Intent*, International Criminal Justice Series 7, DOI 10.1007/978-94-6265-123-4_3

Keywords Collective genocide · Contextual element · In whole or in part · Substantiality requirement · Concrete threat

Contents

3.1 An Overview of the Two-Layered Structure of Genocide: 'Conduct Level' Versus 'Context Level'

Before embarking on a close examination of the concept of genocidal intent from the collectivist viewpoint, it is necessary to understand the unique legal structure of the crime of genocide. I say 'unique' because we can observe an obvious difference in terms of the legal structure of the crime definition when we consider together the case of other core international crimes—i.e., crimes against humanity and war crimes, from which we start our discussion for ease of exposition. The crimes against humanity and war crimes both have a two-layered structure—i.e., the 'conduct level' and the 'context level'.[1] And, those two levels must be legally linked by prosecutors, as required by the nexus requirement. For instance, the crime against humanity of murder (Article 7(1)(a), ICC Statute) consists of a

---

[1] *See* Cassese et al. 2013, pp. 37–38 (explaining the 'twofold dimension'/'double-layered' feature of core international crimes.); Ohlin 2014, p. 331 (discussing the 'essential contribution' requirement of the concept of 'co-perpetration' proposed by the *Lubanga* Trial Judgment within the two layered framework of 'group level' and 'individual level'.).

conduct of murder ('conduct level') and a widespread and systematic attack against a civilian population ('context level'); and the former is required to form part of the latter (nexus).[2] Similarly, in the case of the war crime of willful killing (Article 8(2)(a)(i), ICC Statute), a prosecutor must prove a conduct of killing ('conduct level') and the existence of an international or a non-international armed conflict ('context level').[3] Here again, both must be linked, in the sense that the killing must be committed "in furtherance of or under the guise of the armed conflict" (nexus).[4] For these two core international crimes, an objective conduct element is surrounded by an objective contextual element. Although sometimes only the former gets the label *'actus reus'*, I believe it is more illuminating to view both the conduct and context elements as *actus reus*, and in what follows I will sometimes refer to them as the 'small' and 'large' *actus reus*.

Is the two-layered structure also applicable to genocide? In view of the wording of Article II of the Genocide Convention, though there surely exists the 'conduct level' (e.g., "[k]illing members of the group"), it appears there are no words that indicate the 'context level'.[5] Instead, we find a *mens rea* of 'with intent to destroy,

---

[2] In the case of the ICC, the nexus requirement is phrased as follows in the italicized phrases in the Elements of Crimes: "The conduct was committed *as part of* a widespread or systematic attack directed against a civilian population". (crimes against humanity) (emphasis added); "The conduct took place in the context of and *was associated with* an international armed conflict [or, 'an armed conflict not of an international character']. (war crimes) (emphasis added). For more about the nexus requirement, *see* Prosecutor v. Kunarac et al., Appeals Judgment, 12 June 2002, para 99 (stating that a conduct must be objectively a part of the attack); Prosecutor v. Kunarac et al., Trial Judgment, 22 February 2001, para 100 (stating that a conduct before or after the main attack could still be a part of the attack); Prosecutor v. Krnojelac, Trial Judgment, 14 March 2002, para 55 (stating that a conduct several months after, or several kilometers away from, the main attack could still be a part of the attack); Prosecutor v. Kajelijeli, Trial Judgment, 1 December 2003, para 866 (stating that a conduct needs not necessarily share all the features, such as time and place, with other conducts constituting the attack); Prosecutor v. Semanza, Trial Judgment, 15 May 2003, para 326 (stating that a conduct must objectively form part of the attack by its characteristics, aims, nature, or consequence).

[3] Also note what might be called a quasi-contextual element of war crimes as provided in Article 8(1) of the ICC Statute ("The Court shall have jurisdiction in respect of war crimes in particular when committed as part of a plan or policy or as part of a large-scale commission of such crimes".).

[4] *See generally* Prosecutor v. Kunarac et al., Appeals Judgment, 12 June 2002, para 58 ("the existence of an armed conflict must, at a minimum, have played a substantial part in the perpetrator's ability to commit it, his decision to commit it, the manner in which it was committed or the purpose for which it was committed. Hence, if it can be established, as in the present case, that the perpetrator acted in furtherance of or under the guise of the armed conflict, it would be sufficient to conclude that his acts were closely related to the armed conflict".).

[5] It has been so, say, at least until the adoption of the ICC Elements of Crimes in which it is required that "[t]he conduct took place in the context of a manifest pattern of similar conduct". There are differing views whether this phrase can be considered a contextual element equivalent to the widespread or systematic attack against a civilian population or an armed conflict of an international or a non-international character. For more discussion, *see* Sect. 3.3.2 *infra*.

in whole or in part, a national, ethnical, racial or religious group, as such' in the chapeau of the crime definition of genocide. Thus, on its face, it appears quite problematic to apply the usual formula of a small *actus reus* ('conduct level') circled by a bigger *actus reus* ('context level') to genocide. Instead, within the crime definition, we only see a confusing formula of a small *actus reus* ('conduct level') and a *mens rea* that sounds quite heavy ('intent to destroy, in whole or in part, a national, ethnical, racial or religious group, as such'). In this respect, Claus Kress (while criticizing the purpose-based approach to genocidal intent) stresses the apparent incompatibility between "an *actus reus* list [at the 'conduct' level] formulated from the perspective of the subordinate level with what is typically a leadership standard of *mens rea*".[6] He further elaborates,

> The structure of the crime of genocide poses quite a problem. The definition lacks an explicit 'contextual' element and thus appears at first sight to be drafted from the perspective of the 'lone individual' seeking to destroy a protected group as such. However, it is clear that a single human being will not, except in the most exceptional circumstances, be capable of destroying a protected group or a part thereof.[7]

Consequently, the structure of a small *actus reus* ('conduct level') and a seemingly bigger *mens rea* ('conduct level'? or 'context level'?) renders the definition of genocide inordinately individualistic. This is certainly contradictory to Raphael Lemkin's insight that "the [Genocide] Convention applies only to actions undertaken on a mass scale and not to individual acts [...]".[8] This bizarre structure of the crime definition of genocide has caused a constant conceptual friction because genocide itself is, by its innate nature, definitely a collective crime, as is also the case of other core international crimes. Thus the current crime definition significantly betrays the true nature of genocide: a crime committed by a group against another group. At any rate, given the apparent absence of the 'context level' in the crime definition of genocide, can we say that the legal structure of genocide is only single-layered? In this connection, it is to be noted that crimes against humanity and war crimes can be called 'contextual crimes'. The contextual elements of those crimes constitute a feature that distinguishes these core international crimes from their domestic law counterparts, as almost none of the crimes under national criminal codes contain any legal requirement equivalent to the contextual elements of the former.[9] For scholars and practitioners in the field of international criminal law, however, the contextual elements of the crime of genocide, if there are any, have been a source of confusion usually intermingled with the

---

[6] Kress 2006, p. 496.

[7] Kress 2007, p. 620.

[8] 2 Executive Sessions of the Senate Foreign Relations Committee, Historical Series, p. 370 (1976), *as cited in* LeBlanc 1991, p. 45, footnote 23.

[9] There can be a few exceptions. Under the Korean Penal Code, for example, the only crime that requires a contextual element is the 'crime of causing internal disturbance'. *See* Korean Penal Code (Hyongbeob), Act No. 293, Article 87 (18 September 1953). That is, it requires the proof of a 'riot *of a scale* to destroy the public order of a region' (emphasis added).

subject of genocidal intent.[10] What the contextual element of the 'widespread or systematic attack' (in crimes against humanity) or 'armed conflict' (in war crimes) requires is *a circumstance of a legally meaningful scale* surrounding a specific criminal conduct. While other factual pieces are mostly interchangeable and/or replaceable, the only necessary condition to fulfill this requirement of scale seems to be the involvement of 'many people'. In other words, it is not possible for a solo individual, acting outside the context of group violence, to commit *a* crime against humanity or *a* war crime, because the contextual element within each crime definition precludes it. In the case of genocide, however, a problem arises from the fact that, pursuant to the definition of genocide as provided in the Genocide Convention and other international instruments, it is legally possible for a solo individual to satisfy all the legal requirements of genocide.[11] But, except for this very unlikely situation, it is sound to argue that all the core international crimes including genocide require the involvement of multiple people. William Schabas indeed asserts that "[t]he theory that an individual, acting alone, may commit genocide is little more than a sophomoric *hypothèse d'école*, and a distraction for international judicial institutions".[12] In this respect, it is reasonable to require an equivalent element of 'a circumstance of a legally meaningful scale' also for the

---

[10] For a general overview of the 'contextual element' of genocide, *see* Cryer et al. 2010, pp. 218–219; Cassese et al. 2013, pp. 123–125.

[11] Gerhard Werle and Florian Jessberger explain that the commission of genocide by a solo individual is possible because "the contextual element is shifted to the *mens rea* in the form of genocidal intent" within the structure of genocide. Werle and Jessberger 2014, p. 309. For a historical example of a solo *génocidaire*, *see* Luban 2004, p. 98, footnote 45 ("A real-life example is the strange case of Abba Kovner, a Holocaust survivor, resistance fighter in the Vilna ghetto, and poet, who in 1945 unsuccessfully attempted to poison the Hamburg water supply in revenge for the Holocaust. Kovner said that his ultimate goal was to kill six million Germans".). Luban states that a solo individual can commit genocide "even without organizational responsibility". During the drafting stage of the Genocide Convention, the Iranian delegation stressed the possibility of a genocide committed by a "single individual". Yet, the Belgian delegation, in particular, stated that the idea of solo *génocidaire* is "inconceivable". U.N. GAOR, 6th Comm., 3d Sess., 73d mtg. at 90 and 93, U.N. Doc. A/C.6/SR.73 (13 October 1948). Making probably the most clear-cut opposition to the idea of solo *génocidaire*, William Schabas observes that "[t]o be entirely accurate, nobody has ever actually been convicted of genocide in the absence of evidence that he or she was part of some broader plan or policy of a state or state-like entity". Schabas 2012, p. 131. George Fletcher and Jens David Ohlin also firmly observe that "[g]enocide is not merely one individual seeking to annihilate an entire ethnic group". They further state that "[w]hile it may be theoretically possible for one individual to engage in a genocidal attack, there is no reason to think that such a mass murder would be one of the most serious crimes of concern to the international community as a whole". Fletcher and Ohlin 2005, pp. 545 and 546.

[12] Schabas 2005, p. 877. *See also* Kress 2007, p. 621 (questioning the possibility of genocide committed by a lone perpetrator, observing that (i) there is no "clear international dimension" in such cases; and (ii) "categorizing the conduct of a lone individual as genocide would disconnect the crime of genocide from its historical roots as a crime against humanity".).

crime of genocide.[13] The essential feature of the 'context level' lies in its *anonymous* nature based on the collective undertakings thereof by multiple actors. The level of anonymity is proportional to the degree of organization of the collective performing at the 'context level'. In this respect, an observation made by French Prosecutor M. Charles Dubost at the International Military Tribunal at Nuremberg deserves extended quotation:

> We have already shown that the crime committed by these men is not a simple crime. The common criminal knows his victim; he sees him with his own eyes. He himself strikes and knows the effect of his blow. Even if he is only an accomplice, he is never sufficiently dissociated, morally and psychologically speaking, from the chief perpetrator, not to share to a certain extent his apprehensions and reactions when the blow is delivered and the victim falls. *Genocide, murder or any other crime becomes anonymous when it is committed by the State.* Nobody bears the chief responsibility. Everybody shares it: those who by their presence maintain and support the administration, those who conceived the crime and those who ordained it, as well as he who issued the order. As for the executioner, he says to himself: "Befehl ist Befehl": "An order is an order", and carries out his hangman's task. Those who make the decision do so without shuddering. It is possible that they have no accurate and concrete picture in their minds of the consequences of their orders. The stupefaction of some of the accused immediately after the showing of the film about the camps is understandable in the light of this reflection. As for those who promote the execution of the crime by their general co-operation in the work of Party and State, they feel that they are passive spectators of a scene which does not concern them. They have, in any case, no punishment to fear.[14]

Accordingly, it is absurd to morally blame a specific individual *alone* for the events that occurred at the 'context level' because of its intrinsically collective nature. The drafters of the ICC Elements of Crimes set forth this 'context level' of the crime of genocide by the phrase "a manifest pattern of similar conduct" as follows:

> The conduct took place in the context of *a manifest pattern of similar conduct* directed against that group or was conduct that could itself effect such destruction.[15]

Although the second clause of this Element accommodates the theoretical possibility of a single act effecting a genocide, obviously in real-world cases prosecutors will need to prove the existence of a manifest pattern of similar conduct,

---

[13] It is important to note that recognizing the contextual element of genocide also helps describe and characterize the acts of individual *génocidaires* more precisely. In this respect, Tracy Isaacs, a philosopher, observes as follows: "[…] [I]f we focus too narrowly on individuals, then we risk giving a distorted account of what the individuals do and what they take themselves to be doing. For example, if they understand their own acts as being part of a genocide, then our account of responsibility ought to take that seriously or it leaves something out of individual's own conceptions of what they are doing. At the very least, we should be able to contextualize individual acts of murder within the broader context of genocide in order to be descriptively accurate". Isaacs 2006, pp. 170–171.

[14] 19 Trials of the Major War Criminals Before the International Military Tribunal, p. 564 (1948). (emphasis added).

[15] In the ICC Elements of Crimes, this element is commonly provided for all the five underlying acts of genocide. See Article 6(a), 4th Element; Article 6(b), 4th Element; Article 6(c), 5th Element; Article 6(d), 5th Element; and, Article 6(e), 7th Element.

which should be treated for practical purposes a contextual element. The relevant provisions of the ICC law employ a legal framework very similar to that of the Model Penal Code, which adopts an 'element analysis' approach (as opposed to an 'offence analysis').[16] That is, the ICC law recognizes the three basic 'descriptive' *actus reus* categories of 'conduct', 'consequence' and 'circumstance'[17]; and, for each *actus reus* category, either 'intent ('means to')' for 'conduct' or 'knowledge ('awareness')' for 'circumstance' or both for 'consequence' must attend as a corresponding *mens rea* pursuant to Article 30 of the ICC Statute.[18] One of the distinguishing factors between the 'conduct level' and the 'context level' lies in the fact that we need to address only one kind of *actus reus* with regard to the 'context level'—i.e., 'circumstance'. In other words, as to the 'context level' of crimes against humanity and war crimes, the *actus reus* of a 'circumstance'[19] and the corresponding *mens rea* of 'knowledge' are the only objects of legal analysis.[20]

---

[16] ICC Statute, Article 30; ICC Elements of Crimes, General Introduction, paras 2 and 7. While there can be a single *mens rea* for an offence according to the common law 'offence analysis', the 'element analysis' assumes a distinct *mens rea* for each element of an offence. *See also* Prosecutor v. Bemba, Decision Pursuant to Article 61(7)(a) and (b) of the Rome Statute on the Charges of the Prosecutor Against Jean-Pierre Bemba Gombo, 15 June 2009, para 355 (the ICC Pre-Trial Chamber in *Bemba* also observes that Article 30 of the ICC Statute "is constructed on the basis of an element analysis approach – as opposed to – a crime analysis approach".). Ilias Bantekas observes that the adoption of the 'element analysis' by the drafters of Article 30 of the ICC Statutes reflects the complexity of definitions of international crimes in which we often find multiple consequences and circumstances. He also points out that "[t]his multiple layering of mental elements obviously makes life hard for prosecuting authorities". *See* Bantekas 2010, pp. 38–39. For more discussion on the 'element analysis' and the 'offence analysis', *see* Robinson and Grall 1983. It should however be noted that, as is the case with regard to the strict liability offences, *mens rea* is not always required in respect of every *actus reus*. *See* Duff 1990, p. 9.

[17] Note that, as opposed to the 'descriptive' *actus reus*, there is another kind of *actus reus* in the ICC legal framework—i.e., 'normative' *actus reus* such as, e.g., the 'gravity' element required for the 'crime against humanity of imprisonment or other severe deprivation of physical liberty' (ICC Elements of Crimes, Article 7(1)(e), 2nd Element: "The gravity of the conduct was such that it was in violation of fundamental rules of international law".), and the 'war crime of sexual violence' (*Ibid.*, Article 8(2)(b)(xxii)-6, 2nd Element: "The conduct was of a gravity comparable to that of a grave breach of the Geneva Conventions".).

[18] *See* Ormerod 2011, p. 134 ("[t]he justification for requiring *mens rea* as to every element of the *actus reus* is that it must be presumed that every element contributes to the criminality of it. If it does not, it should not be there. The requirement is therefore described as one of correspondence between the elements of *actus reus* and *mens rea*. This is an important aspect of the subjective approach to *mens rea*".).

[19] 'A widespread or systematic attack against a civilian population' (crimes against humanity); and 'an armed conflict of an international or non-international character' (war crimes).

[20] Though the ICC Elements of Crimes does not rule out the possibility of 'intent' being a relevant *mens rea* for the 'context' level analysis for crimes against humanity, it would be a rare exception because in most cases the legal analysis would be complete with the 'knowledge' without needing to further proceed to examine the 'intent'. *See, e.g.,* ICC Elements of Crimes, Article 7(1)(a), 3rd element: "[t]he perpetrator knew that the conduct was part of or *intended* the conduct to be part of a widespread or systematic attack directed against a civilian population". (emphasis added).

In relation to the crime of genocide, however, there was a disagreement amongst delegations to the drafting committee of the ICC Elements of Crimes over the issue of whether to place the *actus reus* of 'circumstance' within the 'context level'—i.e., something equivalent to 'a widespread or systematic attack' or 'an armed conflict'.[21] The main question that should be addressed in this context is whether, even without being stated explicitly in the crime definition, a contextual element of the crime is implicitly present in the structure of the crime of genocide. I will argue that the answer is yes.[22] Answering this question involves spotting a place for a legal discussion of genocidal intent at the 'context level', which I will do by introducing a conceptual distinction between the collective genocidal intent (collective intent) and the individual genocidal intent (individual intent). In this context, it should be noted that what I am doing here is to conceptually distinguish the individualistic genocidal intent at the 'conduct level' on the one hand and the collective genocidal intent at the 'context level' on the other. Put otherwise, in my view, genocidal intent *itself* is a double intent. The 'double intent structure of the genocidal intent *itself*' that I herewith propose should be distinguished from the 'double intent structure of the crime of genocide' composed of '*mens rea* for underlying acts' (general intent to which Article 30 of the ICC Statute is applicable) and genocidal intent ("intent to destroy").[23] Within the 'double intent structure of the genocidal intent *itself*', to the extent that the term *mens rea* is defined as an individual inner state of mind, the term is applicable to the 'genocidal intent at the conduct level' only. Since the 'genocidal intent at the context level', being of a collective nature, is shared by a multiplicity of individuals, it is not an individual inner state of mind and, thus, cannot be tagged by the term *mens rea*. Consequently, the 'genocidal intent at the context level' should, to some extent, take on an objective characteristic, much like the 'common purpose/plan'[24] or the 'State or organizational policy'[25] elements elsewhere in international criminal law. These two distinct concepts

---

[21] *See* Clark 2001, p. 326 (explaining that, in relation to the 'manifest patter of similar conduct' phrase in the Elements of Crimes, there were disputes amongst delegations to the drafting committee whether to acknowledge it as an element).

[22] For an opposing view, *see* Werle and Jessberger 2014, p. 311. *See also* Ambos and Wirth 2001, p. 703 *et seq.*.

[23] For the 'double intent structure of the crime of genocide', *see e.g.*, Prosecutor v. Al Bashir, Decision on the Prosecution's Application for a Warrant of Arrest against Omar Hassan Ahmed Al Bashir, 4 March 2009, para 139; Ambos 2009, pp. 834–835.

[24] The 'common purpose/plan' element is generally discussed in relation to such modes of liability theories as 'joint criminal enterprise of the *ad hoc* tribunals', 'co-perpetration (control theory) of the ICC' and 'liability scheme under Article 25(3)(d) of the ICC Statute'. Most case law and commentators regard this element as an objective element. For an opposing view, *see* Prosecutor v. Ngudjolo, Concurring Opinion of Judge Christine van den Wyngaert, 18 December 2012, paras 31–39 (claiming that 'common purpose/plan' is a subjective element). I am critical of Judge van den Wyngaert's position in this regard. It seems that Judge van den Wyngaert's observation is premised upon a single-layered structure of core international crimes, which does not fully reflect their unique two-layered structure composed of 'conduct level' and 'context level'.

[25] ICC Statute, Article 7(2)(a).

of genocidal intent, one at the 'conduct level' (individual genocidal intent) and the other at the 'context level' (collective genocidal intent), will form the main theme throughout the remainder of this book, particularly this chapter through Chap. 4. In short, in most of the cases in which there are multiple actors participating in a genocidal campaign, the crime definition of genocide assumes a two-layered structure ('conduct level' and 'context level'). Furthermore, genocidal intent itself is also composed of both individual and collective intent (genocidal intent itself being a 'double intent'), and the collective intent implies that the perpetrator is *acting as part of a collective*. On the other hand, in the extremely exceptional and hitherto hypothetical case of a solo individual committing genocide,[26] it would be of one-layered structure ('conduct level' only).[27]

Summing up, a more precise structural understanding of genocide in terms of its two-layered structure liberates the legal notion of genocide from being mistakenly labeled as a 'crime of *mens rea*' in the sense that its defining feature is the individual perpetrator's *mens rea*. At the same time, it provides a solid starting point to unfold the true identity of genocidal intent being a double intent *itself*, consisting of the 'individual genocidal intent at the conduct level' and the 'collective genocidal intent at the context level'. The two-layered structure of genocide—i.e., the combination of the 'conduct level' and the 'context level'—pays attention to the logic of crimes against humanity within the crime of genocide. Fortunately, such a logic of crimes against humanity within genocide is conspicuous in the relevant jurisprudence of the ICTY and the ICTR as the following sections will demonstrate. While the subjective side of the 'context level' of the crime of genocide (viz. the concept of 'collective genocidal intent') will form the theme of Chap. 4 of this book, this chapter will mainly address the objective aspect of the 'context level' through the theoretical notion of 'collective genocide' as follows.

3.2 Who Are You?: The Hidden Concept of 'Collective Genocide' Governing the Case Law

3.2.1 A Peculiar Judicial Invention of 'Collective Genocide' at the Ad Hoc Tribunals: A Quasi-Element of Genocide?

Can you construct the legal notion of crimes against humanity or war crimes without reference to any individual suspect or specific act? Is there any judicial decision in which judges declare that, overall, crimes against humanity have been

---

[26] The Belgian delegation stated it was "almost inconceivable" during the drafting negotiations of the Genocide Convention. U.N. GAOR, 6th Comm., 3d Sess., 73d mtg. at 90, U.N. Doc. A/C.6/SR.73 (13 October 1948).

[27] Yet, it is probable that such a solo perpetrator would rather be regarded as a lunatic, rather than to be accused of genocide.

committed at the 'context level' by a collective, *before* looking into individual acts of a defendant at the 'conduct level'? The answer is quite simple: There is none. What courts can do prior to their examination of facts concerning the accused's individual conducts is to find that there was an 'a widespread or systematic attack against a civilian population' or 'an international or non-international armed conflict': both are just a circumstance, context and/or a backdrop of individual acts charged in the indictment. International judges say that there was a 'widespread or systematic attack'. But they never say that crimes against humanity were committed in a generic manner. Without looking into specific conducts of an individual defendant, they can never declare that crimes against humanity or war crimes per se have been committed. Contrastingly, that is not the case in relation to the crime of genocide. There is a myriad of international cases where judges do not hesitate to proclaim that 'genocide' has been committed on the basis of overall facts of a campaign of violence without identifying any specific individual actor or actors at the 'conduct level'. Is this practice legitimate?

Despite the absence of any wording explicitly indicating the 'context level' in the crime definition of genocide, the 'context level' has amply been attended to by the jurisprudence of the ICTR and the ICTY. The adjective 'peculiar' used in the heading of this section seems appropriate to describe the *ad hoc* tribunals' approach to tackling the crime of genocide. The reason why it is 'peculiar' is that their rulings on the charge of genocide are heavily and critically dependent on a theoretical notion which is not an element of crime itself. That theoretical notion—which I will call 'collective genocide' for the purpose of this book—is not to be found in the crime definition of genocide at all. Yet it is linguistically commonplace, as for example when we say "the Nazis committed genocide against the Jews" or "the Rwandan Hutus committed genocide against the Tutsis". In these expressions, the word 'genocide' does not refer to specific genocidal acts, but to an entire genocidal campaign. That is what I mean by 'collective genocide'. This 'collective genocide' seems to reflect both dimensions of the objective context of genocidal campaign and the subjective intention of collective genocidal plan, both of them located at the 'context level'. Since the 'subjective intention' here belongs to a collective, as opposed to an individual, the literal meaning of the term 'subjective' dwindles as the concept of a collective intent tends to be objectified.[28] While the theme of collective genocidal intent will be primarily addressed in Chap. 4, this chapter will explore the feature of the objective genocidal campaign at the 'context level' in connection with the theoretical notion of 'collective genocide' stemming from the jurisprudence of the ICTY and the ICTR. It is to be noted that the only case where the concept of 'collective genocide' has been given an explicit name was *Jelisić* Trial Judgment. The Trial Chamber in *Jelisić* used the phrase

---

[28] Concerning the notion of 'common plan' as set forth by the case law of the ICC in connection with its interpretation of the second alternative in Article 25(3)(a) ("jointly with another"), Judge Christine van den Wyngaert argues that, contrary to the prevailing view, the 'common plan' element might not necessarily be of an objective nature. Prosecutor v. Ngudjolo, Concurring Opinion of Judge Christine van den Wyngaert, 18 December 2012, paras 31–39.

"all-inclusive genocide" for what I am labeling 'collective genocide'.[29] Other than this case, the notion of 'collective genocide' has been called by the usual name 'genocide' (or rather has never been called by any special name), which ironically renders the notion hidden and concealed.[30]

3.2.1.1 Akayesu

In *Akayesu*, the first-ever conviction on genocide in the history of the ICTR, the Trial Chamber holds that Jean Paul Akayesu is guilty of genocide. It is crucial to note that the Chamber's finding on the accused's *individual* genocidal intent is based upon its preceding finding of a *collective* genocidal intent. More specifically, before considering the accused's *individual* crime of genocide in the commune Taba,[31] the Chamber first finds a *collective* crime of genocide throughout Rwanda in 1994 in a section entitled, "Genocide in Rwanda in 1994?"[32] Hence, the Chamber concludes that "genocide was, indeed, committed in Rwanda in 1994 against the Tutsi as a group".[33] It is exactly this usage of the term 'genocide' that I call 'collective genocide'. I am not sure whether it can legitimately constitute a *legal finding* because the concept of "genocide" here is not strictly a legal notion—i.e., not related to any specific individual defendant or defendants.[34] Put differently, the generic notion of 'genocide in Rwanda' deviates from the definition of genocide focusing on the 'conduct level' as its necessary ingredient. Rather, it seems more precise to characterize it as being a generic concept deficient of any statutory basis. At this juncture, one might suppose that the section entitled "Genocide in Rwanda in 1994?" only plays a role of explaining the general context in which the alleged crime of the accused is committed. Yet, a careful reading of the section reveals that it is not. For the purpose of finding the accused's individual genocidal intent, the Chamber's reasoning and answer in respect of the question of "Genocide in Rwanda in 1994?" ('collective genocide' and 'collective genocidal intent') actually provides a critical substantive legal ground. That is to say, the Trial Chamber takes a two-step approach to find the individual genocidal intent of the accused. The Chamber examines (i) firstly, whether "the massacres which took place in Rwanda between April and July 1994 […] constitute genocide"[35]; and (ii) secondly, whether the conduct of the accused constitutes genocide.[36] For the purpose of the following analysis, I will continue to use the term

---

[29] For more discussion, *see* Sect. 3.2.2 *infra*.

[30] Even in the *Jelisić* Trial Judgment, the name 'all-inclusive genocide' was used only once within a heading of a section which says, '[t]he intention to commit all-inclusive genocide'.

[31] Prosecutor v. Akayesu, Trial Judgment, 2 September 1998, paras 727–730.

[32] *Ibid.* paras 112–129.

[33] *Ibid.* para 126.

[34] In this respect, Guglielmo Verdirame describes that the decision is made "in absolute terms". *See* Verdirame 2000, p. 585.

[35] Prosecutor v. Akayesu, Trial Judgment, 2 September 1998, paras 112–129.

[36] *Ibid.* paras 727–730.

'collective genocide' for the former—i.e., the genocide at the 'context level'. In this connection, I emphasize again that the notion of 'collective genocide' does not have any statutory basis as, on its face, neither the Genocide Convention nor the statutes of international criminal courts seems to contain any reference to it. Neither is there, in the *Akayesu* Trial Judgment, any serious discussion of the necessity and/or legitimacy of finding the 'collective genocide' led by the Chamber's question of whether "the massacres which took place in Rwanda between April and July 1994 [...] constitute genocide".[37] By putting this question, the Trial Chamber in *Akayesu* abruptly embarks upon a factual and legal analysis of 'collective genocide' at the 'context level' which is not legally required by the crime definition of genocide – and yet, which the Trial Chamber rightly senses is essential for its legal analysis.

It is instructive to note that the Chamber seems to interpret its own self-invented notion of 'collective genocide' as requiring the same legal requirements as the statutory genocide—i.e., (i) the underlying conduct element (killing, causing serious harm, etc. *in general*)[38]; and (ii) the genocidal intent element (vis-à-vis the "perpetrators" *in general*). Reviewing the relevant part of the judgment, it seems accurate to call them 'collective conduct' and 'collective genocidal intent' respectively. Both exist at the 'context level'. Thus, it appears that the Chamber presupposes that the formula of 'collective conduct' plus 'collective genocidal intent' equals 'collective genocide'.[39] In its actual analysis, the first element of 'collective genocide'—i.e., the quasi-requirement of 'collective conduct' concerning 'killing' and 'causing serious bodily harm'—is claimed to be met based on the evidence of 'widespread killing of mainly Tutsi victims'.[40] As regards the second element of the 'collective genocide'—i.e., the quasi-requirement of collective genocidal intent—the Chamber puts the question as follows: "The second requirement is that these killings and serious bodily harm, as is the case in this instance, be committed with the intent to destroy, in whole or in part, a particular group targeted as such".[41] Subsequently, without reference to any specific actors, the Chamber affirms the existence of the collective genocidal intent in view of the facts concerning the overall context of the massacres that took place throughout Rwanda in 1994 and a few representative incidents demonstrating a collective desire to destroy the Tutsi group. In particular, those facts mentioned by the Chamber are: (i) the scale of the massacres[42]; (ii) the systematic nature of the massacres[43]; (iii) the atrociousness of the massacres[44]; (iv) provocative statements

---

[37] *Ibid.* para 112.

[38] *Ibid.* paras 114–116.

[39] Van Sliedregt 2012, p. 18 (observing that the development of corporate responsibility as opposed to individual criminal responsibility tends to presuppose the existence of collective *actus reus* and collective *mens rea* of a legal entity as an actor).

[40] *Ibid.* para 116. The Trial Chamber discusses the 'collective conduct' part only in passing.

[41] *Ibid.*

[42] *Ibid.* para 118.

[43] *Ibid.*

[44] *Ibid.*

made by political leaders[45]; (v) provocative songs and slogans popular among the killers[46]; (vi) the fact that "Achilles' tendons of many wounded persons were cut to prevent them from fleeing"[47]; (vii) the fact that "even newborn babies were not spared"[48]; (viii) the fact that "even pregnant women, including those of Hutu origin, were killed on the grounds that the fetuses in their wombs were fathered by Tutsi men"[49]; (ix) the fact that Tutsi people were selectively sorted out at the roadblocks across the country[50]; and (x) the widespread propaganda campaign calling for killing Tutsi using media before and during the massacres.[51] At this juncture, it is to be remembered that these facts also serve as the main evidentiary basis for the individual genocidal intent of the accused. The extent of the overlap between evidence of collective genocidal intent and individual genocidal intent is quite overwhelming.

In this respect, it is noteworthy that the *Akayesu* Trial Chamber looks bold and even confident in deciding on the self-imposed question of 'collective genocide' and collective genocidal intent on the basis of conducts, consequences and circumstances vis-à-vis *unidentified actors*. Yet, the genocidal intent described in the *Akayesu* Indictment follows the individualistic approach thereto. That is, the Indictment only talks about Akayesu's individual genocidal intent. There is no reference to the 'collective genocide' or the collective genocidal intent in the Indictment. Para 6 of the Indictment—which is the only place where genocidal intent is mentioned—simply states that "in each paragraph charging genocide [from paras 12 to 23], the alleged acts or omissions were committed with intent to destroy, in whole or in part, a national, ethnic or racial group". Since each of those paragraphs charging genocide depicts quite a detailed personal involvement of the accused at the actual crime scenes,[52] it seems quite obvious that the genocidal intent mentioned in para 6 is of an individualistic nature. Again, however, the

---

[45] *Ibid.*

[46] *Ibid.*

[47] *Ibid.* para 119.

[48] *Ibid.* para 121.

[49] *Ibid.*

[50] *Ibid.* para 123.

[51] *Ibid.*

[52] E.g., Akayesu Indictment, para 14 ("AKAYESU led a meeting ... urged the population to eliminate accomplices of the RPF ..."); para 15 ("AKAYESU named at least three prominent Tutsis ..."); para 16 ("AKAYESU ... conducted house-to-house searches ... [Victims] were interrogated and beaten ... in the presence of [AKAYESU] ... AKAYESU personally threatened to kill ..."); para 17 ("AKAYESU ordered the interrogation and beating ..."); para 18 ("AKAYESU blew his whistle to alert local residents to the attempted escape ... AKAYESU ordered and participated in the killings of the three brothers".); para 19 (AKAYESU took 8 detained men ... and ordered the militia members to kill them".); para 20 ("AKAYESU ordered the local people and militia to kill intellectual and influential people".); para 21 ("AKAYESU ... went to the house of Victim Y ... [and] interrogated her ... AKAYESU threatened to kill her if ..."); para 22 ("AKAEYSU picked up Victim W ... [and] forced her to lay on the road in front of his car and threatened to drive over her".); para 23 ("AKAYESU picked up Victim Z in Taba and interrogated him".).

Chamber's deliberation on this para 6 of the Indictment sounds confusing because the genocidal intent dealt with by the Chamber is a *collective* genocidal intent, but not its individualistic counterpart as understood by the Prosecution in the Indictment.[53] In the relevant part of the judgment, most of the facts mentioned, except for the evidence of the accused being present and speaking in a meeting on April 19, 1994, are *not* about Akayesu. Furthermore, the conclusion drawn by the Chamber clearly shows that the concept of genocidal intent being addressed by the Chamber is of a collective nature. Para 169 thus reads,

> In light of this evidence, the Chamber finds beyond a reasonable doubt that the acts of violence which took place in Rwanda during this time were committed with the intent to destroy the Tutsi population, and that the acts of violence which took place in Taba during this time were *a part of* this effort.[54]

The pattern of legal reasoning seen in this paragraph appears to parallel that of crimes against humanity. For example, the Chamber deliberates on the question of whether "the acts of violence which took place in Taba" *forms part of* the 'collective genocide' throughout Rwanda, which reminds us of the issue of nexus between an act and a widespread or systematic attack vis-à-vis crimes against humanity.[55] To sum up, in *Akayesu*, the Trial Chamber engages in a lengthy and detailed analysis of facts[56] in order to answer the self-imposed question of whether the overall context of violence which took place throughout Rwanda between April and July 1997 constitutes genocide.[57] The problem is that the term 'genocide' here seems to be a suspicious notion. Since there existed no explicitly stipulated contextual element of genocide (in its crime definition of the ICTR Statute and the relevant jurisprudence of the ICTR and the ICTY) equivalent to 'a widespread or systematic attack against a civilian population' (crimes against humanity) or 'an armed conflict' (war crimes), the *Akayesu* Trial Chamber had no legal obligation to perform any evidential or legal examination in relation to the general context of the acts of violence throughout Rwanda as it extensively engaged in from paras 112 through 129 of its judgment under the heading of "Genocide in Rwanda in 1994?". Moreover, as I said earlier, in respect of the charge of genocide, the Prosecution did not make any allegation in relation to the

---

[53] Prosecutor v. Akayesu, Trial Judgment, 2 September 1998, paras 168–9.

[54] *Ibid.* para 169. (emphasis added).

[55] Note that the contextual element of crimes against humanity provides, "[f]or the purpose of this Statute, 'crimes against humanity' means any of the following acts when committed *as part of* a widespread or systematic attack directed against any civilian population, with knowledge of the attack". *See* ICC Statute, Article 7(1). (emphasis added). Concerning war crimes, *see* ICC Element of Crimes, Article 8: "The conduct took place *in the context of and was associated with* an international [or non-international] armed conflict". (emphasis added).

[56] Prosecutor v. Akayesu, Trial Judgment, 2 September 1998, paras 112–129.

[57] *Ibid.* para 112. After reviewing the relevant evidence, the Chamber answers the question in the positive as follows: "Consequently, the Chamber concludes from all the foregoing that genocide was, indeed, committed in Rwanda in 1994 against the Tutsi as a group". See *Ibid.* para 126.

'collective genocide' or overall acts of violence in Rwanda in its indictment.[58] Thus it is logical to conclude that there must have been a special reason for the Chamber to engage in such an extensive and detailed examination on the theme of 'collective genocide' and, in particular, 'collective genocidal intent'. One might suppose that the reason might have been a need for an objective reference point for the Chamber to infer individual genocidal intent of the accused. But that raises questions: In order to establish individual genocidal intent, is it necessary to refer to 'collective genocide' and 'collective genocidal intent'? If it is, what would be the legal implication of such necessity? Explaining the purpose of asking such a question, the *Akayesu* Trial Chamber states,

> As regards the massacres which took place in Rwanda between April and July 1994, as detailed above in the chapter on the historical background to the Rwandan tragedy, the question before this Chamber is *whether they constitute genocide*. Indeed, it was felt in some quarters that the tragic events which took place in Rwanda were only part of the war between the Rwandan Armed Forces (the RAF) and the Rwandan Patriotic Front (RPF). The answer to this question would allow a better understanding of the context within which the crimes with which the accused is charged are alleged to have been committed.[59]

From this statement, we can make two observations. Firstly, the Chamber takes it for granted that an overall context of violence ("the massacres which took place in Rwanda between April and July 1994") can constitute the crime of genocide without bringing in any specific defendant or defendants, and thus acknowledging a theoretical notion of 'collective genocide' devoid of any statutory definition. Secondly, one of the rationales behind asking the question of 'collective genocide' is the Chamber's concern to refute the opinion that "the massacres" were just a part of the war in Rwanda and consequently fall into the realm of war crimes, not of genocide. Thus, by characterizing "the massacres" themselves as genocide, the Chamber also solves the problem relating to some claims that "the massacres" are just a part of the war between RAF and the RPF. In this respect, the Chamber concludes,

> Finally, in response to the question posed earlier in this chapter as to whether the tragic events that took place in Rwanda in 1994 occurred solely within the context of the conflict between the RAF and the RPF, the Chamber replies in the negative, *since it holds that the genocide did indeed take place* against the Tutsi group, alongside the conflict.[60]

Although the relevant part of the *Akayesu* Trial Judgment does not provide a clear answer, we can postulate that the Chamber also felt uncomfortable finding the accused guilty of genocide without any reference to the overall context of violence. In my view, the Chamber was compelled to do so due to the *collective* inner dynamic of genocide stemming from the characterizing force of the 'context level'

---

[58] The only remote reference to overall acts of violence made in the indictment can be found in its 'Background' section as follows: "Following the deaths of the two Presidents [of Rwanda and Burundi in a plane crash on April 6, 1994], widespread killings, having both political and ethnic dimensions, began in Kigali and spread to other parts of Rwanda". *See* Akayesu Indictment, para 1.

[59] Prosecutor v. Akayesu, Trial Judgment, 2 September 1998, para 112. (emphasis added).

[60] *Ibid.* para 127.

common to all core international crimes. In this respect, it is very understandable
that subsequent case law of both the ICTR and the ICTY, almost without any
exception, has followed the same path of being heavily dependent on the theoretical notion of 'collective genocide' in addressing the charge of genocide.[61] For
instance, in *Kayishema and Ruzindana*, the individual genocidal intent of the
defendants as the constituent element of the crime of genocide is established on
the basis of the collective genocidal plan as factually found by the Chamber.
Despite the Chamber's legal observation that the genocidal plan is not an element
of genocide,[62] the degree of evidentiary dependence of the individual genocidal
intent on the collective genocidal plan, as revealed in the judgment, is so enormous
that it looks as if the Chamber is legally *required* to find the genocidal plan within
the 'collective genocide' in Rwanda in general and in Kibuye in particular before it
proceeds to find the individual genocidal intent of the accused. The same pattern
repeats itself in the subsequent cases at the ICTR as will be shown below.

3.2.1.2 Kayishema and Ruzindana

The Trial Chamber in *Kayishema and Ruzindana* employs a macro- to micro-anal-
ysis mode to set forth the relevant facts of the case and to explain how the requisite elements of the crime of genocide are met. The process of factual and legal
analysis taken by the Chamber follows a three-step inquiry: (i) are the elements of
genocide met in Rwanda? ('Part V. Factual Findings, Chapter 5.2'); (ii) are the
elements of genocide met in Kibuye? ('Part V. Factual Findings, Chapter 5.2.1');
and, (iii) is the accused's individual genocidal intent element met in the four incidents alleged in the Indictment? ('Part VI. Legal Findings, Chapter 6.2.
Genocide'). While the first two chapters focus on the collective circumstances surrounding the massacres that took place in Rwanda and Kibuye in general ('context
level'), the last chapter addresses the individual genocidal intent of Kayishema and
Ruzindana ('conduct level'). Out of these three inquiries, it is only the third one
that is legally *required* for the Chamber to scrutinize for the purpose of determining whether the accused is guilty of genocide. It appears that that is why only the
third question is included in the 'Legal Findings' section of the judgment. The
Chamber's inquiries (i) and (ii) indicate that the *Kayishema and Ruzindana* Trial
Chamber follows the precedent of *Akayesu* in that it also presumes that the underlying acts element and the genocidal intent element are applicable to the theoretical notion of 'collective genocide' without identifying specific perpetrators.

---

[61] All the case law after *Karemera* at the ICTR has taken a judicial notice of 'collective genocide'. Prosecutor v. Karemera et al., Decision on Prosecutor's Interlocutory Appeal of Decision
on Judicial Notice, 16 June 2006 (taking a judicial notice of 'collective genocide' for the first
time in the history of the ICTR. Subsequent case law just cites this decision without needing to
engage in an actual discussion of 'collective genocide').

[62] Prosecutor v. Kayishema and Ruzindana, Trial Judgment, 21 May 1999, para 94 (The Chamber
opines that it is virtually impossible to commit genocide without genocidal plan.).

Accordingly, the Chamber also applies the formula of 'collective conduct' plus 'collective genocidal intent' equals 'collective genocide'.[63] In this sense, the concept of genocidal intent addressed by the Chamber vis-à-vis the 'collective genocide' cannot be a *mens rea* because there is no specifically identified individualistic 'mind' per se which we can look into. That is why the relevant discussion in *Kayishema and Ruzindana* centers on the notion of 'genocidal plan' rather than 'genocidal intent'. Let us follow the Chamber's analysis from macro to micro.

1st Stage Inquiry: Are the Elements of Genocide Met in Rwanda?

Just like the *Akayesu* Trial Chamber,[64] the Trial Chamber in *Kayishema and Ruzindana* explores the issue of 'collective genocide' by asking whether genocide took place in Rwanda in 1994.[65] The manner in which the Chamber puts and answers the question reveals the pivotal role of the collective genocidal intent at the 'context level'. As to the question whether genocide took place in Rwanda in 1994,[66] the Chamber concludes that "top level Hutu extremists in the former Rwandan government" pursued a "plan of genocide" to destroy the Tutsi group,[67] thereby identifying the collective genocidal intent with the genocidal plan. At the outset of the evidentiary analysis on the issue of the 'collective genocide', the Chamber stresses the importance of asking the question of "whether genocide took place in Rwanda in 1994".[68] The Chamber explains that "the question [of genocide in Rwanda] is *so fundamental to the case against the accused that the Trial Chamber feels obliged to* make a finding of fact on this issue".[69] The Chamber further clarifies the purpose of making such a finding as follows:

> The purpose [...] is [to assess] whether the event in Rwanda as a whole, reveal *the existence of the elements of the crime of genocide*. Such a finding allows for a better understanding of the context within which perpetrators may have committed the crimes alleged in the Indictment.[70]

Thus, as is the case in *Akayesu*,[71] the *Kayishema and Ruzindana* Trial Chamber is of the view that the decision on "whether genocide took place in Rwanda in 1994" can be made by appraising the facts relevant to the overall situation through

---

[63] *See* this chapter, footnote 39 *supra* and accompanying text.

[64] *See* Sect. 3.2.1.1 *supra*.

[65] Prosecutor v. Kayishema and Ruzindana, Trial Judgment, 21 May 1999, paras 273–291 ('Part V. Factual Findings, Chapter 5.2').

[66] *Ibid.* paras 273–274.

[67] *Ibid.* paras 289 and 291.

[68] *Ibid.* para 273.

[69] *Ibid.*

[70] *Ibid.* para 274. (emphasis added).

[71] *See* Sect. 3.2.1.1 *supra*.

the lenses of (i) the underlying acts element at the 'context level', and (ii) the genocidal intent element at the 'context level'. So we can understand that there is the Chamber's hidden assumption that the seemingly theoretical concept of 'collective genocide' at the 'context level' has the same elements as the statutory crime of genocide. It is to be noted that both 'lenses' are of an anonymous nature because they involve unidentified perpetrators in generic terms. In relation to the term 'element' in the cited text above (as used in the phrase "[...] reveals the existence of the elements of the crime of genocide"), it is illustrative to note that what the Chamber states as the reason to look into the issue of 'collective genocide'—i.e., "the question is *so fundamental to the case against the accused* that the Trial Chamber *feels obliged to* make a finding of fact"—sounds very close to the definition of the term 'element of crime'. The Black's Law Dictionary defines 'element of crime' as "[t]he constituent parts of a crime [...] that the prosecution must prove to sustain a conviction".[72] So it seems quite legitimate to state that, in *Kayishema and Ruzindana*, the theme of 'collective genocide' is dealt with as an element of the crime in the same manner as the elements of statutory genocide (the elements of underlying acts and genocidal intent). Though the Chamber adds a caveat that the finding on the 'collective genocide' in Rwanda "is *not* dispositive of the question of the accused's innocence or guilt",[73] the importance of this finding throughout the judgment forming a cornerstone for all the legal findings on the allegation of genocide strongly suggests that the final guilty verdict would have been impossible without the preceding (legal or factual or generic) finding of the 'collective genocide'.

The Chamber draws its conclusion on the question of 'collective genocide' in Rwanda—i.e., "a plan of genocide [developed by top level Hutu extremists] existed and [unidentified multiple] perpetrators executed this plan in Rwanda between April and June 1994"[74]—from "the widespread nature of the attacks",[75] "the sheer number of victims"[76] and "the overwhelming majority of the victims being Tutsi civilians".[77] The "plan of genocide" in this context is certainly of a collective nature as summarized by the Trial Chamber as follows:

---

[72] Black's Law Dictionary, 9th edn., 2009.

[73] Prosecutor v. Kayishema and Ruzindana, Trial Judgment, 21 May 1999, para 273. (emphasis added).

[74] *Ibid.* paras 289 and 291. Refuting the Trial Chamber's finding on the existence of a genocidal plan, Kayishema asserts before the Appeals Chamber that the killings of Tutsi population were caused by "crowd psychology and paranoia" and "an a[t]mosphere of suspicion, revenge or denunciation over problems of land, livestock, weapons and even women". *See* Prosecutor v. Kayishema and Ruzindana, Appeals Judgment, 1 June 2001, para 141. The Appeals Chamber subsequently rejected this claim. See *Ibid.* para 143.

[75] Prosecutor v. Kayishema and Ruzindana, Trial Judgment, 21 May 1999, para 289.

[76] *Ibid.*

[77] *Ibid.* para 291.

In summary, the Trial Chamber finds that the massacres of the Tutsi population indeed were meticulously planned and systematically co-ordinated by top level Hutu extremists in the former Rwandan government at the time in question.[78]

In relation to the existence of the collective "plan of genocide", the Chamber considered the evidence grouped in four categories. It appears that they all indicate a systematic preparation of the genocidal campaign against the Tutsis: the Chamber examined (i) facts immediately after the plane crash of the Rwandan president on 6 April 1994[79]; (ii) facts concerning the anti-Tutsi propaganda campaign prior to April 1994[80]; (iii) facts concerning the civil defence program and the militia[81]; and (iv) facts concerning roadblocks and identification cards.[82]

---

[78] *Ibid.* para 289. (internal quotation marks omitted).

[79] *Ibid.* paras 275–78: (a) the fact that massacres began throughout Rwanda immediately after the plane crash of the President Juvenal Habyarimana on 6 April 1994; (b) the existence of execution lists including the names of "the Tutsi elite, government ministers, leading businessmen, professors and high profile Hutus, who may have favoured the implementation of the Arusha Accords"; and (c) the radio announcement on the morning of 7 April 1994 ordering people to stay at home for the purpose of facilitating "the movement of the soldiers and gendarmes from house to house to arrest and execute real and perceived enemies of the Hutu extremists, specifically those named on execution lists".

[80] *Ibid.* paras 279–82: (a) the spread of extremist ideology prior to April 1994 through the mass media such as the Kangura newspaper, the RTLM radio station and other print and electronic media inciting the Hutu population against the Tutsis; (b) the publication of the "Ten Commandments" for the Hutus in 1991 in which Tutsis were described as the enemy; (c) the production of a report produced by ten military commanders in 1991 that "answered the question how to defeat the enemy in the military, media and political domains"; (d) the production of a military memorandum in September 1992 which "defined the "enemy" as the Tutsi population, thereby transferring the hostile intentions of the RPF to all Tutsis"; (e) the propaganda campaign as to the Tutsi babies urging the Hutus not to make the same mistake as the one they made in 1959 letting the young Tutsis escape; and (f) the fact that the killings "started off like a little spark and then spread" as a result of the anti-Tutsi propaganda.

[81] *Ibid.* paras 283–86: (a) the fact that Rwandan officials controlled the civil defence forces and the militias, including their training in military camps; (b) the fact that both the civil defence program and the militias became an integral part of the machinery carrying out the genocidal plan in 1994; (c) the use of the civil defence program for the purpose of swift distribution of weapons; (d) the fact that 50,000 machetes were ordered and distributed through the civil defence program shortly before the commencement of the 1994 massacres, to the militias and the Hutu civilian population; and (e) almost universal presence of the militia members and other armed civilians at various massacre sites.

[82] *Ibid.* paras 287–88: (a) the fact that roadblocks were erected within hours of the President's death on 6 April 1994 throughout Rwanda, some within thirty to forty-five minutes thereafter; (b) the fact that such roadblocks remained operative for at least following three months during which most massacres took place throughout Rwanda; (c) the existence of roadblocks at the approach to each locality along the way from Goma to Kibuye on 25 June 1994; (d) the existence of 45 roadblocks along the way from Butare to Kibuye in May 1994; (e) the fact that roadblocks were manned by military personnel, soldiers, members of the *Interahamwe* militia and/or armed civilians; (f) the common practice of checking identification cards at each roadblock to separate the Tutsis from the Hutus, and the subsequent killings of those identified as Tutsis.

2nd Stage Inquiry: Are the Elements of Genocide Met in Kibuye?

For the purpose of looking into the question of 'collective genocide' in Kibuye,[83] the Chamber begins its assessment of facts by stating, "[h]aving determined that perpetrators carried out a genocidal plan in Rwanda in 1994, this Chamber now turns to assess the situation in Kibuye Préfecture".[84] What the Chamber seeks to do throughout this chapter, entitled "Genocide in Kibuye", is to see whether the genocidal plan spotted at the level of Rwanda as a whole extends to the local level of Kibuye. Again, the Chamber's factual analysis in this chapter centers around the issue of the genocidal plan. Ultimately, the Chamber reaches a conclusion that "in Kibuye Préfecture, the plan of genocide was implemented by the public officials".[85] Here, it should be noted that the "plan of genocide" mentioned in this chapter is exactly the genocidal plan found in the preceding chapter on "Genocide in Rwanda". From the analysis of evidence in this chapter, we can identify two key phrases through which all the pieces of evidence are connected to show the implementation of the genocidal plan in Kibuye. They are 'immediately after' and 'public officials'. Most evidence considered by the Chamber in this chapter is about facts that happened 'immediately after' the plane clash on 6 April 1994 in which Rwandan president Habyarimana was killed. In this regard, the Chamber is obviously of the view that the temporal proximity between the president's death and the systematic attack against Tutsi population in Kibuye is a strong evidence of an implementation of a pre-established genocidal plan. In particular, the Chamber considers that the pervasive involvement of local 'public officials' in the attack is indicative of the existence of a plan and the systematic implementation thereof. The factual findings made by the Chamber in respect of the interaction among local officials in Kibuye *Préfecture* and the communication between the central authorities and the *préfet* Kayishema also point to a pre-arranged plan. The testimony about the meeting that had taken place during the prime minister Kambanda's visit to Kibuye, in which the fate of seventy-two Tutsi children was discussed sounds very impressive because it clearly indicates the individual purpose-based genocidal intent of one of the most high-level government officials.[86] To sum up, the picture drawn by the Chamber in this chapter is a factual microcosm of that depicted in the preceding chapter on genocide in Rwanda, sharing the same pattern of evidence. Evidence

---

[83] *Ibid.* paras 292–313 ('Part V. Factual Findings, Chapter 5.2.1').

[84] *Ibid.* para 292.

[85] *Ibid.* para 312.

[86] The seventy-two Tutsi children aged between 8 and 15 survived the massacre at the Complex and were hospitalized at the Kibuye hospital. An official from the hospital attending the meeting with the Prime Minister Kambanda and other high-level governmental officials voiced a concern for the children's safety. The Prime Minister asked the Minister of Information to answer this question and he rebuked the hospital official for not supporting the politics of the Interim Government and not recognizing the enemy. On this testimony, the Chamber states, "[t]he Minister of Information gave the impression that the Interim Government recognized these infirm children as enemies. Later, these children were forcibly taken from the hospital and killed". *See* Prosecutor v. Kayishema and Ruzindana, Trial Judgment, 21 May 1999, para 310. On this evidence, Kayishema complained before the Appeals Chamber suggesting that the Trial Chamber's finding on his genocidal intent should be reversed because those seventy-two Tutsi children were

considered by the Chamber concerning its finding of a genocidal plan implemented in Kibuye can be grouped as follows: (i) facts concerning the background of the massacre in Kibuye[87]; (ii) facts concerning initial attacks at the residences of the Tutsis[88]; and, (iii) facts concerning the pervasive involvement of local government officials.[89]

Footnote 86 (continued)

taken to the hospital upon his order. The Appeals Chamber however dismissed this claim specifying that whether the children were "taken to the hospital pursuant to Kayishema's instructions has little direct bearing on" the issue of his genocidal intent. *See* Prosecutor v. Kayishema and Ruzindana, Appeals Judgment, 1 June 2001, para 148.

[87] Prosecutor v. Kayishema and Ruzindana, Trial Judgment, 21 May 1999, paras 293–94 and 307: Such means of proof includes, immediately after the plan crash on April 6, 1994: (a) the Hutu population's open use of accusatory or pejorative terms, such as Inkotanyi (meaning RPF accomplice/ enemy) and Inyenzi (meaning cockroach) referring to Tutsis; (b) "the members of the *Interahamwe* and other armed militant Hutus began a campaign of persecution against Tutsis based on the victims' education and social prominence; (c) "the Tutsi population, as a whole, suffered indiscriminate attacks in their homes" such as setting fire to their houses and looting and killing their cattle; (d) the erection of roadblocks to separate Tutsis using the identification cards and to injure, mutilate, rape and/or kill them; (e) the Hutu attackers singing songs which exhorts extermination of Tutsis; and (f) the Hutu attackers being "armed and led by local government officials and other public figures.

[88] *Ibid.* paras 296–98: Such means of proof includes, immediately after the plane crash on 6 April 1994: (a) In Gitesi commune, Kibuye prefecture on 7 April 1994, wounded Tutsis being pervasive, by the roadside, bushes and places very close to the administrative headquarters of the Prefecture; (b) "a cause-and-effect relationship [...] between the 8 April radio announcement of the purported resumption of the war and the first death in Rwanda and, in particular, in Kibuye prefecture; (c) a local meeting discussing the "Tutsi problem" on 7 or 8 April and participation by many public officials therein; (d) machetes being distributed by a commune secretary; (e) machetes being transported into a commune by Prefectoral trucks and a commune secretary supervising the unloading thereof; (f) after distributing the machetes, local officials leaving for other communes; (g) the massacres of Tutsi civilians immediately following the distribution of weapons (The Chamber specifically points out that "the proximity of the distribution of weapons to the massacres of Tutsi civilians is evidence of the genocidal plan".); and (h) the separation of Tutsi civilians who fled to a local church and subsequent killing.

[89] *Ibid.* paras 309–11: (a) bourgmestres communicating lists of suspected RPF members and supporters from their commune to the Prefect, months before the commencement of the massacres; (b) "written communications [among] the Central Authorities, Kayishema and the Communal Authorities that contain language regarding whether "work has begun" and whether more "workers" were needed in certain commune"; (c) a letter from Kayishema to the Minister of Defence requesting "military hardware and reinforcement to undertake clean-up efforts in Bisesero"; (d) the fact that some of the most brutal massacres followed meetings organized by the Prefectoral authorities and attended by the heads of the Rwandan interim government and/or ordinary citizens of the prefecture to discuss matters of security; (e) the fact that Kayishema requested reinforcement from the central authorities to deal with the security problem in Bisesero (see also *Ibid.* para 529 ; (f) "[a] letter dated 26 June 1994 written by the then *Bourgmestre* of Mabanza, Bagilishema to the *Prefect* of Kibuye, Kayishema, [stating] that there was no need for sending additional attackers to Mabanza because there were no Tutsis left in his commune" (regarding this letter, the Chamber comments, "[t]he letter clearly indicates the knowledge and participation of the civilian authorities in the process of extermination". *Ibid.* para 530.); (g) the Interim Governmental Prime Minister Kambanda's visit to Kibuye on 3 May 1994; (h) the fact that, during the meeting which Kambanda himself attended, the Minister of Information gave an impression that the Interim Government regards Tutsi children as enemies to be wiped out; and (i) the fact that local public officials including the prefect and sous-prefect expressed anti-Tutsi sentiment.

3.2.1.3 Rutaganda and Musema

In *Rutaganda*, the Chamber takes a more sophisticated approach than the previous cases such as *Akayesu* and *Kayishema and Ruzindana*. Thus, the *Rutaganda* Trial Chamber refrains from using the legally undefined term 'genocide in Rwanda'. The fact that the Chamber does not directly call the overall context a 'genocide' is clearly contrary to cases of the *Akayesu* Trial Judgment[90] and the *Kayishema and Ruzindana* Trial Judgment.[91] Yet, although the Chamber does not legally characterize the overall context of violence in Rwanda in 1994 as 'genocide', the end result is not that much different from that of *Akayesu* or *Kayishema and Ruzindana*. All three Trial Chambers link the acts of the accused at the 'conduct level' to the overall context at the 'context level'. Hence, the approach taken by these three Trial Chambers is more akin to that usually employed vis-à-vis the contextual element of crimes against humanity linking the acts of the accused to the overall context ('as part of'). What distinguishes *Rutaganda* from the previous two cases is merely the fact that, as is the case of crimes against humanity in respect of which the contextual element of the 'widespread or systematic attack against a civilian population' is never characterized as 'crimes against humanity' per se, the *Rutaganda* Trial Chamber does not use the term 'genocide' indicating the overall genocidal context.

Following the precedent in *Akayesu* and *Kayishema and Ruzindana*, the logic of crimes against humanity also governs the relevant reasoning of the Trial Chamber in *Rutaganda*. This can be seen from the fact that, in the ensuing paragraph after the Chamber's affirmation of Rutaganda's individual genocidal intent, the Chamber endeavors to establish collective genocide throughout Rwanda. First of all, the Chamber declares that "numerous atrocities [... were] committed against Tutsis in Rwanda" in 1994.[92] The Chamber then "infers a general context within which acts aimed at destroying the Tutsi group were perpetrated" in view of (i) "the widespread nature of such atrocities, throughout the Rwandan territory"[93]; and (ii) the systematic and deliberate selection of the victims for the reason of their being members of the Tutsi group, while excluding others.[94] The rationale behind the Chamber's account of

---

[90] *See* this chapter of the judgment entitled "Genocide in Rwanda in 1994?".

[91] *See* the sections entitled "Genocide in Kibuye" (pp. 113–121) and "Genocide in Rwanda and Kibuye Generally" (pp. 198–199) of the judgment.

[92] Prosecutor v. Rutaganda, Trial Judgment, 6 December 1999, para 399.

[93] *Ibid.* para 400.

[94] *Ibid.* In this respect, the Trial Chamber specifically takes into account the following facts: (i) Prior to the ETO school massacre on 11 April 1997, the Hutus were separated from the Tutsis so that they can escape the attack by solders and members of the *Interahamwe*, and the accused was present during the attack; (ii) Immediately after the ETO school massacre at Nyanza, Rutaganda directed the *Interahamwe* to surround a large number of refugees from whom Hutus were allowed to leave prior to the massacre of the remaining Tutsis; and (iii) on 28 April 1994, members of *Interahamwe* conducted house-to-house searches in the Agakingiro neighbourhood demanding identity cards from the residents, and Tutsis and people belonging to a certain political parties were taken to a place where Rutaganda was present. Subsequently, the accused personally killed a Tutsi man among the people brought. *Ibid.* paras 390–394.

the "general context" can be traced by what it deduces therefrom: "[c]onsequently, the Chamber notes that such acts as are charged against the Accused *were part of* an over-all context within which other criminal acts systematically directed against members of the Tutsi group, targeted as such, were committed".[95] From this statement, we can glimpse that the Chamber wanted to link the individual acts of the accused ('conduct level') to an overall context or circumstances of violence throughout Rwanda ('context level'): the logic of crimes against humanity. What would have been the reason for that? The Chamber might have felt uneasy about finding the accused guilty of geno-cide without first establishing the broader context of violence encompassing his indi-vidual acts. Although the Chamber never uses such a term as 'collective genocide', the phrase "other criminal acts systematically directed against members of the Tutsi group, targeted as such" gives an impression that the Chamber, advertently or inadvertently, wishes to characterize the "overall context" as genocidal. The relevant paragraph reads,

> […] [T]he Chamber finds that, at the time of the events referred to in the Indictment, numerous atrocities were committed against Tutsis in Rwanda. From the widespread nature of such atrocities, throughout the Rwandan territory, and the fact that the victims were sys-tematically and deliberately selected owing to their being members of the Tutsi group, to the exclusion of individuals who were not members of the said group, the Chamber is able to infer a general context within which acts aimed at destroying the Tutsi group were per-petrated. Consequently, the Chamber notes that such acts as are charged against the Accused *were part of an overall context* within which other criminal acts systematically directed against members of the Tutsi group, targeted as such, were committed.[96]

This finding would be legally irrelevant unless the Chamber believed that the overall context matters in establishing the individual crime of genocide. About two months after the issuance of the *Rutaganda* Trial Judgment (December 6, 1999), the ICTR issued its ruling on the *Musama* case (January 27, 2000). In finding the accused guilty of genocide, the *Musema* Trial Chamber also applies the logic of crimes against humanity which links the 'conduct level' to the 'context level'. In the Indictment in *Musema*,[97] we can hardly find any reference to, let alone any allegation of, 'collective genocide'. The Trial Chamber, however, is of the view that some paragraphs of the Indictment "contain *allegations* on the general context in Rwanda in 1994, as well as *general elements* of the crimes which the Accused is charged with committing".[98] Those paragraphs of the Indictment are as follows:

> 4.1 During the events referred to in this indictment, Rwanda was divided into eleven pre-fectures, one of which was Kibuye.

> 4.2 During the events referred to in this indictment, Tutsis were identified as members of an ethnic or racial group.

---

[95] *Ibid.* para 400.

[96] *Ibid.* (emphasis added).

[97] Prosecutor v. Musema, Amended Indictment, 29 April 1999.

[98] Prosecutor v. Musema, Trial Judgment, 27 January 2000, para 354 (emphasis added) ("Paras 4.1, 4.2 and 4.3 of the Indictment, under the heading "A concise statement of the facts", contain allegations on the general context in Rwanda in 1994, as well as general elements of the crimes which the Accused is charged with committing".).

4.3 On 6 April 1994, the plane transporting President Juvénal Habyarimana of Rwanda crashed on its approach to Kigali airport, Rwanda. Attacks and killings of civilians began soon thereafter throughout Rwanda.[99]

Do these paragraphs contain any 'allegations' or '(general) elements of the crimes'? Though it seems obvious that para 4.2 talks about the element of 'a national, ethnical, racial or religious group',[100] what is the element included in para 4.3? Is para 4.3 an allegation to be proven by the Prosecution? Despite that the Chamber clearly treats para 4.3 of the Indictment as an allegation in para 359 of its judgment,[101] para 4.3 rather seems to be a generally accepted fact that has been inserted by the Prosecution as background information.[102] Moreover, what is meant "*general* elements" when the Chamber mentions "general elements of the crimes which the Accused is charged with committing"? For now it is enough to bear in mind that the *Musema* Trial Chamber, on the basis of paras 4.1, 4.2, and 4.3 of the Indictment, wanted to examine evidence about the 'collective genocide' *throughout Rwanda* in the section entitled "Context of the events alleged".[103] Subsequently, with regard to the "general context in Rwanda in 1994",[104] the Chamber reached a somewhat contrived conclusion that "[i]n light of these admissions [made by the accused], these facts are not in dispute. The Chamber finds, therefore, that the allegations set forth in Paras 4.1, 4.2 and 4.3 of the Indictment have been established beyond reasonable doubt".[105] In comparison, it should be noted that, in terms of the geographical areas concerned, all the statements of facts and allegations contained in the ensuing paragraphs of the Indictment are strictly confined *within the area of Bisesero* in Gisovu and Gishyita communes, Kibuye Prefecture.[106] Then, why does the Chamber seem to be obsessed with dealing with the general context of violence *throughout Rwanda*? It seems that the Chamber covertly felt a need or necessity to make a finding on collective genocide.

I think the Chamber's interpretation of para 4.3 of the Indictment as an 'allegation' implicitly manifests that the Chamber was (for some reason) eager to make a legal finding on the "general context in Rwanda in 1994" and "general elements" of the crime of genocide.[107] Though it is not clear what "general elements" means

---

[99] Prosecutor v. Musema, Amended Indictment, 29 April 1999, at 2.

[100] *See* ICC Elements of Crimes, the first common element of genocide: "Such person or persons belonged to a particular national, ethnical, racial or religious group".

[101] Prosecutor v. Musema, Trial Judgment, 27 January 2000, para 359 ("Musema admits that on 6 April 1994, the plane transporting President Juvenal Habyarimana of Rwanda crashed on its approach to Kigali airport, Rwanda and that attacks and killings of civilians began soon thereafter throughout Rwanda, *as alleged in* Para 4.3 of the Indictment".). (emphasis added).

[102] Both the Akayesu Indictment and Rutaganda Indictment places the paragraph equivalent to the para 4.3 under the heading of "Background", not of "General Allegations".

[103] Prosecutor v. Musema, Trial Judgment, 27 January 2000, paras 354–361.

[104] *Ibid.* para 354.

[105] *Ibid.* para 361.

[106] Musema Indictment, paras 4.4.–4.11.

[107] *See* Prosecutor v. Musema, Trial Judgment, 27 January 2000, para 354.

because the *Musema* Trial Judgment does not articulate it any further, we might refer to the similar discussion in *Akayesu* where the Trial Chamber enunciates the two elements of 'collective genocide' we have already seen—i.e., the 'collective conduct' element and the 'collective intent' element.[108] In this respect, it is note-worthy that there is another significant observation made by the *Musema* Trial Chamber by which we can guess the existence of the notion of 'collective geno-cide' in the bench's minds. In para 931 (in a section addressing Musema's individ-ual genocidal intent), the Trial Chamber states,

> Consequently, the Chamber notes that the above acts, with which Musema and his subor-dinates are charged, were committed *as part of a widespread and systematic perpetration of other criminal acts* against members of the Tutsi group.[109]

Let's compare this statement with the definition of crimes against humanity:

> '[C]rime against humanity' means any of the following acts when committed *as part of a widespread or systematic attack* directed against any civilian population [...].[110]

From the *Musema* Trial Chamber's observation in para 931, we can postulate that the Chamber did understand the structure of the crime of genocide as some-thing very similar to that of crimes against humanity, consisting of both the 'con-duct level' and the 'context level', with the former linked to the latter. In other words, what the para 931 reveals is that the Chamber thought that '*collective geno-cide' ("a widespread and systematic perpetration of other criminal acts")* at the 'context level' encompasses Musema's individual genocidal act at the 'conduct level'. The Chamber's understanding of the structure of genocide being an individ-ual act forming part of 'collective genocide' conflicts with the traditional under-standing of genocide in which there is no objective contextual element such as the 'widespread and systematic perpetration of other criminal acts' as phrased by the *Musema* Trial Chamber. In the traditional understanding, the structure of genocide consists of 'underlying conduct' and 'genocidal intent' at the 'conduct level' only.

The preceding examination of the four early genocide cases of the ICTR (*Akayesu, Kayishema and Ruzindana, Rutaganda* and *Musema*) confirms that the Trial Chambers indeed understood the structure of genocide as being two-layered: 'conduct level' and 'context level'. All four Trial Chambers consistently apply the logic of crimes against humanity in which an individual act of the accused at the 'conduct level' is linked to overall genocidal campaign at the 'context level'. It strongly appears that what I call the 'collective genocide' at the 'context level' is indeed conceived by international judges at the ICTR as something that must be addressed and proven as a 'general element'.

---

[108] Prosecutor v. Akayesu, Trial Judgment, 2 September 1998, paras 116–7.

[109] Prosecutor v. Musema, Trial Judgment, 27 January 2000, para 931. See also *Ibid.* para 358 ("In addition to that, Musema admits that in 1994 widespread or systematic attacks were directed against civilians on the grounds of ethnic or racial origin".).

[110] ICC Statute, Article 7(1).

3.2.1.4 Krstić, Popović et al., Karadžić and Tolimir

The notion of 'collective genocide' also appears in the jurisprudence of the ICTY. In its Legal Findings part, where there is no mentioning of the accused's individual genocidal intent, let alone any discussion thereof, the Trial Chamber in *Krstić* concludes that the Bosnian Serb forces' "intent to kill all the Bosnian Muslim men of military age in Srebrenica constitutes intent to destroy in part the Bosnian Muslim group within the meaning of Article 4 [of the ICTY Statute] and therefore must be qualified as a genocide".[111] In reaching this conclusion, it is only the collective *mens rea* that penetrates the Chamber's reasoning on the issue of genocidal intent. The Chamber's focus consistently lies on the Bosnian Serb forces' intent and knowledge. In particular, the Bosnian Serb forces' *knowledge* and even *constructive knowledge* inferred from the evidence forms the legal basis of its finding that genocide was "perpetrated against the Bosnian Muslims, at Srebrenica, in July 1995".[112] Hence, it should be noted that the Chamber's legal finding on the charge of genocide was made at the exclusion of any discussion on individual genocidal intent of the accused.[113] In other words, what we see in the Legal Findings part of the judgment is 'collective genocide' *only*. The Trial Chamber made no efforts to discuss statutory genocide—i.e., genocide committed by an individual—and individual genocidal intent in the entire section on the legal findings. It is impressive to see that, throughout the legal findings section on genocide, the Trial Chamber strictly applies its understanding that genocidal intent "must be discernible in the criminal act itself, *apart from the intent of particular perpetrators*".[114] This observation reminds us of the ICTR Trial Chambers' discussion of collective genocidal intent located at the 'context level' as a 'general element' that we have examined in the previous sub-subsection above. The *Krstić* Trial Chamber's proclamation that genocidal intent "must be discernible in the criminal act itself, *apart from the intent of particular perpetrators*" strongly suggests that the Chamber's notion of genocidal intent is of a collective nature. The Chamber establishes the collective genocidal intent on the basis of the Bosnian Serb force's collective knowledge at the 'context level'. More specifically, in addition to the Bosnian Serb forces'

---

[111] Prosecutor v. Krstić, Trial Judgment, 2 August 2001, para 598. The Appeals Chamber endorses the Trial Chamber's reasoning in this regard. Prosecutor v. Krstić, Appeals Judgment, 19 April 2004, para 20 ("The proof of the mental state with respect to the commission of the underlying act can serve as evidence from which the fact-finder may draw the further inference that the accused possessed the specific intent to destroy".). Note, however, that, ultimately, the Appeals Chamber denied the individual genocidal intent of the accused.

[112] *Ibid.* para 599.

[113] *Ibid.* ("The Trial Chamber has thus concluded that the Prosecution has proven beyond all reasonable doubt that genocide [...] [was] perpetrated against the Bosnian Muslims, at Srebrenica, in July 1995".).

[114] *Ibid.* para 549. (emphasis added).

knowledge of destructive consequences,[115] the legal finding of the forces' collective genocidal intent relies upon its constructive knowledge of their actions' impact on the protected group when the Chamber states,

> Granted, only the men of military age were systematically massacred, but it is significant that these massacres occurred at a time when the forcible transfer of the rest of the Bosnian Muslim population was well under way. The Bosnian Serb forces *could not have failed to know*, by the time they decided to kill all the men, that this selective destruction of the group would have a lasting impact upon the entire group. [...] Furthermore, the Bosnian Serb forces *had to be aware of* the catastrophic impact that the disappearance of two or three generations of men would have on the survival of a traditionally patriarchal society [...].[116]

---

[115] *Ibid.* para 595 ("The Bosnian Serb forces knew [...] that the combination of those killings with the forcible transfer of the women, children and elderly would inevitably result in the physical disappearance of the Bosnian Muslim population at Srebrenica".).

[116] *Ibid.* The *Krstić* Appeals Chamber endorses the Trial Chamber's consideration of the *impact* of killing military-aged men from Srebrenica in determining the question of genocidal intent. For the purpose of both the Trial and Appeals Chambers' deliberation in *Krstić*, it is the Bosnian Muslim population in Srebrenica that legally constitutes the '(substantial) part' to be targeted for destruction, but not the Bosnian Muslim men of military age systematically executed by the VRS. In other words, in terms of the phrase 'in whole or in part' in the crime definition of genocide, 'in whole' corresponds to the Bosnian Muslims *throughout the entire Bosnia*, while 'in part' indicates the Bosnian Muslims *in Srebrenica*. Prosecutor v. Krstić, Appeals Judgment, 19 April 2004, paras 15 and 19. *See also* Prosecutor v. Krstić, Trial Judgment, 2 August 2001, para 560; Prosecutor v. Popović et al., Trial Judgment, 10 June 2010, paras 839–840; Prosecutor v. Blagojević and Jokić, Trial Judgment, 17 January 2005, para 673. In this context, what the *impact* of killing men of military age signifies is that the Appeals Chamber's concept of 'destruction' is destruction in the future, which is at least one generation away. Put otherwise, the execution of 7000 to 8000 Bosnian Muslim men of military age at Srebrenica does not per se satisfy the 'targeting/destroying substantial part' requirement. That is because it is not those men in Srebrenica, but the entire Bosnian Muslim population in Srebrenica that legally constitutes the 'targeting/destroying substantial part' requirement. In this respect, the Appeals Chamber observes: "The physical destruction of the men therefore had *severe procreative implications* for the Srebrenica Muslim community, potentially consigning the community to extinction. This is the type of *physical destruction* the Genocide Convention is designed to prevent". Prosecutor v. Krstić, Appeals Judgment, 19 April 2004, paras 28–9. See also *Ibid.* para 32. Contrary to the Appeals Chamber's position that associated the 'severe procreative implications' with 'physical destruction', it seems to me that what mattered most in the deliberation of the Trial and Appeals Chambers in *Krstić* was the 'biological destruction' expected to occur in the remote future, as signified by the term "severe procreative implications", rather than the immediate 'physical destruction' of the Bosnian Muslim men of military age in Srebrenica. (*Blagojević and Jokić* Trial Chamber regards it as 'physical destruction'. Prosecutor v. Blagojević and Jokić, Trial Judgment, 17 January 2005, para 677). Think of the two typical examples of 'biological destruction': the underlying acts of 'imposing measures intended to prevent births' (ICC Statute, Article 6(d)) and 'forcibly transferring children' (ICC Statute, Article 6(e)), in respect of which a concern for 'severe procreative implication' constitutes the central legislative purpose. Again, I emphasize that this observation stems from the 'in part' component as legally defined by the Trial and Appeals Chambers in *Krstić*. At this juncture, we can take note that how to legally define the 'in part' element has significant implications for the legal characteristic of 'destruction'. Moreover, it also affects the legal classification of the crime of genocide. For this discussion, *see* this chapter, footnote 214 *infra* and Chap. 4, footnote 32 *infra*.

Nine years later in 2010, the relevant legal analysis of the *Popović* et al. Trial Chamber still follows the same pattern as that of the *Krstić* Trial Chamber.[117] Thus, sharing the same factual basis of the Srebrenica massacre with Krstić, the Legal Findings part of the *Popović* et al. Trial Judgment only addresses the issue of 'collective genocide' and collective genocidal intent.[118] As was the case in the *Krstić* Trial Judgment, the *Popović* et al. Trial Chamber, on the basis of its finding on collective genocidal intent, concludes that "genocide was committed by members of the Bosnian Serb forces [...] against the Muslims in Eastern Bosnia, as part of the Bosnian Muslims".[119] The term 'genocide' in this sentence certainly indicates the notion of 'collective genocide'. The Chamber infers the collective genocidal intent possessed by members of the Bosnian Serb Forces, including members of the VRS Main Staff and the Security Branch, in an objective manner from surrounding circumstances that includes: (i) the scale and nature of the murder operation[120]; (ii) the targeting of victims[121]; (iii) the systematic and organized manner of murder operation[122]; (iv) a staggering number of killings occurred on 13 July[123]; (v) widespread locations of detention and killings[124]; (vi) the executioners being many different soldiers belonging to various units[125]; (vii) the killings being carried on for a number of days;[126] (viii) no efforts being made to distinguish between civilians and soldiers[127]; (ix) some children, elderly and infirm being killed[128]; and (x) the frenzied efforts to forcibly transfer the remainder of the population other than military-aged males.[129]

In 2012, the Trial Chamber in *Karadžić*, in its oral decision on Karadžić's motion for a judgment of acquittal pursuant to Rule 98 *bis* of the Rules of Procedure and Evidence, also relied on the notion of 'collective genocide' when it held that "the Chamber finds that there is evidence on which, if accepted, a reasonable trier of fact could be satisfied beyond reasonable doubt that genocide charged pursuant to Article 4 of the [ICTY] Statute was carried out by Bosnian Serb forces in Srebrenica".[130] In reaching this conclusion, the Trial Chamber found only the collective genocidal

---

[117] The *Krstić* Trial Judgment was dated on 2 August 2001 and the *Popović* et al. Trial Judgment was on 10 June 2010.

[118] Prosecutor v. Popović et al., Trial Judgment, 10 June 2010, paras 837–866.

[119] *Ibid*. para 863.

[120] *Ibid*. para 856.

[121] *Ibid*

[122] *Ibid*.

[123] *Ibid*. para 859.

[124] *Ibid*. paras 858–859.

[125] *Ibid*. para 858.

[126] *Ibid*. para 859 (in particular, the Chamber notes that this fact shows a "grim determination to ensure that each and every prisoner would be killed".).

[127] *Ibid*. para 860.

[128] *Ibid*.

[129] *Ibid*. para 862.

[130] Prosecutor v. Karadžić, Transcript, 28 June 2012, pp. 28751–28752.

intent of the Bosnian Serb forces ("the specific intent of such [physical] perpetrators")[131] inferred from the "systematic nature and scale of the crimes committed, as well as the systematic targeting of the group".[132] In this connection, the Chamber mentioned specific facts such as: (i) organized killings "on a large scale, similarly to a military operation"[133]; (ii) "the assistance of local authorities in the burial of bodies after the mass executions"[134]; (iii) "the number of victims killed"[135]; (iv) "the facts that only Bosnian Muslim men and boys were targeted for summary executions"[136]; and (v) "the Bosnian Serb forces tried to kill each and every able-bodied Bosnian Muslim man in Srebrenica".[137] It appears that the *Karadžić* Trial Chamber had no hesitation in using the term 'genocide' when it, in effect, found 'collective genocide' on the basis of collective genocidal intent inferred from collective conducts.[138]

Most recently, following the pattern of the previous ICTY case law, the *Tolimir* Trial Chamber also finds the collective genocidal intent before addressing the question of individual genocidal intent of the accused. Thus, in relation to the killings of able-bodied men and forced transfer of civilian population in Srebrenica and Žepa, the Trial Chamber infers the "specific intent of the Bosnian Serb Forces"[139] from the "scope and nature of […] the killings" of military-aged men and overall context of violence including (i) "the circumstances under which the separation of men in Potocari occurred on 12 and 13 July 1995"[140]; (ii) "the opportunistic killing of one Bosnian man […] [committed] in Potocari on 13 July [1995]"[141]; (iii) "the capture of thousands of Bosnian Muslim men from the column on [13 July 1995]"[142]; and (iv) identification documents of the detained men being collected and burnt.[143] The Trial Chamber ultimately declares the finding of 'collective genocide' when it states that "the Chamber […] found that these criminal acts were committed *with the intent to physically destroy the protected group*, thus amounting to the crime of genocide".[144]

---

[131] *Ibid.* at 28751.

[132] *Ibid.*

[133] *Ibid.*

[134] *Ibid.*

[135] *Ibid.*

[136] *Ibid.*

[137] *Ibid.*

[138] In a later part of the oral decision, the Trial Chamber briefly discusses Karadžić's individual genocidal intent. In finding the individualistic genocidal intent, the Chamber uses the concept of 'shared intent' within the joint criminal enterprise doctrine as a springboard. Thus, the Chamber concludes that "[…] the accused shared the intent of the other members of this joint criminal enterprise to carry out its objectives, including the specific intent to commit genocide […]". Prosecutor v. Karadžić, Transcript, 28 June 2012, p. 28758.

[139] Prosecutor v. Tolimir, Trial Judgment, 12 December 2012, para 769.

[140] *Ibid.*

[141] *Ibid.*

[142] *Ibid.*

[143] *Ibid.*

[144] Prosecutor v. Tolimir, Trial Judgment, 12 December 2012, para 1157.

As seen from these four cases of *Krstić, Popović et al., Karadžić,* and *Tolimir,* the factual and legal analysis of the ICTY in relation to the crime of genocide demonstrates that the Trial Chambers of the ICTY have also had in mind, advertently or inadvertently, the two-layered structure of genocide consisting of 'conduct level' and 'context level'. The case law of the ICTY obviously grasps the crime of genocide in a collective sense (as opposed to an individualistic sense) through the two main concepts of 'collective genocide' and collective genocidal intent. In the next section, let us consider another case of the ICTY in which the Trial Chamber acquitted the accused for lack of evidence showing the 'collective genocide' at the 'context level'.

3.2.2 The Reason for the Jelisić Acquittal: The Absence of 'Collective Genocide'

The factual basis of the *Jelisić* case is different from the *Krstić* case, the *Popović et al.* case and the *Karadžić* case. While the former deals with the events that occurred in Brcko area in 1992, the latter cases are about the Srebrenica massacre in 1995.[145] Defendants who were charged with genocide vis-à-vis the atrocities other than the Srebrenica massacre have been consistently acquitted by the ICTY (on the charge of genocide). Those cases include *Jelisić, Stakić, Sikirica, Brđanin,* and *Karadžić* (Rule 98 *bis* Decision, concerning Count 1). As evident from the evidentiary analysis of the *Jelisić* Appeals Chamber,[146] the Prosecution adduced sufficient evidence before the *Jelisić* Trial Chamber, particularly that of the accused's 'words and deeds', which points at the accused's individual intent to destroy the Muslim group in Brcko area. But the reason why the Trial Chamber, after all, acquitted the accused of the charge of genocide is hinted at by its remark as follows: "The Trial Chamber observes, however, that it will be very difficult in practice to provide proof of the genocidal intent of an individual if the crimes committed are not widespread and if the crime charged is not backed by an organisation or a system".[147] This observation, especially the phrases "widespread ... by an organisation or a system", also reminds us of the contextual element of crimes against humanity.[148] Ultimately, what the Trial Chamber set forth as a reason for its acquittal decision is the absence of 'collective genocide' at the 'context level'

---

[145] Another case law in which the Trial Chamber found the accused guilty of genocide in relation to the Srebrenica massacres is the *Tolimir* case.

[146] Prosecutor v. Jelisić, Appeals Judgment, 5 July 2001, pp. 61–72.

[147] Prosecutor v. Jelisić, Trial Judgment, 14 December 1999, para 101.

[148] ICC Statute, Article 7(2)(a) elaborates on the contextual element of crimes against humanity as follows: "'Attack directed against any civilian population' means a course of conduct involving the multiple commission of acts referred to in para 1 against any civilian population, pursuant to or in furtherance of *a State or organizational policy* to commit such attack". (emphasis added).

which should have provided the Chamber with a contextual basis of finding the accused guilty of genocide at the 'conduct level'.[149] In the end, on the basis of the totality of evidence, the Trial Chamber concludes that "the acts of Goran Jelisić are not the physical expression of an affirmed resolve to destroy in whole or in part a group as such".[150] In supporting this conclusion, the Chamber implicitly observes that the Prosecution failed to prove the 'collective genocide' in Brcko by stating that "[a]ll things considered, the Prosecutor has not established beyond all reasonable doubt that *genocide was committed in Brcko during the period covered by the indictment*".[151] Here, the term "genocide" should be regarded as indicating the 'collective genocide' in respect of which no specific individual perpetrator or perpetrators are identified by the Trial Chamber. The word "genocide" as used by the Chamber in this cited phrase means an overall genocidal campaign launched by anonymous multiple actors with collective genocidal intent at the 'context level'. In view of the relevant part of the judgment, it is especially peculiar to see that the question of whether there existed 'collective genocide' was the pivotal factor in determining the issue of individual genocidal intent of the accused ("affirmed resolve to destroy").[152] In other words, notwithstanding the facts demonstrating a reduced level of the accused's "affirmed resolve to destroy" such as the proof of (i) the accused's "disturbed personality", (ii) acts of random selection of victims, and (iii) issuing laissez-passer to several victims, the main reason for the Trial Chamber's acquittal decision was the lack of evidence showing the 'collective genocide' in Brcko. In this manner, the *Jelisić* Trial Judgment strongly suggests that the essential feature of genocide is 'collective genocide' at the 'context

---

[149] In a similar vein, I think the *Karadžić* Trial Chamber also granted the accused's motion for a judgment of acquittal (concerning Count 1: Genocide in 1992) for this very reason of the absence of evidence showing 'collective genocide'. Have a look at the following text from the Chamber's oral decision (note, in particular, the phrase "in light of the scale and the context of the alleged crimes"): "The Chamber has considered these examples as well as the other evidence received in relation to the accused *in light of the scale and the context of the alleged crimes* in the municipalities in 1992, and the inability to infer genocidal intent from other factors. Following this review, the Chamber finds that notwithstanding the statement of the accused, there is no evidence upon which, if accepted, a reasonable trier of fact could find that the acts of killing, serious bodily or mental harm, and conditions of life inflicted on the Bosnian Muslims and/or Bosnian Croats were perpetrated with the *dolus specialis* required for genocide". Prosecutor v. Karadžić, Transcript, 28 June 2012, p. 28769. In comparison, the Trial Chamber, in the same decision, rejects the accused's motion for acquittal in respect of 'Count 2: Genocide in 1995 at Srebrenica'. This contrast of the Chamber's decision between 'Count 1: Genocide in 1992' and 'Count 2: Genocide in 1995 at Srebrenica' evidently demonstrates the significance of 'collective genocide' in determining on the charge of genocide. That is especially so because the Chamber did not make a particular reference to any difference in terms of Karadžić's inner states of mind in 1992 and in 1995. The phrase "notwithstanding the statement of the accused" in the cited paragraph above even suggests that Karadžić's inner state of mind did not play any significant role for the Chamber's decision on the two charges of genocide.

[150] Prosecutor v. Jelisić, Trial Judgment, 14 December 1999, para 107.

[151] *Ibid.* para 108.

[152] *Ibid.* para 107.

level', rather than the accused's individual genocidal intent at the 'conduct level'.[153] In this respect, it deserves note that the Chamber employs the term "all-inclusive genocide" in order to indicate the 'collective genocide'. In the relevant case law of the *ad hoc* tribunals, this is, to my knowledge, the only occasion where the hidden notion of 'collective genocide' is given a particular name. Thus, the Chamber states, "the Prosecutor has not proved beyond all reasonable doubt that *all-inclusive genocide* was committed in Brcko or elsewhere in May 1992 [...]".[154] A review of the relevant part of the judgment reveals that the key component of this 'all-inclusive genocide' is a collective plan to destroy a group (collective genocidal intent).[155] Moreover, the concept of this 'all-inclusive genocide' functions much like the 'widespread or systematic attack' element of crimes against humanity as the Chamber implies when it concludes the section entitled "the intention to commit 'all-inclusive' genocide" as follows:

> In consequence, the Trial Chamber considers that, in this case, the Prosecutor has not provided sufficient evidence allowing it to be established beyond all reasonable doubt that there existed *a plan to destroy* the Muslim group in Brcko or elsewhere *within which the murders committed by the accused would allegedly fit*.[156]

The italicized phrase clearly represents the logic of crimes against humanity within genocide which requires the underlying acts at the 'conduct level' to be linked to the 'collective genocide' at the 'context level'. For the *Jelisić* Trial Chamber, the terms 'intent' is a synonym for 'plan' as far as the 'collective genocide' or 'all-inclusive genocide' is concerned.[157] The importance of 'collective genocide' at the 'context level' is also emphasized by Claus Kress as follows:

> [W]hen examining the various incidents of atrocities, the Court [International Court of Justice] seemed to inquire into the possible genocidal intent of unnamed individual perpetrators as though such intent could have existed in the absence of a collective genocidal act. In adopting this mode of analysis, the Court made the same error as the Darfur Commission when it considered it possible that certain unnamed individuals acted with genocidal intent *irrespective of the existence of a collective genocidal act*. Instead, the Court should have made it clear that, under normal circumstances, the genocidal intent of the individual perpetrator presupposes his or her knowledge of a collective genocidal act.[158]

---

[153] For a more detailed discussion, *see* Sect. 3.3.3 *infra*.

[154] Prosecutor v. Jelisić, Summary of Trial Chamber Judgment, 14 December 1999, p. 3.

[155] Prosecutor v. Jelisić, Trial Judgment, 14 December 1999, paras 88–98.

[156] *Ibid.* para 98. (emphasis added).

[157] There is another possible way of reading the Trial Chamber's strategy. It might be reasoning as follows: Without a widespread pattern of genocidal acts, it would be impossible for a single individual to destroy a group in whole or in part, or even to contribute to such destruction – because the destruction itself cannot happen. If the individual is sane and rational, he will understand that he cannot singlehandedly destroy the group, and therefore he cannot *intend* to destroy the group. (A rational person cannot intend the impossible.) Therefore, he could not have had genocidal intent. -- If this is the Trial Chamber's reasoning, it is inquiring about the collective genocide only as evidence of Jelisić's individual intention.

[158] Kress 2007, p. 623. (emphasis added).

I understand that the term 'collective genocidal act' in this paragraph conceptually contains both the collective act and collective genocidal intent. In my view, what Kress rightly argues in this paragraph is that, without the 'collective genocide' at the 'context level', an intrinsic logic of genocide does not permit the existence of individual genocidal intent at the 'conduct level'. In this sense, the conceptual framework of genocidal intent has a vertical structure, in particular, a top-down liability-attribution structure. This understanding tends to cast a doubt on the individualistic approach to genocidal intent which assumes a concept of genocidal intent *within* the mind of a perpetrator. That is, what the vertical structure of genocidal intent postulates is an individual genocidal intent *imputed from outside* an individual mind—i.e., from collective genocidal intent that exists at another level.[159] In this scheme of thought, the author or originator of genocidal intent is impersonal.[160]

In short, employing the term "intention to commit all-inclusive genocide"[161] (collective genocidal intent) as opposed to the term "Jelisić's intention to commit genocide"[162] (individual genocidal intent), the *Jelisić* Trial Chamber understands the concept of genocidal intent as basically of a collective nature. Hence, the issue of 'collective genocide' and collective genocidal intent governs the whole section on genocidal intent. Citing an annual report of the International Law Commission,[163] it seems the Chamber explains that genocidal intent can be inferred from the collective conduct committed against a group "as an incremental step in the overall objective of destroying the group".[164] In this connection, it is very important to observe that the Chamber further pronounces two components of genocidal intent when it states,

> It is in fact the *mens rea* which gives genocide its speciality and distinguishes it from an ordinary crime and other crimes against international humanitarian law. The underlying crime or crimes must be characterised as genocide when committed with the intent to destroy, in whole or in part, a national, ethnical, racial or religious group as such. Stated otherwise, [t]he prohibited act must be committed against an individual because of his membership in a particular group and as an incremental step in the overall objective of destroying the group. Two elements which may therefore be drawn from the special intent are:
>
> – that the victims belonged to an identified group;
> – that the alleged perpetrator must have committed his crimes as part of a wider plan to destroy the group as such.[165]

---

[159] There is a seemingly opposing view. George Fletcher and Jens David Ohlin suggest that genocidal intent is to be attributed from an individual perpetrator to the group to which he belongs. Fletcher and Ohlin 2005, p. 546.

[160] Larry May explains that the 'collective intent' involving genocide "is not mere aggregation of [individual] intents, but some type of nonaggregated collective intent". May 2010, p. 116.

[161] Prosecutor v. Jelisić, Trial Judgment, 14 December 1999, p. 28.

[162] *Ibid.* at 31.

[163] Report of the International Law Commission on the Work of Its Forty-Eight Session, May 6-July 26, 1996, at 45, U.N. Doc. A/51/10.

[164] Prosecutor v. Jelisić, Trial Judgment, 14 December 1999, para 66.

[165] *Ibid.* (internal quotation marks omitted).

In accordance with these two elements, the Chamber's subsequent discussion of genocidal intent includes two chapters corresponding to the two elements respectively: (i) a chapter on discriminatory intent[166]; and (ii) a chapter on "all-inclusive genocide" and genocidal plan.[167] The "[t]wo elements" in the cited text above certainly sound like *actus reus*, rather than *mens rea*. This apparent contradiction in which the Chamber appears to understand that the *mens rea* of genocidal intent consists of "two elements" of an objective characteristic demonstrates the reason why collective genocidal intent, rather than individual intent, occupies the center place of the Chamber's discussion on genocidal intent. I think the term *mens rea* as used in connection with genocidal intent in the paragraph cited above is a 'false friend'—i.e., it actually means the objective element of collective genocidal intent which has two objective components. Furthermore, as suggested by the phrase "as part of a wider plan to destroy a group as such", it is to be remembered that the *Jelisić* Trial Chamber constructs the structure of the crime of genocide in a very similar way to that of crimes against humanity, distinguishing the 'conduct level' and the 'context level'. Another paragraph that seems to testify that the Chamber's notion of collective genocidal intent is of an objective characteristic reads,

> [...] the underlying crime is also characterised by the fact that it *is part of* a wider plan to destroy, in whole or in part, the group as such. [...] By killing an individual member of the targeted group, the perpetrator does not thereby only manifest his hatred of the group to which his victim belongs but also knowingly commits this act *as part of* a wider-ranging intention to destroy the national, ethnical, racial or religious group of which the victim is a member.[168]

To sum up: a close reading of the case law of both the ICTR and the ICTY confirms that their genocide jurisprudence contains an unacknowledged contextual element of 'collective genocide', not found in the statutory definition of genocide, that is essential to establishing the individual crime of genocide. In the following section, I shall argue that two-layered understanding the crime of genocide proposed here also sheds light on the "in whole or in part" element of the crime definition.

3.3 'Collective Genocide' and the Substantiality Requirement

3.3.1 Historical Development of the Substantiality Requirement

In relation to the interpretation of the phrase "in whole or in part" in the definition of genocide, it has become a settled jurisprudence of international criminal law

---

[166] *See* Chapter IV.B.1 entitled "Acts committed against victims because of their membership in a national, ethnical, racial or religious group" covering paras 67 through 77 of the Trial Judgment.

[167] *See* Chapter IV.B.2 entitled "The intent to destroy, in whole or in part, the group as such" covering paras 78 through 108 of the Trial Judgment.

[168] Prosecutor v. Jelisić, Trial Judgment, 14 December 1999, para 79. (emphasis added).

that the crime of genocide requires a showing of 'targeting a substantial part' of a protected group (hereinafter 'substantiality requirement'). It was as early as 1950 that Raphael Lemkin used the adjective 'substantial' in terms of the required extent of the 'destruction in part'. In his letter to the Committee on Foreign Relations of the U.S. Senate on the issue of the ratification of the Genocide Convention, Lemkin clarified that "destruction in part must be of a *substantial* nature [...] so as to affect the entirety".[169] He was also of the view that "the [Genocide] Convention applies only to actions undertaken on a mass scale and not to individual acts [...]".[170] Ten years later, Nehemiah Robinson, an early commentator on the Genocide Convention, also observed,

> Therefore, the intent to destroy a multitude of persons of the same group because of their belonging to this group, must be classified as Genocide even if these persons constitute only part of a group either within a country or within a region or within a single community, *provided the number is substantial*; the Convention is intended to deal with *action against large numbers*, not individuals even if they happen to possess the same group characteristics. It will be up to the courts to decide in each case *whether the number was sufficiently large*.[171]

The Whitaker Report of 1985 interprets the phrase "in part" in the definition of genocide as suggesting "a reasonably significant number, relative to the total of the group as a whole, or else a significant section of a group such as its leadership".[172] In 1988, the Proxmire Act of the United States, officially called the Genocide Convention Implementation Act of 1987, takes a more direct way to solidify the substantiality requirement by inserting it into the definition of its own version of genocide itself: "with the specific intent to destroy, *in whole or in substantial part*, a national, ethnic, racial, or religious group as such".[173] In 1996, the International Law Commission further elaborated the meaning of "in part" by stating,

> [T]he intention must be to destroy a group "in whole or in part". It is not necessary to intend to achieve the complete annihilation of a group from every corner of the globe. None the less the crime of genocide by its very nature requires the intention to destroy *at least a substantial part* of a particular group.[174]

---

[169] 2 Executive Sessions of the Senate Foreign Relations Committee, Historical Series, p. 370 (1976), *as cited in* LeBlanc 1991, p. 44, footnote 21.

[170] 2 Executive Sessions of the Senate Foreign Relations Committee, Historical Series, p. 370 (1976), *as cited in* LeBlanc 1991, p. 45, footnote 23. *See also* Lemkin 1947, p. 151 ("[...] especially in cases where such tensions result in large scale criminality".).

[171] Robinson 1960, p. 63. (emphasis added). A commentator supports the substantiality requirement suggested by Robinson mainly in view of the aim of the Genocide Convention to "deal with action against large numbers of people". LeBlanc 1984, p. 372.

[172] Benjamin Whitaker, Revised and Updated Report on the question of the Prevention and Punishment of the Crime of Genocide, UN Doc. E/CN.4/Sub.2/1985/6, 2 July 1985, para 29.

[173] The Genocide Convention Implementation Act of 1987, 18 U.S.C. § 1091(a) (1988). (emphasis added). *See also* 18 U.S.C. § 1093(8) (2006) ("the term "substantial part" means a part of a group of such numerical significance that the destruction or loss of that part would cause the destruction or loss of that part would cause the destruction of the group as a viable entity within the nation of which such group is a part".).

[174] Report of the International Law Commission on the Work of Its Forty-Eight Session, May 6-July 26, 1996, at 45, U.N. Doc. A/51/10.

In this paragraph, it appears what is signified by the phrase "genocide by its very nature" is connected to the observation made by Lemkin that the Genocide Convention "applies only to actions undertaken on a mass scale [...]". In the same vein, the Special Rapporteur Ruhashyankiko states, "[...] the *prime object* of [the Genocide Convention] is clearly defined: the prevention and punishment of genocide as an act committed with intent to destroy *a large number of persons* belonging to the groups specified or the group in its entirety".[175]

On the basis of the views opined by these commentators, the jurisprudence of the ICTY and the ICTR firmly established the substantiality requirement. Acknowledging that "there is no numeric threshold of victims necessary to establish genocide",[176] the case law of the *ad hoc* tribunals is consistent in requiring a targeting of a *substantial part* of a protected group for the purpose of fulfilling the "in whole or in part" requirement, which would ultimately satisfy the genocidal intent element. The *Krstić* Appeals Chamber observes, "[...] [T]he substantiality requirement both captures genocide's defining character as a crime of massive proportions and reflects the Convention's concern with the impact the destruction of the targeted part will have on the overall survival of the group".[177] In the jurisprudence of the ICTY, after a period of confusion,[178] it was the *Jelisić* Trial Chamber that first addressed the substantiality requirement. To answer the self-imposed question of "what proportion of the group is marked for destruction, and beyond what threshold could the crime be qualified as genocide?",[179] the Trial Chamber observes, "[g]iven the goal of the [Genocide] Convention to deal with mass

---

[175] Nicodème Ruhashyankiko, Study on the Question of the Prevention and Punishment of the Crime of Genocide, UN Doc. E/CN.4/Sub.2/416 (1978), para 54. (emphasis added). *See also* Lippman 1998, p. 464 ("[r]equiring an intent to exterminate a "substantial part" of a group is intended to limit genocide to mass atrocities".); Bantekas 2010, p. 207 ("Since genocide is a mass-victim offence, the part targeted must be a substantial part of the group".); Nersessian 2010, p. 41 ("Most authorities indicate that 'in part' really means 'in *substantial* part'. The reading-in of 'substantial' arises out of the search for a practical way to distinguish genocide (a large-scale crime against a protected group) from ordinary 'hate' or 'bias' crimes (attacks on individuals because of their membership in that group). The modifier is one way to distinguish matters of international concern and to reserve 'genocide' for large-scale atrocities".).

[176] Prosecutor v. Semanza, Trial Judgment, 15 May 2003, para 316. This view had been subsequently cited by other judgments with approval. *See e.g.*, Prosecutor v. Muhimana, Trial Judgment, 28 April 2005, para 498; Prosecutor v. Gacumbitsi, Trial Judgment, 17 June 2004, para 253.

[177] Prosecutor v. Krstić, Appeals Judgment, 19 April 2004, para 8.

[178] An early case law of the ICTY in which the 'targeting substantial part' requirement stemming from the phrase 'in whole or in part' was not fully taken into account by judges is: Prosecutor v. Karadžić and Mladić, Review of the Indictments pursuant to Rule 61 of the Rules of Procedure and Evidence, 11 July 1996, para 92 ("According to [the] definition [of genocide], genocide requires that acts be perpetrated against a group with an aggravated criminal intent, namely, that of destroying the group in whole or in part. The degree to which the group was destroyed in whole or in part is not necessary to conclude that genocide has occurred. That one of the acts enumerated in the definition was perpetrated with a specific intent suffices".). Certainly, this position is not valid any more due to the subsequent jurisprudential development of the substantiality requirement.

[179] Prosecutor v. Jelisić, Trial Judgment, 14 December 1999, para 80.

crimes, it is widely acknowledged that the intention to destroy must target at least a substantial part of the group".[180] Proposing two tests of the quantitative approach and the qualitative approach to determine the substantiality requirement, the *Krstić* Trial Chamber states that "an intent to destroy only part of the group must nevertheless concern a substantial part thereof, either numerically or qualitatively".[181] The *Sikirica* Trial Chamber also explains that "[t]his part of the definition [i.e.—"in part"] calls for evidence of an intention to destroy a reasonably substantial number relative to the total population of the group".[182] The jurisprudence on the ICTR side also says the same. The Trial Chamber in *Kayishema and Ruzindana* states that "'in part' requires the intention to destroy a considerable number of individuals who are part of the group".[183] The *Bagilishema* Trial Judgment observes that "[a]lthough the destruction sought need not be directed at every member of the targeted group, the Chamber considers that the intention to destroy must target at least a substantial part of the group".[184] This line of jurisprudence has been consistently affirmed by subsequent case law[185] to the extent that the recent case law of the ICTR uses a set phrase of "in whole or in substantial part" instead of "in whole or in part".[186] The ICJ also acknowledges the substantiality requirement when it states, "the intent must be to destroy at least a substantial part of the particular group".[187]

---

[180] *Ibid.* para 82.

[181] Prosecutor v. Krstić, Trial Judgment, 2 August 2001, para 634.

[182] Prosecutor v. Sikirica et al., Judgement on Defence Motions to Acquit, 3 September 2001, para 65. The Chamber expresses its preference of the term "reasonably substantial" to "reasonably significant" without explaining why. *Ibid.*

[183] Prosecutor v. Kayishema and Ruzindana, Trial Judgment, 21 May 1999, para 97.

[184] Prosecutor v. Bagilishema, Trial Judgment, 7 June 2001, para 64.

[185] *See e.g.,* Prosecutor v. Simba, Trial Judgment, 13 December 2005, para 412; Prosecutor v. Muvunyi, Trial Judgment, 12 September 2006, para 479; Prosecutor v. Karemera et al., Trial Judgment, 2 February 2002, para 1606; Prosecutor v. Ndahimana, Trial Judgment, 30 December 2011, para 803.

[186] Prosecutor v. Nzabonimana, Trial Judgment, 31 May 2012, paras 1707, 1716, 1724, 1726, 1728, 1732, 1734 and 1736 ("intent to destroy, in whole or in substantial part, the Tutsi ethnic group, as such"); Prosecutor v. Nyiramasuhuko et al., Trial Judgment, 24 June 2011, paras 5773, 5792 and 5844 ("intent to destroy, in whole or in substantial part, the Tutsi group"); Prosecutor v. Ndindiliyimana et al., Trial Judgment, 17 May 2011, paras 2078 and 2081 ("specific intent to destroy, in whole or in substantial part, the Tutsi group"); Prosecutor v. Munyakazi, Trial Judgment, 5 July 2010, para 499 ("intent to destroy, in whole or in substantial part, the local population of Tutsi civilians"); Prosecutor v. Setako, Trial Judgment, 25 February 2010, para 472 ("intent to destroy, in whole or in substantial part, the Tutsi group"); Prosecutor v. Nsengimana, Trial Judgment, 17 October 2009, para 836 ("intent to destroy, in whole or in substantial part, the Tutsi group"); Prosecutor v. Rukundo, Trial Judgment, 27 February 2009, para 575 ("intent to destroy, in whole or in substantial part, the Tutsi ethnic group".); Prosecutor v. Bagosora et al., Trial Judgment, 18 December 2008, paras 2125, 2134 and 2138 ("intent to destroy, in whole or in substantial part, the Tutsi group.).

[187] Application of Convention on Prevention and Punishment of Crime of Genocide (Bosn. & Herz. v. Serb. & Montenegro), 2007 I.C.J. 91, para 198 (Feb. 26).

3.3.2 Objectifying 'in Whole or in Part'?: Contextual Element of Genocide

As to this consistent case law interpretation of the phrase "in whole or in part", it should be borne in mind that the primary objective of the substantiality requirement in the relevant international jurisprudence is to define the genocidal intent element. The main difficulty involving the substantiality requirement is the true nature of the genocidal intent element to be established thereby: Is it an individual genocidal intent or its collective counterpart? I believe the answer is that the genocidal intent is both individual and collective. An individual cannot truly intend what he knows is impossible especially when his 'bad mind' involves committing a core international crime. Therefore, he cannot intend to destroy a substantial part of a group unless he is acting within the context of a genocidal campaign capable of destroying a substantial part of the group. Individual genocidal intent makes sense only in the context of collective genocidal intent, that is, the genocidal intent with which the genocidal campaign is being waged by a collective.

At this juncture, it is to be noted that the two-layered structure of the crime of genocide has another advantage besides providing a better analysis of genocidal intent as a combination of collective and individual intent. That is, the two-layered structure also facilitates a more solid and objectified understanding of the "in whole or in part" component of genocidal intent.[188] Moreover, with the adoption of the 'manifest pattern of similar conduct' element in the ICC Elements of Crimes, it appears this objectified approach to the "in whole or in part" requirement keeps pace with the relevant development of the law of genocide. The chapeau of Article 6 of the ICC Statute, reproducing verbatim the definition of genocide from Article II of the Genocide Convention, provides,

> [...] "genocide" means any of the following acts committed *with intent to destroy, in whole or in part*, a national, ethnical, racial or religious group, *as such*: (emphasis added)

It seems the plain reading of this definition tells us that the *mens rea* of genocidal intent has three components: (i) "to destroy"; (ii) "in whole or in part"; and (iii) "group, as such". That is, apparently, the general picture that we usually visualize when we hear the word 'genocide'—i.e., 'mass killing (destruction)' of 'numerous victims ("in whole or in part")' 'because they are members of a particular group ("group, as such")'—does not belong to *actus reus*, but solely to the *mens rea* of the crime of genocide. Put otherwise, literally speaking, one might say that the egregious event we usually depict in our mind in connection with the term 'genocide' is not required to take place in reality in order to constitute the crime of genocide. Instead, on the basis of a literal understanding of the crime definition, it

---

[188] The *Krstić* Appeals Chamber is of the view that the genocidal intent and the requirement of 'targeting a whole or a substantial part of a group' constitute the two key elements of genocide. Prosecutor v. Krstić, Appeals Judgment, 19 April 2004, para 37. For more discussion, *see* this Chapter, footnote 220 *infra* and accompanying text.

is legally sufficient if the atrocious event is harbored by the perpetrator in his or her mind (with a single commission of an underlying act). Such was the view of the *Mpambara* Trial Chamber when it stated,

> The *actus reus* of genocide does not require the actual destruction of a substantial part of the group; the commission of even a single instance of one of the prohibited acts is sufficient, *provided that the accused genuinely intends* by that act to destroy at least a substantial part of the group.[189]

In a similar vein, Antonio Cassese and his co-authors observe,

> Clearly, the murder of dozens of Muslims, Kurds, or Jews may be termed genocide if the required special intent is present, regardless of whether the general purpose of destroying the group as such is achieved.[190]

The *travaux préparatoires* of the Genocide Convention also recorded that the French delegation ardently argued that, if there existed a genocidal intent, an attack on a single individual could still constitute the crime of genocide.[191]

Most of other delegations, however, opposed the French proposal, observing *inter alia* that, "when a single individual was affected, it was a case of homicide [i.e., just a domestic crime as opposed to an international crime], whatever the intention of the perpetrator of the crime might be".[192] Ultimately, the French dele-

---

[189] Prosecutor v. Mpambara, Trial Judgement, 12 September 2006, para 8. (emphasis added). As will be addressed in detail in Sect. 3.4 *infra*, the ICC Pre-Trial Chamber in *Al Bashir* also mistakenly understands that the case law of the ICTY and the ICTR is of the view that the crime of genocide becomes applicable upon a completion of an underlying act against a single victim with genocidal intent.

[190] Cassese et al. 2013, p. 45.

[191] U.N. GAOR, 6th Comm., 3d Sess., 73d mtg. at 90–92, U.N. Doc. A/C.6/SR.73 (Oct. 13, 1948). The French delegation explained that its amendment proposal specially kept in mind the victim of genocide (as opposed to the perpetrator thereof). Indeed, the French delegation submitted an amendment to the Draft Article of the Ad Hoc Committee in which it was proposed that the phrase "acts committed with the intention to destroy a [...] group" be replaced with the phrase "an attack on life directed against a human group, or against an individual as a member of a human group [...]". *Ibid.* at 91. Pieter Drost is of a similar view. He argues that, if a perpetrator's *mens rea* is directed against a multiplicity of victims, his act of killing only one member of a group can still constitute genocide. In Drost's understanding, genocide is indeed a 'crime of *mens rea*'. He further observes that, provided that killing only one member of a group is committed "with a connecting aim" (or "with the intent to commit similar acts in the future and in connection with the first crime"), a single homicide constitutes genocide. Drost 1959, pp. 84–86. This idea has been well reflected in the German Code of Crimes against International Law (CCAIL) of 2002 which provides the underlying acts of genocide as follows: "1. Kills *a member* of the group"; "2. Causes serious bodily or mental harm to *a member* of the group [...]"; and "Forcibly transfers *a child* of the group to another group". (emphasis added). In the Genocide Convention and other international instruments, these italicized nouns were provided in the plural form. English translation of the CCAIL is available at http://www.iuscomp.org/gla/statutes/VoeStGB.pdf. Accessed 23 December 2015. For more explanation of the CCAIL, *see* Wirth 2003, p. 156.

[192] U.N. GAOR, 6th Comm., 3d Sess., 73d mtg. at 92, U.N. Doc. A/C.6/SR.73 (13 October 1948). For a similar view, *see* Shaw 1989, p. 806 ("The killing of an individual or small number of individuals remains murder, depending upon the circumstances of the case, and it would be unwise to blur the line between this and the unique crime of genocide".).

gation agreed with the views of other delegations.[193] It is at this juncture that the Norwegian proposal of inserting the phrase "in whole or in part" was widely acclaimed by many delegations.[194] Thus, the drafting history reveals that the phrase "in whole or in part" currently included in the definition of genocide does not contemplate a "part" consisting of a single victim or even a small number of victims, despite the confusing wording of "one or more persons" in the ICC Elements of Crimes.[195] In other words, contrary to the *Mpambara* Trial Chamber's observation that "[t]he *actus reus* of genocide does not require the actual destruction of a substantial part of the group", something in the concept of genocide, be it *actus reus*, *mens rea* or whatever, requires a material fact of at least more than an attack on a single member of a group or a small number of group members.

In this context, it should be borne in mind that excluding an attack on a lone victim from the conceptual realm of genocide is correct only when the attack is considered at the 'context level'. Thus, if the entire campaign kills only one member of the targeted group, it cannot constitute a genocidal context, and the killing cannot count as genocide regardless of the individual perpetrator's subjective intention. But if the campaign as a whole kills a substantial part of the group, a specific defendant's individual act of killing only one person could still constitute genocide.[196] Such was the reasoning of the Trial Chamber in *Ndindabahizi* when it claimed,

> Whether by killing [a single victim named] Nors the attackers intended to destroy the Tutsi ethnic group, in whole or in part, must be assessed *within the context of* ethnic killing in Rwanda at the time. [...] The fact that only a single person was killed on this occasion does not negate the perpetrators' clear intent, which was to destroy the Tutsi population of Kibuye and of Rwanda, in whole or in part. Accordingly, the killers of Nors committed genocide.[197]

The phrase "within the context of" (reminding us of the wording "the conduct took place *in the context of* a manifest pattern of similar conduct" in the ICC Elements of Crimes) clearly points at the logic of crimes against humanity (the

---

[193] U.N. GAOR, 6th Comm., 3d Sess., 73d mtg. at 93, U.N. Doc. A/C.6/SR.73 (13 October 1948).

[194] *Ibid.* at 92–93.

[195] ICC Elements of Crimes, Article 6(a), 1st element; Article 6(b), 1st element; Article 6(c), 1st element; Article 6(d), 1st element; Article 6(e), 1st element.

[196] Prosecutor v. Akayesu, Trial Judgment, 2 September 1998, para 521 ("[...] for any of the acts charged under Article 2(2) of the Statute to be a constitutive element of genocide, the act must have been committed against one or several individuals [...]").

[197] Prosecutor v. Ndindabahizi, Trial Judgement, 15 July 2004, paras 470–471. (emphasis added).

nexus between the 'conduct level' and the 'context level') within genocide.[198] In this respect, the relevant discussion during the drafting negotiations of the ICC Elements of Crimes is summarized by a commentator as follows:

> [...] the five forms of genocide are referred to in the plural (e.g., killing of *members* of the group or forcibly transferring *children* of the group to another group) [in the definition of genocide], whereas it was agreed [during the drafting negotiations of the ICC Elements of Crimes] that the Elements of Crimes, which deal with individually accused persons, would have recognized *a single act* (e.g., a single murder) as genocide, *if the requisite context was present*.[199]

We learn from this explanation that the wording of "one or more persons" in the Elements of Crimes was cautiously selected by the drafters. In doing so, they took into account the two-layered structure of genocide. That is, in the paragraph cited above, while the phrase "a single act (e.g., a single murder)" signifies the 'conduct level', "if the requisite context was present" indicates the 'context level'. The five underlying acts against a single victim in the Elements of Crimes ("*one* or more persons") are reconciled with the plural form of genocide in Article 6 of the ICC Statute (e.g., "killing *members* of the group"; and "forcibly transferring *children*") through the 'context level' of "a manifest pattern of similar conduct".[200] In this sense, the substantiality requirement (interpreting the phrase "in whole or in part" as 'targeting at least a substantial part of group') comes to be significantly overlapping with the objective 'context level', not exclusively confined to the subjective *mens rea* of the individual perpetrator. In sum, the 'in whole or in part' requirement, be it a *mens rea* or an *actus reus*, tends to provide a conceptual platform for an objective contextual element of genocide to take root. I believe the substantiality requirement and the contextual element of genocide should be conceptually dealt

---

[198] *See also* Prosecutor v. Mpambara, Trial Judgement, 12 September 2006, para 8 ("[genocidal] [i]ntent may be proven by [...] drawing inference from circumstantial evidence, such as *any connection to a wide-scale attack* against the targeted group".). (emphasis added). Payam Akhavan is of the view that the introduction of the 'manifest pattern of similar conduct' requirement to the ICC Elements of Crimes "seems to merge genocide more closely with crimes against humanity [...]". Akhavan 2012, p. 46. It is further to be noted that Akhavan thinks this new requirement "amends and restricts the scope of genocide as envisaged in both international conventional and customary law". *Ibid.* Yet, in view of the supplementary role of the ICC Elements of Crimes as provided in Article 9(1) of the ICC Statute and also of the absence of any ICC case law from which we can deduce the new requirement's legal effect, it seems to me that it is too early to talk about whether it amends and restricts the scope of genocide.

[199] Oosterveld 2001, p. 45. (emphasis added).

[200] For a similar view, *see* Jørgensen 2001, p. 299 ("Article 6(1) of the ICC Elements of Crimes provides that genocide may be committed if the perpetrator killed *one or more* persons. Thus it seems that, in principle, an individual perpetrator may be found guilty of genocide on the basis of a single act of killing as long as this act is part of a pattern resulting in the destruction of a significant part of the targeted group".).

with together,[201] which would result in an objectification of the "in whole or in part" requirement. Or, rather, it might be more accurate to say that the objectified understanding of the "in whole or in part" requirement better reflects the "very nature" of genocide applicable "only to actions undertaken on a mass scale" that inherently and necessarily accompanies the 'context level'. In this connection, the substantiality requirement plays a similar role to that of the qualifier 'widespread or systematic' in the contextual element of crimes against humanity. We can see the 'targeting of a substantial part' and 'widespread or systematic' with our bare eyes. Their existences are to be verified objectively. In short, the requirement of 'in whole or in part' that is, literally speaking, contained within the *mens rea* of 'intent to destroy' has been objectified firstly through the substantiality requirement developed by the case law of the ICTY and the ICTR, and secondly by virtue of the 'manifest pattern of similar conduct' requirement of the ICC Elements of Crimes.[202]

It was destined to be so because genocide is not a 'crime of *mens rea*', but an international crime that can be committed only within objective contextual circumstances of a legally meaningful scale. As the British delegation voiced during the drafting negotiations of the Genocide Convention, killing only one person is just a domestic crime of homicide however egregious the killer's mind had been.[203] Thus, the proposition that the crime of genocide is "completed by, *inter alia*, killing or causing serious bodily harm to a single individual"[204] is valid only when a substantial part of a group is objectively targeted at the 'context level'.

---

[201] A similar view was expressed by the *Gacumbitsi* Appeals Chamber as follows: "In the Appeals Chamber's view, it is appropriate and consistent with the Tribunal's jurisprudence to consider, in determining whether the Appellant meant to target a sufficiently substantial part of the Tutsi population to amount to genocide, that the Appellant's actions took place within the context of other culpable acts systematically directed against the Tutsi population". Prosecutor v. Gacumbitsi, Appeals Judgment, 7 July 2006, para 44. The *Gacumbitsi* Appeals Chamber explains that the primary purpose of considering whether a substantial part of a group is targeted is to make a decision on the issue of genocidal intent. The Chamber also clarifies that, in order to determine whether the substantial part of a group is targeted, the nexus between the accused acts and the context of a systematic attack on a group launched by other participants can be taken into account by the Trial Chamber. In other words, the reasoning takes a route of (i) affirming the context, and then (ii) affirming a substantial part having been targeted, and then, ultimately (iii) affirming the genocidal intent. Thus the ultimate destination in the relevant discussion of the *Gacumbitsi* Appeals Chamber vis-à-vis the substantiality requirement is the decision on genocidal intent. *See also* Prosecutor v. Krstić, Trial Judgment, 2 August 2001, para 581 ("Since in this case primarily the Bosnian Muslim men of military age were killed, a second issue is whether this group of victims represented a sufficient part of the Bosnian Muslim group *so that* the intent to destroy them qualifies as an "intent to destroy the group in whole or in part" under Article 4 of the Statute".). (emphasis added).

[202] William Schabas claims that, given the "weight of the opinion of states" reflected in the Elements of Crimes, international judges should consider the manifest pattern element seriously. Schabas 2012, p. 142.

[203] *See* this chapter, footnote 192 *supra*.

[204] Prosecutor v. Al Bashir, Decision on the Prosecution's Application for a Warrant of Arrest against Omar Hassan Ahmed Al Bashir, 4 March 2009, para 119 (the ICC Pre-Trial Chamber in *Al Bashir* observes that, according to the case law of the ICTY and the ICTR, "the crime of genocide is completed by, *inter alia*, killing or causing serious bodily harm to a single individual with the intent to destroy in whole or in part the group to which such individual belongs".).

3.3.3 Essence of Genocide? Destruction, Result and Substantiality

It is widely understood that the mental state of the perpetrator (genocidal intent) is decisive in determining whether an act constitutes genocide, while the result of actual destruction has hardly been emphasized.[205] This individual mental state is characterized by its destructive orientation towards a protected group. Here is the point where we can understand why the crime of genocide is called "a crime of *mens rea*".[206] In particular, it is generally said that the mental element framework of the crime of genocide is twofold: the general *mens rea* scheme under Article 30 of the ICC Statute (intent or knowledge) applicable to the underlying acts and the "intent to destroy"—i.e., genocidal intent. As some commentators put it, while *mens rea* in the first category must attend a specific *actus reus* (e.g., as for Article 6(a) of the ICC Statute, intent to engage in the 'conduct' of killing, and intent or knowledge in respect of the 'consequence' of death),[207] the genocidal intent does

---

[205] *See e.g.*, Robinson 1960, p. 59 ("The majority of the Human Rights Commission, however, was of the opinion that there was no Genocide without intent and that, if intent was absent, act would become simple homicide. Therefore, according to the wording of Article II, acts of destruction would not be classified as Genocide unless the intent to destroy the group existed or could be proven *regardless of the results achieved*".).

[206] *See* Lemkin 1947, p. 147 ("All [genocidal] actions are subordinated to the criminal intent to destroy or to cripple permanently a human group".); Prosecutor v. Al Bashir, Decision on the Prosecution's Application for a Warrant of Arrest against Omar Hassan Ahmed Al Bashir, 4 March 2009, p. 43, footnote 140; Cassese 2002, p. 338; Cryer et al. 2010, pp. 182–185; Zahar and Sluiter 2007, pp. 172–173. Prosecutor v. Stakić, Trial Judgment, 31 July 2003, para 522 ("The key factor is the specific intent to destroy the group rather than its actual physical destruction. [...] [I]t is not necessary to establish, with the assistance of a demographer, the size of the victimised population in numerical terms. It is the genocidal *dolus specialis* that predominantly constitutes the crime".).

[207] The general rule of criminal law both in the Anglo-American and the Continental traditions is that criminal responsibility should be based on a connection between guilty act (*actus reus*) and guilty mind (*mens rea*). *See, e.g.*, Bohlander 2009, p. 60 ("The required intent is always tied to the ambit of the individual offence and according to § 16 [of the German Criminal Code] it means being aware of the statutory elements of the offence".); Simester and Sullivan 2010, p. 126 ("The first step [to establish whether a defendant has *mens rea*] is to determine what *mens rea* standard is required in respect of each separate element of the *actus reus*".); American Law Institute, Model Penal Code, § 2.02 (1) ("[...] a person is not guilty of an offense unless he acted purposely, knowingly, recklessly or negligently, as the law may require, with respect to each material element of the offense".); Request from the Governments of Belgium, Finland, Hungary, Mexico, the Republic of Korea and South Africa and the Permanent Observer Mission of Switzerland to the United Nations regarding the text prepared by the International Committee of the Red Cross on the mental element in the common law and civil law systems and on the concepts of mistake of fact and mistake of law in national and international law, Preparatory Comm'n for the Int'l Criminal Court, Working Group on Elements of Crimes, at 4, U.N. Doc. PCNICC/1999/WGEC/INF/2/Add.4 (15 December 1999) ("In all modern criminal law systems an actor must fulfill two elements to be held criminally responsible: (1) through his behavior he must have caused a certain state of affairs forbidden by criminal law (*actus reus*); (2) he must have had a defined state of mind

not attend any.[208] That is to say, the 'destruction' is not a material element of 'consequence' in the legal structure of the crime of genocide.[209] Instead, according to this analysis, the notion of 'destruction' is conceptually contained in the *mens rea* of genocidal intent and forms part thereof as a component.[210]

Yet, as seen thus far, the jurisprudence of the ICTY and the ICTR treats 'destruction' as a quasi-element of genocide by requiring that at least a *substantial part* of a group be targeted.[211] Hence, the relevant case law often uses such a phrase as "with intent to destroy a substantial part of the targeted group".[212] Indeed, the International Law Commission defines the term 'destruction' as the "material destruction of a group either by physical or by biological means".[213] Consequently, in practice, this quasi-element of 'destruction' plays a role of turning the crime of genocide into a sort of 'result-crime' by requiring the proof of the

---

Footnote 207 (continued)

in relation to the causing of the event or state of affairs (*mens rea*)".); Report of the Preparatory Comm'n for the Int'l Criminal Court, Finalized Draft Text of the Elements of Crimes, Article 6, U.N. Doc. PCNICC/2000/1/Add.2 (2 November 2000), General Introduction, para 2 ([…] a person shall be criminally responsible and liable for punishment for a crime within the jurisdiction of the Court only if the material elements are committed with intent and knowledge".).

[208] Kress 2005, p. 568 ("Where an intent has no point of reference in the *actus reus*, as is the case with genocidal intent …"). *See also* Choi and Kim 2011, pp. 602–603.

[209] *See* Prosecutor v. Ndindabahizi, Trial Judgement, 15 July 2004, para 454 ("The actual destruction of a substantial part of the group is not a required material element of the offence, but may assist in determining whether the accused intended to bring about that result".).

[210] Prosecutor v. Krajišnik, Trial Judgment, 27 September 2006, para 854 ("Destruction as a component of the *mens rea* of genocide"); Zahar and Sluiter 2007, p. 179 ("… 'destruction', as a component of the *mens rea* of genocide").

[211] For seemingly a differing view, *see* Cupido 2014, pp. 7–8 ("[…] the ad hoc tribunals assume a close *evidentiary* relationship between the accused's genocidal intent and the existence of a collective act. This does not, however, imply that the finding of a genocidal campaign or plan also forms a *legal* element of genocide".). (emphasis in original). Accordingly, Marjolein Cupido acknowledges the *theoretical* possibility of one-man genocide. Yet, she also considers that one-man genocide "diverges to such an extent from the prototypical genocide [e.g., Holocaust] that it will be difficult to classify [the one-man genocide]" under the category of the crime of genocide. *Ibid.* at 34.

[212] Prosecutor v. Gacumbitsi, Trial Judgment, 17 June 2004, para 258. *See also* Prosecutor v. Krajišnik, Trial Judgment, 27 September 2006, para 853 ("Thus the indictment alleges intent to achieve destruction "in part". This can be proven only if the intent to destroy a substantial part of the protected group is proven".); United Nations Diplomatic Conference of Plenipotentiaries on the Establishment of an International Criminal Court, Rome, 15 June – 17 July 1998, Official Records, Reports and other documents, A/CONF. 183/13 (Vol. III), p. 14, footnote 10 ("The reference to "intent to destroy, in whole or in part, a … group, as such" was understood to refer to the specific intention to destroy more than a small number of individuals who are members of a group".).

[213] Report of the International Law Commission on the Work of Its Forty-Eight Session, May 6-July 26, 1996, at 46, U.N. Doc. A/51/10. Explaining the drafting history of excluding the 'cultural genocide' from the crime definition in the Genocide Convention, the ILC further emphasizes that the term 'destruction' "must be taken only in its material sense, its physical or biological sense". *Ibid.* It is to be noted that the ILC classifies subparagraphs (a) to (c) of Article II of the Genocide Convention as "acts of physical genocide"; and (d) and (e) as "acts of biological genocide". *Ibid.*

destructive consequences of such targeting upon at least a substantial part of a group[214] – and, as we have seen, that normally requires that a genocidal campaign larger than the actions of the individual perpetrator must be taking place. That tends to relocate the nature of that 'destruction' closer to an *actus reus*. This apparent contradiction between the normative character (*mens rea*) and the practical function (*actus reus*) of the quasi-element of 'destruction' can be reconciled in the conceptual framework of the two-layered structure of genocide. That is because, in the two-layered structure, the quasi-element of the 'targeting a substantial part of a group' no longer stands in the dubious spot between *mens rea* and *actus reus*. Instead, it comes to legitimately form part of an objective contextual element of genocide. That yields a more refined legal construction of the key features of the crime of genocide—in particular, the aspect of a collective campaign of violence accompanying a partial destruction of a group—as observed by Claus Kress as follows,

> [I]t is not such a desire of an individual that hallmarks genocide as the horrible crime it is. It is the dimension of the collective genocidal goal that every individual participant takes the conscious decision to further. The laudable intention not to distort the character of genocide as "one of the worst crimes known to humankind" by an unduly generous interpretation is thus *better served by a stringent construction of the words "destroy" and "in part"* than by insisting on a flawed understanding of genocidal intent.[215]

---

[214] In this context, it is to be noted that I use the term 'result-crime' with caution, because of the extended scope of the notion of 'result', which conceptually puts the crime of genocide on the verge of the offence of endangerment. That is, the 'destruction' as a result of a genocidal campaign conceptually encompasses a destructive consequence in the remote future at least one generation away. Such was the case when the Trial Chamber and the Appeals Chamber in *Krstić* took into account the "severe procreative implications" to be caused by the mass killing of the Bosnian Muslim men of military age at Srebrenica in respect of the expected destruction of the part ('in part': 'Bosnian Muslims in Srebrenica') of the group ('in whole': 'Bosnian Muslims'). Prosecutor v. Krstić, Appeals Judgment, 19 April 2004, para 28. In this respect, as I pointed out previously, what mattered most in *Krstić* was the 'biological destruction' expected to occur in the remote future, because the 'part' that conceptually connected to the 'destruction' was not the men of military age at Srebrenica, but the Bosnian Muslims in Srebrenica. If the 'part' as conceived by the Prosecution and the Chambers had been the men of military age at Srebrenica, it should have been the 'physical destruction' (as opposed to the 'biological destruction') that guided the relevant legal discussion. In this regard, *see also* this chapter, footnote 116 *supra*. Accordingly, the crime of genocide as interpreted by the Trial and Appeals Chamber in *Krstić* might rather be characterized as a 'conduct-crime' (as opposed to 'result-crime') and 'offence of causing a danger (endangerment offence)' (as opposed to 'offence of causing a definite harm'). In general, the concept of 'biological destruction' presumes the destructive consequence in the remote future from the time of 'imposing measures intended to prevent births within the group' (ICC Statute, Article 6(d)) or 'forcibly transferring children of the group to another group' (ICC Statute, art 6(e)), which renders the crime of genocide based on these two underlying acts 'an offence of causing a danger (endangerment offence)'.

[215] Kress 2006, p. 497. Note that Kress is making this argument for the purpose of advocating the knowledge-based approach to interpreting genocidal intent, while challenging the purpose-based approach.

The way I see it, what is stressed in this paragraph is that the essence of genocide as being a *collective* endeavor geared towards a destruction of a group best *manifests itself* through the substantiality requirement, rather than through the element of individualistic genocidal intent. In this sense, the crime of genocide, particularly at the 'context level', should be understood as a result-crime[216] in respect of which the extent of a destructive *consequence* is required to be quantitatively or qualitatively measured through the scale of 'targeting a substantial part of a group'.[217] In a similar vein, characterizing genocide as an "intentional result crime",[218] Hans Vest states that "[a]s such an extended mental element, the intent to destroy is referring to the conduct *and* result of a collective action".[219] Although it is true that, literally speaking, the phrase "in whole or in part" is a component of *mens rea* ("with intent to destroy…"), the fundamentally *collective* nature of the crime of genocide ceaselessly pushes the "in whole or in part" requirement away

---

[216] It is to be noted that I confine this legal characterization of 'result-crime' only to the cases of 'physical destruction'. In respect of 'biological destruction', I would rather legally classify those cases as 'conduct-crime' and 'endangerment crime', in view of the attribute of 'remote harm' involved therein. Given the recent worldwide trend of introducing 'remote harm' offences in response to global terrorist activities, the Genocide Convention should be regarded as a pioneer in criminalizing conduct of 'remote harm' as reflected in the underlying acts of 'biological destruction' more than a half century ago.
As to my argument for viewing genocide as a result-crime, the word 'targeting' might pose some conceptual difficulties. What I mean is that the act of 'targeting' itself seems to be well compatible with the notion of 'conduct- crime' (as opposed to 'result-crime'). A close example would be the war crime of 'intentionally directing attacks against the civilian population' as provided in Article 8(2)(b)(i) of the ICC Statute which is generally classified as a 'conduct-crime' in respect of which no showing of 'result' is required. The mere fact of using weapons of mass destruction (without a proof of subsequent actual destruction of a substantial part of a group) might constitute strong evidence of intent to *target* a substantial part of the group. Yet, I think that, in view of the very nature of genocide being a crime of mass scale, it still makes sense to regard a destruction of a substantial part of a group as a collective result of actions undertaken on a mass scale. Moreover, it seems that the requirement of 'context level', such as the element of 'a manifest pattern of similar conduct' provided in the ICC Elements of Crimes further supports my position.

[217] For a summary of the relevant jurisprudence of the 'quantitative approach' and the 'qualitative approach' to interpreting the 'substantial part' requirement, *see* Nersessian 2010, pp. 41–46. As regards the 'qualitative approach', note that Raphael Lemkin, in explaining the new term 'genocide', also reports the targeting of "leading personalities" and "intellectuals" in Poland, Bohemia-Moravia, and Slovenia. Lemkin 2008, pp. 88–89.

[218] Vest 2007, p. 783. Given the ingrained slogan of genocide being a 'crime of *mens rea*', this characterization might sound disturbing. Let us however ask ourselves again. What is really the 'central feature' of the crime of genocide? Underlying acts? Genocidal intent? Destruction? When George Fletcher includes the crime of homicide in the third category of the pattern of criminality (viz. the 'pattern of harmful consequences')—in addition to his famous two patterns of criminality (viz. the 'pattern of manifest criminality' and the 'pattern of subjective criminality')—he observes that the "central feature of homicide is the death of one person at the hands of another", not the "manifest danger of threatening to kill nor the intent to kill". What about genocide? Out of Fletcher's three patterns of criminality, which one do you think should apply to the crime of genocide? Denno 2004, p. 782, footnote 10.

[219] Vest 2007, p. 784.

from the realm of individual inner state of mind. In this manner, the "in whole or in part" requirement dressed with the substantiality requirement stands as an independent and distinct element in parallel with the genocidal intent element. In this respect, the *Krstić* Appeals Chamber makes it clear that the genocidal intent and the requirement of 'targeting a whole or a substantial part of a group' constitute the *two* key "requirements" of genocide. The Chamber states,

> The gravity of genocide is reflected in the stringent *requirements* which must be satisfied before this conviction is imposed. *These requirements* – the demanding proof of specific intent *and* the showing that the group was targeted for destruction in its entirety or in substantial part – guard against a danger that convictions for this crime will be imposed lightly. Where these requirements are satisfied, however, the law must not shy away from referring to the crime committed by its proper name.[220]

Obviously, this construction of the substantiality requirement as a distinct key element of genocide conflicts with some of the case law of the *ad hoc* tribunals. An example is the *Stakić* Trial Judgment in which the Trial Chamber observes,

> The key factor is the specific intent to destroy the group rather than its actual physical destruction. As pointed out by the Trial Chamber in *Semanza*, "there is no numeric threshold of victims necessary to establish genocide". This Trial Chamber emphasizes that in view of the requirement of a surplus of intent, it is not necessary to prove a de facto destruction of the group in part [...]. It is genocidal *dolus specialis* that predominantly constitutes the crime.[221]

---

[220] Prosecutor v. Krstić, Appeals Judgment, 19 April 2004, para 37. (emphasis added). In this regard, also consider the two factors determinative of the meaning of *mens rea* as observed by Jerome Hall as follows: "The principle of *mens rea* is the ultimate evaluation of criminal conduct [...]. Its paramount role in penal theory also results from the fact that *mens rea* is the fusion ("concurrence") of the elementary functions of intelligence and volition. [...] [T]he connotation "blameworthy" [accompanied by the term *mens rea*] has played a great role in the history of penal law. In that history, *mens rea* is meaningful in relation to harm-doing, and to characterize *mens rea* as "evil mind" or "evil will" makes sense only if actual harm, sought or hazarded, is *held in view*. [...] As suggested above, two factors determine the meaning of *mens rea*—an actual harm and the mental state of the actor who voluntarily commits it. Current professional literature has emphasized the latter, the so-called "subjective" aspect of the principle of *mens rea* in its reference to the defendant who caused a proscribed harm. What has escaped adequate attention is that, as is evident at least as regards the more serious crimes, an actual harm, a social disvalue, was committed". Hall 1960, pp. 70–73. (emphasis added). The way I see it, within the crime definition of genocide, it is the distance between the "actual harm" (destruction of a group) and the inner "fusion" (genocidal intent) that makes the crime of genocide unique. Put otherwise, in the crime definition, the "actual harm" of destruction exists only as a component of *mens rea*, which makes the crime of genocide a type of 'conduct-crime' (as opposed to 'result-crime') at least from a theoretical point of view. Therefore, in terms of the crime definition of genocide, it is difficult to *hold* the "actual harm" of destruction *in view*. Accordingly, it follows that it makes little sense to characterize *mens rea* as "evil mind" or "evil will" vis-à-vis the crime of genocide. The relevant jurisprudence reveals that it is only when the judicial creation or implicit element of 'collective genocide' is "held in view" that "actual harm" of genocide becomes legally meaningful. In sum, in relation to the crime of genocide, the key *mens rea* of genocidal intent is a feeble and unstable legal notion that needs to be buttressed by the implicit element of 'collective genocide', which leads us to doubt that whether the concept of genocidal intent fits into the traditional definition of *mens rea* as the "fusion ('concurrence') of the elementary functions of intelligence and volition" as explained by Jerome Hall.

[221] Prosecutor v. Stakić, Trial Judgment, 31 July 2003, para 522. In this paragraph, the term 'surplus of intent' means the genocidal intent element.

This line of jurisprudence recognizes the 'targeting substantial part' only as a proof of genocidal intent as follows:

> The actual destruction of a substantial part of the group is not a requirement of the offence, but may assist in determining whether the accused intended to bring about the result.[222]

Yet, this position recognizing the 'targeting of a substantial part' only as a proof of genocidal intent can make sense only if the actual destruction of at least a substantial part of a group is just one of many evidentiary routes to establish the genocidal intent element – otherwise, it is effectively an element of the crime. As explored throughout this chapter thus far, ruling out the exceptional case of solo *génocidaire*, there is no way to prove genocidal intent without first establishing the fact of 'targeting a substantial part', which renders it an element of crime. Namely, the case law of the ICTR and the ICTY testifies aloud that the objective scale of destruction at the 'context level' is a necessary condition in determining whether the crime of genocide is committed. As signified by Lemkin's observation that "the [Genocide] Convention applies only to actions undertaken on a mass scale",[223] the 'context level' of genocide is established through the showing of destructive consequences that must meet the substantiality requirement.[224] Without the destruction of a substantial part of a group at the 'context level', the strongest degree of genocidal intent harbored by each and every member of the whole population of an attacking group means nothing. In this sense, the *two* key requirements formulation declared by the *Krstić* Appeals Chamber is valid.

3.4 'Collective Genocide' and Threat

3.4.1 Objective Threat Inherent in the Contextual Element

As to the issue of balance between a criminal offender's inner attitude and the risk of harm, George Fletcher asks, "[t]he basic question is whether the actor's attitude

---

[222] Prosecutor v. Rukundo, Trial Judgment, 27 February 2009, para 556. *See also* Prosecutor v. Brđanin, Trial Judgment, 1 September 2004, para 697 ("In view of the specific intent required for genocide, it is not necessary to prove the de facto destruction of the group in whole or in part. Nevertheless, the de facto destruction of the group may constitute evidence of the specific intent and may also serve to distinguish the crime of genocide from the inchoate offences in Article 4(3) of the Statute, such as the attempt to commit genocide"); Prosecutor v. Milosević, Decision on Motion for Judgement of Acquittal, 16 June 2004, para 125 ("Since the acts in Article 4(2) of the Statute are only required to be committed with an intent to destroy the protected group, it is clear that the actual destruction of the group need not take place. However, the extent of the actual destruction, if it does take place, will more often than not a factor from which the inference may be drawn that the underlying acts were committed with the specific intent to destroy, in whole or in part, a specific group as such".).

[223] R. Lemkin, 'United States Senate, Committee on Foreign Relations, Subcommittee on Genocide Convention, April 12, 1950', 2 Executive Sessions of the Senate Foreign Relations Committee, Historical Series (1976), p. 370.

[224] With the exception of genocide based on the underlying acts of 'biological destruction' as provided in Article 6(d) and 6(e) of the ICC Statute. *See* this chapter, footnotes 116 and 214 *supra*.

alone can warrant classification at a higher level of culpability than would be supported by the risks he creates. Can the lust for [a criminal result] compensate for a low risk of harm?"[225] If we ask the same question concerning the crime of genocide in respect of which the mental element of "intent to destroy" occupies the central position of the whole discussion surrounding the crime definition, what would be the answer? Can the strong inner attitude of an actor provide grounds to convict him of genocide despite the low level of risk objectively created by his own action or even by collective acts of a group to which he belong? As we have examined in the previous section, the answer from commentators and international case law is an ambivalent no. Although the genocidal intent element is still considered the essence of the crime of genocide, it should be acknowledged that the completion of genocide requires more than genocidal intent—i.e., it also requires a destruction of at least a substantial part of a group at the 'context level'.[226] In other words, it is an objective *scale* of 'collective act and consequence' at the 'context level' that is determinative of the completion of the crime of genocide. Just as many domestic jurisdictions punish an assault inflicted by more than one person more seriously than that by only one person because of the aggravated danger involving the former, the *scale* of a criminal transaction is the most obvious index of the related 'danger/threat/risk'. The contextual elements of core international crimes—as a parameter of the objective *scale* at the 'context level'—signify the level of 'danger/threat/risk' involved therein. The 'widespread or systematic attack' element or the 'international or non-international armed conflict' element can be paraphrased as the required level of *threat towards a collective* as objectively reflected in the scale of an overall context of violence. Despite the fact that defendants charged with crimes against humanity and war crimes are to be convicted of specific underlying acts (e.g., a conviction of crime against humanity of torture, or a conviction of war crime of pillaging), the real concern of legislators of the rules on core international crimes consists in the *threat towards a collective*. In this regard, a participant in the drafting process of the ICC Elements of Crimes records,

> Because genocide is universally recognized as an extremely serious crime, it was generally agreed that the context of the crime requires that there be a certain *scale or other real danger* to a group. [...] [T]he United States and others argued that some 'contextual element' was also needed *to capture the notion of scale or threat* to a group.[227]

In the same vein, Claus Kress explains the crux of the contextual element of genocide by stating that "it is important to fully appreciate what the common [contextual]

---

[225] Fletcher 2000, p. 448 (in the context of discussing *dolus eventualis.*).

[226] Despite the fact that the phrase *'targeting* a substantial part' (rather than 'destruction of a substantial part') has been used more frequently in the relevant case law, I think this expression is too feeble to deny the irrefutable and fundamental result-based reality of genocide, in particular, with regard to the crime of genocide involving 'physical destruction'. On the other hand, to the extent that genocide by way of 'biological destruction' is to be classified as a concrete endangerment offence in respect of which the pertinent risk is required to be materialized, it seems there is no problem to classifying this type of genocide also as a 'result-crime'.

[227] Oosterveld 2001, p. 45.

element of the crime of genocide essentially suggests: that this crime presupposes a *real danger* for the targeted group [...]".[228] Kress also applies the notion of "real danger" to the contextual elements of crimes against humanity and war crimes when he observes that "there can be no doubt that crimes against humanity imply a *real danger* for the targeted civilian population because of the requirement of a(n emerging) widespread or systematic attack. [...] In the case of war crimes, *this danger* stems from the fact that an armed conflict must exist".[229] In short, it is considered that the objective *scale* of a genocidal campaign *reaching* the required level of the contextual element of genocide itself essentially entails the threat towards a collective. In this manner, the question of 'danger/threat/risk' is closely interlinked with the issue of objective contextual element of genocide. Since it is a threat *towards a collective* accompanied by an objective scale of violence, the notion of threat in this context is of an *objective* characteristic and conceptually exists at the 'context level'.

3.4.2 'Concrete Threat' as Content of 'Collective Genocide'?: Al Bashir Decision

In the section entitled "Contextual elements of the crime of genocide", the ICC Pre-Trial Chamber in *Al Bashir* characterizes the crime of genocide as a 'concrete endangerment' crime.[230] The Pre-Trial Chamber states,

> In the view of the Majority, according to this contextual element [i.e., 'a manifest pattern of similar conduct' or 'conduct that could itself effect a destruction'], the crime of genocide is *only completed when* the relevant conduct presents a *concrete threat* to the existence of the targeted group, or a part thereof. In other words, the protection offered by the penal norm defining the crime of genocide – as an *ultima ratio* mechanism to preserve the highest values of the international community – is only triggered when the threat against the existence of the targeted group, or part thereof, becomes concrete and real, as opposed to just being latent or hypothetical.[231]

It is to be noted that the purpose of this observation made by the Majority of the Pre-Trial Chamber is to interpret the 'manifest pattern of similar conduct' element ('contextual element' as referred to by the Chamber).[232]

---

[228] Kress 2009, p. 300. (emphasis added).

[229] *Ibid.* at 297, 301–302. (emphasis added).

[230] For the same view, *see* Ambos 2009, p. 835, footnote 8 ("[The *Al Bashir* decision], in essence, characterizes genocide as a crime of (concrete) endangerment [...]").

[231] Prosecutor v. Al Bashir, Decision on the Prosecution's Application for a Warrant of Arrest against Omar Hassan Ahmed Al Bashir, 4 March 2009, para 124. (emphasis added).

[232] Strictly speaking, when the Majority says "according to this contextual element", it is referring to the Elements of Crimes as paraphrased in the previous paragraph of the decision (*Ibid.* para 123) in which the scope of the term "contextual element" covers both (i) the manifest pattern of similar conduct; and (ii) conduct that could itself effect a destruction of a group. In this section, I will mostly address the first meaning of the term, because the alternative of conduct that could itself effect the destruction of a group is – as we have seen repeatedly – largely hypothetical.

Accordingly, refuting the view that characterizes the 'manifest pattern of similar conduct' element as a jurisdictional element (as opposed to an element of the crime itself),[233] the Chamber introduces the notion of 'concrete threat' to clarify the meaning of the manifest pattern element at the 'context level'. Classifying genocide as a concrete endangerment offence conceptually locates the crime of genocide closer to a result-crime, as it is generally accepted that concrete endangerment offences are result-crimes (as opposed to conduct-crimes). Theoretically speaking, therefore, it seems the Chamber's decision requiring a 'concrete threat' is in line with my observation in the Sect. 3.3.3, which places emphasis on the character of result-crime inherent in the structure of genocide (destructive consequence at the 'context level').[234] Another aspect of the Majority's opinion that deserves note is the object to which the 'concrete threat' is supposed to be posed—i.e., the "existence of the targeted *group, or a part thereof*".[235] Accordingly, the 'concrete threat' is evidently not directed towards an individual member of a protected group. Given the title of the section in which this discussion on 'concrete threat' is going on ("The contextual element of the crime of genocide"), I think it is sound to say that the "targeted group, or a part thereof" means at least a substantial part of the targeted group at the 'context level'.[236] Thus, in my view, the notion of 'concrete threat' as used by the Majority carries a connotation of a scale and collective endeavors at the 'context level'. In this sense, a term such as 'campaign' might have better represented the implication of 'concrete threat' than the singular noun 'conduct' in the phrase "only completed when the relevant conduct presents a concrete threat to [...]".

---

[233] Prosecutor v. Al Bashir, Decision on the Prosecution's Application for a Warrant of Arrest against Omar Hassan Ahmed Al Bashir, 4 March 2009, p. 44, footnote 142. The Majority of the Chamber notes that some commentators regard the manifest pattern element as a jurisdictional element due to the absence of corresponding knowledge element in the ICC Elements of Crimes. The Majority, however, is of the view that it is not a jurisdictional element because the general mental element framework provided under Article 30 of the ICC Statute is still applicable. For an opposing view, *see* Werle 2009, p. 272.

[234] Note however that, as will be explained throughout this section, I do not support the Majority in *Al Bashir* in respect of their adoption of the concept of 'concrete threat'.

[235] *See also* Greenawalt 1999, pp. 2291 and 2293–2294 ("[...] the campaign of persecution poses a very serious threat *to future survival of either the group* as a whole, or a clearly defined segment of the group (such as the Kosovo Albanians or the Iraqi Kurds)"; "by proscribing targeted actions that *threaten the survival of at least a substantial part* of specified groups".).

[236] From Kress's observation that, at the initial stage of a genocidal campaign, "the threat to the targeted group as such, or a substantial part thereof, will not yet be concrete", we can deduce that he is of a similar view. Kress 2009, p. 306. For more discussion on Kress's observations in relation to the initial stage of a genocidal campaign, *see* this chapter, text accompanying notes 250–254 *infra*.

3.4.3 Rethinking the Criticisms of the Al Bashir Decision's 'Concrete Threat'

On the other hand, interpreting the manifest pattern element as "a systematic, clear pattern of conduct in which the alleged genocidal conduct occurs[,]"[237] Judge Anita Ušacka, in her dissenting opinion, criticizes the Majority's 'concrete threat' requirement by stating,

> [...] I disagree with the meaning given to the term ['a manifest pattern of similar conduct'] by the Majority [...]. In my view, [the concrete threat] interpretation converts the term ['a manifest pattern of similar conduct'] into a 'result-based' requirement, which would then duplicate the purpose of the second part of the sentence, "or was conduct that could itself effect such destruction".[238]

Citing Judge Ušacka's dissenting opinion with approval, Robert Cryer and Claus Kress argue against the 'concrete threat' requirement. Cryer calls the 'concrete threat' an "odd gloss".[239] Kress also rejects the "unfortunately worded" 'concrete threat' requirement "because it suggests an unduly stringent [contextual] threshold".[240]

As I see it, Judge Ušacka is correct in saying that the 'concrete threat' requirement turns the manifest pattern element into a 'result-based' requirement. That is because, in order to decide whether a risk has reached the level of 'concrete threat' to the existence of at least a substantial part of a group, one must assess the risk *created* by the manifest pattern of similar conduct at the 'context level'.[241] Yet, purely at a textual level, it is hard to agree with the latter portion of Judge Ušacka's opinion which states that treating the manifest pattern element as a result-based requirement "would then duplicate the purpose of the second part of the sentence [...]". In this respect, Robert Cryer and Kevin Jon Heller are of the view that what Judge Ušacka points out is that interpreting the manifest pattern element as requiring 'concrete threat' would erase the distinction between the first prong (concerning multiple perpetrators) and

---

[237] Prosecutor v. Al Bashir, Separate and Partly Dissenting Opinion of Judge Anita Ušacka, 4 March 2009, para 19.

[238] *Ibid.* at 9, footnote 26 and accompanying text.

[239] Cryer 2009, p. 290.

[240] Kress 2009, pp. 299–300.

[241] Claus Kress understands the term 'result-based requirement' in Judge Ušacka's dissenting opinion in a slightly different manner when he explains: "As Judge Ušacka rightly observes in her dissent, the precondition of a 'concrete threat' come close to a 'result-based requirement', i.e. the requirement of a situation where the genocidal campaign has advanced up to a point where actual destruction may soon result". *Ibid.* at 306. On the other hand, I understand that, in relation to the crime of genocide, the 'concrete threat' itself incorporates actual destructions pursuant to the 'in whole or in part' (in particular, the 'targeting a substantial part') requirement. While Kress seems to focus on the risk soon to come, I place an emphasis on the risk already created. As will be addressed in the later part of this section, my approach is more consistent with the practice of the *ad hoc* tribunals that uses the threat feature of genocide as a proof of the substantiality requirement. In my view, in terms of the crime of genocide involving multiple perpetrators, the notion of 'destruction' at the 'context level' is composed of a spectrum of numerous small destructions at the 'conduct level'.

the second prong (concerning a solo perpetrator) of the contextual element.[242] Accordingly, Cryer observes that "it collapses the first, disjunctive 'manifest pattern of conduct' requirement in the [contextual e]lement into the second, result-based alternative, that the conduct was such that itself could effect destruction of the group (or a part of it)".[243] I think, however, that this reading is mistaken, because the second prong of the contextual element—i.e., "or was conduct that could itself effect such destruction"—is not actually a result-based requirement. It seems a literal interpretation of the phrase "could itself effect" refers to the case of a solo *génocidaire*, and comes closer to describing an abstract endangerment offence, which is generally considered a conduct crime.[244] Put otherwise, the term "could itself effect" far more comfortably fits the concept of a 'latent or hypothetical threat', rather than a 'concrete threat'.[245] In this fashion, the formulation of this second prong of the contextual element connotes a serious danger of an objective possibility of destruction, rather than a destructive consequence. Furthermore, this second prong should be applicable for the purpose of *ex ante* pre-emption of a solo perpetrator who, for instance, personally has a nuclear weapon.[246] In sum, the second prong should not be interpreted as result-based. At this juncture, the following record of the drafting history of the Elements of Crimes concerning the second prong of the contextual element sheds light on this issue:

> [...] the reference to 'would destroy' was altered to 'could destroy'. *The result-based "would destroy" requirement was criticized* by many for raising the standard of proof far too high, since the use of "would" implied that the Prosecutor would have to prove that, if the action had continued, the perpetrator would have succeeded in destroying the group.

---

[242] Cryer 2009, p. 291; Heller 2009.

[243] Cryer 2009, p. 291.

[244] For an opposing view, *see* Heller 2009 ("The 'concrete threat' requirement makes complete sense in terms of the second prong of the contextual element, where we are concerned with separating the truly dangerous lone *génocidaires* from the ones not worthy of international prosecution".); Cryer et al. 2010, p. 218 ("[The contextual element of genocide] does however require either a pattern of crimes, or a concrete danger to a group, thereby ruling out isolated hate crimes".).

[245] Note that the Majority contrasts the two notions of the "concrete and real" threat with the "latent or hypothetical" threat. Prosecutor v. Al Bashir, Decision on the Prosecution's Application for a Warrant of Arrest against Omar Hassan Ahmed Al Bashir, 4 March 2009, para 124.

[246] I keep this position in theory, solely in order to explicate the second prong of the contextual element. As a matter of practice, however, in view of the crucial significance of the substantiality requirement, I am doubtful about the actual applicability of this position. For the purpose of *ex ante* preemption of a solo perpetrator who possesses a weapon of mass destruction, the charge of attempt of genocide, rather than genocide proper, would be more attractive to prosecutors and judges. For views suggesting the need for such an *ex ante* preemption of a solo *génocidaire*, *see* Rückert and Witschel 2004, p. 66 (summarizing the discussions during the drafting process of the Elements of Crimes, states, "[a] single (initial) perpetrator, who killed only one person, but had used a chemical weapon (which, due to whatever circumstance, did not result in more than one death, but could have killed thousands) would fall within the scope of application".); Cryer et al. 2010, p. 218 ("It would also capture those who had the means to destroy a group but for whatever reason managed to cause only a single death or a few deaths, such that there would be no objective 'pattern'").

This was a more difficult test than that found in *Akayesu*. Most States agreed that "could destroy" was a better formulation that did not impose an unnecessary burden on the Prosecutor, and still demonstrated that the conduct should *be of a seriousness that could possibly result in destruction.*[247]

In the end, as opposed to the view of Judge Ušacka and the commentators cited above, the real distinction between the first prong and the second prong of the contextual element does not consist in whether one prong or another is result-based or not. The distinction is more fundamental. The first prong presumes a repetition of *multiple acts* by a number of perpetrators at the 'context level', whilst the second prong accompanies only a solo perpetrator's *single action* at the 'conduct level' with a great potential to be able to effect the destruction of a targeted group. Thus, contrary to Judge Ušacka, the distinction between the first and second prongs will not be undermined by treating the first prong as result-based. Accordingly, her valid proposition that the 'concrete threat' interpretation of the manifest pattern element converts this element into a result-based requirement hardly stands as an argument against the 'concrete threat' interpretation given by the Majority of the Pre-Trial Chamber.

In this connection, I would like to look into another argument advanced by Claus Kress which also challenges the 'concrete threat' requirement. In a section entitled "No Requirement of a Concrete Threat", Kress explains,

Contrary to what the [Majority of the *Al Bashir* Pre-Trial] Chamber appears to hold, the last (common) Element ["The conduct took place in the context of a manifest pattern of similar conduct directed against that group or was conduct that could itself effect such destruction".] does not require the occurrence of so dangerous a situation either. Under this Element's second alternative, it is sufficient that the conduct in question *can effect* the destructive result. Accordingly, it must suffice for the first alternative too, that the genocidal campaign is of nature *capable to bring about* the planned destruction. This interpretation is confirmed by the fact that the Introduction to the Elements of Crimes on Genocide underline[s] that the 'term "in the context of" would include the initial acts in an emerging pattern'. This means that the crime of genocide is completed with the initial act of a genocidal campaign. At this moment, in time, however, the threat to the targeted group as such, or a substantial part thereof, will not yet be *concrete.*[248]

The thrust of this argument is that, contrary to the Majority, the genocidal context is *not* required to be so dangerous as to reach the level of 'concrete threat': rather, a latent capability to bring about the destructive consequence is sufficient to meet the element of 'a manifest pattern of similar conduct'. The phrases italicized by Kress ("can effect"; "capable to bring about" and "not yet be concrete") seem to suggest that both genocide by multiple perpetrators and genocide by a solo perpetrator should be regarded as abstract endangerment offences, which would characterize genocide as a conduct crime. I think the difficulty involving this scheme is that, in relation to the crime of genocide, it is not easy to mark the exact 'conduct' that, upon

---

[247] Oosterveld 2001, pp. 46–47. (emphasis added).

[248] Kress 2009, p. 306. (emphasis in original).

its performance, instantly constitutes genocide as an abstract endangerment offence (as a conduct crime). With respect to the extremely rare case of solo *génocidaire*, it might be possible to designate *the* conduct. For instance, in the case of the Holocaust survivor Abba Kovner whose desire was to kill six million Germans by poisoning the Hamburg water supply, *the* conduct would have been his act of putting the poisonous substance into the water supply system.[249] Contrastingly, in relation to genocide involving a multiplicity of perpetrators on a mass scale, it would be almost impossible to specify *the* conduct which creates the abstract endangerment *towards the destruction of a group, or a part thereof.* In this respect, within the sentence in the cited paragraph above "it must suffice for the first alternative too, that the genocidal *campaign* is of nature capable to bring about the planned destruction", Kress's use of the term "campaign" instead of 'conduct' is precise. What I want to emphasize here is that the notion of 'the threat to the existence of a group', be it a 'concrete threat' or an 'abstract threat', should always be considered at the 'context level' from the perspective of 'collective genocide'. I acknowledge that the notion of abstract or concrete endangerment offence in this context does not work in the same manner as that of domestic jurisdictions. Yet, even when we interpret the 'conduct' (or "campaign" as Kress says) that is "capable to bring about" the destructive result as a collective conduct, the concept of 'conduct' or 'campaign' in this context is too fluid to specify the point in time when the crime of genocide as an abstract endangerment offence becomes complete. Thus, it seems to me that, given the context-fixing role played by the 'targeting a substantial part' requirement that conceptually encompasses the manifest pattern element, it would be better not to introduce the domestic criminal law notion of abstract endangerment into the law of genocide. In this connection, it is important to note that the context-fixing role of the 'targeting a substantial part' requirement was almost completely neglected by the *Al Bashir* Pre-Trial Chamber, a point I will discuss further below. Before we move on to this issue, let me briefly comment on another question stemming from Kress's observation cited above.

In particular, I am troubled by the proposition that "[t]his means that the crime of genocide is completed with the initial act of a genocidal campaign" on the basis of which Kress rejects the 'concrete threat' requirement, whilst rendering or tending to render the crime of genocide an abstract endangerment offence. Or rather, I disagree with the proposition if "the crime of genocide" therein indicates the notion of 'collective genocide' at the 'context level'[250]; I agree with Kress's proposition only if "the crime of genocide" refers to the one charged in relation to a specific individual perpetrator's specific act.

Let me explain further. In my view, when the Elements of Crimes states that "[t]he term 'in the context of' would include the initial acts in an emerging pattern",[251] it is not talking about the timing of the completion of the crime of genocide. Rather,

---

[249] For the Abba Kovner's tale, *see* Luban 2004, p. 98, footnote 45.

[250] Note that throughout this chapter, I am demonstrating and arguing that, without this theoretical notion of 'collective genocide', no genocide conviction is possible. For a more detailed discussion, *see* Sect. 4.1.1 *infra*.

[251] ICC Elements of Crimes, Introduction to Genocide, (a).

the Elements of Crimes is here spelling out the nexus requirement between an individual perpetrator and the genocidal context. That is, what the Elements of Crimes wants to ensure with this clarification of the term "in the context of" is that the perpetrators of the initial acts cannot escape from prosecution under the rule of genocide on the grounds that, when they committed the relevant initial acts, "the contextual element of a 'manifest pattern of similar conduct' was not yet met ("you cannot charge me with genocide because when I acted there existed only an emerging pattern, not a manifest pattern".).[252] The way I see it, the decision on the establishment of the contextual elements of crimes against humanity and genocide should be made *retrospectively* from an objective perspective. Consequently, Kress's argument against the 'concrete threat' requirement in reference of the 'initial acts' does not stand up to scrutiny, because the explanation in the Elements of Crimes about the "initial acts in an emerging pattern" has been made for practice guidelines and policy purposes,[253] rather than for purposes of substantiation of a legal requirement. It seems to me that the laudable aspiration to halt genocide at an early stage must not be addressed through the legal definition of genocide.[254] Rather, it is a matter of political policy and practice. If genocide is halted at an early stage before it manifests a pattern of conduct fulfilling the substantiality requirement, genocide in a legal sense does not exist. The bad men will not be charged of the crime of genocide because it is too soon to know whether the contextual element of the crime of genocide exists.

3.4.4   Threat Only as Proof, but Not Content of 'Collective Genocide'

Thus far, I have demonstrated that various attacks on the notion of 'concrete threat' vis-à-vis the crime of genocide from the dissenting judge in *Al Bashir* and

---

[252] Participants in the relevant discussions during the drafting process of the Elements of Crimes reports: "[A] bullet was added to the introduction [to Genocide in the Elements of Crimes], clarifying that the term 'in the context of' would include the initial acts in an emerging pattern. Thus, the perpetrator of the first act of murder would be covered by the definition. Delegations agreed that, especially given the particular danger and gravity of an initial act ('igniting the genocide'), the perpetrator should not go free due to the fact that there cannot be any genocidal context for the first act". Rückert and Witschel 2004, p. 66.

[253] In particular, it is evident that the item (c) of the Introduction to Genocide was written for practical guidelines and policy purposes. The item (c) states that "[n]otwithstanding the normal requirement for a mental element provided for in article 30, and recognizing that knowledge of the circumstances will usually be addressed in proving genocidal intent, the appropriate requirement, if any, for a mental element regarding this circumstance will need to be decided by the Court on a case-by-case basis".

[254] *See* David Luban's explanation of Raphael Lemkin's original purpose of proposing the genocidal intent element: "Lemkin hoped (in vain, it seems) that future genocides would be halted in their early stages, before great loss of life ensued, in which case the bare intent would nevertheless suffice to convict perpetrators. Thus, Lemkin saw the intent requirement as easing the prosecutor's burden rather than making it more onerous". Luban 2004, p. 97, footnote 44.

commentators have not been successful. So shall we adopt the 'concrete threat' interpretation of the manifest pattern element as proposed by the Majority in *Al Bashir*? My answer to this question is that that would not be feasible either. Let me show why. I will argue that both the Majority and the dissenting judge (Judge Ušacka) unduly neglected the 'substantial part' requirement of the definition of genocide. Had the Majority focused on this requirement, it would not have found it necessary to introduce the 'concrete threat' interpretation, because the concreteness of the threat is already implicit in the substantial part requirement as I have interpreted it: not as a subjective *mens rea*, but as an objective recognition of an ongoing genocidal campaign.

At this juncture, it is important to note that the Majority's opinion in *Al Bashir* also features the question of point in time when the crime of genocide becomes complete. Actually it was precisely the Majority's concern over the same exact question that compelled the judges to pronounce the 'concrete threat' requirement. But the Majority's concern was based on a misunderstanding of the case law of the ICTY and the ICTR, which resembles Kress's apparent misconception about the completion of genocide with 'initial acts'. With regard to genocide by multiple perpetrators, the Majority in *Al Bashir* observes,

> The Majority highlights that the case law of the ICTY and the ICTR has interpreted th[e] definition [of genocide] as excluding any type of contextual element, such as a genocidal policy or plan. Hence, for the case law of the ICTY and the ICTR, the crime of genocide is completed by, *inter alia*, killing or causing serious bodily harm to a single individual with the intent to destroy in whole or in part the group to which such individual belongs. As a result, according to this case law, for the purpose of completing the crime of genocide, it is irrelevant whether the conduct in question is capable of posing any concrete threat to the existence of the targeted group, or a part thereof. As a consequence, according to the case law of the ICTY and the ICTR, the protection offered to the targeted groups by the penal norm defining the crime of genocide is dependent on the existence of an intent to destroy, in whole or in part, the targeted group. As soon as such intent exists and materializes in an isolated act of a single individual, the protection is triggered, regardless of whether the latent threat to the existence of the targeted group posed by the said intent has turned into a concrete threat to the existence in whole or in part of that group.[255]

Compare this with the following case law from the ICTY Appeals Chamber (which we have already considered in the previous section):

> The gravity of genocide is reflected in the stringent *requirements* which must be satisfied before this conviction is imposed. *These requirements* – the demanding proof of specific intent *and* the showing that the group was targeted for destruction in its entirety or in substantial part – guard against a danger that convictions for this crime will be imposed lightly.[256]

Contrary to the understanding of the Majority in *Al Bashir*, the case law of the ICTY and the ICTR has never firmly expressed the view that crime of genocide is complete when there is "an isolated act of a single individual" committed with

---

[255] Prosecutor v. Al Bashir, Decision on the Prosecution's Application for a Warrant of Arrest against Omar Hassan Ahmed Al Bashir, 4 March 2009, paras 119–120.

[256] Prosecutor v. Krstić, Appeals Judgment, 19 April 2004, para 37. (emphasis added).

genocidal intent.[257] Instead, as we have already studied in the previous section,[258] the relevant case law has been consistent in ensuring that a single underlying act, however egregious the actor's intent, is not sufficient to constitute the crime of genocide if the requirement of 'targeting at least a substantial part' ('in whole or in part') is not met – and it can only be met in a context where a substantial part of the group could, realistically, be destroyed. This is also confirmed by the fact that, in relation to all the cases (other than Srebrenica) in which the crime of genocide was charged by the Prosecution, the ICTY acquitted all the defendants of genocide charges.[259]

In this respect, it is surprising to see that both the Majority and Judge Ušacka in her dissenting opinion almost completely neglected any serious discussion of the substantiality requirement.[260] I guess that the reason behind this oversight was, as I explained in Sect. 3.3.3, the contradiction between the normative character (*mens rea*) and the practical function (*actus reus*) of the quasi-element of 'destruction', which renders the substantiality requirement quite elusive.[261]

This leads to the question whether, if the substantiality requirement had been given due consideration by the Majority, the judges would still have set forth the 'concrete threat' requirement? Does the substantiality requirement negate the need of the 'concrete threat' requirement? What is the relationship between these two notions? To answer these questions, let us consult the jurisprudence of the *ad hoc* tribunals. Though only a few, there are some relevant sources at the ICTY and the ICTR.

---

[257] I acknowledge that there exists a possibility of misunderstanding. For instance, after concluding that the Government of Sudan had not pursued a policy of genocide, the Darfur Commission of Inquiry added that "[t]he Commission does recognize that in some instances individuals, including Government officials, may commit acts with genocidal intent". International Commission of Inquiry on Darfur, Established Pursuant to Resolution 1564 (2004), Report to the United Nations Secretary–General, 25 January 2005, paras 520 and 641. Moreover, the *Jelisić* Trial Chamber states, "[s]uch a case [of genocide being committed by an isolated act of a single individual] is theoretically possible". Prosecutor v. Jelisić, Trial Judgment, 14 December 1999, para 100. Nevertheless, this observation must be read together with the Chamber's further explanation in the immediately following paragraph which says that "[t]he Trial Chamber observes, however, that it will be very difficult in practice to provide proof of the genocidal intent of an individual if the crimes committed are not widespread and if the crime charged is not backed by an organization or a system". *Ibid.* para 101. Citing para 100 of the *Jelisić* Trial Judgement, William Schabas observes that the case of a *solo génocidaire* is "entirely speculative and hypothetical[.]" Schabas 2012, p. 131. It is interesting to note that Schabas suggests that the contextual element of genocide in the ICC Elements of Crimes was provided in response to the *Jelisić* Trial Chamber's observation that genocide by a solo perpetrator is "theoretically possible". Schabas emphasizes that, during the drafting negotiations of the Elements of Crimes, the draft contextual element only appeared in March 2000, four months after the issuance of the *Jelisić* Trial Judgment in December 1999. *Ibid.* at 141.

[258] *See* Sect. 3.3 *supra*.

[259] *See* Schabas 2012, p. 131 ("At the Yugoslavia Tribunal, the handful of genocide convictions have all related to the Srebrenica massacre, which was apparently organized and coordinated at the highest levels of the Bosnian Serb military and political leadership".).

[260] Note that even the separate section entitled "'In part': the substantial part requirement" in Judge Ušacka's dissenting opinion does not contain any meaningful discussion of the substantiality requirement.

[261] *See* this chapter, footnote 214 *supra* and accompanying text.

In 1996, in its annual report, the International Law Commission briefly mentioned the threat feature of genocide in relation to the underlying act of 'causing serious bodily or mental harm'. The ILC observed that "[t]he bodily harm or the mental harm inflicted on members of a group must be of such a *serious nature as to threaten* its destruction in whole or in part". [262] On the other hand, in the jurisprudence of the *ad hoc* tribunals, the 'danger/threat/risk' factor has hardly been discussed as a separate legal requirement of genocide. Indeed, the ICC Pre-Trial Chamber in *Al Bashir* summarizes the case law of the ICTY and the ICTR by stating that "according to this case law, for the purpose of completing the crime of genocide, it is irrelevant whether the conduct in question is capable of posing any concrete threat to the existence of the targeted group, or a part thereof".[263] There are a few exceptions in which the threat feature is addressed by the case law of the *ad hoc* tribunals with regard to the crime of genocide. However, contrary to the approach taken by the *Al Bashir* Pre-Trial Chamber, the *ad hoc* tribunals have not discussed the theme of threat in connection with the contextual element of genocide (context level). Instead, seemingly affected by the view of the ILC just quoted, the threat feature has been dealt with by the *ad hoc* tribunals only in their treatment of one particular underlying genocidal act: 'causing bodily or mental harm' (conduct level). Out of those few exceptional cases where the threat feature of genocide was discussed,[264] let me delve into the *Rukundo* case which provides the most vivid contrast between the 'conduct level' and 'context level'.

---

[262] Report of the International Law Commission on the Work of Its Forty-Eight Session, May 6-July 26, 1996, at 46, U.N. Doc. A/51/10. (emphasis added). For an opposing view, *see* Jessberger 2009, p. 99 ("there are no indications in the definition [of 'serious bodily or mental harm'] as to a requirement that the harm be of such as serious nature as to threaten the group with destruction".).

[263] Prosecutor v. Al Bashir, Decision on the Prosecution's Application for a Warrant of Arrest against Omar Hassan Ahmed Al Bashir, 4 March 2009, para 119.

[264] *See* Prosecutor v. Rukundo, Dissenting Opinion of Judge Park, 27 February 2009; Prosecutor v. Nyiramasuhuko et al., Trial Judgement, 24 June 2011, paras 5866–5873 (the *Nyiramasuhuko* Trial Chamber considered whether bodily and mental harm inflicted on Tutsi civilians sought refuge at Butare *Prefecture* Office was "of such a serious nature as to threaten the destruction in whole or in part of the Tutsi ethnic group", particularly in relation to rape.); Prosecutor v. Karadžić, Transcript, 28 June 2012, pp. 28762–28770. In this oral decision on Karadžić's motion for a judgment of acquittal pursuant to Rule 98 *bis*, the Trial Chamber dealt with the threat feature in relation to the underlying act of 'causing serious bodily or mental harm' vis-à-vis Count 1 (Genocide in 1992). The bodily or mental harm was allegedly inflicted on thousands of Bosnian Muslims and Bosnian Croats by Bosnian Serb forces at numerous detention centers in some municipalities in Bosnia from March to December 1992. Ultimately the Trial Chamber granted the Karadžić's motion for acquittal concerning Count 1 (Genocide in 1992) on the grounds that the "nature, scale and context" of alleged 'killing', 'causing serious bodily or mental harm', and 'inflicting conditions of life' "[...] do not reach the level from which a reasonable trier of fact could infer that they were committed with genocidal intent". *Ibid.* at 28768. In my opinion, the real focus of the Chamber's consideration with regard to the Count 1 (Genocide in 1992) lay in the question of 'collective genocide'. Thus, as to Count 1, the Chamber seemed to be of the view that the objective scale/context of the criminal campaign did not reach the level of a targeting/destruction of a substantial part of Bosnian Muslims or Bosnian Croats. Note that, in relation to Count 2 (Genocide at Srebrenica in 1995), the Trial Chamber rejected the motion for acquittal. *Ibid.* at 28751–28752.

In his dissenting opinion in the *Rukundo* Trial Judgment, Judge Seon Ki Park disagrees with the majority's conviction on the charge of genocide (by causing serious mental harm) in relation to the accused's sexual assault at the St. Leon Minor Seminary. In finding the accused guilty of genocide (partly) on the basis of this incident, the Majority did not discuss the threat feature at all.[265] Rukundo tried but failed to have forceful sexual intercourse with a young Tutsi woman in a locked room at the seminary, with only Rukundo and the victim present therein. Though Rukundo eventually gave up his attempt to have sexual intercourse with the victim, he rubbed himself against her fully clothed body until he ejaculated. The crux of Judge Park's argument is that the seriousness of the mental harm inflicted upon the victim in this specific incident was not grave enough to *threaten* the Tutsi group's destruction, in whole or in part.[266] Thus, he is of the view that "to support a conviction for genocide, the bodily harm or the mental harm inflicted on members of a group must be of such a serious nature as to *threaten* its destruction in whole or in part".[267] It seems Judge Park's dissenting opinion manifests the pervasive confusion about the objective contextual element of genocide, viz., about the dimension of the 'context level'. In this connection, Judge Park apparently fails to note that it is not a specific incident but an objective context of overall violence at the 'context level' that can be said to "be of such a serious nature as to threaten" a group's destruction. In *Akayesu*, as explained by Judge Park, the Trial Chamber observes that "sexual violence was an integral part of the process of destruction, specifically targeting Tutsi women and specifically contributing to their destruction and to the destruction of the Tutsi group as a whole".[268] Yet, as clearly suggested by the fact that the *Akayesu* Trial Chamber places emphasis on the *systematic* commission of rape against Tutsi women,[269] it is important to note that "sexual violence" here does not indicate a specific incident at the 'conduct level', but points at an overall context of violence against Tutsis involving widespread sexual offences at the 'context level'. Thus, the *Akayesu* Trial Chamber concludes that "[s]exual violence was a step in the process of destruction of the

---

[265] For the relevant finding of the majority, *see* Prosecutor v. Rukundo, Trial Judgment, 27 February 2009, paras 574–76.

[266] Prosecutor v. Rukundo, Dissenting Opinion of Judge Park, 27 February 2009, para 5.

[267] *Ibid.* para 3. (emphasis added). In this regard, the only authority cited by Judge Park is the Appeals Judgment in *Seromba* which expresses, just in passing, the same *verbatim* view. *See* Prosecutor v. Seromba, Appeals Judgement, 12 March 2008, para 46. There are quite many judgments at the ICTR which approvingly cite this proposition in *Seromba* (which copied the ILC's observation) in 'Law' part without actually applying it to the relevant facts. *See e.g.,* Prosecutor v. Nzabonimana, Trial Judgement, 31 May 2012, para 1703; Prosecutor v. Karemera et al., Trial Judgment, 2 February 2002, para 1609.

[268] Prosecutor v. Akayesu, Trial Judgment, 2 September 1998, para 731.

[269] *Ibid.* para 732 ("The rape of Tutsi women was systematic and was perpetrated against all Tutsi women and solely against them. A Tutsi woman, married to a Hutu, testified before the Chamber that she was not raped because her ethnic background was unknown. As part of the propaganda campaign geared to mobilizing the Hutu against the Tutsi, the Tutsi women were represented as sexual objects".).

[T]utsi group – destruction of the spirit, the will to live, and of life itself".[270] This observation is obviously made from the contextual and collective perspective.

This incident of Rukundo's attempted rape was further deliberated in the *Rukundo* Appeals Judgment in which the Trial Chamber's conviction was reversed.[271] It is to be noted, however, that both the majority and the dissenting Judge Pocar in the Appeals Judgment did not discuss the threat feature at all, disregarding Judge Park's dissenting opinion. Instead, the relevant discussion in the Appeals Judgment centered around Rukundo's genocidal intent in this specific incident inferred from (i) the context of mass violence against Tutsis in the area, and (ii) Rukundo's pattern of genocidal conduct. Why did all the judges of the Appeals Chamber disregard the threat feature in relation to this specific incident? I think it was because the 'threat to the existence of a group, or a part thereof' is a theme for the 'context level', not for the 'conduct level'. In particular, for the purpose of determining whether serious bodily or mental harm has been caused, it seems the test of 'threat to the destruction of a group' proposed by the International Law Commission is not compatible with the established jurisprudence of the *ad hoc* tribunals which states that 'serious bodily or mental harm' should be determined on a case-by-case basis.[272] In this respect, emphasizing this case-by-case approach to deciding on the required mental harm, a recent case law from the ICTR further clarifies that 'serious mental harm' is not necessarily required to reach the level of "*more than* minor or temporary impairment of mental faculties".[273] Indeed, the potential facts or evidence illustrated by international judges as falling into the category of 'serious bodily or mental harm' are the ones usually confined to a specific incident at the 'conduct level' such as "sexual violence, rape, mutilations and interrogations combined with beatings, and/or threats of death, were all acts that amount to serious bodily harm".[274] They are directed towards individual body and mind. The case law even observes that serious bodily harm is "self-explanatory" as is clearly the case with "seriously injur[ing] the health, caus[ing] disfigurement or caus[ing] any serious injury to the external, internal organs or senses".[275] Introducing into the 'conduct level' another layer of consideration—i.e., whether the bodily or mental harm was "of such a serious nature as to threaten [a group's] destruction in whole or in part"—entails a risk of complicating the already convoluted structure of the crime definition of genocide. The danger/threat/risk factor involving the destruction of at least a substantial part of a group is to be assessed at the 'context level'.

---

[270] *Ibid.* para 732.

[271] Prosecutor v. Rukundo, Appeals Judgment, 20 October 2010, paras 227–238; Prosecutor v. Rukundo, Partially Dissenting Opinion of Judge Pocar, 20 October 2010, paras 1–13. For an analysis of the Appeals Chamber's reasoning on Rukundo's attempted rape incident, *see* Oosterveld 2012, pp. 200–202 (while criticizing the majority, highly appreciates Judge Pocar's dissenting opinion).

[272] Prosecutor v. Kayishema and Ruzindana, Trial Judgment, 21 May 1999, paras 108 and 110.

[273] Prosecutor v. Kanyarukiga, Trial Judgement, 1 November 2010, para 637. (emphasis added).

[274] Prosecutor v. Kayishema and Ruzindana, Trial Judgment, 21 May 1999, para 108.

[275] *Ibid.* para 109.

It is only the *predisposition or tendency* towards the physical or biological destruction of a group that is required to be shown at the 'conduct level' especially in respect of a specific conduct of an individual actor. In other words, the notion of threat to the destruction of a group does not fit a specific actor's specific act at the 'conduct level'. Such a dissonant conceptual combination should be avoided. In this regard, the reformulation of the 'threat feature (originally proposed by the ILC)' in the recent ICTY case *Tolimir* is a welcome development: "The [bodily or mental harm] must be of such a serious nature as to contribute or tend to contribute to the destruction of all or part of the group[.]"[276] The threshold has been lowered from 'of such a serious nature as to *threaten the destruction*' to 'of such a serious nature as to *contribute or tend to contribute to the destruction*'. While a Hutu footsoldier's specific conduct of injuring his Tutsi neighbor does not and cannot by itself threaten the destruction of the Tutsi ethnic group, the conduct's innate predisposition or tendency towards the destruction certainly enable it to contribute or tend to contribute to the destruction of the group. As hinted by the lowest *actus reus* provision in Article 25 of the ICC Statute ("[i]n any other way contribute to" in Article 25(3)(d)),[277] the threshold of an 'act of contributing to the

---

[276] Prosecutor v. Tolimir, Trial Judgment, 12 December 2012, para 738. For an actual application of this new formulation, see *Ibid.* para 755 (in its legal findings section, the Trial Chamber observes, "[t]here is no doubt in mind of the Chamber that the suffering inflicted on the Bosnian Muslim men in the days and hours before their deaths was of the most serious nature, and that these horrific confrontations with death have had a long-standing impact on those that survived. […] The Chamber is satisfied, moreover, that *this harm was of such a nature as to contribute or tend to contribute to* the destruction of all or part of the group in that their suffering prevented these members of the group from leading a normal and constructive life".). (emphasis added). I am, however, a bit troubled with the reason given by the Trial Chamber for its determination that the harm was of such a nature as to contribute or tend to contribute to the destruction. I don't think the question of whether the affected members of a group can lead a normal and constructive life is directly related to the result/danger of *a physical or biological destruction* of a group which is one of the ultimate parameters of the crime of genocide.

[277] Werle 2009, p. 185 (as to *actus reus* of Article 25(3)(d), explains, "[a]ny contribution to the group crime ("in any other way contributes") not covered by another form of participation [provided under Article 25], especially assistance, establishes the criminal responsibility of the accessory. This catch-all rule includes financing and other forms of indirect support for crimes against international law".). Werle also observes that this 'contribution' in the sense of Article 25(3)(d) is the "weakest from of liability". Werle 2007, p. 971. Similarly, the ICC Pre-Trial Chamber in *Lubanga* regards Article 25(3)(d) as a "residual form of accessory liability[.]" Prosecutor v. Lubanga, Decision on the Confirmation of Charges, 29 January 2007, para 337. For an opposing view, *see* Vest 2014, p. 305. It is to be noted that, in respect of Article 25(3)(d), the ICC Pre-Trial Chamber in *Mbarushimana* sets the threshold of 'contribution' at a higher level by requiring a "significant contribution" (lower than 'essential' or 'substantial' though). In doing so, the Chamber refers to the cases of lardlords, grocers, utility providers, secretaries, janitors and even taxpayers. Prosecutor v. Mbarushimana, Decision on the Confirmation of Charges, 16 December 2011, paras 277 and 285. On appeal, although the majority of the Appeals Chamber declined to discuss the merit of this legal question, Judge Silvia Fernández de Gurmendi, in her separate opinion, expressed an opposing view, observing that the phrase 'in any other way' "indicates that there should not be a minimum threshold or level of contribution under this mode of liability". Prosecutor v. Mbarushimana, Separate Opinion of Judge Silvia Fernández de Gurmendi, 30 May 2012, para 7 *et seq.* To the contrary, it seems

destruction' should be considered lower than an 'act of threating the destruction'.[278] In this respect, it is to be noted that the *Krajišnik* Trial Judgment (which originally suggested the new 'contribute to' formulation) associates the 'contribute to' formulation with all five underlying acts of genocide.[279] This is very understandable in view of the fact that predisposition and tendency towards destruction is a fundamental common feature of all five underlying acts. This predisposition and tendency has been paraphrased by the *ad hoc* tribunals for other underlying acts than 'causing serious bodily or mental harm' as follows: (i) 'objective probability of the conditions of life leading to the physical destruction of the group' (as to the underlying act of 'deliberately inflicting on the group conditions of life calculated to bring about its physical destruction in whole or in part')[280]; and (ii) 'under such circumstances as to lead to the death of all or part of the displaced population' (as to forcible transfer taking on the underlying act of 'causing serious bodily or mental harm').[281] Regarding the remaining three underlying acts of 'killing', 'imposing measures intended to prevent births', and 'forcibly transferring children', the Trial Chamber in *Krajišnik* elucidates,

> [I]n the context of genocide[,] the act must contribute, or tend to contribute, to the destruction of the protected group or part thereof. Murder has that effect, as do the two types of *actus reus* [of] measures to prevent births in the group and transfer of children out of the group.[282]

Footnote 277 (continued)

Judge Christine van den Wyngaert agrees with the 'significant contribution' standard. Prosecutor v. Ngudjolo, Concurring Opinion of Judge Christine van den Wyngaert, 18 December 2012, para 44. For a critical overview of this jurisprudence in *Mbarushimana*, *see* DeFalco 2013. As regards the *Mbarushimana* Pre-Trial Chamber's concern on lardlords, grocers, and utility providers etc., *see* Fletcher 2000, §8.5.2 and §8.8.2; Ohlin 2007, p. 79 ("[…] these contributions are best viewed as commodities because they are readily available on the open market. [...] if one merchant does not sell the gasoline, another merchant will".). Note however that Ohlin regards Article 25(3)(d) as a codification of the joint criminal enterprise doctrine.

[278] For a differing view which seems to suggest that the two thresholds of 'threatening the destruction' and 'contributing to the destruction' are identical, *see* Prosecutor v. Karadžić, Transcript, 28 June 2012, pp. 28765–28766 ("[Evidence] indicates that Bosnian Serb forces caused serious bodily or mental harm to many Bosnian Muslims and/or Bosnian Croats during their detention in multiple detention facilities. However, in order to support a conviction for genocide, the bodily or mental harm inflicted on members of a group must be *of such a serious nature as to threaten its destruction in whole or in part*. In that regard, the Chamber has not heard evidence, even taken at its highest, which could support a conclusion by a reasonable trier of fact that the harm caused reached *a level where it contributed to or tended to contribute to the destruction* of the Bosnian Muslims and/or Bosnian Croats in whole or in part or that it was committed with the intent to destroy those groups".) (emphasis added).

[279] Prosecutor v. Krajišnik, Trial Judgment, 27 September 2006, parsa. 859–863.

[280] Prosecutor v. Tolimir, Trial Judgment, 12 December 2012, para 742; Prosecutor v. Karadžić, Transcript, 28 June 2012, p. 28767.

[281] Prosecutor v. Tolimir, Trial Judgment, 12 December 2012, para 739; Prosecutor v. Karadžić, Transcript, 28 June 2012, p. 28766.

[282] Prosecutor v. Krajišnik, Trial Judgment, 27 September 2006, para 861.

In this manner, it appears the case law of the ICTY and the ICTR is struggling to detach the notion of threat from the level of underlying acts, which should be commended. The *ad hoc* tribunals' experience in terms of the threat feature of genocide thus far demonstrated leads to a conclusion that the right venue to discuss the notion of 'danger/threat/risk' to the existence of a protected group is the 'context level'—i.e., the 'manifest pattern of similar conduct' element. It should be remembered again that, when the *Al Bashir* Pre-Trial Chamber employed the notion of 'concrete threat' in substantiating the contextual element of genocide in the form of 'a manifest pattern of similar conduct', the Chamber almost completely neglected to give due consideration to the well-established substantiality requirement. This neglect is problematic because the substantiality requirement is an authoritative interpretation of the 'context level' ("in whole of in part") of genocide resulting from serious scholarly and jurisprudential debates for more than fifty years.[283] As Claus Kress has rightly observed, what the contextual element of core international crimes itself "essentially suggests" is a "real danger".[284] In this sense, it would not be a complete exaggeration to say that what the Majority of *Al Bashir* actually did was to interpret the notion of 'real danger' (the contextual element of genocide) with the notion of 'real danger' ('concrete threat').

The notion of 'danger/threat/risk', be it concrete or abstract, implies an existence of a source, author or originator. Thus, it is the preposition 'from' that always, explicitly or implicitly, accompanies the concept of 'danger/threat/risk'. That is to say, the notion of 'danger/threat/risk' *is dependent on* an objective reality as its origin. Accordingly, addressing the 'danger/threat/ risk' without giving a due consideration to that objective reality as its origin is destined to cause confusion. From a different angle, the 'danger/threat/risk' factor can provide a good lead to the origin. One can infer the existence of the origin from the pertaining 'danger/threat/risk'. This conceptual framework entailing the 'danger/threat/risk' and its origin well fits the relationship between the 'concrete threat' and the substantiality requirement. More specifically, it is the 'destruction of at least a substantial part' that has originally generated the *effect* of 'concrete threat'. Thus, the 'concrete threat' should not be considered the *content or substance* of the 'destruction of at least a substantial part'. Rather, the 'concrete threat' is a *lead or proof* that is pointing at the fulfilment of the substantiality requirement. I think, in this context, the case of the Srebrenica massacres provides us with a good point of reference because, in that case, the decision on whether a substantial part of the Bosnian Muslim group was targeted was the one of the most challenging issues.[285] In this respect, the Trial Chamber in *Krstić* observes,

---

[283] For this history, *see* Sect. 3.3.1 *supra*.

[284] *See* this chapter, footnote 228 *supra* and accompanying text.

[285] For the *Krstić* Appeals Chamber's decision rejecting the Defence's argument of 'part of a part' ('men of military age in Srebrenica' forming part of 'Bosnian Muslims in Srebrenica' which also forms part of 'Bosnian Muslims in general'), *see* Prosecutor v. Krstić, Appeals Judgment, 19 April 2004, paras 18–19. *See also* Prosecutor v. Krstić, Partial Dissenting Opinion of Judge Shahabuddeen, 19 April 2004, paras 43-44.

[T]he Trial Chamber has concluded that [...] the military aged Bosnian Muslim men of Srebrenica do in fact constitute a substantial part of the Bosnian Muslim group, *because the killing of these men inevitably and fundamentally would result in* the annihilation of the entire Bosnian Muslim community at Srebrenica.[286]

This paragraph clearly tells us that the 'danger/threat/risk' to the existence of the Bosnian Muslim group was used as a *proof* for the substantiality requirement. Furthermore, the *Karadžić* Trial Chamber also suggests an idea that the 'danger/threat/risk' to the existence of a protected group can be a *proof* for the substantiality requirement when it states, "[h]owever, the evidence the Chamber received in relation to the municipalities, even if taken at its highest, does not reach the level from which a reasonable trier of fact could infer that a significant section of the Bosnian Muslim and/or Bosnian Croat groups and a substantial number of members of these groups were targeted for destruction *so as to have an impact on the existence* of the Bosnian Muslims and/or Bosnian Croats as such".[287]

At this juncture, let us return back to the questions I put earlier in this subsection: if the substantiality requirement had been given due consideration by the Majority in *Al Bashir*, would the judges have still set forth the 'concrete threat' requirement? Does the substantiality requirement negate the need of the 'concrete threat' requirement? What is the relationship between the substantiality requirement and the notion of 'concrete threat'? My reasoning thus far leads me to an answer that the Majority in *Al Bashir* was mistaken in employing the notion of 'concrete threat' for the purpose of interpreting the contextual element of genocide ('a manifest pattern of similar conduct'). The 'concrete threat' should not be considered the substance of the contextual element of genocide in the form of 'manifest pattern of similar conduct'. Rather, in view of the significant conceptual overlap between the substantiality requirement and the 'context level' of genocide as explicated in the previous subsection,[288] I think that the substantiality element, which is an objectified incarnation of the 'in whole or in part' component of the genocidal intent element, is sufficient to satisfy the manifest pattern element. In this regard, an objection based on the apparent conduct-based description of the 'manifest pattern of similar *conduct*' element should be considered naïve in that that manifest pattern, however palpable it is, means nothing for the purpose of constituting the crime of genocide if it does not accompany the destruction of at least a substantial part (which is a collective 'result' rather than 'conduct'). Without the showing of the destructive result at the 'context level' that manifests itself as 'collective genocide',

---

[286] Prosecutor v. Krstić, Trial Judgment, 2 August 2001, para 634. This finding was subsequently endorsed by the Appeals Chamber. Prosecutor v. Krstić, Appeals Judgment, 19 April 2004, para 28.

[287] Prosecutor v. Karadžić, Transcript, 28 June 2012, p. 28765. (emphasis added). At the stage of deciding on Karadžić's motion for a judgment of acquittal, the *Karadžić* Trial Chamber had to decide on Count 1 (Genocide in 1992) which was even more challenging than the Srebrenica massacres (Count 2: Genocide in 1995) in terms of the substantiality requirement. The cited observation was made in the course of deliberating on Count 1 in respect of which the Chamber ultimately granted the accused's motion for acquittal.

[288] *See* this chapter, footnotes 200–201 *supra* and accompanying text.

the legal establishment of the crime of genocide is not possible. Moreover, the purpose-based genocidal intent theory expounded in Chap. 2 is not operative without acknowledging the result element at the 'context level'. In this respect, Hans Vest's claim that genocide is an "intentional result crime" is perceptive.[289] It deserves note, in this context, that, in paraphrasing the meaning of the notion of 'special intent', the Appeals Chamber of the Special Tribunal for Lebanon states,

> Under international law, when a crime requires special intent (*dolus specialis*), its constitutive elements can only be met, and the accused consequently be found guilty, if it is shown beyond reasonable doubt that he specifically intended to reach the *result* in question, that is, he entertained the required special intent.[290]

To sum up, only when the decision on the substantiality requirement is difficult, can the 'danger/threat/risk' towards the future survival of a protected group play a role of a factual springboard to infer the 'destruction of a substantial part'. In a case where the destructive result itself is evident as was the case in Rwanda, the value of the 'danger/threat/risk' feature as a proof for the substantiality requirement would be significantly decreased. This line of reasoning is also consistent with the view of Raphael Lemkin when he stated that "destruction in part must be of a substantial nature [...] *so as to affect* the entirety".[291]

3.5 'Collective Genocide' and the Degraded Importance of Individualistic Genocidal Intent

The common definition of genocide in the Genocide Convention and other international instruments reveals that the crime of genocide per se is of a collective nature. The five underlying acts listed therein do not constitute separate

---

[289] For a relevant discussion, *see* text accompanying notes 205–219 *supra*. In this respect, a proposal by Mr. Morozov representing the USSR presented during the drafting negotiations of the Genocide Convention is noteworthy. Underlining the "risk of ambiguity" potentially to be posed by the wording of "committed with the intent to ...", Mr. Morozov advanced a proposal to constitute the crime of genocide as a result crime. U.N. GAOR, 6th Comm., 3d Sess., 73d mtg. at 96, U.N. Doc. A/C.6/SR.73 (Oct. 13, 1948) ("Rather [...] than stipulate the intent to destroy, the article should define acts of genocide as acts 'resulting in' destruction".). Mr. Morozov's proposal to characterize the crime of genocide as a result-crime, which placed an emphasis on the objective aspect of genocide, was quite a radical one. His proposal faced immediate opposition from the delegations from the United States and Belgium. But the French delegation support the USSR proposal stating that "[t]he idea of the USSR was apparently to guard against the possibility that the presence in the definition of the word "intent" might be used as a pretext, in the future, for pleading not guilty on the grounds of absence of intent. In the circumstances, the objective concept seemed to be more effective than the subjective concept". See *Ibid.* at 97.

[290] Prosecutor v. Ayyash, Interlocutory Decision on the Applicable Law: Terrorism, Conspiracy, Homicide, Perpetration, Cumulative Charging, 16 February 2011, para 248.

[291] 2 Executive Sessions of the Senate Foreign Relations Committee, Historical Series, at 370 (1976), *as cited in* LeBlanc 1991, p. 44, footnote 21. (emphasis added).

offences.[292] They are only the 'acts or types of acts' that can constitute the crime of genocide.[293] By contrast, the items listed under the provision of crimes against humanity or war crimes are not, strictly speaking, 'acts or types of acts' but offences per se. For instance, 'torture' as provided in Article 7(1)(f) of the ICC Statute itself constitutes a crime or an offence. 'Torture', however, is not an 'act or type of act against humanity'. Instead, it is the act of inflicting severe physical or mental suffering that can constitute the offence of 'torture'.[294] This inherently collective nature of genocide has also silently controlled the manner in which international judges render their decisions on the charge of genocide. For instance, compare the way in which convictions on the charges of genocide, crimes against humanity and war crimes are phrased in the 'disposition' section of *Popović* et al. case:

- Vujadin Popović

The Accused Vujadin Popović is found GUILTY pursuant to Article 7(1) of the Statute, through committing, of the following counts:

> Count 1: Genocide
> Count 3: Extermination, as a crime against humanity;
> Count 5: Murder, as a violation of the laws and customs of war;
> Count 6: Persecution, as a crime against humanity.[295]

On the ICTR side, for example, the *Rukundo* Trial Judgment renders its verdict by stating:

For the reasons set out in this judgment, having considered all evidence and arguments, the Trial Chamber finds unanimously as follows in respect of Emmanuel Rukundo:

---

[292] *See* U.N. GAOR, 6th Comm., 3d Sess., 73d mtg. at 89-90, U.N. Doc. A/C.6/SR.73 (Oct. 13, 1948) (rejecting, by 28 votes to 14, with 1 abstention, the USSR proposal to replace the phrase "the following [...] acts" with "the following crimes" in the definition of genocide contained in the Ad Hoc Committee Draft Convention on Genocide). Note however that it is not clear what exactly the reason for this rejection is. The only objection recorded in this report is that of the Philippines which states, "the convention clearly defined genocide as a crime and that repetition was therefore unnecessary". *See also* Akhavan 2005, p. 992 ("Since the underlying acts – such as killing or causing serious bodily or mental harm – are not international crimes as such [...]").

[293] Compare the wordings between Article III of the Genocide Convention and equivalent provisions in Article 4 of the Law on the establishment of the ECCC. *See also* Vest 2007, p. 793 ("[t]his part of the crime may be termed the 'individual act' underlying the crime of genocide".). Article III: "The following acts shall be punishable: (a) Genocide; (b) Conspiracy to commit genocide; (c) Direct and public incitement to commit genocide; (d) Attempt to commit genocide; (e) Complicity in genocide". Article 3: "The following acts shall be punishable under this Article: [1] attempts to commit acts of genocide; [2] conspiracy to commit acts of genocide; [3] participation in acts of genocide".

[294] ICC Statute, Article 7(2)(e) ("'Torture' means the intentional infliction of severe pain or suffering, whether physical or mental, upon a person in the custody or under the control of the accused; except that torture shall not include pain or suffering arising only from, inherent in or incidental to, lawful sanctions[.]").

[295] Prosecutor v. Popović et al., Trial Judgment, 10 June 2010, p. 832.

Count 1: GUILTY of Genocide
Count 2: GUILTY of Murder as a Crime against Humanity
Count 3: GUILTY of Extermination as a Crime against Humanity[296]

Evidently, neither Chambers bothers to specify the underlying act of genocide in its verdict, while they do enumerate the particular offence for crimes against humanity and war crimes. This practice also applies in the charging practice of the Prosecution of both tribunals. When specifying the 'count' in the indictment, prosecutors do not say 'Count 1: Killing as a Genocide' or 'Count 1: Causing serious bodily or mental harm as a Genocide'. They just say 'Count 1: Genocide'. For international judges and prosecutors, the uncountable noun of 'genocide' is a generic term.[297]

It seems to me that it is for this reason that the ICC Elements of Crimes employs the term 'by' to link the crime of genocide and the five underlying acts when it says, for instance, 'genocide *by* killing'. For crimes against humanity and war crimes, however, the document uses the term 'of'—e.g., 'crime against humanity *of* murder' and 'war crime *of* willful killing'.[298] Furthermore, contrary to other core international crimes like crimes against humanity and war crimes, the term 'genocide' is always used in the singular form. At least within a singular situation of a mass atrocity, international criminal law does not know such a word as 'genocides'. In this respect, we can guess that there might be a certain similarity between genocide and the crime of aggression because the term 'aggression' is likewise hardly used in a plural form within a given situation.[299]

Though it has never been said overtly, the term 'genocide' as used by international criminal courts has double meaning—i.e., 'collective genocide' and 'individual (conviction of) genocide'. The former encompasses the latter, providing an overall factual circumstance in which an individual perpetrator is to be legally found guilty of individual genocide. The notion of 'collective genocide' in this sense connotes both multiple perpetrators and multiple victims. Since there is no specific statutory basis to define the notion of 'collective genocide',[300] it is, legally speaking, a theoretical concept. Yet, a review of relevant case law reveals that the function of this concept is real and significant. I have shown that the role played by 'collective genocide' is similar to the contextual element of crimes against humanity ("a widespread or systematic attack on a civilian population") in that acts of individual genocide must form part of 'collective genocide'.[301] The difference is

---

[296] Prosecutor v. Rukundo, Trial Judgment, 27 February 2009, p. 176.

[297] For more discussion on the generic notion of genocide, *see* Sect. 4.2.1 *infra*.

[298] Note, however, that the para 10 of the 'General introduction' to the ICC Elements of Crimes states as follows: "The use of short titles for the crimes has no legal effect".

[299] In this respect, note that I argue hereinbelow that genocide and aggression share the characteristic of being a leadership crime. *See* Sect. 4.2.3 and Chap. 5 *infra*.

[300] The closest would be "a manifest pattern of similar conduct directed against that group" as provided in the ICC Elements of Crimes.

[301] For the purpose of this book, I ignore the very unrealistic scenario of 'one-man genocide' in respect of which the ICC Elements of Crimes provides, "conduct that could itself effect such destruction".

that, while the contextual element of crimes against humanity can be established by *actus reus* only ("a course of conduct involving multiple commission of acts referred to in para 1" plus "a State or organizational policy"),[302] the case law treats 'collective genocide' as if it requires both the underlying acts element (collective acts) and the genocidal intent element (collective intent).[303] The evidentiary significance of 'collective genocide' attributed thereto by the jurisprudence of the *ad hoc* tribunals is quite overwhelming, as the Appeals Chamber in *Karemera* et al. observes that "[w]hether genocide occurred in Rwanda is of obvious relevance to the Prosecution's case; it is a *necessary*, although not sufficient, part of that case".[304] In this context, the word "necessary" strongly implies that 'collective genocide' has been practically dealt with by the case law as an element of the crime of genocide, just like the element of 'a widespread or systematic attack' vis-à-vis crimes against humanity. Moreover, in this decision in *Karemera*, the Appeals Chamber took judicial notice of 'collective genocide' in Rwanda, which freed subsequent case law from a burden of finding 'collective genocide' again and again. In this respect, 'collective genocide' should not be considered an element of the crime to be proved by the Prosecution during each trial within a given situation.

Accordingly, 'collective genocide' puts us in a noteworthy situation: this notion is a "necessary" part of a case, but not an element of crime. The ICTR Trial Chambers' finding of 'collective genocide' throughout Rwanda in 1994 either from evidentiary examination (before *Karemera*) or from taking a judicial notice (after *Karemera*) has been a necessary condition for them to find an individual defendant guilty of genocide on the basis of factual findings of specific incidents alleged in the Indictment. Such individual conviction of genocide has always been rendered against the background of 'collective genocide'.[305] In a sense, the crime of genocide itself is of a collective nature, rather than individual. Except for the word "intent", every key word in the definition of genocide is of a collective nature. The definition of the crime of genocide says:

In the present Convention, genocide means any of the following acts committed with intent to destroy, in whole or in part, a national, ethnical, racial or religious group, as such:

---

[302] *See* ICC Statute, Article 7(2)(a).

[303] *See* Sects. 3.2.1.1–3.2.1.3 *supra*. For example, paras 116 and 117 of the *Akayesu* Trial Judgment states, "[c]onsequently, in view of these widespread killings the victims of which were mainly Tutsi, the Chamber is of the opinion that the first requirement for there to be [collective] genocide has been met, the killing and causing serious bodily harm to members of a group. The second requirement is that these killings and serious bodily harm, as is the case in this instance, be committed with the intent to destroy, in whole or in part, a particular group targeted as such".

[304] Prosecutor v. Karemera et al., Decision on Prosecutor's Interlocutory Appeal of Decision on Judicial Notice, 16 June 2006, para 36. (emphasis added). With regard to the issue of taking judicial notice of genocide, *see* Sluiter and Vriend 2012; Jørgensen 2007; Heller 2007; Mamiya 2007.

[305] In contrast, in trial judgments in which the verdict was acquittal, there is hardly a discussion on collective genocide or judicial notice thereof. *See e.g.*, Prosecutor v. Mpambara, Trial Judgement, 12 September 2006.

(a) Killing members of the group;
(b) Causing serious bodily or mental harm to members of the group;
(c) Deliberately inflicting on the group conditions of life calculated to bring about its physical destruction in whole or in part;
(d) Imposing measures intended to prevent births within the group;
(e) Forcibly transferring children of the group to another group.[306]

The phrase "inflicting on the group" in (c) well explains the manner of all those five genocidal acts—i.e., 'inflicting collective killing on the group', 'inflicting collective bodily or mental harm on the group', 'inflicting collective measures to prevent births on the group', and 'inflicting collective loss of children on the group'. At this point, a reference to an old document might be illustrative. Seven months after the publication of Raphael Lemkin's book *Axis Rule in Occupied Territory* in which the term 'genocide' was coined by Lemkin for the first time, Justice Robert Jackson, taking part in the London Conference, referred to:

> Genocide or destruction of racial minorities and subjugated populations by such means and methods as (1) underfeeding; (2) sterilization and castration; (3) depriving them of clothing, shelter, fuel, sanitation, medical care; (4) deporting them for forced labour; (5) working them in inhumane conditions.[307]

Comparing the underlying acts of the current definition of genocide and of the description in Justice Jackson's report, I would argue that specific acts that constitute the crime of genocide are not the main concern of the international community that drafted the Genocide Convention.[308] The underlying acts provided in the definition themselves are of a collective nature. What is crucial is the collective dimension of genocide in both theoretical and practical terms. Thus, one might even argue that: (i) the crime of genocide itself is a collective crime; (ii) an individual alone cannot commit the crime of genocide; (iii) instead, an individual can only participate in the crime of genocide; (iv) accordingly, the crime of genocide

---

[306] Convention on the Prevention and Punishment of the Crime of Genocide, 9 December 1948, 78 U.N.T.S. 277, Article II.

[307] 'Planning Memorandum Distributed to Delegations at Beginning of London Conference, June 1945', *in* Report of Robert H. Jackson, United States Representative to the International Conference on Military Trials 68 (1949), *as cited in* Schabas 2012, p. 65.

[308] Though not in the realm of criminal law, strictly speaking, in the jurisprudence of the European Court of Justice and the Court of First Instance, the 'European cartel offence' is regarded as constituting a single infringement when the Court of First Instance states as follows: "It would be thus artificial to split up such continuous conduct, characterized by a single purpose, by treating it as consisting of a number of separate infringements. The fact is that the applicant took part – over a period of years – in an integrated set of schemes constituting a single infringement, which progressively manifested itself in both unlawful agreements and unlawful concerted practices". Cases 1/89 etc., Rhone-Poulenc v. Commission (1991) ECR II-867, at 1074–5, *as cited in* Harding 2013, p. 253. Christopher Harding place the 'European cartel offence' under the generic category of 'joint criminal enterprise' on the basis of the common features between the two such as 'common plan', 'manifested unlawful practices', and 'knowing participation'. He further emphasizes the importance of 'participation in the cartel' as a legal basis of imposing liability and sanctions, rather than specific acts of fixing prices and quotas. *Ibid.*

has the characteristics of JCE, the 'common purpose/plan' of which can only be a genocidal plan to destroy a group;[309] (v) in this sense, "with intent to destroy" can only mean a collective plan.[310] In this scenario, genocidal intent stops being a *mens rea*, but transforms to an *actus reus*, just as the 'common purpose/plan' element is in the doctrine of JCE. This transformation makes sense because criminal law usually requires collective mind to be interpreted as a material element, rather than a mental element.[311]

References

Akhavan P (2005) The crime of genocide in the ICTR jurisprudence. J Int Crim Justice 3:989–1006

Akhavan P (2012) Reducing genocide to law: definition, meaning, and the ultimate crime. Cambridge University Press, Cambridge

Ambos K (2009) What does "intent to destroy" in genocide mean? Int Rev Red Cross 91:833–858

Ambos K, Wirth S (2001) Sentencing, cumulative charging, genocide and crimes against humanity. In: Klip A, Sluiter G (eds) Annotated leading cases: international criminal tribunal for Rwanda 1994–1999, vol 2, 703 et seq

Bantekas I (2010) International criminal law, 4th edn. Hart Publishing, Oxford

Bohlander M (2009) Principles of German criminal law. Hart, Oxford

Cassese A (2002) Genocide. In: Cassese A, Gaeta P, Jones JRWD (eds) The Rome Statute of the international criminal court: a commentary, vol I. Oxford University Press, Oxford, pp 335–352

Cassese A, Gaeta P, Baig L, Fan M, Gosnell C, Whiting A (2013) Cassese's international criminal law. Oxford University Press, Oxford

Choi TH, Kim S (2011) Nationalized international criminal law: genocidal intent, command responsibility, and an overview of the South Korean implementing legislation of the ICC Statute. Mich State J Int Law 19:589–637

Clark RS (2001) The mental element in international criminal law: the Rome Statute of the international criminal court and the elements of offences. Crim Law Forum 12:291–334

Cryer R (2009) The definitions of international crimes in the Al Bashir arrest warrant decision. J Int'l Crim Justice 7:283–296

Cryer R, Friman H, Robinson D, Wilmshurst E (2010) An introduction to international criminal law and procedure. Cambridge University Press, Cambridge

Cupido M (2014) The contextual embedding of genocide: a casuistic analysis of the interplay between law and facts. Melbourne J Int Law 15:1–36

DeFalco RC (2013) Contextualizing actus reus under Article 25(3)(d) of the ICC Statute. J Int Crim Justice 11:715–735

Denno DW (2004) When two become one: views on Fletcher's 'two patterns of criminality'. Tulsa Law Rev 39:781–801

---

[309] As to the relationship between crime and mode of liability, note the ICC Statute, Article 8(2) (e)(viii) ('ordering the displacement of the civilian population') in which a form of participation—i.e., 'ordering' is specifically provided as a conduct type of a criminal offence. *See also* the introductory part of Sect. 4.2.3 *infra*.

[310] *See* Chap. 4, footnote 193 *infra* and accompanying text regarding the terms "common intention", "common plan", and "common genocidal plan" as used by the *Kayishema and Ruzindana* Trial Judgment.

[311] E.g., 'agreement' required by the offence of conspiracy is an *actus reus*. *See generally* Okoth 2014.

Drost P (1959) The crime of state: genocide. Leyden, Sythoff

Duff RA (1990) Intention, agency and criminal liability: philosophy of action and the criminal law. Basil Blackwell, Oxford

Fletcher GP (2000) Rethinking criminal law. Oxford University Press, Oxford

Fletcher GP, Ohlin JD (2005) Reclaiming fundamental principles of criminal law in the Darfur case. J Int Crim Justice 3:539–561

Greenawalt AKA (1999) Rethinking genocidal intent: the case for a knowledge-based interpretation. Colum Law Rev 99:2259–2294

Hall J (1960) General principles of criminal law, 2nd edn. Bobbs-Merrill, Indianapolis

Harding C (2013) Criminal enterprise: individuals, organisations and criminal responsibility. Routledge, London

Heller KJ (2007) Prosecutor v. Karemera et al., Decision on prosecutor's interlocutory appeal of decision on judicial notice. Am J Int Law 101:157–163

Heller KJ (2009) The majority's problematic interpretation of genocide's contextual element. http://opiniojuris.org/2009/03/06/the-majoritys-problematic-interpretation-of-genocides-contextual-element. Accessed 23 Dec 2015

Isaacs T (2006) Individual responsibility for collective wrongs. In: Harrington J, Milde M, Vernon R (eds) Bringing power to justice? The prospects of the international criminal court. McGill-Queen's University Press, Montreal, pp 167–190

Jessberger F (2009) The definition and the elements of the crime of genocide. In: Gaeta P (ed) The UN genocide convention: a commentary. Oxford University Press, Oxford, pp 87–111

Jørgensen N (2001) The definition of genocide: joining the dots in the light of recent practice. Int Crim Law Rev 1:285–313

Jørgensen N (2007) Genocide as a fact of common knowledge. Int Comp Law Q 56:885–898

Kress C (2005) The Darfur report and genocidal intent. J Int Crim Justice 3:562–578

Kress C (2006) The crime of genocide under international law. Int Crim Law Rev 6:461–502

Kress C (2007) The international court of justice and the elements of the crime of genocide. Eur J Int Law 18:619–629

Kress C (2009) The crime of genocide and contextual elements: a comment on the ICC pre-trial chamber's decision in the Al Bashir case. J Int Crim Justice 7:297–306

LeBlanc LJ (1984) The intent to destroy groups in the genocide convention: the proposed U.S. understanding. Am J Int Law 78:369–385

LeBlanc LJ (1991) The United States and the genocide convention. Duke University Press, Durham

Lemkin R (1947) Genocide as a crime under international law. Am J Int Law 41:145–151

Lemkin R (2008) Axis rule in occupied Europe: laws of occupation, analysis of government, proposals for redress, 2nd edn. The Law Book Exchange Ltd, Clark

Lippman M (1998) The convention on the prevention and punishment of the crime of genocide: fifty years later. Ariz J Int Comp Law 15:415–514

Luban D (2004) A theory of crimes against humanity. Yale J Int Law 29:85–167

Mamiya R (2007) Taking judicial notice of genocide? The problematic law and policy of the Karemera decision. Wis Int Law J 25:1–22

May L (2010) Genocide: a normative account. Cambridge University Press, Cambridge

Nersessian DL (2010) Genocide and political groups. Oxford University Press, Oxford

Ohlin JD (2007) Three conceptual problems with the doctrine of joint criminal enterprise. J Int Crim Justice 5:69–90

Ohlin JD (2014) Searching for the hinterman: in praise of subjective theories of imputation. J Int Crim Justice 12:325–343

Okoth JRA (2014) The crime of conspiracy in international criminal law. Asser Press, The Hague, T.M.C

Oosterveld V (2001) The context of genocide. In: Lee RS (ed) The international criminal court: elements of crimes and rules of procedure and evidence. Transnational Publishers, Ardsley, pp 44–49

Oosterveld V (2012) Contextualizing sexual violence in the prosecution of international crimes. In: Bergsmo M (ed) Thematic prosecution of international sex crimes. Torkel Opsahl Academic EPublisher, Beijing, pp 189–206

Ormerod D (2011) Smith and Hogan's criminal law, 13th edn. Oxford University Press, Oxford

Robinson N (1960) The genocide convention: a commentary. Institute of Jewish Affairs, New York

Robinson PH, Grall JA (1983) Element analysis in defining criminal liability: the model penal code and beyond. Stanford Law Rev 35:681–762

Rückert W, Witschel G (2004) Genocide and crimes against humanity in the elements of crimes. In: Fischer H, Kress C, Lüder SR (eds) International and national prosecution of crimes under international law. Berliner Wissenschafts, Berlin, pp 59–94

Schabas W (2005) Darfur and the "odious scourge': the commission of inquiry's findings on genocide. Leiden J Int Law 18:871–885

Schabas W (2012) Unimaginable atrocities: justice, politics, and rights at the war crimes tribunals. Oxford University Press, Oxford

Shaw MN (1989) Genocide and international law. In: Dinstein Y (ed) International law at a time of perplexity: essays in honour of Shabtai Rosenne. Martinus Nijhoff, Leiden, pp 797–820

Simester AP, Sullivan GR (2010) Simester and Sullivan's criminal law: theory and doctrine, 4th edn. Hart Publishing, Oxford

Sluiter G, Vriend K (2012) Defending the 'undefendable'? Taking judicial notice of genocide. In: van der Wilt HG et al (eds) The genocide convention: the legacy of 60 years. Martinus Nijhoff, Leiden, pp 81–93

van Sliedregt E (2012) Individual criminal responsibility in international law. Oxford University Press, Oxford

Verdirame G (2000) The genocide definition in the jurisprudence of the ad hoc tribunals. Int Comp Law Q 49:578–598

Vest H (2007) A structure-based concept of genocidal intent. J Int Crim Justice 5:781–797

Vest H (2014) Problems of participation—unitarian, differentiated approach or something else? J Int Crim Justice 12:295–309

Werle G (2007) Individual criminal responsibility in article 25 ICC Statute. J Int Crim Justice 5:953–975

Werle G (2009) Principles of international criminal law. Asser Press, The Hague, T.M.C

Werle G, Jessberger F (2014) Principles of international criminal law, 3rd edn. Oxford University Press, Oxford

Wirth S (2003) Germany's new international crimes code: bringing a case to court. J Int Crim Justice 1:151–168

Zahar A, Sluiter G (2007) International criminal law: a critical introduction. Oxford University Press, Oxford

Chapter 4
Collective Genocidal Intent and Genocide as a Criminal Enterprise

Abstract In this chapter, this book turns its focus to the conceptual counterpart of individual genocidal intent—that is, 'collective genocidal intent' called by various names such as 'genocidal plan/plan of genocide', 'wider plan to destroy', 'wider-ranging intention to destroy', 'overall intent', and so on in the relevant jurisprudence of the *ad hoc* tribunals. I demonstrate that, without collective genocidal intent, there is no individual genocidal intent. I also point out that what the *ad hoc* tribunals inferred from the overall context of violence had not been individual genocidal intent, but its collective counterpart. In the course of analyzing the notion of collective genocidal intent, this chapter finds a possibility of conceptual congruence between 'collective genocidal intent' of genocide and the 'common/purpose plan' element of JCE. The common characteristic of collective criminality is horizontally linking the two substantive theories of genocide and JCE. It is also noted that, both theories share a similar vertical structure: i.e., the combinations of 'context level' and 'conduct level' for genocide, and the level of 'JCE members' and that of 'non-JCE members' for JCE. Within this horizontal and vertical structure of both theories, I employ the two sets of parallel notions: 'collective genocidal intent' corresponding to 'common purpose/plan' on one hand, and 'individual genocidal intent' corresponding to 'shared intent' on the other. Within this conceptual framework, I detect the inherent logic of JCE within genocide. Under the conceptual force of the logic of JCE within the concept of genocide, individual genocidal intent is presumed (and thereby watered down) on the basis of objective features of individual participation, contribution and rank, in the same manner as 'shared intent' is presumed under the JCE doctrine. It is only when evidentiary weight of such objective aspects of an individual actor is strong enough to convince international judges that they proceed to presume individual genocidal intent. In this way, the catchphrase of the 'crime of *mens rea*' proves empty. At this juncture, the flow of arguments of this book compelled me to make a difficult observation: that is to say, genocide being a leadership crime. The weight and importance of collective criminality at the 'context level' (reflected in the two essential notions of 'collective genocide' and 'collective genocidal intent') which forcefully operates through the inherent logic of JCE within the concept of genocide left no other option. In this context, admitting principal liability for subordinate

© T.M.C. ASSER PRESS and the author 2016
S. Kim, *A Collective Theory of Genocidal Intent*, International Criminal Justice Series 7, DOI 10.1007/978-94-6265-123-4_4

actors means unfair labeling of criminal liability of leadership actors and subordinate actors by grouping them together without proper differentiation. This would result in a deflation of criminal liability of leadership-level actors, while inflating that of subordinates. At the same time, it is emphasized that this does not exonerate subordinate actors: they can still be convicted as aiders and abettors of genocide.

Keywords Collective genocidal intent · Common purpose/plan · Individual genocidal intent · Shared intent · Joint criminal enterprise · Leadership crime

Contents

4.1 Unveiling Collective Genocidal Intent

4.1.1 Without Collective Genocidal Intent, No Individual Genocidal Intent

With respect to core international crimes, the ICTY Appeals Chamber in *Tadić* observes that "[m]ost of the time these crimes do not result from the criminal propensity of single individuals but constitute manifestations of collective criminality: the crimes are often carried out by groups of individuals acting in pursuance of a common criminal design".[1] In the same vein, we have already seen above that Raphael Lemkin was of the view that "the [Genocide] Convention applies only to actions undertaken on a mass scale and not to individual acts [...]",[2] the spirit of which has been preserved by subsequent international case law primarily by way of applying the substantiality requirement. This collective dimension of the crime of genocide, however, has been the source of pervasive confusion surrounding the genocidal intent element apparently worded from the individualistic perspective. Challenging the

---

[1] Prosecutor v. Tadić, Appeals Judgment, 15 July 1999, para 191.

[2] *See* Chap. 3, footnote 8 *supra*.

individualistic understanding of the notion of genocidal intent, John R.W.D. Jones observes that "it is not warranted to infer that the reference to the specific intent of genocide in the [Genocide] Convention was intended to refer to the *mens rea* requirement of an accused charged before a criminal tribunal".[3] He further argues that "requiring proof that an accused *personally* intended the destruction of a group not only runs counter to the concept of genocide as a mass crime, but risks becoming hopelessly embroiled in an examination of the accused's motives".[4] In the previous chapter, we have gone through the relevant case law of the *ad hoc* tribunals and concluded that the hidden notion of 'collective genocide' has been the cornerstone of substantive legal analysis of the crime of genocide. We have also witnessed that international judges do not hesitate to apply the elements of genocide originally stipulated from the individualistic standpoint to the anonymous collective genocidal campaign at the 'context level'. The term "general elements" used by the *Musema* Trial Chamber was a clear example of such a practice devoid of any statutory legal grounds.[5] Similarly, the *Kayishema and Ruzindana* Trial Chamber also puts a question that "whether the events in Rwanda as a whole, reveal the existence of the elements of the crime of genocide".[6] At any rate, an examination of the relevant case law clearly demonstrates that international judges have widely used the notion of genocide in an abstract sense, without having any particular individual perpetrators in mind. In doing so, as we have studied earlier, the judges have perceived the concept of genocide in a collective sense which is composed of two components of 'collective act' and 'collective genocidal intent'. In the most memorable paragraph of the *Krstić* Trial Judgment concerning the notion of genocidal intent, the Chamber observes,

> As a preliminary, the Chamber emphasises the need to distinguish between the individual intent of the accused and the intent involved in the conception and commission of the crime. The gravity and the scale of the crime of genocide ordinarily presume that several protagonists were involved in its perpetration. Although the motive of each participant may differ, the objective of the criminal enterprise remains the same. In such cases of joint perpetration, the intent to destroy, in whole or in part, a group as such *must be discernible*

---

[3] Jones 2003, p. 478.

[4] *Ibid.* at 468.

[5] Prosecutor v. Musema, Trial Judgment, 27 January 2000, para 354. In Sect. 3.2.1.3 *supra*, I concluded that the 'general elements' in *Musema* means 'collective genocide' that consists of 'collective acts' and 'collective genocidal intent'.

[6] Prosecutor v. Kayishema and Ruzindana, Trial Judgment, 21 May 1999, para 274. Exactly the same mode of analysis which inquires whether the elements of genocide have been fulfilled in a collective context has been applied by the International Commission of Inquiry on Darfur as follows: "Arguably, two elements of genocide might be deduced from the gross violations of human rights perpetrated by Government forces and the militias under their control. These two elements are: first, the *actus reus* consisting of killing, or causing serious bodily or mental harm, or deliberately inflicting conditions of life likely to bring about physical destruction; and, second, [...] the existence of a protected group being targeted by the authors of criminal conduct. [...] However, one crucial element appears to be missing, at least as far as the central Government authorities are concerned: genocidal intent". International Commission of Inquiry on Darfur, Established Pursuant to Resolution 1564 (2004), Report to the United Nations Secretary–General, 25 January 2005, para 518.

in the criminal act itself, apart from the intent of particular perpetrators. It is then necessary to establish whether the accused being prosecuted for genocide share the intention that a genocide be carried out.[7]

As I see it, in this paragraph, the phrase "must be discernible in the criminal act itself, apart from the intent of particular perpetrators" is the key to understanding the notion of collective genocidal intent. Given the prevalent practice of addressing the collective genocidal intent only in an indirect manner, it is even refreshing to see such a clear-cut distinction made by the *Krstić* Trial Chamber between the individual genocidal intent ("individual intent of the accused") and the collective genocidal intent ("the intent involved in the conception and commission of the crime"). In the relevant international jurisprudence and scholarly discussions, we can hardly find such a straightforward distinction between these two pivotal concepts.[8] Within the context of this paragraph, it seems clear that the Chamber refers to the concept of collective genocidal intent four times as follows: (i) "the intent involved in the conception and commission of the crime"; (ii) "the objective of the criminal enterprise"; (iii) "the intent to destroy, in whole or in part, a group as such"; and (iv) "the intention that a genocide be carried out". If I take up the Chamber's words in this cited paragraph, the notion of collective genocidal intent is an "intent to destroy [...] apart from the intent of particular perpetrators". Since it is an intent 'apart from the intent', it exists external to the 'individual inner state of mind (the realm of *mens rea*)'.[9] And, since it exists externally, the collective genocidal intent "must be discernible in the criminal act itself [...]". The term 'criminal act' in this sentence of course means collective actions performed by a collective at the 'context level'. As a consequence, the notion of collective genocidal intent should be considered an objective element at the 'context level'. In the relevant case law, the notion of

---

[7] Prosecutor v. Krstić, Trial Judgment, 2 August 2001, para 549. (emphasis added).

[8] Literatures that pay serious attention to the notion of collective genocidal intent include: Jones 2003, p. 467, Verdirame 2000, pp. 584–588; Fletcher and Ohlin 2005, pp. 545–548 (in particular, observing that "[i]n cases recognized by history as true genocide, the ethnic group as a whole carries the intent to destroy".); Bantekas 2010, p. 210 (citing the same paragraph from *Krstić*, states, "[t]he execution of genocide involves two levels of intent: that of the criminal enterprise as a collectivity and that of the participating individuals".); Kress 2007. pp. 622–623 (citing the same paragraph from *Krstić*, Claus Kress also states, "[...] the fundamental distinction between collective and individual genocidal intent, which was so well expressed by the Trial Chamber in *Krstić*[.] [...] The [International] Court [of Justice] did recognize the possibility of a collective genocidal intent in theory. It failed, however, to shed light on the relevance of such a collective intent for the intent of individual perpetrators".). What led Kress to recognize the distinction between collective and individual genocidal intent was the necessity of contextual element of genocide as an objective reference point for individual genocidal intent. He observes that, without a contextual element, an individual "cannot have a *realistic* genocidal intent". (emphasis in original). *Ibid.* at 622. *See also*, as regards the core international crimes in general, Gadirov 2014, p. 355 (recommending the future case law of the ICC to "distinguish the executive collective intentions from subsidiary particular intentions, rather than downplaying the collective character of mass atrocities".).

[9] Quoting philosopher David J. Velleman's account of shared intention which, states that "intentions may be extramental, existing outside of mental states", philosopher Brook Jenkins Sadler says she is "sympathetic to the idea that intentions are not necessarily mental states". Sadler 2006, p. 125, footnote 29.

collective genocidal intent has been referred to as "genocidal plan/plan of geno-cide",[10] "wider plan to destroy",[11] "wider-ranging intention to destroy",[12] "overall intent",[13] "scheme to perpetrate the crime of genocide",[14] "intention to commit all-inclusive genocide",[15] "[Bosnian Serb forces'] intent to kill all the Bosnian Muslim men of military age in Srebrenica",[16] "specific intent of the Bosnian Serb Forces",[17] "specific intent of such [physical] perpetrators",[18] "a lethal plan to destroy the male population of Srebrenica once and for all",[19] "criminal plan to kill the Bosnian Muslim men originated earlier by General Mladić and other VRS officers",[20] "kill-ing plan",[21] "the intention of the perpetrators of these killings",[22] "the resolve of the perpetrators of these massacres",[23] "an intention to wipe out the Tutsi group in its entirety"[24] and so forth. Quoting the same paragraph from *Krstić* (para 549), Claus Kress observes,

> This statement correctly underscores the need to distinguish between a 'collective' and an 'individual' intent for the typical case of genocide. The collective intent can best be defined as the goal or the objective behind a concerted campaign to destroy, in whole or in part, a protected group. Such goal or objective may well have originated from the desire of one or more individual directors but it will then acquire an impersonal, objective exist-ence (most usefully referred to as the "overall genocidal plan") [...].[25]

It seems to me that, as Kress insightfully points out, it was the anonymous, impersonal and objective nature of both the collective genocidal intent and the

---

[10] Prosecutor v. Kayishema and Ruzindana, Trial Judgment, 21 May 1999, paras 291, 292 and 312.

[11] Prosecutor v. Jelisić, Trial Judgment, 14 December 1999, para 79.

[12] *Ibid.*

[13] Prosecutor v. Munyakazi, Trial Judgment, 5 July 2010, para 496.

[14] Prosecutor v. Gacumbitsi, Trial Judgment, 17 June 2004, para 288.

[15] Prosecutor v. Jelisić, Trial Judgment, 14 December 1999, para 28.

[16] Prosecutor v. Krstić, Trial Judgment, 2 August 2001, para 598.

[17] Prosecutor v. Tolimir, Trial Judgment, 12 December 2012, para 769. *See also* Prosecutor v. Blagojević and Jokić, Trial Judgment, 17 January 2005, para 674 ("one single scheme to commit genocide of the Bosnian Muslims of Srebrenica").

[18] Prosecutor v. Karadžić, Transcript, 28 June 2012, p. 28751. Yet, given that collective geno-cidal intent is to be generally formulated at the leadership level, this description of collective genocidal intent sounds crude and inappropriate.

[19] Prosecutor v. Krstić, Trial Judgment, 2 August 2001, para 622.

[20] *Ibid.* para 631 ("General Krstić participated in the full scope of the *criminal plan to kill* the Bosnian Muslim men originated earlier by General Mladić and other VRS officers".). (emphasis added).

[21] *Ibid* para 632 ("On 15 July, General Krstić's participation in the *killing plan* reached an aggressive apex".). (emphasis added).

[22] Prosecutor v. Akayesu, Trial Judgment, 2 September 1998, para 118.

[23] *Ibid.* para 119.

[24] *Ibid.* para 121.

[25] Kress 2006, pp. 495–496.

substantiality requirement that has advertently or inadvertently compelled international judges to find 'collective genocide' before considering the individual genocidal intent of the accused.[26] In this context, it is crucial to note that collective genocidal intent is not only to be distinguished from its individualistic counterpart, but also to be regarded as a necessary condition for the latter to ever exist.[27] In other words, there can be no individualistic genocidal intent without there first being the collective genocidal intent.[28] It was exactly at this point where the International Commission of Inquiry on Darfur went astray. After concluding that "the Government of Sudan has not pursued a policy of genocide", the Report says,

> One should not rule out the possibility that in some instances *single individuals*, including Government officials, may entertain a genocidal intent, or in other words, attack the victims with the specific intent of annihilating, in part, a group perceived as a hostile ethnic group. If any single individual, including Governmental officials, has such intent, it would be for a competent court to make such a determination on a case by case basis. Should the competent court determine that in some instances certain individuals pursued the genocidal intent, the question would arise of establishing any possible criminal responsibility of senior officials either for complicity in genocide or for failure to investigate, or repress and punish such possible acts of genocide.[29]

What the Commission of Inquiry neglected to consider in this paragraph is the top-down vertical nature of genocidal intent.[30] That is to say, an individual inner state of mind *alone*, however egregious it may be, cannot have any legal significance in terms of the law of genocide, because without a collective genocidal context to give it effect, the individual intent is empty.[31] In this respect, to the extent

---

[26] For detailed examples of such international judges' efforts to find 'collective genocide', *see* Sect. 3.2.1 *supra*.

[27] For a similar view, *see* Schabas 2005, p. 877 ("Although there is no shortage of authority claiming that a state plan or policy is not an element of the crime of genocide, the behavior of the Security Council and the Darfur Commission shows that state plan or policy is not only an essential ingredient of the crime, it is the question that lies at the very heart of the debate".).

[28] The most conspicuous example would be the three underlying acts as provided in Articles 6(c), (d), and (e) of the ICC Statute. Cassese and his co-authors rightly point out that, in relation to these three acts, a plan or policy is required to be proven. Cassese et al. 2013, p. 141. *See also* Bantekas 2010, p. 209.

[29] International Commission of Inquiry on Darfur, Established Pursuant to Resolution 1564 (2004), Report to the United Nations Secretary–General, 25 January 2005, para 520. (emphasis in original).

[30] For a similar view, *see* Kress 2007, p. 623. The top-down vertical nature of genocidal intent is reflected in the mode of its analysis taken by the *ad hoc* tribunals, as we have extensively studied in Sect. 3.2 *supra*. Guglielmo Verdirame also observes: "[A] method for the judicial application of the *dolus specialis* in genocide has been crystallised by the *ad hoc* Tribunals. First, contextual elements are assessed. In particular, the existence of a genocidal plan and the commission of a genocide in a given situation are considered. Secondly, the Tribunals examine the genocidal intent of the individual, which is distinct but yet connected to the collective genocidal intent underlying the plan". Verdirame 2000, p. 588.

[31] For a similar discussion in relation to a hypothetical ultimate mastermind's individual mind, *see* Sect. 4.2.2.5 *infra*.

that the term '*mens rea*' is used to indicate the individualistic inner state of mind of an individual perpetrator, the famous slogan of genocide—i.e., the 'crime of *mens rea*'—is an absolute misconception. Rather, as we have extensively studied in the previous chapter, the crime of genocide does require the *objective* contextual element involving a physical and/or biological destruction of at least a substantial part of a group resulting from the collective genocidal intent, which is also of an *objective* characteristic, existing external to the individual state of mind.[32] Due to the quasi-element nature of the collective dimension of genocide at the 'context level', there is no room for an individualistic *mens rea* alone to secure a genocide conviction without the establishment of the 'collective genocide' beforehand. The validity of this proposition is demonstrated by the consistent acquittal decisions of the genocide charges rendered by the ICTY vis-à-vis the atrocities *other than* the Srebrenica massacre of 1995. Before addressing the individual genocidal intent of the accused, the ICTY Trial Chambers take the step of considering whether there existed a 'collective genocide' and collective genocidal intent without having any *identified* individual perpetrator or perpetrators in mind.[33] That is, the Trial Chambers always try to find an *anonymous* collective genocidal intent on the basis of collective actions and at least a partial destruction of the group targeted.[34] In this sense, defying the slogan of 'crime of *mens rea*', the Chambers heavily rely on the *objective* facts at the 'context level' in rendering a decision on genocide

---

[32] It is to be noted that 'biological destruction' takes time. That is, in the case of 'biological destruction', the 'destruction' is to be conceived as a 'remote harm' or a 'threat in the remote future'. For instance, the destructive consequence of 'imposing measures intended to prevent births within the group' (ICC Statute, Article 6(d)) or 'forcibly transferring children of the group to another group' (ICC Statute, Article 6(e)) would not be realized on the spot. For more discussion, *see* Chap. 3, footnotes 116 and 214 *supra*.

[33] *See e.g.*, Prosecutor v. Karadžić, Transcript, 28 June 2012, pp. 28768–29770. In entering a judgment of acquittal on count 1 (genocide in certain municipalities in 1992), the Trial Chamber holds that "notwithstanding the [provocative] statements of the accused, there is no evidence upon which, if accepted, a reasonable trier of fact could find that the acts of killing, serious bodily or mental harm, and conditions of life inflicted on the Bosnian Muslims and/or Bosnian Croats [occurred in certain municipalities in 1992] were perpetrated with the *dolus specialis* required for genocide". In this respect, it is to be noted that the focus of the Chamber discussion is not on the accused's individual genocidal intent, but on the collective genocidal intent. Thus, the Chamber observes that "the [collective] nature, scale and context of these culpable acts, be it in all the municipalities covered by the indictment or the seven municipalities in which genocide is specifically alleged, do not reach the level from which a reasonable trier of fact could infer that they were committed with [collective] genocidal intent". *Ibid.* at 28768.

[34] I use the word 'anonymous' because it is when the phrase "intent to destroy" is used in international judgments without any indication of its possessor, be it collective or individual, that it is very likely that the phrase points to the collective genocidal intent as is the case in *Tolimir* as follows (see the italicized phrase): "The Chamber [...] found that these criminal acts were committed *with the intent to physically destroy the protected group*, thus amounting to the crime of genocide. The Chamber now turns to the question of whether the Accused had the requisite *mens rea* for the crime of genocide, namely, a specific intent "to destroy, in whole or in part, a national, ethnical, racial or religious group, as such". Prosecutor v. Tolimir, Trial Judgment, 12 December 2012, para 1157.

charges. In addition to the reason for acquittal in the *Jelisić* case that we have reviewed in detail in the previous chapter,[35] let us have a close look at the *Karadžić* case. In *Karadžić*, on the second count of genocide ('count 2' concerning the Srebrenica massacre in 1995 in respect of which the substantiality requirement was met), the Trial Chamber reaches an affirmative conclusion with regard to the anonymous collective genocidal intent ("specific intent of such [physical] perpetrators")[36] inferred from the targeting/destruction of a substantial part of the Bosnian Muslim group in Srebrenica (killings of thousands of Bosnian Muslim men of military age),[37] and moves on to the next step of the inquiry, asking about Karadžić's individual genocidal intent.[38] Yet, in relation to the first count of genocide ('count 1' concerning the alleged genocidal atrocities in certain municipalities in 1992), the Chamber did not even engage in the inquiry into the accused's individual genocidal intent, because the first-step evidentiary examination on the 'collective genocide' and anonymous collective genocidal intent produced a negative answer.[39] In this respect, the *Karadžić* Trial Chamber concludes,

> Finally, having reviewed the totality of the evidence which the Chamber has received with respect to the killing, of serious bodily or mental harm to, the forcible displacement of, and conditions of life inflicted on Bosnian Muslims and/or Bosnian Croats in detention facilities in the municipalities, the Chamber finds that there is no evidence that *these actions* reached a level from which a reasonable trier of fact could draw an inference that they were committed with an intent to destroy in whole or in part the Bosnian Muslims and/or Bosnian Croats as such.[40]

---

[35] *See* Sect. 3.2.2 *supra*.

[36] I have already said this description of collective genocidal intent is crude and inappropriate. *See* this chapter, footnote 18 *supra*.

[37] Prosecutor v. Karadžić, Transcript, 28 June 2012, pp. 28751–28752 ("Accordingly, the Chamber finds that there is evidence on which, if accepted, a reasonable trier of fact could be satisfied beyond reasonable doubt that genocide charged pursuant to Article 4 of the Statute was carried out by Bosnian Serb forces in Srebrenica".).

[38] *Ibid.* at 28757–29758.

[39] In this respect, the Appeals Chamber is of the view that the Trial Chamber "also expressly considered evidence concerning Karadžić himself and other alleged JCE members". Prosecutor v. Karadžić, Rule 98 *bis* Appeals Judgement, 11 July 2013, para 82. Despite that the Trial Chamber indeed makes a vague reference to Karadžić and other members of the Bosnian Serb leadership, the Appeals Chamber misses the Trial Chamber's overall structure of evidentiary analysis consisting of the two-step inquiry upon (i) the anonymous collective genocidal intent of the physical perpetrators; and (ii) the accused's individual genocidal intent within the framework of JCE I, which follows the analysis pattern of the ICTY's other case law on genocide. In this context, para 83 of the Appeals Judgment deserves a close reading where the Appeals Chamber reinforces its position which I consider to be far-fetched because there is no reason for the Trial Chamber to employ a different analytic method in relation to count 1 (genocide in certain municipalities in 1992) and count 2 (genocide in Srebrenica in 1995), especially in view of the fact that the Prosecution alleges the JCE I for both counts. *See* Prosecutor v. Karadžić, Third Amended Indictment, paras 37–39 and paras 42–44 (Feb. 27, 2009).

[40] Prosecutor v. Karadžić, Transcript, 28 June 2012, pp. 28768–28769. (emphasis added).

As signified by the word "these actions", the Chamber's acquittal decision on this charge of genocide ('count 1') was made on the basis of its consideration of the *objective* aspects of the relevant atrocities. Accordingly, the Trial Chamber made it clear that, although it took note of evidence that the accused's statements and speeches signified his individual genocidal intent,[41] the Chamber acquitted him of the charge of genocide "in light of the scale and the context of the alleged crimes in the municipalities in 1992".[42] Put otherwise, it was the threshold of 'targeting/destruction of at least a substantial part' and the collective genocidal intent inferred therefrom that led the *Karadžić* Trial Chamber to determine that "these actions" did not reach the level of 'collective genocide'. The same pattern of deliberation has been followed by Trial Chambers in other cases dealing with charges of genocide in relation to incidents other than the Srebrenica massacre. In this respect, what the International Commission of Inquiry on Darfur opined above vis-à-vis the legal possibility of constructing the crime of genocide substantively on the basis of "single individuals" entertaining an individual genocidal intent is an evident contrast to the established practice of the ICTY. In my view, the Commission was preoccupied, and thereby misled, by the perception of genocide being a 'crime of *mens rea*'. The possibility of a positive legal finding of genocide apart from the 'collective genocide' suggested by the Darfur Commission is straightforwardly contradictory to the *Krstić* Trial Chamber's principle of genocidal intent being "discernible in the criminal act itself". On the other hand, it is important to note that the main conclusion made by the Commission of Inquiry— i.e., "the Government of Sudan has not pursued a policy of genocide"[43]—is consistent with the practice of the ICTY, affirming the pivotal role of collective

---

[41] I make this observation on the basis of a combined reading of pages 28763 and 28769 of the transcript, paying special attention to the Chamber's utterance of "notwithstanding the [genocidal] statements of the accused". The relevant text in 28763 states: "The Prosecution submits that what is of relevance is whether there was *dolus specialis*. In that respect, the Prosecution responds by reference to statements of the accused that he shared the intent to destroy the Bosnian Muslim and/or Bosnian Croat groups in part and that he encouraged the destruction of this protected group by the organs under his authority and control". On the other hand, the relevant text in 28769 states: "As stated earlier, the Prosecution in its response to the accused also refers to evidence of statements and speeches made by him and other members of the Bosnian Serb leadership which, according to the Prosecution, contained rhetorical warning of disappearance, elimination, annihilation or extinction of Bosnian Muslims in the event that war broke out. The Chamber has considered these examples as well as the other evidence received in relation to the accused in light of the scale and the context of the alleged crimes in the municipalities in 1992, and the inability to infer genocidal intent from other factors. Following this review, the Chamber finds that[,] *notwithstanding the statements of the accused*, there is no evidence upon which, if accepted, a reasonable trier of fact could find that the acts of killing, serious bodily or mental harm, and conditions of life inflicted on the Bosnian Muslims and/or Bosnian Croats were perpetrated with the *dolus specialis* required for genocide". (emphasis added). In view of the context, this *dolus specialis* clearly indicates the collective genocidal intent.

[42] Prosecutor v. Karadžić, Transcript, 28 June 2012, p. 28769.

[43] International Commission of Inquiry on Darfur, Established Pursuant to Resolution 1564 (2004), Report to the United Nations Secretary–General, 25 January 2005, para 518.

genocidal intent in determining whether the crime of genocide has been committed.[44] Borrowing the words of Larry May, now we can say with confidence that collective genocidal intent tantamount to a 'plan or policy to destroy' is the "most important element of genocide".[45] As I just said, the Darfur Commission concludes that "the Government of Sudan has not pursued a policy of genocide" because "one crucial element [of genocidal intent] appears to be missing".[46] The term 'policy of genocide' in this context certainly indicates the collective genocidal intent of an anonymous and objective nature.[47] Hence, in the relevant analysis of the report, the main hypothetical possessor of genocidal intent is not an individual, but a collective entity—i.e., the government of Sudan. In the Report, the "Government of Sudan" is represented by such terms as "attackers", the Government forces, the Janjaweed militias, the Government commissioner and the leaders of the militias. Thus, those few facts that the Commission mentions as indicative of the existence of genocidal intent are all of a collective nature, not individualistic: "the scale of atrocities"; "the systematic nature of the attacks"; and

---

[44] Yet, in contrast to the Darfur Commission of Inquiry's main conclusion involving the notion of collective genocidal intent ('governmental policy'), the Commission defines the concept of genocidal intent in an individualistic manner. *See* Chap. 2, footnote 27 *supra* and accompanying text.

[45] May 2010, pp. 126–127 ("It is indeed crucial that there be a plan that has as its purpose the destruction of protected group in whole or in substantial part. This is the collective intent that is the most important element of genocide".). See also *Ibid.* at 211–212 ("Genocide requires just this collective intent, and planning satisfies the requirement".). In discussing the Holocaust, May defines that a "plan plus the initiation [...] is a form of collective intent". *Ibid.* at 116. Larry May also uses the term "larger intent" for the purpose indicating collective genocidal intent (*Ibid.* at 209–10), while using the term "single intent" for individual genocidal intent (*Ibid.* at 119). William Schabas, on the other hand, prefers to use the term 'policy' for collective genocidal intent, e.g., as follows: "Neither the Darfur Commission nor the ICJ was looking for the specific intent of individual offenders. Rather, they were looking for the specific intent of a State, like Sudan, or a State-like entity, like the Bosnian Serbs. States, however, do not have specific intent. Individuals have specific intent. States have policy. The term specific intent is used to describe the inquiry, but its real subject is State policy". Schabas 2007, p. 970. The delegation of the United States to the drafting negotiations of the ICC Elements of Crimes also submitted a proposal specifying the collective genocidal intent using the term 'policy'. Proposal Submitted by the United States of America (Draft Elements of Crimes), U.N. Doc. PCNICC/1999/DP.4 (Feb. 4, 1999), at 5–6 ("That the person or persons were killed in conscious furtherance of a widespread or systematic policy or practice aimed at destroying such group".). For an example in which the term 'intention' is used in connection with a collective, see the phrase "intention of the group" as provided in Article 25(3)(d)(ii) of the ICC Statute. *See also* Application of Convention on Prevention and Punishment of Crime of Genocide (Bosn. & Herz. v. Serb. & Montenegro), 2007 I.C.J. 91, para 190 (Feb. 26) (suggesting a collective interpretation of intent by using a phrase "the intent, as a matter of policy").

[46] International Commission of Inquiry on Darfur, Established Pursuant to Resolution 1564 (2004), Report to the United Nations Secretary–General, 25 January 2005, para 518 (the Commission concluded that the intent behind the plan to attack civilian villages was "to drive the victims from their homes, primarily for purposes of counter-insurgency warfare".).

[47] For a similar view, *see* Fletcher and Ohlin 2005, p. 545 ("The Report of the International Commission of Inquiry concludes that there was no genocide in Sudan because there was no genocidal intent at the collective level [...]".).

"racially motivated statements by perpetrators that have targeted members of the African tribes only".[48] Further, it is interesting to note that the Commission's conclusion is drawn mainly on the basis of evidence demonstrating the absence of collective genocidal intent (reflected in a policy of genocide). Such facts are: (i) the fact that "the attackers refrained from exterminating the whole population that had not fled, but instead selectively killed groups of young men"[49]; (ii) the fact of forcible detention in IDP camps ("the populations surviving attacks on villages are not killed outright")[50]; (iii) the fact that the Government of Sudan allows humanitarian assistance for IDP camps;[51] (iv) the fact that "in a number of instances villages with a mixed composition (African and Arab tribes) have not been attacked".[52] and (v) an instance of killing an individual for the motive of appropriating the victim's property.[53] Thus, the Darfur Commission interpreted these facts as deviating from the *pattern of conduct* from which the collective genocidal intent—i.e., 'policy of genocide' or 'centralized guidance directing at the destruction of a group'—is supposed to be inferred.[54] On the ICTY's side, for instance, for the purpose of inferring the collective genocidal intent of the Bosnian Serb forces, the Trial Chamber in *Tolimir* places an emphasis on the *systematic pattern of killing* that made it possible for the Bosnian Serb forces to kill at least 5749 Bosnian Muslim men from Srebrenica "in a period of only several days".[55] The pattern of killings as found by the Chamber follows such steps as (i) deployment

---

[48] International Commission of Inquiry on Darfur, Established Pursuant to Resolution 1564 (2004), Report to the United Nations Secretary–General, 25 January 2005, para 513.

[49] *Ibid.*

[50] *Ibid.* para 515.

[51] *Ibid.*

[52] *Ibid.* para 516.

[53] *Ibid.* para 517.

[54] I borrow the phrase 'centralized guidance' from the Dusseldörf Higher Regional Court in *Jorgić* case. Ambos 2014, p. 17 (the Dusseldörf Higher Regional Court "argued in *Jorgić* that genocide requires a 'structurally organized centralized guidance'. The German Federal Constitutional Court (*Bundesverfassungsgericht*) adopted the same view".). Nikola Jorgić was the first defendant ever convicted of genocide by a German national court. The *Jorgić* judgment rendered by Dusseldörf Higher Regional Court in 1997 reflects the collective theory of genocidal intent. The court issued the genocide conviction against the backdrop of ethnic cleansing in Bosnia and Herzegovina. Despite the killings personally committed by Jorgić himself, the *actus reus* found by the court seems to be a form of participation in a campaign of ethnic cleansing. Hence, the court makes detailed findings with regard to the role played by Jorgić in the context of ethnic cleansing. On the other hand, the genocidal intent found by the court is a collective genocidal intent possessed by the "Serb political and military leadership, which had orchestrated the cleansing campaign". This collective genocidal intent was inferred from the "Serbs' systematic method, statements by then-president of the Republic of Srpska, Radovan Karadžić, and the circumstances of the campaign". This summary of *Jorgić* case is based on the description of the case in: Werle 2007.

[55] Prosecutor v. Tolimir, Trial Judgment, 12 December 2012, para 769.

of armed forces to "specifically selected remote locations to take part in [the] kill-ings";[56] (ii) the killings being committed "in an efficient and orderly manner"[57]; (iii) "machinery and manpower being swiftly put in place to remove, transport and bury thousands of bodies"[58]; (iv) the "bodies [being] later dug up and reburied in a further effort to conceal what had occurred"[59]; and (v) "several layers of leader-ship [being] involved in the organization and coordination of the killing opera-tion".[60] In this sense, the collective genocidal intent found by the *Tolimir* Trial Chamber comes closer to the plan or policy collectively devised and implemented by the Bosnian Serb forces. In the following subsection, let us have a closer look at the issue of 'pattern of conduct' as an indicative of the existence of the collec-tive genocidal intent.

4.1.2 Inferring My Intent from 'Acts of Others'?: Collective Genocidal Intent and the Pattern of Conduct

Collective genocidal intent being the 'most important element of genocide' explains the hidden rationale behind the common, and dubious, practice of infer-ring individual genocidal intent from the *context* of genocidal campaigns. It is to be remembered, however, that, in most of the cases, international judges have not expressly recognized the specific notion of collective genocidal intent per se. Instead, they have extensively taken into account proof of collective genocidal intent in finding the individual genocidal intent of the accused, which resulted in complaints from the defendants arguing that 'you infer my intent from the acts of others' as we will further examine in this subsection. Drawing the final conclusion on the issue of the genocidal intent of the accused, the *Akayesu* Trial Chamber states,

> [...] *The Chamber has already established that genocide was committed against the Tutsi group in Rwanda in 1994*, throughout the period covering the events alleged in the Indictment. Owing to the very high number of atrocities committed against the Tutsi, their widespread nature not only in the commune of Taba, but also throughout Rwanda, and to the fact that the victims were systematically and deliberately selected because they belonged to the Tutsi group, with persons belonging to other groups being excluded, the Chamber is also able to infer, beyond reasonable doubt, the genocidal intent of the accused in the commission of the above-mentioned crimes.[61]

---

[56] *Ibid.* para 770.

[57] *Ibid.*

[58] *Ibid.*

[59] *Ibid.*

[60] *Ibid.*

[61] Prosecutor v. Akayesu, Trial Judgment, 2 September 1998, para 730. (emphasis added).

Despite the Chamber's observation that an individual genocidal intent can also be inferred from the "acts and utterances of the accused",[62] what the Chamber claims here and throughout the relevant parts of the judgment is that an individual's genocidal intent can be inferred from the overall context of the atrocities. In this manner, the *Akayesu* Trial Chamber here engages in a risky practice of combining the 'conduct level' and 'context level'. The means of proof of genocidal intent set forth by the Chamber are: (i) "the general context of the perpetration of other culpable acts systematically directed against that same group, whether these acts were committed by the same offender or by others[63]"; (ii) "the scale of atrocities committed [...] in a region or a country[64]"; (iii) "the general nature" of such atrocities committed in a region or a country[65]; and (iv) "the fact of deliberately and systematically targeting victims on account of their membership of a particular group, while excluding the members of other groups".[66] In addition, the *Akayesu* Trial Chamber approvingly cites a decision from the ICTY that sets forth the potential proof of genocidal intent as follows: (i) "the general political doctrine which gave rise to the acts possibly covered by the definition in Article 4 [of the ICTY Statute][67]"; (ii) "the repetition of destructive and discriminatory acts[68]"; and (iii) "the perpetration of acts which violate, or which the perpetrators themselves considers to violate the very foundation of the group [i.e.,] acts which are not in themselves covered by the list in Article 4(2) [of the ICTY Statute] but which are committed as part of the same pattern of conduct".[69] It is to be noted that all these potential means of proof of individual genocidal intent are of a collective nature. But the cognitive gap between a 'mental state of an individual suspect' and 'collective conduct and circumstances' should not be ignored. How can you blame me for my alleged bad intent on the basis of what others did? In this respect, the validity of the established practice of the ICTY and the ICTR judges inferring individual genocidal intent from the overall context of violence should be questioned.

What is the rationale behind the international tribunals' practice of inferring genocidal intent from the overall context of violence? Ultimately, what they do

---

[62] *Ibid.* para 728.

[63] *Ibid.* para 523. A representative example of "other culpable acts systematically directed against the same group" is the forcible transfer of women, children and elderly from Srebrenica by the VRS. In this respect, the *Krstić* Appeals Chamber endorses the *Krstić* Trial Chamber's reliance on the proof of the forcible transfer in finding the collective genocidal intent of some members of the VRS Main Staff, making it clear that the "other culpable acts" encompasses conducts that do "not constitute in and of itself [one of the five] genocidal act[s]" listed in the Genocide Convention and other international instruments. Prosecutor v. Krstić, Appeals Judgment, 19 April 2004, para 33.

[64] Prosecutor v. Akayesu, Trial Judgment, 2 September 1998, para 523.

[65] *Ibid.*

[66] *Ibid.*

[67] *Ibid.* para 524.

[68] *Ibid.*

[69] *Ibid.*

infer is collective genocidal intent which is the 'most important element of genocide', not its individualistic counterpart. Otto Triffterer argues that any type of
contextual elements should not be introduced to the crime definition of genocide,
in order to facilitate the punishment of genocide at an early stage where contextual
circumstances such as 'a manifest pattern of similar conduct' have not yet developed.[70] He suggests that such a contextual element would narrow down the "scope
of punishable crimes of genocide and/or the jurisdiction of the [c]ourt".[71] This
position is based on the assumption that, at the early stage of genocidal campaign,
it is possible to spot the genocidal intent of an allegedly culpable individual. On
analysis, this assumption proves untenable. The experience of the ICTY and the
ICTR plainly tells us that the element of genocidal intent still remains difficult to
prove even when the atrocious situation has developed into a large-scale and well-
organized campaign of violence.

The reality goes even further. The relevant jurisprudence reveals that overall
circumstances including the existence of collective genocidal intent at the 'context
level' have attained the status of *sine qua non* in determining the existence of individual genocidal intent.[72] While it is absolutely reasonable to deliberate on the
substantiality requirement and collective genocidal intent on the basis of the collective facts, it is troublesome to note that international judges do not hesitate to
infer individualistic genocidal intent from the 'acts of others' spotted at the 'context level'. In this regard, the *Akayesu* Trial Chamber proclaims,

> On the issue of determining the offender's specific intent, the Chamber considers that
> intent is a mental factor which is difficult, even impossible, to determine. This is the rea-
> son why, in the absence of a confession from the accused, his intent can be inferred from a
> certain number of presumptions of fact. The Chamber considers that it is possible to
> deduce the genocidal intent inherent in a particular act charged from the general context
> of the perpetration of other culpable acts systematically directed against that same group,
> whether these acts were committed by the same offender or *by others*.[73]

The *Akayesu* Trial Chamber further affirms that,

> The Chamber is of the opinion that it is possible to infer the genocidal intention that pre-
> sided over the commission of a particular act, *inter alia*, from all acts or utterances of the
> accused, or from the general context in which other culpable acts were perpetrated sys-
> tematically against the same group, regardless of whether such other acts were committed
> by the same perpetrator or *even by other perpetrators*.[74]

Yet, the proposition that it is possible to infer individual intent from the acts of
others is, to a significant extent, counterintuitive. Even when parents rebuke their
child *for his own bad conduct*, it is not uncommon for the child to respond by

---

[70] Triffterer 2001, pp. 406–408.

[71] *Ibid.* at 408.

[72] In a similar vein, William Schabas is of the view that "[t]o be entirely accurate, nobody has
ever actually been convicted of genocide in the absence of evidence that he or she was part of
some broader plan or policy of a state or state-like entity". Schabas 2012, p. 131.

[73] Prosecutor v. Akayesu, Trial Judgment, 2 September 1998, para 523. (emphasis added).

[74] *Ibid.* para 728. (emphasis added).

saying "I didn't mean it". That is, judging a person's state of mind *from his own acts* is still a perilous exercise subject to an ample possibility of misjudgment.[75] Furthermore, given the gravity and the extreme level of stigmatization involving the crime of genocide, imputing a criminal liability to an individual suspect based on his individual genocidal intent inferred from acts of others seems hardly justifiable. As to the *Akayesu* principle of inferring individual genocidal intent from acts of others, John R.W.D. Jones rightly observes,

> Yet this reasoning, while specifically persuasive, is flawed. The fact that others are committing the same act does not per se permit the inference that the accused, while committing a similar act, was motivated by a specific intent. If a large number of murders of a specific religious group are being committed, and A then perpetrates a murder of that religious group, the only logical inference is that A's murder is part of a pattern of murders. It would not ordinarily permit any inference as to what was passing through A's mind when he committed the murder.[76]

Not surprisingly, such practice of inferring individual *mens rea* from the acts of others has been argued against on appeal. For example, in *Rutaganda*, the accused complained that the Trial Chamber erroneously inferred his individual genocidal intent from the "general context of the perpetration of acts *by others*".[77] Ultimately, the Appeals Chamber dismissed the appeal on the grounds that the Trial Chamber "based its finding that the Appellant had the specific intent on the analysis of *his own acts and conduct*"[78] such as "his direct participation in the widespread massacres committed against the members of the Tutsi group, and his ordering and abetting the commission of crimes against the Tutsis".[79] At this juncture, it is noteworthy that, through this observation, the *Rutaganda* Appeals Chamber actually acknowledges the reasonableness and rationality of the accused's complaint. Similarly, in *Gacumbitsi*, the Appeals Chamber also rejects the accused's appeal based on the same grounds by stating that "[i]n establishing the Appellant's mental state[,] the Trial Chamber relied *principally* on the Appellant's own actions and utterances[.]"[80] The Appeals Chamber further notes that [t]he only aspect of the Trial Chamber's analysis that relates to the actions of others is its reference to "the scale of the massacres", which is necessary for deciding whether Gacumbitsi's genocidal intent is directed toward *a substantial part* of the Tutsi group.[81] In both cases of *Rutaganda* and *Gacumbitsi*, however,

---

[75] There is even an assertion that "[e]ven an admission of a person regarding her state of mind is untrustworthy". Shapira-Ettinger 2007, p. 2591.

[76] Jones 2003, p. 475. For a similar view, *see* Obote-Odora 2002, p. 383 (commenting on the *Akayesu* Trial Judgment, opines that "[s]pecific intent of the accused should not be inferred or presumed from the criminal acts of other persons".).

[77] Prosecutor v. Rutaganda, Appeals Judgment, 26 May 2003, para 522. (emphasis added).

[78] *Ibid.* para 530. (emphasis added).

[79] *Ibid.* para 529.

[80] Prosecutor v. Gacumbitsi, Appeals Judgment, 7 July 2006, para 44. (emphasis added).

[81] *Ibid.*

the Appeals Chamber did not state that the Trial Chamber based its finding of the Appellant's individual genocidal intent "on the analysis of his own acts and conduct" *only*, thereby leaving the issue still open. Thus, the Appeal Chamber's reason for the dismissal of the appeal is incapable of refuting the Appellant's assertion that, if it had not been for the inference from the "general context of the perpetration of acts by others", the Trial Chamber might not have been able to find his individual genocidal intent regardless of whether "his own acts and conduct" was also taken into account or not. This observation is important because what the Appellant claims encompasses a situation where the Trial Chamber's inference of his individual genocidal intent was possible *only when both* the evidence of "his own acts and conducts" *and* "general context of the perpetration of acts by others" were considered. What was, in *Rutaganda*, such evidence of general context from which the Trial Chamber made the inference of the Appellant's genocidal intent? That was facts relating to the systematic selection of victims which is legally meaningful only at the 'context level'. Given the relevant part of the Trial Judgment, it seems that the Trial Chamber would have had significant difficulties in finding Rutaganda's individual genocidal intent had it not been for the evidence that "[t]he victims were *systematically* selected because they belonged to the Tutsi group and for the very fact that they belonged to the said group".[82] The *systematic* selection of the Tutsi victims not only involved "acts by other" but also had been a widespread practice performed by Hutu attackers throughout Rwanda from April to July 1994, as the Trial Chamber elaborates as follows,

> [...] [T]he Chamber finds that, at the time of the events referred to in the Indictment, numerous atrocities were committed against Tutsis in Rwanda. From the widespread nature of such atrocities, throughout the Rwandan territory, and the fact that *the victims were systematically and deliberately selected* owing to their being members of the Tutsi group, to the exclusion of individuals who were not members of the said group, the Chamber is able to infer a general context within which acts aimed at destroying the Tutsi group were perpetrated.[83]

To sum up, it appears that the ICTR Appeals Chamber has failed to answer the question put by defendants with regard to the pervasive practice of inferring genocidal intent from the general context ("relevant facts and circumstances").[84] In this respect, the *Krstić* Trial Chamber's position that genocidal intent, which should be understood as an intent of a criminal enterprise—i.e., the objective element of collective intent—"must be discernible" from the collective acts of violence "itself" can be an explanation for the dubious practice of inferring genocidal intent from

---

[82] Prosecutor v. Rutaganda, Trial Judgment, 6 December 1999, para 399. (emphasis added).

[83] *Ibid.* para 400. (emphasis added).

[84] *Jelisić* Appeals Judgment specifies the "relevant facts and circumstances" as, "[...] the general context, the perpetration of other culpable acts systematically directed against the same group, the scale of atrocities committed, the systematic targeting of victims on account of their membership of a particular group, or the repetition of destructive and discriminatory acts". Prosecutor v. Jelisić, Appeals Judgment, 5 July 2001, p. 47, as cited in Prosecutor v. Rutaganda, Appeals Judgment, 26 May 2003, para 525.

the general context of violence. According to the reasoning of the *Krstić* Trial Judgment, such practice of *ad hoc* tribunals makes perfect sense because what they are really inferring from the overall context is a collective genocidal intent, not its individualistic counterpart. In the same vein, the *Krstić* Appeals Chamber observes,

> The Defence also argues that the record contains no statements by members of the VRS Main Staff indicating that the killing of the Bosnian Muslim men was motivated by genocidal intent to destroy the Bosnian Muslims of Srebrenica. The absence of such statements is not determinative. Where direct evidence of genocidal intent is absent, the intent may still be inferred from the factual circumstances of the crime. *The inference that a particular atrocity was motivated by genocidal intent may be drawn, moreover, even where the individuals to whom the intent is attributable are not precisely identified.* If the crime committed satisfies the other requirements of genocide, and if the evidence supports the inference that the crime was motivated by the intent to destroy, in whole or in part, a protected group, a finding that genocide has occurred may be entered.[85]

Thus, the position of the ICTY Appeals Chamber is squarely contradictory to that of the ICTR Appeals Chamber.[86] That is to say, while the latter is of the view that individual genocidal intent is to be "principally"[87] inferred from the accused's "own actions and utterances", the former observes that genocidal intent "may still be inferred from the factual circumstances of the crime" despite the absences of such "direct evidence of genocidal intent". Furthermore, the ICTY Appeals Chamber's view is in outright contrast to that of the ICTR Appeals Chamber because the former denies any need to identify the "individuals to whom the intent is attributable". Without such identification, however, individual "actions and utterances" that the ICTR Appeals Chamber emphasizes for the purpose of inferring genocidal intent are meaningless. Hence, although both Appeals Chambers are using the same term 'genocidal intent', its content is different. That is, the italicized part in the paragraph strongly suggests that the notion of genocidal intent addressed by the *Krstić* Appeals Chamber is an objective element that exists outside the inner state of mind of the accused. Thus, despite the differing conclusions drawn on the question of whether the accused is guilty of genocide,[88] both the

---

[85] Prosecutor v. Krstić, Appeals Judgment, 19 April 2004, para 34. (emphasis added).

[86] This is difficult to understand since the ICTY and the ICTR share the same panel of the Appeals Chamber stationed in The Hague. This common appeals body has made a great contribution to maintaining consistency between the jurisprudence of the ICTY and the ICTR. For instance, explaining the two tribunals' coherent jurisprudence of the contextual element of crimes against humanity despite the distinct component provided in the chapeau of the relevant articles in the ICTY Statute ("when committed in armed conflict") and the ICTR Statute ("when committed […] on national, political, ethnic, racial or religious grounds") respectively, M. Cherif Bassiouni attributes this jurisprudential consistency to the common appeals body. *See* Bassiouni's 'foreword' in Agbor 2013, pp. xxvi–xxv.

[87] *See* this chapter, footnote 80 *supra* and accompanying text.

[88] While the *Krstić* Trial Chamber convicted the accused of genocide proper, the *Krstić* Appeals Chamber reversed this conviction and convicted the accused of aiding and abetting genocide.

Trial and the Appeals Chambers in *Krstić* agree that there is another layer of geno-cidal intent in addition to individualistic genocidal intent of the accused, which concerns the collective dimension. In this respect, it is regrettable that, while infer-ring genocidal intent from the acts of others, the relevant international judgments themselves have not been clear about the distinction between collective genocidal intent and individual genocidal intent. Had they been clear in explaining what they do infer from a general context of violence is not individual genocidal intent, but its collective counterpart, there would have not been such appeals made by the Defence on the practice of inferring genocidal intent from the acts of others.[89] With regard to the practice of inferring individual genocidal intent from the acts of others, John R.W.D. Jones again criticizes,

> As a matter of criminal law, this is curious. If the accused is, *ex hypothesi*, regarded merely as an individual, then the ease or difficulty of proving his mens rea *should not depend on the criminal behavior of others*. The [*Jelisić* Trial] Chamber's approach only makes sense if the special intent associated with genocide is considered an attribute of the overall plan in which the accused wilfully participated, rather than as a question of his *mens rea*.[90]

In other words, it is only in a case where the item thus inferred from the acts of others is the "overall plan" in which the accused participates, that the practice of the *ad hoc* tribunals inferring genocidal intent from the acts of others "makes sense". In this context, the 'overall plan' should be considered the collective geno-cidal intent which exists external to the inner state mind of the accused. This reminds us of what M. Cherif Bassiouni already proposed in 1993 that, as to "decision makers and commanders", genocidal intent can be shown by an "objec-tive legal standard", more specifically a "particular objective pattern of conduct".[91]

The notion of collective genocidal intent has been widely called 'genocidal plan or policy'. The relevant case law has consistently demonstrated that interna-tional judges, advertently or inadvertently, inferred such 'genocidal plan or policy' from the 'objective pattern of conduct'. Such 'pattern of conduct' has been under-stood to indicate the 'improbability of random occurrence' of the relevant acts, which in turn points at its systematic nature.[92] Accordingly, though in the context of discussing the contextual element of crimes against humanity, the *Kunarac* Trial

---

[89] An example of such challenge from defendants, *see* Prosecutor v. Rutaganda, Appeals Judgment, 26 May 2003, para 522 ("The Appellant asserts that the Trial Chamber, in particular, erred in law in finding that the specific intent could be inferred from the 'general context of the perpetration of acts by others'".).

[90] Jones 2003, p. 473. (emphasis added). For similar views, *see* Cryer et al. 2010, p. 226 ("Less reasonably, the ICTR has also stated that intent may be deduced from the behaviour of oth-ers[.]"). (emphasis in original).

[91] Bassiouni 1993, pp. 233–236. *See also* Vajda 2015, p. 166 ("Reliance on a 'pattern of acts' argument [in proving the genocidal intent element] moves the focus away from the intent of indi-vidual perpetrators to the intent of a 'higher authority' […]".).

[92] Prosecutor v. Kunarac et al., Trial Judgment, 22 February 2001, para 429. *See also* Prosecutor v. Tolimir, Trial Judgment, 12 December 2012, para 698.

Chamber states that the 'pattern of conduct'—"that is the non-accidental repetition of similar criminal conduct on a regular basis—are a common expression of such systematic occurrences".[93]

This observation is also significant for the law of genocide in that it provides a useful clue to substantiate the 'manifest pattern of similar conduct' element newly introduced by the ICC Elements of Crimes. Thus, in view of the *Kunarac* Trial Chamber's explanation of the 'pattern of conduct', one might spot the hidden ingredients of 'improbability of random occurrence' pointing at the 'organized and/or systemic nature of the collective conduct' within the 'manifest pattern of similar conduct' element. These ingredients ultimately suggest the 'common policy' and the collective genocidal intent. This is evident from the reasoning of the *Akayesu* Trial Chamber, which states that "[t]he concept of 'systematic' may be defined as thoroughly organized and following a regular pattern on the basis of a *common policy* involving substantial public and private resources".[94] In short, it seems to me that the 'manifest pattern of similar conduct' element can be regarded as either (i) providing a legal space to formulate the collective genocidal intent; or (ii) a substantiation of the collective genocidal intent contained in the 'intent to destroy' element. Either way, the manifest pattern element is closely related to collective genocidal intent.[95]

---

[93] *Ibid.* para 429. This view had been subsequently endorsed by the Appeals Chamber. Prosecutor v. Kunarac et al., Appeals Judgment, 12 June 2002, para 94.

[94] Prosecutor v. Akayesu, Trial Judgment, 2 September 1998, para 580. (emphasis added). Note that the Chamber makes this observation in explaining the contextual element of crimes against humanity. It is to be also noted that Darryl Robinson and others place the feature of 'improbability of random occurrence' at the center of proving the 'State or organizational policy' element under Article 7(2)(a) of the ICC Statute. Drawing on international and national case law, they argue that the policy element is to be readily inferred by the "manner in which the acts occur", and thus to be "satisfied by showing the improbability that the acts occurred randomly". For this purpose, they ultimately suggest the test of "plausibility of a hypothesis of coincidence". Prosecutor v. Gbagbo, Amicus Curiae Observations of Professors Robinson, deGuzman, Jalloh and Cryer, 9 October 2013, paras 22–36. M. Cherif Bassiouni also expresses a similar view in the context of discussing the crime of genocide. Bassiouni thus admits that genocidal intent can be shown by "the cumulative effect of the objective conduct" and/or "a particular objective pattern of conduct". Bassiouni 1993, p. 234.

[95] On the other hand, in terms of the issue of proving the collective genocidal intent through the 'manifest pattern of similar conduct', it deserves note that the ICJ observes that "for a pattern of conduct to be accepted as evidence of [the] existence [of genocidal intent], it would have to be such that it could only point to the existence of such intent". Application of Convention on Prevention and Punishment of Crime of Genocide (Bosn. & Herz. v. Serb. & Montenegro), 2007 I.C.J. 91, paras 373 and 376 (Feb. 26). Recently, the ICJ clarified that the phrase "could only point to" signifies the 'only reasonable inference' standard of inferring genocidal intent from the facts other than direct evidence. Application of the Convention on the Prevention and Punishment of the Crime of Genocide (Croatia v. Serbia), I.C.J. para 148 (Feb. 3, 2015). As regards the 'only reasonable inference' test for inferring genocidal intent, *see* Prosecutor v. Brđanin, Trial Judgment, 1 September 2004, para 970.

4.1.3 "Group as Such": Importance of Collective Motive/Reason for Targeting

It is not an exaggeration to say that the *Akayesu* Trial Judgment sets the tone for all the subsequent international case law on the issue of genocidal intent. More specifically, it has almost been blindly believed that this case is the authority for the purpose-based concept of genocidal intent.[96] A reading of the following two paragraphs, however, seems to suggest something different. The paras 520 and 521 of the Trial Judgment in *Akayesu* state,

> 520. With regard to the crime of genocide, the offender is culpable only when he has committed one of the offences charged under Article 2(2) of the Statute with the clear intent to destroy, in whole or in part, a particular group. The offender is *culpable because he knew or should have known* that the act committed would destroy, in whole or in part, a group.
> 521. *In concrete terms*, for any of the acts charged under Article 2(2) of the Statute to be a constitutive element of genocide, the act must have been committed against one or several individuals, *because* such individual or individuals were members of a specific group, and specifically *because* they belonged to this group. Thus, the victim is chosen not because of his individual identity, but rather *on account of* his membership of a national, ethnical, racial or religious group. The victim of the act is therefore a member of a group, chosen as such, which, hence, means that the victim of the crime of genocide is the group itself and not only the individual.

In para 520, the apparently purpose-based definition of genocidal intent ("clear intent to destroy") seems to be immediately contradicted by a knowledge (and/or constructive knowledge)-based explanation that "[t]he offender is culpable because *he knew or should have known* that the act committed would destroy, in whole or in part, a group".[97] Indeed, the Prosecution in *Sikirica* et al. invoked this paragraph to make a case for the knowledge-based interpretation of genocidal intent.[98] More significantly, the phrase "would destroy" even tends to connote the cognitive standard of 'probability/likeliness/possibility' for *dolus eventualis*/recklessness.[99] As such, para 520 even gives an impression that the 'clear intent to destroy' requirement might be compatible with 'reckless genocide'.[100]

The next paragraph (para 521) is more enlightening as it explicates the meaning of the previous paragraph "[i]n concrete terms". A careful reading of the paragraph brings to light that one of the key features of genocidal intent concerns the 'reason for

---

[96] For a critique of this belief on the basis of the *Akayesu* Trial Chamber's evidentiary consideration vis-à-vis the genocidal intent element, *see* Sect. 2.6.1 *supra*.

[97] In relation to this sentence, a commentator opines that the *Akayesu* Trial Chamber "confused special and general intent". Akhavan 2005, p. 993. Another commentator understands that the sentence shows that the Chamber applied the knowledge-based approach. Mundorff 2009, p. 100. It seems neither of these observations pay due regard to the explanatory para 521.

[98] Prosecutor v. Sikirica et al., Prosecutor's Second Revised Pre-Trial Brief, 13 October 2000, para 142.

[99] *See* the chart on page 51 *supra*.

[100] For a similar view, *see* Haren 2006, p. 221.

targeting'—i.e., the selection of victims *for their membership in a protected group*.[101] In this context, the dispute over whether it is individual 'purpose' or 'knowledge' that is capable of meeting the threshold of genocidal intent recedes in importance. That is because the 'reason for targeting' is meaningful only when it is understood at the 'context level', as implied by the absence of a grammatical 'subject' in para 521—i.e., the person or thing that performs the action of the verbs "committed" and "chosen". The use of the passive voice in para 521 clearly signals that the law of genocide actually is not interested in the 'reason for targeting' at the 'conduct level' which is commonly called an individual 'motive' of a criminal act.[102] Unless there is a collective reason for targeting at the 'context level', selecting victims for their membership in a group at the 'conduct level' alone cannot constitute the element of 'intent to destroy a group *as such*'. Accordingly, genocidal intent is inseparable from a group or collective motive of targeting individual members of a protected group.

In this sense, a political or historical background pertaining to the groups involved in a genocidal atrocity is a decisive and reliable source to ascertain the existence of the genocidal intent at the 'context level'—i.e., the collective genocidal intent. As Kirsten Fisher observes,

> Intention, more than action, is the element of the crime that becomes clouded in situations in which collectives commit grievous wrongs. It is difficult to attach intention to the collective, when attempting to determine collective responsibility, and it is difficult to decipher the intentions of individuals in respect to the collective action. Understanding how one person, his action and his intentions, fits within the larger context is a layered activity. His intentions might not be comprehensible taken apart from the context in which he operates or operated. To understand the context, it is likely essential to understand the community of which the agent is a member and the motivations, purposes and aspirations of the community. It is important to understand the community as an entity, a collective, with purpose.[103]

Genocidal intent grasped in this manner is hardly compatible with individualistic approaches thereto—be it purpose-based or knowledge-based. Indeed, the *Akayesu* Trial Judgment, which rendered the first genocide conviction at the ICTR, begins its substantive deliberation with a chapter entitled 'Historical Context of

---

[101] *See also* Prosecutor v. Krstić, Trial Judgment, 2 August 2001, para 561 ("The Prosecution and the Defence, in this case, concur in their belief that the victims of genocide must be targeted *by reason of* their membership in a group. This is the only interpretation coinciding with the intent which characterises the crime of genocide. The intent to destroy a group as such, in whole or in part, presupposes that the victims were *chosen by reason of* their membership in the group whose destruction was sought".). (emphasis added).

[102] William Schabas also points out the evidentiary difficulties associated with proving individual motives. Schabas 2009, p. 305. Schabas further observes that "[i]ndividual offenders should not be entitled to raise personal motives as a defence to genocide [...]". *Ibid.* at 306.

[103] Fisher 2012, p. 72. Similarly, emphasizing the historical paradigm of genocide between "embattled groups", George Fletcher and Jens David Ohlin place emphasis on the "intent of the larger collective" and the "intent of nations". They distinguish the 'intent of the smaller group' and the 'intent of the larger collective'. The rationale behind this distinction is that the former is used for the actual prosecution of genocide as a proxy for the latter. Fletcher and Ohlin state that "the ethnic hatred at the heart of genocide stems from the intent of nations". Fletcher and Ohlin 2005, pp. 547–548.

the Events in Rwanda in 1994'.[104] It is only after this elaborated account of the relevant historical context that the Trial Chamber considers the 'collective genocide' in Rwanda as I have extensively discussed in Chap. 3 hereinabove. The Trial Chamber in *Kayishema and Ruzindana* also takes into account the historical and political context preceding the massacres. In this regard, the Chamber singles out Hutu extremists' "plans to avoid power sharing" to draw the key conclusion of Part II, "Historical Context of the 1994 Events in Rwanda" as follows:

> The ethnic tensions were used by those in power in 1994 to carry out their *plans to avoid power sharing*. The responsible parties ignored the Arusha Accords and used the militias to carry out their *genocidal plan* and to incite the rest of the Hutu population into believing that all Tutsis and other persons who may not have supported the war against the RPF were in fact RPF supporters. It is against this backdrop that [...] thousands of people were slaughtered and mutilated in just three short months.[105]

The fact that the 'reason for targeting' in a collective sense at the 'context level' is the essential feature of the genocidal intent element is also deduced from a comparison between the elements of genocide and those of extermination as a crimes against humanity. The first element of the latter in the ICC Elements of Crimes thus provides that "[t]he perpetrator killed one or more persons, including by inflicting conditions of life calculated to bring about the *destruction* of *part* of a population".[106] Out of the three components of genocidal intent ((i) "to destroy"; (ii) "in whole or in part"; and (iii) "group, as such"), the only component that is not common with the first element of extermination as a crime against humanity is the "group, as such"—i.e., the collective 'reason for targeting'. Consequently, the collective 'reason for targeting' is the only distinguishing factor between the crime of genocide and extermination as a crime against humanity. In sum, the importance of the 'reason for targeting', which is legally meaningful only in a collective sense at the 'context level', proclaims that the notion of collective genocidal intent is a crucial *element* of the crime of genocide.[107]

---

[104] Prosecutor v. Akayesu, Trial Judgment, 2 September 1998, paras 78–111.

[105] Prosecutor v. Kayishema and Ruzindana, Trial Judgment, 21 May 1999, para 54. (emphasis added).

[106] ICC Elements of Crimes, Article 7(1)(b), 1st Element. (emphasis added).

[107] In the same vein, William Schabas states that "it should be necessary for the prosecution to establish that genocide, taken in its collective dimension, was committed on the grounds of nationality, race, ethnicity, or religion". Schabas 2009, p. 306. For 'collective reason for targeting' emphasized in Raphael Lemkin's writings, *see* Lemkin 2008, p. 79 ("However, if the confiscations are ordered against individuals *solely because* they are Poles, Jews, or Czechs, then the same confiscations tend in effect to weaken the national entities of which those persons are members".); *Ibid.* at 93 ("*De lege ferenda*, the definition of genocide in the Hague Regulations thus amended should consist of two essential part: in the first should be included every action infringing upon the life, liberty, health, corporal integrity, economic existence, and the honor of the inhabitants when committed *because* they belong to a national, religious, or racial group; and in the second, every policy aiming at the destruction or the aggrandizement of one of such groups to the prejudice or detriment of another".); Lemkin 1947, p. 147 ("The acts are directed against groups, as such, and individuals are selected for destruction *only because* they belong to these groups".). (emphases added).

4.2   Genocide as a Criminal Enterprise: A Genocide-'Joint Criminal Enterprise' Analogy

4.2.1   The Inherent Logic of Joint Criminal Enterprise Within Genocide: Parallel Notions of 'Common Purpose/Plan' and Collective Genocidal Intent

At the outset, I would like to ensure that there are two sets of corresponding notions that provide a conceptual framework of the 'genocide-joint criminal enterprise' analogy: (i) the parallel between 'collective genocidal intent' (objective element of genocide) and 'common purpose/plan' (objective element of JCE) on the one hand; and (ii) the parallel between 'individual genocidal intent' (subjective element of genocide) and 'shared intent' (subjective element of JCE) on the other. I will show below that the close interaction of these four notions suggests an existence of an inherent logic of JCE within the crime of genocide itself.

Although it might sound strange, a review of the relevant international case law strongly suggests that the tribunals have inferred a built-in mode of liability scheme within the notion of genocide, which very much resembles the doctrine of JCE. Sometimes, it appears that genocide suggests itself as a form of criminal enterprise. Perhaps this was the reason that the proponents of the knowledge-based approach did not feel uncomfortable engaging in the task of attributing individual criminal liability while discussing elements of crimes itself.[108] Feeling a touch of a built-in mode of liability within genocide is natural, because genocide and JCE share a similar conceptual structure in which the notion of 'collective intention' is located at the center governing all other elements. That 'collective intention' at the center is called 'collective genocidal intent' for the crime of genocide, and 'common purpose/plan' for the JCE. Hence, the 'collective genocidal intent' and 'common purpose/plan' are the crux of genocide and JCE respectively.[109]

In the relevant case law of the *ad hoc* tribunals, the three notions of individual genocidal intent, collective genocidal intent and 'common purpose/plan' have not been clearly distinguished. Thus, for instance, John R.W.D. Jones criticizes the ICTR case law for "equivocat[ing] over whether the intent to destroy the group must be an attribute of the [genocidal] plan or an attribute of the individual participating in the plan".[110] He suggests the need to clarify whether genocidal intent is to be captured by a "plan embodying the intent to destroy the group" or by an "individualized intent or *mens rea* on the part of the individual [perpetrator]".[111] To illustrate the

---

[108] For more discussion, *see* Sect. 2.3 *supra*.

[109] Regarding JCE, *see e.g.*, Ambos 2007, pp. 167–68 (the common purpose/plan element being the "core feature" of JCE.); Cupido 2014a, p. 153 (the common purpose/plan element being the "basis" and "criteria" of attribution of liability in JCE). *See also* Sliedregt 2012a, pp. 1175–1176.

[110] Jones 2003, p. 477.

[111] *Ibid.* at 478.

problem, let me again quote the *Krstić* Trial Judgment, which I have already quoted in the previous section, focusing on a different phrase as italicized below:

> As a preliminary, the Chamber emphasises the need to distinguish between the individual intent of the accused and the intent involved in the conception and commission of the crime. The gravity and the scale of the crime of genocide ordinarily presume that several protagonists were involved in its perpetration. Although the motive of each participant may differ, *the objective of the criminal enterprise* remains the same. In such cases of joint perpetration, the intent to destroy, in whole or in part, a group as such must be discernible in the criminal act itself, apart from the intent of particular perpetrators. It is then necessary to establish whether the accused being prosecuted for genocide *share the intention* that a genocide be carried out.[112]

The conceptual framework of the crime of genocide and genocidal intent outlined in this paragraph can be paraphrased in the following terms: a person is guilty of genocide when a criminal enterprise's collective genocidal intent discernible in the collective criminal act itself is shared by him. In this manner, the quoted paragraph explicitly demonstrates that the object of sharing in terms of the notion of 'shared intent' ("share the intention") within the conceptual structure of genocide is the collective genocidal intent which is to be identified objectively ("discernible in the criminal act itself"). In one sense, the concept of 'shared intent' in this quoted paragraph from *Krstić* should be distinguished from the 'shared intent' as a *mens rea* of JCE. That is because the quoted paragraph belongs to a section on 'legal findings of the crime of genocide' (pp. 188–212), not to the section on 'legal findings of individual criminal responsibility' (pp. 213–231).[113] Nevertheless, this formula of collective genocidal intent to be *shared by* the accused is identical with that of JCE in which the 'common purpose/plan' is to be *shared by* the members of JCE. Moreover, the *Krstić* Trial Chamber gives a quasi-definition of genocide that well reflects the collective nature of the crime when it states, "[g]enocide refers to any *criminal enterprise* seeking to destroy, in whole or in part, a particular kind of human group, as such, by certain means".[114] The repeated use of the language of "criminal enterprise" plainly illustrates the conceptual overlap between genocide at the contextual level and JCE doctrine.

The Chamber further explains that "[t]he preparatory work of the Genocide Convention clearly shows that the drafters envisaged *genocide as an enterprise* whose goal, or objective, was to destroy a human group, in whole or in part".[115]

---

[112] Prosecutor v. Krstić, Trial Judgment, 2 August 2001, para 549. (emphasis added).

[113] I say "should be distinguished" for the purpose of substantive law. In practice, I believe that the 'shared intent' originates in the concept of genocide and its counterpart as the *mens rea* of 'JCE to destroy a group' are identical, both representing the individual genocidal intent.

[114] Prosecutor v. Krstić, Trial Judgment, 2 August 2001, para 550. (emphasis added).

[115] *Ibid.* para 571. (emphasis added). The Trial Chamber immediately applies this understanding to its discussion as follows: "[A]n enterprise attacking only the cultural or sociological characteristics of a human group [...] would not fall under the definition of genocide". *Ibid.* para 580. In this respect, compare the phrase "genocide as an enterprise" with the term "genocidal enterprise" used by the *Krstić* Appeals Chamber when it draws a conclusion that "[...] Krstić was not a participant in a genocidal enterprise [...]". In my opinion, the term 'enterprise' in the former is of a descriptive nature, whilst that in the latter is of a normative nature. For more discussion of this distinction, *see* this chapter, footnotes 125–130 *infra* and accompanying text.

This understanding is indeed consistent with that of Raphael Lemkin and the United States Military Tribunal at Nuremberg. Lemkin defines the notion of genocide *in generic terms* when he observes that "genocide is a composite crime".[116] He further explains that "genocide is […] a composite of different acts of persecution and destruction".[117] The generic and collective concept of genocide defined in this manner is to be "practiced"[118] or "occurred",[119] rather than to be 'committed'. In like manner, "within the purview of genocide",[120] there can be a multitude of "genocide practices".[121] This generic notion of genocide was also described in an indictment for the United States Military Tribunal at Nuremberg,[122] albeit concerning the charge of crimes against humanity, as "a systematic program of genocide".[123] The official record of the *Ulrich Greifelt* et al. case further explains that the notion of genocide "was taken by the prosecution and the Tribunal as a *general concept defining the background* of the total range of specific offenses […]".[124]

This understanding of the concept of genocide reminds me of the expression 'descriptive umbrella' which Christopher Harding used in indicating the 'joint criminal enterprise in a purely descriptive sense' (as opposed to the 'joint criminal enterprise in a normative sense' which provides a "basis for legal liability" for the purpose of prosecution of individual perpetrators).[125] While the 'joint criminal

---

[116] Lemkin 1947, p. 150.

[117] Lemkin 2008, p. 92.

[118] *See* Lemkin 1947, p. 151 ("practiced genocide").

[119] *See e.g.*, Prosecutor v. Krstić, Appeals Judgment, 19 April 2004, para 34 ("[…] a finding that genocide has occurred may be entered".).

[120] Lemkin 2008, p. 92.

[121] Lemkin 1947, p. 151.

[122] Of course, at that time the legal definition of genocide as embodied in the Genocide Convention had not yet been formulated and adopted into international law. So, at the time of the *Greifelt* indictment, the generic notion of genocide was not yet in any tension with the statutory definition of genocide. It might almost be said that at the time of *Greifelt* the generic notion was the only one that existed.

[123] United States v. Ulrich Greifelt et al. ('RuSHA Case'), Case No. 8, Indictment, at 5 (1947–1948), available at http://www.loc.gov/rr/frd/Military_Law/pdf/NT_Indictments.pdf. Accessed 23 December 2015. In this regard, the Tribunal concurred with the prosecution's view. *Trial of Ulrich Greifelt and Others, in* 13 Law Reports of the War Criminals, p. 37 (UN War Crimes Commission ed., 1949).

[124] *Trial of Ulrich Greifelt and Others, in* 13 Law Reports of the War Criminals, p. 36 (UN War Crimes Commission ed., 1949). (emphasis added). In another occasion, the official record again uses the expression "the general concept of genocide". *Ibid.* at 40.

[125] Harding 2013, pp. 250–251. Note that, in this context, Christopher Harding is using the term 'joint criminal enterprise' in a generic sense beyond the boundary of international criminal law, encompassing the "European cartel offence", the "ICTY joint criminal enterprise", and the domestic/transnational "organized crime", *Ibid.* at 251–258. Harding states that 'JCE in a descriptive sense' is used "to factually refer to the organizational structure within which a range of offending activities […] take place". On the other hand, 'JCE in a normative sense', as explained by Harding, is used "as a basis for legal liability" in respect of which the "enterprise and its objectives become essential components of both the *actus reus* and *mens rea*" of the offences of direction and participation normally committed by high-ranking actors.

enterprise in a purely descriptive sense' connotes a factual description of collective conduct, the 'joint criminal enterprise in a normative sense' indicates the legal doctrine through which a person is to be found guilty of a crime committed as part of the collective conduct (or committed in furtherance of the collective intent). In my view, genocide can be perceived as a 'joint criminal enterprise in a descriptive sense' that includes or can include a 'joint criminal enterprise in a normative sense'.[126] When the doctrine of JCE is explicitly applied, surely the 'joint criminal enterprise in a normative sense' officially exists and operates. On the other hand, even when the doctrine of JCE is not overtly applied, the 'joint criminal enterprise in a normative sense' inherent in the notion of genocide can still be at work behind the curtain, as is the case of the ICTR case law which I will discuss below.[127] In this respect, Kai Ambos observes,

> As to genocide, this means that the low-level perpetrator participates in an overall genocidal plan or enterprise, i.e. his individual acts constitutes, together with the acts of the other low-level perpetrators, the realization of the genocidal will or purpose represented by the leaders or mastermind of the enterprise. The existence of the enterprise interconnects the acts of the low-level perpetrators and, at the same time, links them to the mastermind's will, i.e. both the acts of the subordinate and the thoughts of the superiors complement each other.[128]

The idea of the existence of the 'joint criminal enterprise in a normative sense' within genocide was also expressed by George Fletcher and Jens David Ohlin when they identified three groups in the law of genocide: (i) the perpetrators'

---

[126] As to the idea of 'JCE within a JCE', *see* Prosecutor v. Kvočka, Trial Judgment, 2 November 2001, para 307 ("A joint criminal enterprise can exist whenever two or more people participate in a common criminal endeavor. This criminal endeavor can range anywhere along a continuum from two persons conspiring to rob a bank to the systematic slaughter of millions during a vast criminal regime comprising thousands of participants. Within a joint criminal enterprise there may be other subsidiary criminal enterprises".). In addition, Christopher Harding's observation on the notion of JCE at the ICTY deserves extended quotation: "Since the language of joint enterprise has been in that context used interchangeably with the vocabulary of 'common plan' or 'design', in practice the joint enterprise has been used to cover a range of factual situations: for instance, an organised system of repression, such as a concentration camp; a plan to rid the Prijedor region of its non-Serb population (the Tadić enterprise); or a general programme of ethnic cleansing in a large region of Bosnia. Thus, the ICTY joint enterprise is a much more variable concept, in terms of its scale of activity and its range of purposes [...]. What is important, therefore, is to identify clearly and precisely in individual cases the enterprise in question, as something factually relevant to the role of the particular defendant. The problem, however, is that in a context of ongoing strife and fighting it is possible to identify a myriad of structures as organisations and enterprise, varying greatly in scope and function, and to a large extent the choice of enterprise for purposes of framing a charge may be very much in the discretion of the prosecutor". Harding 2013, pp. 260–261.

[127] *See* Sect. 4.2.2.3 *infra*.

[128] Ambos 2009, p. 848.

group; (ii) the victims' group; and (iii) "the smaller group engaged in the common criminal purpose" in a similar vein to JCE.[129] The third group indicates a 'JCE in a normative sense' because Fletcher and Ohlin recognized the third group for the purpose of facilitating the individual criminal prosecution.[130]

Given the purpose of JCE which targets "crucial organisational actors"[131] whose conducts "are not in themselves necessarily unacceptable or delinquent"[132] until they are "placed in the context of being in support of illegal organisational goals",[133] one might say that the 'JCE in a normative sense' within genocide tends to push the crime of genocide to the verge of being a leadership crime. In this respect, in relation to high-level actors' genocidal liability, it is their "directing and facilitating activities which *contribute significantly* to"[134] the collective genocidal conduct that the law of genocide mostly concerns. In this sense, such terms of 'participation', 'contribution', 'role' and 'rank'/'hierarchical class'—generally considered *actus reus* of JCE—become crucial in considering the genocidal liability of actors at the executive level, which is also evident in the relevant case law of the ICTY and the ICTR.

Moreover, spotting a 'JCE in a normative sense' within the notion of genocide also help us understand the practice of the *ad hoc* tribunals. That is, the analogous manner in which international judges have dealt with the matters of genocidal intent and JCE testifies the existence of a 'JCE in a normative sense' within genocide, stemming from its inherently collective nature and the practical need to prosecute individual actors. Let us then examine the relevant case law in the following subsection.

---

[129] Fletcher and Ohlin 2005, pp. 546–547. It seems that, within the conceptual framework of Fletcher and Ohlin, the intent structure of genocide is three-layered: (i) individual intent; (ii) intent of the smaller collective such as JCE; and (iii) intent of the larger collective such as a nation. *Ibid.* at 547–548. Fletcher and Ohlin explicitly identify the "smaller group" with JCE. *Ibid.* at 546 ("[...] the third group is the smaller group engaged in the common criminal purpose [...] contemplated by [...] joint criminal enterprise".). See also *Ibid.* at 547 ("[...] smaller groups that are the subject of joint criminal enterprise [...]".).

[130] *Ibid.* at 547.

[131] Harding 2013, pp. 247–248.

[132] *Ibid.* 259.

[133] *Ibid.*

[134] *Ibid.* 248. (emphasis added). Similarly, in respect of the essential feature of collective criminality, Kirsten Fisher states that "[c]onceivably, the description that is most apt at capturing what really happened is that they performed an action that *contributed* to a horrendous moral wrong by a collective of which they are, through their *contribution*, a part". Fisher 2012, p. 72. (emphasis added).

4.2.2 Applying Joint Criminal Enterprise to Genocide: Watering Down Individual Genocidal Intent Through Objectification?

4.2.2.1 Joint Criminal Enterprise and Presumption of Individual Genocidal Intent

Throughout this subsection, I will refer to the case law of the ICTY and the ICTR in advancing my argument. As well known, JCE is the theme mode of liability representing the case law of the ICTY. As such, it is no wonder that JCE has been applied in all the ICTY cases that I will look into in this subsection. In contrast, there are relatively few cases at the ICTR in which the doctrine of JCE has been employed, and, in the two cases that I will discuss below, JCE was not applied. Nevertheless, in this subsection, I will show that the end result is not that much different between the two tribunals. That is to say, regardless of whether JCE is explicitly applied, the inherent logic of JCE within the notion of genocide effectuates the same outcome: that, apparently, individual genocidal intent is to be *objectified* or to be *proven objectively*. Although it is not one hundred percent clear whether this objectification is a matter of substantive law or the law of evidence,[135] one might argue that such process of objectifying individual genocidal intent through the mediums of 'participation, 'contribution', 'role' and 'rank'/'hierarchical class' of an actor has resulted in a watered-down individual genocidal intent—at least from the point of view of purely individualistic theories of genocidal intent, and in particular, the purpose-based theory.[136] On the other hand, another might claim that such an objective approach is just a natural evidentiary practice directed toward the purpose-based concept of genocidal intent. For reasons given in Sect. 4.1.2, I am skeptical of this latter claim. My own conclusion is that the watering down of individual genocidal intent through objectification has become part of the substantive law of genocide, rather than merely an evidentiary practice.

The doctrine of joint criminal enterprise is basically a 'collective intent' theory. Due to the practice of presuming the individual intention of a member of JCE under the umbrella of 'common purpose/plan' as will be shown below, the subjective element of JCE in the form of 'shared intent' is very likely to be blurred. Thus, when JCE is applied to genocide (especially when the 'common purpose/

---

[135] For a discussion of the tricky relationship between substantive law and evidence law, *see* Shapira-Ettinger 2007.

[136] For a case law in which the term '*mens rea*' is paraphrased as "the role the participant wishes to assume", *see* Prosecutor v. Stakić, Decision on Rule 98 *bis* Motion for Judgment of Acquittal, 31 October 2002, para 50.

plan' is defined as a plan to destroy a protected group),[137] individual genocidal intent of a member of JCE in the form of 'shared intent' (*mens rea* of JCE) is also, to some extent, destined to be watered down through the intrinsic 'collective intent' mechanism of both genocide and JCE which carries with it the presumption of individual intent.[138] When I say 'watered down', this term should be understood descriptively, not as a term of criticism. I am not concerned about *mens rea* of individual genocidal intent per se being diluted or reduced as a matter of substantive law. Rather, what I want to emphasize is the primarily objective manner in which the relevant case law finds the individual genocidal intent dressed with 'shared intent' by considering such *objective* mediums as 'participation, 'contribution', 'role' and 'rank'/'hierarchical class', which renders or tends to render the *subjective* character of individual genocidal intent dressed with 'shared intent' nominal. One might depict this practice as an example of legal manipulations crossing back and forth over the line between substantive law and evidence law through an 'evidentiary backdoor'.[139] Alternatively, one might argue that it is just a legitimate evidentiary practice to find the subjective element of individual genocidal intent. In this context, it is not surprising to read the following observation (on JCE) in which the *ad hoc* tribunals' practice of presuming the 'shared intent' element (the *mens rea* of JCE) is rightly pointed out:

> The conceptual idea of JCE, why the acts of one person can give rise to the criminal responsibility of another person, is based on one subjective and one objective element: the subjective element is the agreement and the shared intent to pursue a common plan that aims at or includes the commission of criminal acts; the objective element is the accused's participation in that plan. But the emphasis lays on the subjective element, on the common

---

[137] In those cases where JCE is applied to genocide, it is not always the case that the 'common purpose/plan' element of JCE represents the collective genocidal intent. For instance, while 'JCE to commit genocide' was applied in *Krstić* (the 'common purpose/plan' of which was to destroy the 'Bosnian Muslims in Srebrenica'), it was 'JCE to Murder' that guided the relevant discussion of genocide in *Popović* et al. Certainly, the 'common purpose/plan' in the latter case was to "murder the able-bodies Bosnian Muslim men from Srebrenica". Prosecutor v. Popović et al., Trial Judgment, 10 June 2010, para 1072. Strictly speaking, this might cause a problem. That is because throughout the relevant case law of the ICTY dealing with the Srebrenica massacre, the collective genocidal intent has been defined as an intent to destroy the 'Bosnian Muslims in Srebrenica' (not the 'Bosnian Muslim men of military age in Srebrenica') constituting a 'substantial part' of the Bosnian Muslims. But, in *Popović* et al., the question of whether the content of 'common purpose/plan' element of JCE incorporates collective genocidal intent does not matter that much because the issue of collective genocidal intent is sufficiently addressed in the 'legal findings related to crimes' section of the judgment (as opposed to 'legal findings related to modes of liability' section). *Ibid.* paras 837–866. In other words, in *Popović* et al., although the 'JCE in a normative sense' in the 'modes of liability' section does not precisely cover the collective genocidal intent, the 'legal findings related to crimes' section dealing with genocide covers it.

[138] The proposition that individual genocidal intent of a member of JCE is to be dressed with the 'shared intent' element of JCE explains the reason why the question of individual genocidal intent of the accused has been addressed in the 'legal findings of individual criminal responsibility' section (rather than 'legal findings of the crime of genocide' section) of the relevant judgments, in particular, at the ICTY.

[139] *See* the sources cited in Chap. 2, footnote 92 *supra*.

understanding of the persons. As all participants *intend* to achieve the goal of the enterprise together, and as each of them *wants* the other participants to contribute to the common goal, they are responsible *to the same degree* despite their varying role in the JCE.
[…] In the actual application of the concept, the judges seem to have reversed the importance of the objective and subjective elements of JCE. While many Chambers set a much
higher standard for the objective element – requiring, in addition to participation, that the
accused *played an influential part* within the joint criminal enterprise and that he was in a
position of authority vis-à-vis the direct perpetrators – they do not examine whether there
existed a shared intent […].[140]

What this paragraph stresses is that the rationale behind imposing "the same
degree" of responsibility among the members of a JCE—i.e., the *subjective* aspect
that they all "intend" and "want" the same goal[141]—conflicts with the actual practice of *ad hoc* tribunals in which such *objective* aspects as 'role/participation/con-
tribution' ("played an influential part") and the 'rank' ("position of authority")
guide the relevant deliberation on the individual responsibility based on JCE.
Accordingly, when the logic of JCE within genocide is activated, it is likely that,
as a matter of practice, individual genocidal intent defined in a strictly individualistic manner loses its original conceptual force because of the inner dynamic of
JCE that underscores the evidentiary weight of objective elements ('rank',
'participation/contribution' and 'common purpose/plan'), while presuming the
subjective element ('shared intent').[142] Despite such a grave effect of significantly
overshadowing the essence of the 'crime of *mens rea*', there has hardly been a
serious challenge to the practice of applying the JCE doctrine to genocide cases. It
seems to me that that was because the collective genocidal intent represented by

---

[140] Haan 2005, pp. 195–196. (emphasis added). For approving comment on Haan's observation,
see Sliedregt 2012b, p. 141. Note that, as to the issue of whether 'agreement' or 'understanding'
to commit particular crimes between a member of JCE and physical perpetrators is an element
of JCE, the *Brđanin* Appeals Chamber clarified that such 'agreement' or 'understanding' is not
required. Prosecutor v. Brđanin, Appeals Judgment, 3 April 2007, paras 415–419. For this reason,
I omit the phrase "between the accused person and the direct perpetrator at all" at the end of the
quoted paragraph. By the way, it is not clear why Haan mentions 'agreement' as a subjective element of JCE. In the relevant jurisprudence of the ICTY concerning JCE, the term 'agreement' is
used in connection with the objective element of common plan. *See e.g.*, Prosecutor v. Blagojević
and Jokić, Trial Judgment, 17 January 2005, para 699.

[141] The ICC Pre-Trial Chamber in *Lubanga* classifies JCE as a subjective theory in terms
of distinction between principals and accessories. Prosecutor v. Lubanga, Decision on the
Confirmation of Charges, 29 January 2007, para 329. Moreover, in explicating the subjective theory, the Pre-Trial Chamber stresses the importance of 'shared intent' by stating that 'principals'
are those who have 'shared intent', "regardless of the level of contribution […]". *Ibid.*

[142] In the context of discussing ordinary crimes in national jurisdictions, Keren Shapira-Ettinger
argues that presuming *mens rea* is a common practice through the law of evidence, whilst substantive law ostensibly claims that *mens rea* is proved beyond reasonable doubt. Shapira-Ettinger
2007, pp. 2585–2586 ("Instead of producing evidence of a defendant's state of mind, we allow
the fact finders to use *presumptions* in order to deduce the existence of relevant mental occurrences according to their own experience. In doing so, we admit that our legal system does not
speak with a single voice: substantive rules regarding the mental element requires the actual
occurrences of a subjective mental state, whereas the law of evidence can provide only an
assumption that the required state may have occurred".). (emphasis added).

the 'common plan/purpose' element of JCE (especially when the 'common purpose/plan' is defined as a plan to destroy a protected group) has exerted some soothing effects. One might also say that the inherent quality of genocide being a collective crime has provided an inadvertent psychological justification for tolerating the weakening of the individual genocidal intent element that results from the application of JCE. Given the presumptive nature or inclination of the 'shared intent' element of JCE, if genocide had truly been a 'crime of *mens rea*', JCE should not have been applied thereto.[143] After all, JCE is a theory under which individual intent is very likely to be presumed or blurred behind the eye-catching features of its individual members' high rank and leadership role against the backdrop of mass atrocities. Therefore, the extensive use of the JCE doctrine in relation to genocide charges in international case law again compels us to cast doubt on the validity of the slogan of genocide being a 'crime of *mens rea*'. Keeping in mind this overall picture of legal implications of applying JCE to genocide, let us look into the ICTY case law.

4.2.2.2   Joint Criminal Enterprise and the Objective Approach to Individual Genocidal Intent at the ICTY

The Trial Chamber in *Krstić* found the accused, the commander of the Drina Corps whose zone of responsibility covered Srebrenica, guilty of genocide proper in respect of the Srebrenica massacre. While the Chamber addresses only the collective genocidal intent in its 'legal findings on the crime of genocide' section to the exclusion of individual genocidal intent, it buries the latter issue in its discussion of modes of liability, in particular, of the "genocidal joint criminal enterprise".[144] A similar pattern of deliberation was repeated by the *Popović* et al. Trial Chamber and the *Tolimir* Trial Chamber. In *Krstić*, the buried individual genocidal intent of the accused takes the form of a 'shared intent' (the *mens rea* of JCE). In

---

[143] Note, however, the ICTR case law that still reflects the logic of JCE even when JCE is not applied, as will be discussed in Sect. 4.2.2.3 *infra*.

[144] Prosecutor v. Krstić, Trial Judgment, 2 August 2001, paras 621–645. More specifically the relevant section is entitled, "genocidal joint criminal enterprise to kill the military-aged men". Since the Trial Chamber defines the 'in part' element as indicating the 'Bosnian Muslims in Srebrenica', the title of the section should have been 'genocidal joint criminal enterprise to destroy the Bosnian Muslims in Srebrenica', rather than 'genocidal joint criminal enterprise to kill the military-aged men'. *Ibid*. para 560. In this respect, the *Krstić* Appeals Chamber clarifies that "the Trial Chamber treated the killing of the men of military age as evidence from which to infer that Radislav Krstić and some members of the VRS Main Staff had the requisite intent to destroy all the Bosnian Muslims of Srebrenica, the [substantial] part of the protected group [of Bosnian Muslims]". Prosecutor v. Krstić, Appeals Judgment, 19 April 2004, para 19. On the other hand, in view of the conceptual possibility of 'JCE within a JCE', we cannot state that the term "genocidal joint criminal enterprise to kill the military-aged men" is completely incorrect. For the relevant case law that addressed the issue of 'JCE within a JCE', *see* this chapter, footnote 126 *supra*.

Popović et al. and *Tolimir*, though the term 'shared intent' is not as obviously used as in *Krstić*,[145] we can still quite convincingly conclude that the *Krstić* scheme of 'shared intent' as the *mens rea* of JCE incorporating 'individual genocidal intent' was also applied. That is because the Trial Chambers in both cases find the individual genocidal intent in the context of discussing JCE.[146] The *Krstić* Trial Chamber ultimately holds, in the section on "genocidal joint criminal enterprise",[147] that Krstić "shared the genocidal intent" as follows:

> The Trial Chamber concludes beyond reasonable doubt that General Krstić participated in a joint criminal enterprise to kill the Bosnian Muslim military-aged men from Srebrenica from the evening of 13 July onward. General Krstić may not have devised the killing plan, or participated in the initial decision to escalate the objective of the criminal enterprise from forcible transfer to destruction of Srebrenica's Bosnian Muslim military-aged male community, but there can be no doubt that, from the point he *learned of* the widespread and systematic killings and became clearly *involved in* their perpetration, he *shared the genocidal intent* to kill the men. This cannot be gainsaid given his *informed participation in the executions through the use of Drina Corps assets.*[148]

In the paragraph cited above, the term "genocidal intent", as an object of sharing, indicates collective genocidal intent manifested as a 'common purpose/plan' to destroy the Bosnian Muslims in Srebrenica.[149] In this way, the *mens rea* of individual genocidal intent taking the form of 'shared intent' (as a *mens rea* of JCE) is established on the basis of Krstić's knowledge ("learned of") and 'participation/contribution' ("involved in"; "participation in the executions through the use of

---

[145] That was because, in *Popović* et al. and *Tolimir*, the JCE was defined as 'JCE to Murder' and 'JCE to Forcibly Remove' (as opposed to 'JCE to destroy a protected group' or 'JCE to commit genocide'). Thus, the 'shared intent' as a *mens rea* of JCE in these two cases—i.e., 'shared intent to murder' and 'shared intent to forcibly remove'—are not precisely identical with the individual genocidal intent. Yet, the notion of collective genocidal intent amply emphasized by the Trial Chambers in both cases plays a role of a melting pot in which such subtleties are adjusted or ignored.

[146] Prosecutor v. Popović et al., Trial Judgment, 10 June 2010, para 1180 ("Accordingly, the Trial Chamber is satisfied beyond reasonable doubt that Popović participated in the JCE to Murder with genocidal intent. He is therefore guilty of genocide").

[147] Prosecutor v. Krstić, Trial Judgment, 2 August 2001, paras 621–645.

[148] *Ibid.* para 633. (emphasis added). This paragraph belongs to a section on individual criminal responsibility (JCE).

[149] In *Krstić*, contrary to *Popović et al.* and *Tolimir*, the concept of collective genocidal intent and the 'common purpose/plan' as an element of JCE are identical, because the JCE is defined as 'JCE to destroy a protected group'. On the other hand, even though the quoted paragraph associates the notion of 'destruction' with the "Srebrenica's Bosnian Muslim military-aged male community", I believe it is a mistake for the reason set out in this chapter, footnote 144 *supra*. The collective genocidal intent in *Krstić* was to destroy 'a substantial part' of the Bosnian Muslims, and that 'substantial part' was the Bosnian Muslims in Srebrenica. Thus, the concept of 'destruction' should be directed toward the Bosnian Muslims in Srebrenica. In this regard, apparently, the *Krstić* Trial Chamber was not careful enough throughout its judgement. *See* Prosecutor v. Krstić, Trial Judgment, 2 August 2001, paras 560 and 634; Prosecutor v. Krstić, Appeals Judgment, 19 April 2004, paras 15 and 19.

Drina Corps assets").[150] Despite its apparent departure from the individualistic notion of genocidal intent, in particular, the purpose-based genocidal intent, it is hard to immediately repudiate the reasoning of the *Krstić* Trial Chamber in this regard. It seems that that is because the Chamber's flow of argument sounds intuitively correct as it well reflects the nature of genocide as a generic concept within which there exists an inherent logic of JCE. In this respect, one might argue that the presumptive nature or inclination of the 'shared intent' as a *mens rea* of JCE provides a backdoor to prove the individual genocidal intent in an objective manner.[151] Put differently, it is the concept of 'sharing' that links the external dimension of genocidal intent (collective genocidal intent in the form of 'common purpose/plan') and its internal dimension (individual genocidal intent). Since the notion of 'sharing' postulates its object (to be shared) outside the sharer's individual state of mind, that object is destined to partake of an objective characteristic. Within the legal framework developed by the *Krstić* Trial Chamber, the 'sharing' occurs both subjectively and objectively. That is, the Chamber's method of finding the accused's individual genocidal intent—which I will henceforth call the '*Krstić* formula'—requires two sets of facts, one concerning the 'individual knowledge' (subjective aspect) and the other concerning the 'individual participation' (objective aspect) of the accused.[152] Let us examine these two aspects in more detail below.

First, in relation to the objective side, viz., the 'participation/contribution', according to the Trial Chamber, Krstić's 'individual participation' indicates his

---

[150] The *Krstić* Appeals Chamber's summary of the Trial Chamber's analysis in this respect is more or less similar. *See* Prosecutor v. Krstić, Appeals Judgment, 19 April 2004, paras 42 and 83.

[151] William Schabas also points out the *Krstić* Trial Chamber's practice of presuming the accused's individual genocidal intent. Commenting on the *Krstić* Trial Judgment, Schabas observes that "[t]he Trial Chamber seemed to have *presumed* that General Krstić knew of the summary executions. This is certainly a mental element that falls shy of the standard of *dolus specialis* in continental law systems. Nevertheless, it would appear consistent with the text of the definition, to the extent that General Krstić had knowledge of the plan to destroy the Bosnian Muslims of Srebrenica and participated actively in it". Schabas 2001, p. 50. (emphasis added).

[152] For a similar view submitted by the Prosecution, *see* Prosecutor v. Krstić, Trial Judgment, 2 August 2001, para 637 ("The Prosecution submits that "knowledge" of the genocidal intent accompanied by substantial contribution to the genocidal plan or enterprise amounts to a shared intent".). It seems that the *Krstić* formula, to some extent, resembles the notion of criminal organizations employed to punish Nazi members other than those at the leadership level on the basis of their membership therein after the World War II as explained by Elies van Sliedregt as follows: "Through the notion of criminal organizations, an offshoot of the concept of conspiracy and the other pillar of the collective criminality theory, it was possible to prosecute the thousands of 'second-level' Nazi members who had been involved in the commission of crimes, if only by *knowing* of the criminal acts of their fellow members and party leaders, and *acquiescing* in them. [...] According to the judgment, knowledge of the criminal nature of the organization and some degree of voluntariness is required before one can be convicted of 'membership of a criminal organization". Sliedregt 2012b, pp. 26–30 (emphasis in original). For a careful proposal to employ the Nuremberg notion of membership responsibility in a criminal organization for the operation of the ICTR, *see* Jørgensen 2001.

contribution by way of "arrang[ing] for men under his command to commit kill-ings".[153] For the purpose of imputing the acts of Drina Corps to Krstić, the Trial Chamber extensively demonstrates that the troop was under Krstić's 'effective control'.[154] The relevant activities performed by the Drina Corps can be summa-rized as "tangible and substantial assistance and technical support to the detention, killing and burial [of the Bosnian Muslim men of military age]".[155] The Trial Chamber further explains that "[t]he need for their involvement was unavoidable because the Main Staff had limited assets and resources of its own and had to uti-lise the Drina Corps resources and expertise for complicated operations like these detentions, executions and burials on Drina Corps territory".[156] From an objective perspective, therefore, one might say that Krstić's participation/contribution through the Drina Corps under his command was *necessary* for the success of the Srebrenica massacre: without the Drina Corps, it would not have been possible to complete the massacre.[157] Accordingly, it seems that Krstić's participation/contri-bution would make him a perpetrator not only under a JCE theory, but even under the more demanding control theory of co-perpetration, which requires an 'essen-tial contribution' on his part.[158] In this respect, the following paragraph is illuminating:

> In the present case, General Krstić *participated in a joint criminal enterprise* to kill the military-aged Bosnian Muslim men of Srebrenica with the awareness that such killings would lead to the annihilation of the entire Bosnian Muslim community at Srebrenica. His intent to kill the men thus amounts to a genocidal intent to destroy the group in part. General Krstić did not conceive the plan to kill the men, nor did he kill them personally. However, he fulfilled a key co-ordinating role in the implementation of the killing cam-paign. In particular, at a stage when his participation was clearly *indispensable*, General Krstić exerted his authority as Drina Corps Commander and arranged for men under his command to commit killings. He thus was an *essential participant* in the genocidal kill-ings in the aftermath of the fall of Srebrenica. In sum, in view of both his *mens rea* and *actus reus*, General Krstić must be considered a principal perpetrator of these crimes. General Krstić is guilty of genocide pursuant to Article 4(2)(a).[159]

---

[153] Prosecutor v. Krstić, Trial Judgment, 2 August 2001, para 644. See also, *Ibid*. paras 623–624, and 632.

[154] *Ibid*. paras 624–632.

[155] *Ibid*. para 624. For more specifics about the Drina Corps' role during the massacre, see *Ibid*. para 623.

[156] *Ibid*. para 624.

[157] According to the control theory, in order to make an 'essential contribution', one must be in a position to frustrate the implementation of the common plan by not participating therein. *See* Prosecutor v. Lubanga, Decision on the Confirmation of Charges, 29 January 2007, para 347.

[158] For an overview of the 'essential contribution' element of the ICC's control theory, *see* Jain 2014, pp 87–89. In particular, note the ambiguity and confusion within the relevant ICC jurispru-dence involving the object of 'essential contribution'—i.e., the question of whether it is a contri-bution to the common plan or to the specific crime. *Ibid*. at 88.

[159] Prosecutor v. Krstić, Trial Judgment, 2 August 2001, para 644. (emphasis added).

Reading this paragraph, the importance that I attach to the *objective aspect* looks even more valid. That is because Krstić's role was "indispensable" to the Srebrenica massacre, which led the Trial Chamber to characterize his participation as "essential". In this connection, given the element of 'essential contribution' for the control theory of the ICC, one might even conclude that the Trial Chamber understood that Krstić was in a position to 'frustrate' implementation of the genocidal common purpose/plan.[160]

Second, as to Krstić's 'knowledge', the Trial Chamber acknowledges his knowledge of (i) the overall context of violence (including the forcible transfer and the mass execution at Srebrenica),[161] (ii) the genocidal intent of some members of the Main Staff,[162] and (iii) the destructive consequence.[163] In spite of the fact that the *Krstić* Trial Chamber appears to take into account the 'level of knowledge' in finding the objectified and consequently reduced *mens rea* of individual genocidal intent of the accused in the form of 'shared intent', the probative value of the knowledge feature seems to be *secondary to* those objective mediums of 'participation/contribution' and 'rank' which constitute the *primary* evidentiary basis of the 'shared intent'. In this respect, the *Popović* et al. Trial Judgment provides a useful illustration. In relation to the codefendant Drago Nikolić who assumed the important post of Chief of Security of the Zvornik Brigade despite his relatively low rank of second lieutenant, the Trial Chamber extensively recognizes his knowledge of almost all aspects of the killing operation in which he participated including his superior's genocidal intent and the context of genocidal campaign.[164] Yet, despite this robust recognition of Nikolić's knowledge, the Trial Chamber "specifically focused on the scope of Nikolić's *acts and participation* for the purpose of determining whether and to what extent [his individual] genocidal intent

---

[160] For the 'essential contribution' element, *see* Ohlin 2014, p. 331.

[161] *Ibid*. paras 608, 618, 622 and 648.

[162] *Ibid*. para 648.

[163] *Ibid*. paras 634 and 644. In respect of the issue of the accused's knowledge of the destructive consequences expected to materialize in the future, the Chamber's indiscreet approach to the notion of knowledge that extended its scope to 'constructive knowledge' has triggered appeal from the accused. Thus, responding to the accused's complaint that such phrases as "must have known", "could not have failed to know", and "could only surmise" demonstrate the Trial Chamber's failure to accord to him the presumption of innocence, the Appeals Chamber observes that such language is "indicative of the nature of the case against Krstić being one based upon circumstantial evidence. While the Trial Chamber should have used less ambiguous language when making findings concerning Krstić's knowledge and intent, the regrettable choice of phraseology alone is not sufficient to overturn the Trial Chamber's findings". Prosecutor v. Krstić, Appeals Judgment, 19 April 2004, paras 80–81. Subsequently, however, the *Popović* et al. Trial Chamber also took into account the accused's constructive knowledge. Prosecutor v. Popović et al., Trial Judgment, 10 June 2010, para 866 (considering the constructive knowledge of the devastating impact on the community in finding genocidal intent.).

[164] Prosecutor v. Popović et al., Trial Judgment, 10 June 2010, paras 1404–1407. For a more detailed description of Nikolić's knowledge, *see* Chap. 2, footnotes 144–149 *supra* and accompanying text.

could be inferred".[165] That is, it was such objective features of 'participation/contribution' that guided the deliberation of the *Popović* et al. Trial Chamber on the issue of Nikolić's individual genocidal intent, as clarified by the Chamber when it observes: "[t]he central issue [...] is whether *those actions* [performed by Nikolić], combined with his knowledge of the genocidal intent of others, [...] are sufficient to satisfy the Trial Chamber beyond reasonable doubt that Nikolić not only knew of the intent but that he shared it".[166] In this context, it seems the knowledge feature just sets a stage for the subsequent determination of individual genocidal intent in respect of which the objective aspects of 'acts and participation' plays a pivotal role.[167] After all, the Trial Chamber denies Nikolić's individual genocidal intent in view of (i) his acts and contribution being geographically and temporally limited[168]; (ii) his low rank within the VRS ("2nd Lieutenant, the lowest rank of officer") and low-level authority[169]; and (iii) the existence of another reasonable inference to be drawn from Nikolić's acts and participation which renders the 'only reasonable inference' test not met.[170] Instead, the Chamber finds Nikolić guilty of aiding and abetting genocide on the basis of his knowledge of the collective genocidal intent and his substantial contribution to the commission of genocide.[171] Thus, as I see it, this example expressly demonstrates the *primary* importance of

---

[165] I quote here the *Popović* et al. Appeals Chamber's description of the Trial Chamber's deliberation on the issue of Nikolić's individual genocidal intent. Prosecutor v. Popović et al., Appeals Judgment, 30 January 2015, para 517.

[166] Prosecutor v. Popović et al., Trial Judgment, 10 June 2010, para 1408 ("The Trial Chamber has found above that Nikolić played an important role in the JCE to Murder in terms of planning and organising detentions and executions. His contribution can properly be described as persistent and determined. The central issue, however, is whether those actions, combined with his knowledge of the genocidal intent of others, considered in the totality of the evidence, are sufficient to satisfy the Trial Chamber beyond reasonable doubt that Nikolić not only knew of the intent but that he shared it".).

[167] Indeed, the *Popović* et al. Trial Chamber states that the consideration of Nikolić's knowledge is the "starting point" of the analysis of his individual genocidal intent. Prosecutor v. Popović et al., Trial Judgment, 10 June 2010, para 1401.

[168] *Ibid.* para 1410 ("While Beara and Popović can properly be described as architects of this genocidal operation, Nikolić was brought into carry out specific tasks assigned to him, in implementation of a monstrous plan, designed by others. His criminal acts, though horrific in nature, were confined to his sphere of responsibility – some specific detention and execution sites in Zvornik".).

[169] *Ibid.* para 1412.

[170] *Ibid.* para 1414 ("Having considered and weighed all of the above factors individually and cumulatively, the Trial Chamber is not satisfied that the only reasonable inference to be drawn from Nikolić's acts is that he shared the genocidal intent. Another reasonable inference is that Nikolić's blind dedication to the Security Service led him to doggedly pursue the efficient execution of his assigned tasks in this operation, despite its murderous nature and the genocidal aim of his superiors. In these circumstances the stringent test for specific intent is not met and the Trial Chamber therefore finds that Nikolić did not participate in the JCE to Murder with genocidal intent".).

[171] *Ibid.* para 1415.

objective factors in deciding on the question of individual genocidal intent (especially when the logic of JCE is activated). While Nikolić had the similar level of knowledge as those like Popović and Beara who were convicted of genocide as principals, it was the limited level of his 'acts and participation' and his low-level rank and authority that was determinative in the *Popović* et al. Trial Chamber's decision that he did not share the collective genocidal intent. Subsequently, the Appeals Chamber affirmed the Trial Chamber's decision in this regard.[172] Thus, the *Popović* et al. case obviously supports the proposition that the objective aspects prevail over subjective knowledge in determining the question of individual genocidal intent taking the form of the 'shared intent' element of JCE.

Compare this with another codefendant in *Popović* et al.: Beara (Colonel and Chief of Security of the VRS Main Staff). At the outset, it should be noted that, since the JCE in this case is 'JCE to Murder', but not 'JCE to Commit Genocide (or JCE to destroy a protected group)', it appears that the Trial Chamber distinguishes the notion of 'shared intent' as a *mens rea* of JCE on one hand and the individual genocidal intent on the other. Hence, the former is defined as the 'shared intent' to carry out the common purpose to murder the able-bodied Bosnian Muslim men.[173] Given that the content of the 'shared intent' as a *mens rea* of JCE is supposed to be determined by that of 'common purpose/plan', it was already at the time when the JCE in this case is characterized as 'JCE to Murder' (instead of 'JCE to commit genocide') that individual genocidal intent becomes distinct from the shared intent. Indeed, in relation to Nikolić, the Trial Chamber concludes that he was a member of the 'JCE to Murder', because of his 'shared intent' to carry out the common purpose to murder the military-aged men in Srebrenica,[174] while rejecting his individual genocidal intent. As we have already seen, in *Krstić*, the 'shared intent' was identified with individual genocidal intent, because in that case the applicable JCE was defined as 'JCE to commit genocide'.[175]

The *Popović* et al. Trial Chamber finds Beara guilty of genocide on the basis of his participation in 'JCE to Murder' with individual genocidal intent.[176] Beara, the Chief of Security of the VRS Main Staff, is described by the Chamber as one of the "architects of this genocidal operation" in Srebrenica.[177] Beara was important because it was the Security Branch of the VRS that was "tasked with a central coordinating role" in the implementation of the 'common purpose/plan' to murder the able-bodied Bosnian Muslim men from Srebrenica.[178] Beara was physically

---

[172] Prosecutor v. Popović et al., Appeals Judgment, 30 January 2015, paras 525–530.

[173] Prosecutor v. Popović et al., Trial Judgment, 10 June 2010, paras 1165 and 1298.

[174] *Ibid.* para 1392.

[175] For more discussion on the interrelationship among 'common purpose/plan', 'shared intent' and 'individual genocidal intent', *see* Chap. 4, footnote 137 *supra*.

[176] Prosecutor v. Popović et al, Trial Judgment, 10 June 2010, paras 1180 and 1318.

[177] *Ibid.* para 1410.

[178] *Ibid.* para 1299.

and functionally far closer to the killing operation at Srebrenica than Krstić.[179] Following the pattern of *Krstić* Trial Judgment, the *Popović* et al. Trial Chamber addresses the issue of individual genocidal intent of the accused in its discussion of modes of liability, particularly, of the JCE. Thus, within the context of discussing JCE, the overall framework of finding individual genocidal intent in *Popović et al.* follows the *Krstić* formula of 'knowledge' plus 'participation/contribution'. Thus, the *Popović et al.* Appeals Chamber points out that it was "the Trial Chamber's findings on the knowledge, words, and actions of Beara that underpin the finding on his genocidal intent".[180] The Appeals Chamber further sets forth the "decisive factors" for the Trial Chamber's decision on Beara's genocidal intent as follows: (i) "the scale and scope of killing operation carried out with Beara's knowledge, pursuant to his instructions and under his supervision[181]"; (ii) "his extensive and forceful participation in all components of the killing operation[182]"; (iii) "his demonstrated determination to kill as many Bosnian Muslims as possible[183]"; and (iv) "his vital contribution in overcoming hurdles and challenges to effective implementation".[184] It is to be noted that most of these "decisive factors" in establishing Beara's individual genocidal intent are of an objective characteristics.

Following the order "from the top" including Mladić,[185] Colonel Beara, as the Chief of Security of the VRS Main Staff, significantly contributed to the common plan to murder the able-bodied Bosnian Muslim male from Srebrenica, sharing the intent to murder on a massive scale as demonstrated by his actions and words.[186] The Chamber finds that, while having been aware of the common plan to murder, Beara played a "pivotal and high level role" in the murder operation,[187] explaining that "[t]he evidence is clear that from [the morning of 12 July 1995] onward, Beara played a key role in orchestrating the murder operation by planning, coordinating and overseeing the detention, transportation, execution and burial of the able-bodied Bosnian Muslim males".[188] In pursuant to the *Krstić* formula, the Chamber infers Beara's individual genocidal intent from his 'knowledge' and 'participation/contribution' as follows:

> Far more telling are the inferences which can be drawn from his detailed *knowledge* of the killing operation itself and Beara's high level and far reaching *participation* in it. As the most senior officer of the Security Branch—the entity charged with a central directing

---

[179] Prosecutor v. Krstić, Appeals Judgment, 19 April 2004, paras 102–106 (detailing Krstić's contact with Beara who were at the actual execution sites).

[180] Prosecutor v. Popović et al., Appeals Judgment, 30 January 2015, para 485.

[181] *Ibid.* para 490.

[182] *Ibid.*

[183] *Ibid.*

[184] *Ibid.*

[185] Prosecutor v. Popović et al., Trial Judgment, 10 June 2010, paras 1299–1300.

[186] *Ibid.* paras 1301–1302.

[187] *Ibid.* para 1300.

[188] *Ibid.* para 1299.

role—he had perhaps the clearest overall picture of the massive scale and scope of the killing operation. Further, from his walk through Bratunac on the night of 13 July, his personal visits to the various execution sights and the extensive logistical challenges he faced throughout, he had a very personal view of the staggering number of victims destined for execution. Steeped in knowledge, Beara became a driving force behind the murder enterprise. His vigorous efforts to organise locations and sites, recruit personnel, secure equipment and oversee executions[,] all evidence his grim determination to kill as many as possible as quickly as possible.[189]

Both Beara and Nikolić had thorough knowledge of what was happening at Srebrenica. In the case of Nikolić, that wasn't enough to support an inference of individual genocidal intent, but in the case of Beara it was. That raises the question of why. My diagnosis is that under the *Krstić* formula, subjective knowledge alone will not support an inference of genocidal intent, but subjective knowledge supplemented by objective participations/ranks factors will.

4.2.2.3   The Inherent Logic of Joint Criminal Enterprise and the Objective Approach to Individual Genocidal Intent at the ICTR

Thus far, we have studied the objectification of individual genocidal intent through the mediums of 'participation/contribution' and 'rank' when JCE is applied to genocide cases. Let us then look into the ICTR case law that yields the same outcome of finding individual genocidal intent in an objective manner despite the fact that JCE is not applied. We will observe that not applying JCE to genocide cannot constrain the operation of the inherent logic of JCE within genocide. In other words, international judges at the ICTR still apply the logic of JCE when this mode of liability is either not pleaded by the Prosecution (*Kayishema and Ruzindana*) or expressly rejected by the Trial Chamber (*Munyakazi*). Let us begin with *Kayishema and Ruzindana*.

As we have already seen, the *Kayishema and Ruzindana* Trial Chamber applies the three-layered mode of analysis vis-à-vis the (i) 'collective genocide' in Rwanda, (ii) 'collective genocide' in Kibuye, and (iii) individual genocidal intent of the accused.[190] For the analysis of (i) and (ii), the Chamber pays more attention to the collective and objective aspect of genocidal intent using the term 'plan', 'genocidal plan', or 'plan of genocide'.[191] The conclusion drawn by the Chamber in relation to the first two stages is that there indeed existed a 'plan' to destroy the Tutsi group in Rwanda and that 'plan' was implemented in Kibuye *Prefecture* by

---

[189] *Ibid*. paras 1313–1314. (emphasis added).

[190] *See* Sect. 3.2.1.2 *supra*.

[191] Prosecutor v. Kayishema and Ruzindana, Trial Judgment, 21 May 1999, paras 289–312. Note that both of the element of 'agreement' in the Anglo-American offence of conspiracy and the element of 'common purpose/plan' in JCE are generally classified as an objective element.

local public officials.[192] On the other hand, at the third stage of evidentiary review under (iii), the Chamber more frequently uses such terms as 'intent', 'special intent', 'specific intent' and 'genocidal intent' than 'plan'. But, although the term 'intent' in its general usages connotes a state of mind of a person, as commonly expressed by the legal term *mens rea*, it is not exactly the case in the *Kayishema and Ruzindana* Trial Judgment, particularly in its 'Legal Findings' section on genocide. One might rather say that the concept of 'intent' as used by the *Kayishema and Ruzindana* Trial Chamber sometimes means 'individual genocidal intent', but also means 'collective genocidal plan' at other times. In such a manner, 'intent' becomes an extremely confusing concept because it moves so erratically around the territories of subjective elements (individual genocidal intent) and objective elements (collective genocidal plan). In explaining the genocidal intent element, the *Kayishema and Ruzindana* Trial Chamber also employs the concepts of '*common* intention', '*common* plan', or '*common* genocidal plan' as follows:

> However, the delineation of power on party political grounds, whilst perhaps theoretically sound, should only be considered in light of the Trial Chamber's findings that the administrative bodies, law enforcement agencies, and even armed civilians were engaged together in a *common genocidal plan*. The focus in these months [between April and July 1994] was upon a unified, *common intention* to destroy the ethnic Tutsi population.[193]

Obviously, these terms represent the collective genocidal intent shared by multiple participants, but they also remind us of the 'common purpose/plan' element of JCE which is generally regarded as an objective element. What is the relationship, if any, between the collective genocidal intent and the 'common plan/purpose' element of JCE? In this regard, the concluding paragraph of the section addressing the defendants' *individual* genocidal intent is illustrative:

> The Trial Chamber is satisfied, from all the evidence accepted, that the perpetrators of the culpable acts that occurred within Kibuye *Prefecture*, during the period in questions, were acting with a *common intent and purpose*. That intent was to destroy the Tutsi ethnic group within Kibuye. Both Kayishema and Ruzindana played pivotal roles in carrying out *this common plan*.[194]

In this paragraph where the terms "common intent and purpose" and "common plan" are being used interchangeably, it is interesting to see that the *Kayishema and Ruzindana* Trial Chamber's reasoning on the issue of accused's *individual* genocidal intent advances in exactly the same way as that explaining JCE does. Accordingly, in this concluding remark on the defendants' individual genocidal

---

[192] *Ibid.* paras 289–291 and 312. On the basis of the Trial Judgment, the Appeals Chamber summarizes the Prosecution's case during trial stating, "a genocide of the Tutsi population was planned and executed by public officials, both one a national and regional level, in Rwanda during 1994". *See* Prosecutor v. Kayishema and Ruzindana, Appeals Judgment, 1 June 2001, para 139.

[193] Prosecutor v. Kayishema and Ruzindana, Trial Judgment, 21 May 1999, para 487. (emphasis added). The Chamber also does not distinguish "common intent" and "common plan" in para 545 of the judgment.

[194] *Ibid.* para 545. (emphasis added).

intent, we see all the objective elements of JCE such as (i) a plurality of persons (*actus reus*); (ii) common purpose/plan (*actus reus*); and (iii) significant contribution ("played pivotal roles"—*actus reus*). At this juncture, it should be borne in mind that, in this case, the Prosecution did not plead JCE and, accordingly, the Chamber did not even mention JCE at all throughout the judgment. So, one might assume that the Chamber, advertently or inadvertently, noticed a similarity between the logic of JCE and that of the crime of genocide. In other words, given the significance of the 'common purpose/plan' element in JCE and the collective genocidal intent element in genocide respectively, it should have been these two seemingly corresponding elements that led the Chamber to find individual genocidal intent through the logic of JCE.[195] In the Trial Chamber's logic here, Kayishema is guilty of genocide because he participated in collective intent to destroy a group through his pivotal role. In this respect, one might argue that the Chamber is using the logic of JCE in skipping a direct tackling of individual genocidal intent—i.e., direct tackling by reference to the accused's individual intent or knowledge. On the other hand, another might claim that the Chamber's argument is a legitimate direct tackling of individual genocidal intent as a progeny of the collective genocidal intent in a situation of mass criminality to which JCE is the most evolved version of the top-down vertical liability attribution scheme.[196] Either way, and regardless of whether it was intended by the Chamber, the logic of JCE seemed to provide it with a legal backdoor to find individual genocidal intent of the accused. It appears that, in this manner, the element of individual genocidal intent becomes nominal. It is not an exaggeration to say that, in the *Kayishema and Ruzindana* courtroom, the subjective element of individual genocidal intent is replaced by the objective element of 'pivotal or instrumental role' played by the accused in carrying out the objective element of common plan to destroy the Tutsi group.

The most significant implication of spotting the inherent logic of JCE within the notion of genocide is that it reveals the hidden truth that the objective element of collective genocidal intent (which is equivalent to the objective element of 'common purpose/plan' of JCE) is the key element of genocide. With regard to the JCE applied to a specific intent crime, the established jurisprudence states that "[w]here

---

[195] It is interesting to note that, despite the fact that the Trial Chamber did not even mention the term 'joint criminal enterprise', the *Kayishema and Ruzindana* Appeals Chamber explicitly referred to that term by mistake in affirming the Trial Chamber's conviction for genocide in relation to the codefendant Ruzindana as if the Trial Chamber had officially applied the JCE doctrine. Prosecutor v. Kayishema and Ruzindana, Appeals Judgment, 1 June 2001, para 193 ("As noted above, the Trial Chamber found that Ruzindana played a pivotal role in carrying out the common plan which was the destruction of the Tutsi ethnic group in Kibuye. In addition, the Trial Chamber also found that […] [Ruzindana's] actions also assisted in and contributed to the execution of the joint criminal enterprise […]. Ruzindana's submissions have failed to challenge these findings".).

[196] *See* Chap. 4, footnote 251 *infra* and accompanying text.

the underlying crime [of JCE] requires a specific intent, the accused, as a JCE member, must *share* the specific intent".[197] There is nothing wrong with this statement as a proclamation of a substantive legal principle. The bottom line is the manner in which this substantive principle is to be proven. Thus, what *Kayishema and Ruzindana* suggests is that, even when JCE is not explicitly applied, the inherent logic of JCE renders the inquiry into individual genocidal intent nominal by presuming its occurrence in the form of 'shared intent' within the mind of the accused through his instrumental role in the implementation of collective genocidal intent.

The *Munyakazi* case of the ICTR is another example where, despite the fact that the Trial Chamber expressly declined to apply the JCE doctrine, the logic of JCE was still employed in determining the question of individual genocidal intent. The *Munyakazi* Trial Chamber's relevant legal reasoning closely resembles the logic of JCE by putting the "overall intent of the attackers [...] to eliminate"[198] (which is functionally equivalent to 'common purpose/plan' of JCE) at its center. Munyakazi, a leader of the *Interahamwe* militia in Bugarama commune, Cyangugu prefecture, led attacks on Shangi Parish on 29 April 1994 (killing approximately 5000–6000 Tutsi refugees) and Mibilizi Parish on 30 April 1994 (killing approximately 60–100 Tutsi refugees).[199] The Trial Chamber, while rejecting the JCE,[200] concludes that Munyakazi "committed" the killings pursuant to Article 6(1) of the ICTR Statute.[201] The Chamber finds the accused guilty of genocide on the basis of the facts concerning the two incidents at Shangi Parish and Mibilizi Parish.[202] As to the genocidal intent element, the Chamber moves vertically from the "overall [genocidal] intent of the attackers" to Munyakazi's individual genocidal intent in a top-down manner. Thus, the Chamber first infers the "overall intent of the attackers to eliminate members of a protected group on the basis of its ethnic composition"[203] from (i) the fact that those who sought refuge at the parishes were predominantly Tutsi civilians[204]; (ii) the number of victims[205]; (iii) the fact that very few refugees survived either attack[206]; and (iv) the fact that the reason why the militiamen led by Munyakazi attacked the two parish was to complete the previous killings of refugees initiated by other units but left significant number of

---

[197] Prosecutor v. Ngirabatware, Trial Judgment, 20 December 2012, para 1301. (emphasis added).

[198] Prosecutor v. Munyakazi, Trial Judgment, 5 July 2010, para 496.

[199] *Ibid.* para 496.

[200] For lack of relevant evidence, the Chamber declined to apply the doctrine of joint criminal enterprise. *See* Prosecutor v. Munyakazi, Trial Judgment, 5 July 2010, paras 436–436 and 489–490.

[201] *Ibid.* paras 490–491 and 496.

[202] *Ibid.* para 501.

[203] *Ibid.* para 496.

[204] *Ibid.* para 499.

[205] *Ibid.* para 496.

[206] *Ibid.*

survivors.[207] In relation to Munyakazi's individual genocidal intent, the Chamber makes two findings that (i) the accused knew that the attacks on the two parishes "were part of the context of widespread attacks on Tutsi civilians";[208] and (ii) the accused "shared the specific intent to eliminate the protected group that had sought refuge at these two parishes".[209]

In short, the Chamber first establishes the collective genocidal intent ("overall [genocidal] intent of the attackers") and then demonstrates that, knowing the overall context of violence against Tutsis, the accused "shared" the collective genocidal intent through his "leadership role" in the two attacks.[210] As we have already studied, the combination of 'individual knowledge' and 'individual participation/ contribution ('leadership role')' employed to find the individual genocidal intent (in the form of 'shared intent') in both *Kayishema and Ruzindana* and *Munyakazi* closely resembles the manner of finding individual genocidal intent in JCE cases at the ICTY—i.e., the '*Krstić* formula'. It should be again remembered that, in the *Munyakazi* case, the Trial Chamber rejected the JCE for lack of evidence.[211] Thus, whereas it is certain that the Chamber's finding that Munyakazi "shared the specific intent [of the attackers]" has nothing to do with JCE, the term "share" still suggests a particular characteristic of the genocidal intent element as understood by the Chamber. Namely, the Chamber's concept of genocidal intent is of a collective nature to be *shared* by the Accused.

In short, we have seen that the logic of JCE permeates the law of genocide, even in cases where JCE was not the explicit basis of genocide liability. The logic of JCE derives proof of individual genocidal intent from shared collective intention, which is inferred from the defendant's membership, rank/position and participation/contribution in a genocidal enterprise. As further confirmation, we next examine an example where the weakening of these objective factors led to the conclusion of no genocidal intent.

---

[207] *Ibid.* para 499.

[208] *Ibid.* para 500.

[209] *Ibid.* Note that the Chamber makes reference to motive when it states, "*Whether Munyakazi led the attacks because he shared an animosity towards Tutsis or because he sought to curry favour with political associates or authorities*, the Trial Chamber finds that[,] in leading the attacks, Munyazaki shared the specific intent to eliminate the protected group that had sought refuge at these two parishes". (emphasis added).

[210] *Ibid.* para 422 ("[…] evidence with respect to Munyakazi's leadership role is well corroborated".). *See also* Prosecutor v. Munyakazi, Appeals Judgment, 18 December 2014, para 139 (The Appeals Chamber summarizes the reasoning of the Trial Chamber observing, "[i]n view of the nature and scope of the crimes, the Trial Chamber inferred that the attackers, including Munyakazi, acted with genocidal intent".); *Ibid.* 142 (In rejecting Munyakazi's appeal concerning his genocidal intent, the Appeals Chamber places emphasis on his active participation in the attacks taking a leadership role.).

[211] Prosecutor v. Munyakazi, Trial Judgment, 5 July 2010, paras 489–490.

4.2.2.4 Krstić Appeals: Lowered Level of Participation/Contribution and the Reduced Level of Genocidal Liability

The *Krstić* Trial Chamber's objective approach to finding individual genocidal intent is well expressed in the following observation:

> In short, the Trial Chamber sees no basis for refusing to accord the status of a co-perpetrator to *a member of a joint genocidal enterprise* whose participation is of an extremely significant nature and at the leadership level.[212]

We can see from this quotation that, in *Krstić*, the origin of such an objectified analysis of individual genocidal intent drawing upon 'participation/contribution' and 'rank/position of authority' lies in the accused's *membership* in a genocidal joint criminal enterprise. Such membership was recognized on the basis of the Trial Chamber's positive finding of 'shared intent' as a *mens rea* of JCE ("joint genocidal enterprise"), which the Chamber presumed on the basis of its confidence in the evidentiary weight of the objective aspects of the accused's 'participation/contribution' and 'rank/authority'. In this sense, it is not completely misleading to say that such objective features determine the accused's membership in 'JCE to commit genocide' through the 'shared intent' element. If you *shared* the collective intent of the "joint genocidal enterprise", you are its member, and the decision on whether you shared the collective intent is based on the objective aspects of your 'participation/contribution' and 'rank/position of authority'. On the other hand, when a trier of fact is not convinced by relevant evidence regarding those objective aspects, it cannot move forward to find or, rather, presume the 'shared intent' that carries with it the individual genocidal intent. At this juncture, the only option left to the trier of fact is to examine the *mens rea* of 'shared intent' more closely as a *mens rea* per se. In such a situation, it is very likely that the Chamber would deny the establishment of 'shared intent/individual genocidal intent', because of its inability to presume it due to the feeble objective foundations of the case. That is precisely what happened in the *Krstić* Appeals Chamber when it lowered the accused's principal liability initially determined by the Trial Chamber to that of an accessory—i.e., 'aiding and abetting genocide'.[213] That is to say, the Appeals Chamber was not able to apply the 'JCE to commit genocide' to Krstić, because evidence did not permit the Chamber to reach a positive conclusion about the accused's membership therein since it was not possible to presume his 'shared intent', which resulted from the Chamber's lack of confidence in the objective aspects of Krstić's acts and participation.

Indeed, in the *Krstić* Appeals Judgment, I think what principally led the Appeals Chamber to lower the level of liability from 'committing genocide' to

---

[212] Prosecutor v. Krstić, Trial Judgment, 2 August 2001, para 642. (emphasis added). For case laws which take a similar approach to principal liability of genocide, *see* Prosecutor v. Stakić, Decision on Rule 98 *bis* Motion for Judgment of Acquittal, 31 October 2002, para 50; Prosecutor v. Blagojević and Jokić, Trial Judgment, 17 January 2005, para 776.

[213] Prosecutor v. Krstić, Appeals Judgment, 19 April 2004, para 138.

'aiding and abetting genocide' was the reduced level of the Drina Corps' role during the Srebrenica massacre as newly assessed by the Appeals Chamber. Contrary to the Trial Chamber's finding that the Drina Corps *carried out* the executions (direct participation in the executions), the Appeals Chamber concluded that the corps only *facilitated* the executions (indirect participation in the executions).[214] Indeed, the Trial Chamber's finding that Krstić "shared the [collective] genocidal intent" was primarily based on the Drina Corps' direct participation in the actual executions of the Bosnian Muslim men, as clearly expressed by the Trial Chamber when it stated "[The fact that] he shared the genocidal intent […] cannot be gainsaid given his informed participation in the executions through the use of Drina Corps assets".[215] By contrast, its finding of reduced level of 'participation/contribution' kept the Appeals Chamber from moving on to presume the accused's individual genocidal intent dressed with the notion of 'shared intent'. Thus, it was not the *mens rea* per se, but the objective facts that surrounded the *mens rea* that guided and directed the relevant legal deliberation and determined whether to apply the JCE or to turn to consider a lower-level liability such as 'aiding and abetting'.[216] As seen from the *Krstić* case, such objective facts are not limited to the accused's personal realm (e.g., Krstić's own acts and utterances), but extend to acts of others (e.g., actions performed by the Drina Corps) through such imputation/attribution mechanisms as the 'effective control' test and/or principal liability theories.[217] It seems the case law of the *ad hoc* tribunals that we have studied thus far in this subsection well reflects Bassiouni's observation that "[i]ntent to commit Genocide […] can be proven by objective legal standards with respect to decision makers and commanders.[218]

---

[214] *Ibid*. paras 77–78.

[215] Prosecutor v. Krstić, Trial Judgment, 2 August 2001, para 633.

[216] For examples of the 'implicit' application of JCE, see *Kayishema and Ruzindana* and *Munyakazi* discussed in Sect. 4.2.2.3 *supra*.

[217] In a case where the accused was physically present at the crime scene, it might be enough to consider the objective facts within the accused's personal realm. Such was the case in *Mpambara* in which the doctrine of JCE was officially pleaded by the Prosecution. Mpambara, as a *bourgmestre* of Rukara Commune during the Rwandan genocide, was personally present at crime scenes. Ultimately, the Trial Chamber acquitted the accused of genocide, because it was not established beyond reasonable doubt that he participated in JCE to commit genocide and, consequently, that he did not have the 'shared intent'. For the purpose of the Chamber's acquittal decision in the context of applying the JCE doctrine, it was the objective features of Mpambara's individual acts and participation that was determinative. Such alleged objective acts of the accused include: (i) distributing weapons and inciting genocide at Paris Centre on 9 April 1994; (ii) colluding with another person to kill Tutsi refugees; (iii) distributing rocks on the Parish church on 12 April 1994; and (iv) deliberately leaving Rukara unprotected. Prosecutor v. Mpambara, Trial Judgement, 12 September 2006, para 164.

[218] Bassiouni 1993, pp. 235–236.

4.2.2.5 A Hypothetical Consideration of the Ultimate Mastermind's Genocidal Intent

The importance of objective features in determining the question of individual genocidal intent—which stems from the collective criminality of genocide—is also confirmed by having another look into the hypothetical question of individual genocidal intent of the ultimate mastermind. Apparently, the relevant case law says that, for the purpose of prosecuting individuals for their alleged crime of genocide, it is not required to identify the ultimate mastermind who originally conceived the initial 'intent to destroy'. Thus, such a challenge made by Karadžić that there exists no evidence "as to who made the decision on the genocide and the killings [in Srebrenica] in general" does not allow a genocide suspect escape criminal prosecution.[219]

I would say that such an ultimate mastermind exists only in the hypothetical realm because not only it is almost impossible in practice to precisely identify him or her, but also even the initial 'intent to destroy' is rather to be regarded as being of a collective nature. Assuming that it was Hitler himself who initially conceived the 'intent to destroy' the Jewish people in Europe,[220] such intent cannot be identified as genocidal intent without coupling it with other people's 'intent to destroy'. That is, Hitler's original intent does not have any legal significance until it is associated with the intent of other agents, which makes *their* intent an object of criminal law.[221] From that time on, when intentions meet together, what criminal law is interested in is not Hitler's intent, but his group's intent which is only to be shared, not to be solely possessed, even by Hitler.[222] Though the legal concept of 'possession'

---

[219] Prosecutor v. Karadžić, Transcript, 28 June 202, p. 28754.

[220] *See e.g.*, Lemkin 2008, p. 89, footnote 45 (citing the Joint Declaration by members of the United Nations, dated Dec. 17, 1942 which refers to "Hitler's oft-repeated intention to exterminate the Jewish people in Europe".).

[221] For a similar view, in the context of discussing the crime of aggression, *see* May 2006, pp. 311–312 and 315–316 ("Crimes against peace, unlike war crimes for instance, are crimes committed by States, yet criminal trials do not have States in the dock. The most obvious person to put in the dock when States commit crimes would be the State's head. But even this person, the president of a State for instance, typically does not act as an individual but as a representative of the people, or of the ruling elite. Even the head of a State is not clearly responsible, as an individual, for waging aggressive war. [...] So even if Hitler had been in the dock at Nuremberg, there would still have been serious questions about whether it was Hitler, *qua* individual person, who had the criminal intent to engage in aggressive war, or whether it was Hitler as head of State who had that intention".).

[222] In this respect, Hans Vest rightly points out the importance of the 'group intent' aspect when he observes that "[...] it is dangerous to technically speak of 'intending' consequences of a collective act, as 'intention' is in the ordinary legal meaning referring to the result of one's own conduct. Consequently, individuals can only intend to destroy (part of) a national, ethnic, racial or religious group 'with the help of others'". Vest 2007, p. 790. Indeed, during the drafting negotiations of the Genocide Convention, such expression as "with intent to co-operate in destroying a national, racial or religious group [...]" was considered for the genocidal intent element. UN GAOR, 6th Comm., 3d Sess., U.N. Doc. A/C.6/217, at 2 (Oct. 5, 1948) (Belgium's proposed amendments to the Ad Hoc Committee Draft Convention on Genocide). In a subsequent session,

connotes a full power to control,[223] neither Hitler nor any individual agent himself or herself has such a power with regard to the group's intent.[224] Such power only belongs to a criminal enterprise.[225] In this sense, the French legislation that replaces *mens rea* ('intent to destroy') with *actus reus* ('concerted plan aimed at the total or partial destruction') appears to be insightful in that it exposes the hidden truth that genocidal intent is an intent from a collective to a collective.[226] Nobody would argue that the concept of "concerted plan aimed at the total or partial destruction" is of an individualistic nature. An individual person's mental state, however evil it may be, is outside the realm of criminal law until it is (i) expressed through his own conduct, or (ii) joined together with another guilty mind.

This possibility of collectivizing even the initial 'intent to destroy' of the ultimate mastermind reminds us of Lemkin's remark that "[genocide] is intended rather to signify a *coordinated plan* of different actions aiming at the destruction".[227] In this respect, Carl-Friedrich Stuckenberg rightly observes that "[i]f the distinctive feature of genocide is seen rather in the – usually collective – enterprise to produce a special kind of large-scale harm, then the genocidal intent is nothing else than the

---

Footnote 222 (continued)

the Belgian delegation modified its original proposal whereby replace the word "co-operate" with the word "participate". Mr. Kaeckenbeeck of the delegation explained that "the Belgian delegation had put forward its amendment on the ground that it was almost inconceivable that a crime aimed particularly at the destruction of a race or group could be the work of a single individual. [...] The purpose of the Belgian delegation was to emphasize the collective character of genocide". U.N. GAOR, 6th Comm., 3d Sess., 73d mtg. at 90, U.N. Doc. A/C.6/SR.73 (Oct. 13, 1948).

[223] Black's Law Dictionary (9th edn., 2009) defines the term 'possess' as "[t]o have in one's actual control; to have possession of".

[224] Similarly, Alexander Greenawalt observes, "This aspect of genocidal intent [i.e., the question of superior order] poses a particular problem given the type of "administrative massacre" presented by the Holocaust, where a state deploys an entire bureaucracy and military chain of command to realize the genocidal plan. In such scenarios almost everyone, including high-ranking perpetrators, is a subordinate on some level". Greenawalt 1999, pp. 2280–2281.

[225] For a view that acknowledges the possibility of a single individual's full control over a genocidal apparatus, *see* Cupido 2014b, p. 25.

[226] For a similar view, *see* Ohlin 2007, p. 73 ("[I]t is the ethnic group as a whole that carries the intention to carry out the crime [of genocide]".). With regard to the 'concerted plan' formulation in the French Criminal Code, *see* Elliott 2001, p. 140 (The French Criminal Code of 1992 replaced the 'intent to destroy (*mens rea*)' with the element of 'concerted plan (*actus reus*)' by providing the definition of genocide as follows: "Genocide consists in the execution of a *concerted plan* aimed at the total or partial destruction of a national, ethnic, racial or religious group, or of a group determined by any other arbitrary criteria, to commit or to have committed, against members of this group, one of the following acts: [1] A voluntary attack on life; [2] A serious attack on their physical or psychological integrity; [3] Submission to living conditions likely to lead to the total or partial destruction of the group; [4] Measures aiming to prevent reproduction; [5] Forced transfer of children ...") (emphasis added). *See also* U.N. GAOR, 6th Comm., 3d Sess., 73d mtg. at 95, U.N. Doc. A/C.6/SR.73 (Oct. 13, 1948) (Mr. Chaumont of the French delegation "thought the expression 'aimed at the ... destruction' was preferable to "in the intent to destroy", used by the Ad Hoc Committee [Draft Convention on Genocide]".).

[227] Lemkin 2008, p. 79.

plan that animates this enterprise [...]".[228] In this manner, from the perspective of 'genocide as a criminal enterprise', the objective nature of genocidal intent emerges plainly. That is, in this picture, genocidal intent primarily belongs to a collective, but not to an individual, which locates the genocidal intent outside the individual inner state of mind. In sum, the objective and collectivized nature of even the ultimate mastermind's 'intent to destroy' suggests that, since genocidal intent is to be *shared* by actors, rather than to be possessed, an individual *génocidaire*'s own mental state might not be determinative of his genocidal culpability *as much as we have thought it to be*. Due to the logic of JCE inherent in genocide, it is, doctrinally speaking, the 'shared intent' (in the sense of sharing the collective genocidal intent) that is decisive in the determination of individual guilt of genocide.

As we have studied thus far, however, practically (or evidentiarily) speaking, it is the objective aspects of individual 'participation/contribution' and 'rank' that guide and direct such determination, because the 'shared intent' is mostly presumed on the basis of the evidentiary strength of such objective features. It is also in this context that such judicial inventions as the *Krstić* formula, which places primary emphasis on the objective act, participation and contribution emerge for the purpose of determining the criminal liability of superior/leadership actors vis-à-vis the crime of genocide.[229] In this manner, as Verena Haan observed in relation to the way in which JCE is actually applied at the *ad hoc* tribunals,[230] the objective elements of 'participation/contribution' and 'rank' occupy the central post of the relevant legal deliberation. All these observations lead to a conclusion that genocide is a leadership crime in respect of which only the high-level actors can share the collective genocidal intent by dint of the inherent logic of JCE within genocide: without an instrumental participation/contribution from a leadership position, the presumption of 'shared intent' is not feasible.

4.2.3 The Top-Down Verticality of Genocidal Intent: The JCE Logic Within Genocide Rendering Genocide a Leadership Crime

Since the elements of crimes set forth by the jurisprudence of the *ad hoc* tribunals or the ICC Elements of Crimes are basically articulated from the perspective of a physical perpetrator (in most cases, subordinate actors),[231] it is rather the elements of modes of liability than the elements of crimes that critically determine guilt and culpability of the usual suspects of core international crimes—i.e., superior/

---

[228] Stuckenberg 2014, pp. 319–320.

[229] For the *Krstić* formula, *see* Sect. 4.2.2.2 *supra*.

[230] *See* this chapter, footnote 140 *supra* and accompanying text.

[231] An obvious exception would be Article 8(2)(e)(viii) of the ICC Statute in respect of which the ICC Elements of Crimes provides: "1. The perpetrator ordered a displacement of a civilian population. [...] 3. The perpetrator was in a position to effect such displacement by giving such order. [...]".

leadership actors. More specifically, within the category of the elements of crimes, it is only the subjective elements of crimes that are directly applicable to superior/leadership actors.[232] In the case of objective elements of crimes, they are to be applied to them only in an indirect manner. Such indirect application is caused by the physical distance between the actual commission of the crime and the superior/leadership actors.[233] The legal space created by this indirect applicability of objective elements of crimes is exactly the place where the elements of modes of liability figure in the determination of guilt and culpability of superior/leadership actors. Through each mode of liability's own objective elements and subjective elements tailored to the complicated fact pattern of collective criminality, the relevant legal analysis of guilt and culpability of superior/leadership actors is to be further advanced to a more refined level. Various trials of such tailoring have been called the 'membership in a criminal organization',[234] the 'joint criminal enterprise', the 'control theory' and so forth. In this context, let us have a look at the question posed by Gideon Boas and his co-authors. As to the issue of potential possessor of genocidal intent, they ask:

> Relatively little attention has been paid, however, when discussing the elements of the crimes themselves, to whether all the elements must be satisfied by the conduct of a single actor, or whether a crime may be constituted by the cumulative contributions of more than one actor. With regard to the crime of genocide, the judgements of the *ad hoc* Tribunals have not been clear in articulating which actor, among the possible culprits, is required to have the specific intent to commit genocide.[235]

A similar question was also considered by Mark Osiel when he observed that "[i]t is sometimes possible for each element of a given offense to be committed by a different person, so that no single participant realizes all of the constituent elements".[236] In relation to the question of potential possessors of individual genocidal intent, we

---

[232] For example, the ICC Pre-Trial Chamber in *Lubanga* says that the first subjective element of its control theory of co-perpetration is "[t]he suspect must fulfil the subjective elements of the crime in question". Prosecutor v. Lubanga, Decision on the Confirmation of Charges, 29 January 2007, para 349. For a critical overview of the relevant ICC jurisprudence concerning the question of subjective elements of the control theory, *see* Jain 2013, pp 860–862.

[233] I take the term 'distance' from the eloquent explanation of the relationship between the crime and modes of liability contained in Zahar and Sluiter 2007, pp. 219–221.

[234] Charter of the International Military Tribunal in the Agreement for the Prosecution and Punishment of the Major War Criminals of the European Axis, Article 9, 8 August 1945, 59 Stat. 1544, 82 U.N.T.S. 279.

[235] Boas et al. 2008, p. 157.

[236] Osiel 2009, pp. 23–24. Actually, this observation should not be considered a special principle only applicable to core international crimes. The idea is basically the one behind the general theory of co-perpetration in national jurisdictions around the world. Think of the textbook example of three persons robbing a bank together. One threatens the casher with a gun; another actually takes the money; the third one at the driver seat in a car outside the bank waiting for his friends. They are all perpetrators of the offence of bank robbery, and it is not important which element of crime is met by which person. In this regard, Gabriel Hallevy explains that the doctrine of co-perpetration "treats all members of the joint enterprise *as one body* that is liable for the commission of the offense". Hallevy 2014, p. 51. (emphasis added).

can think of two substantive law mechanisms to solve the problem: (i) allocating the genocidal intent element to a specified individual or a group of individuals through the inherent logic of JCE within genocide; or (ii) allocating the genocidal intent element to a specified individual or a group of individuals through the JCE doctrine. The former only involves the realm of crime, while the latter concerns both territories of crime and mode of liability. In either case, principal liability is to be attributed only to the person who was assigned the genocidal intent element by one of these two mechanisms. The outcome would be the same: both mechanisms allow allocating principal liability only to those actors whose 'participation/contribution' and 'rank' are, in an evidentiary sense, weighty enough to presume the 'shared intent' that carries with it the individual genocidal intent element. Given the inherent logic of JCE within genocide, the general practice of international prosecutors charging the doctrine of JCE in relation to the crime of genocide might be regarded as just transcribing the collective liability scheme already existing in the crime itself. At the heart of that liability attribution mechanism, there exists the collective genocidal intent effectively stretching out its hands to each participant of a genocidal criminal enterprise. Afterwards, on the basis of the factual strength of such objective aspects of 'participation/contribution' and 'rank', the collective genocidal intent labels each participant either a principal or an accessory by presuming the 'shared intent/individual genocidal intent' for the former, and by rejecting to presume it for the latter.[237]

Now one thing is clear: owing to the inherent logic of JCE within genocide, it is not possible to attribute principal liability to the low-level actors. In a similar vein, the *Stakić* Trial Chamber observes:

[I]n most cases, the principal perpetrator of genocide are those who devise the genocidal plan at the highest level and take the major steps to put it into effect. The principal perpetrator is the one who fulfils "a key co-ordinating role" and whose "participation is of an extremely significant nature and at the leadership level".[238]

In relation to core international crimes in general, Jens David Ohlin states:

The Joint Intentions Theory will convict as principals only those individuals who desire that the group commit the crime and who participate in the group-level deliberation that resulted in that joint intention and coordinated elements of the plan by meshing sub-plans.[239]

---

[237] This observation fits well with Marjolein Cupido's explanation of the liability-attributing function of the 'common purpose/plan' element: "The normative approach requires the formulation of specific criteria of attribution that help to determine who exactly is 'most responsible'. In relation to JCE and join perpetration, the 'common plan' element qualifies as such a criterion of attribution: it forms the basis for the attribution of criminal acts committed by other participants to the accused. The analysis of the ICTY and ICC case law illustrates that the courts' application of the 'common plan' element shows signs of what Hart defines as 'role responsibility'. [...] The ICTY and the ICC accordingly assess the accused's knowledge of, and contribution to, the common plan in light of his or her social status and position of responsibility". Cupido 2014a, p. 153.

[238] Prosecutor v. Stakić, Decision on Rule 98 *bis* Motion for Judgment of Acquittal, 31 October 2002, para 50. *See also* Prosecutor v. Krstić, Trial Judgment, 2 August 2001, para 642; Prosecutor v. Blagojević and Jokić, Trial Judgment, 17 January 2005, para 776.

[239] Ohlin 2014, p. 340. *See also* Ohlin's proposal of a mode of liability of 'co-perpetrating a joint criminal enterprise and its three elements. Ohlin 2011, pp. 714–715.

The view of attributing principal liability of genocide only to leadership-level actors fits in with the inherent logic of JCE within genocide. As the JCE is a commission liability scheme for its members who are generally political and military high-ranking officials,[240] the unique generic nature of the crime of genocide stemming from its inherent logic of JCE exerts a conceptual force that restrict the scope of principal liability only to the leadership-level actors. In this context, it is important to note that this theory does not exonerate the mid- or low-level actors. They can still be convicted as aiders and abettors.[241] I explained above the logic of JCE's function of assigning (or rather distributing) elements of crimes to different actors. In that respect, with regard to the elements of the crime of genocide listed in the ICC Elements of Crimes, the element that subordinate actors do not satisfy is "[t]he perpetrator intended to destroy, in whole or in part, that national, ethnical, racial or religious group, as such". That is because the low-level actors do not occupy a role that would allow them to destroy the group, and therefore they cannot truly form that intention.

In this respect, there remains no *raison d'être* of the knowledge-based approach any more as a principal liability theory for low-level actors.[242] The question of whether physical perpetrators at the lower echelon of genocidal enterprise possess genocidal intent is no longer relevant to the attribution of principal liability of genocide. For example, facing a charge of genocide, Karadžić asserts the absence of genocidal intent on the part of physical perpetrators of genocidal acts at Srebrenica as follows:

> We can even see here statements by insiders and others who were familiar with these events and we even have statements by the perpetrators, those who killed prisoners of war, that they did not know anyone who had the intent of destroying the Muslims in Srebrenica and neither did they have that intent.[243]

> The repenting perpetrators who admitted to the killings of prisoners of war confirmed that the thought never crossed their minds of exterminating Muslims as a group.[244]

In response, the *Karadžić* Trial Chamber actually embarks on the relevant evidence review, which implies that the Chamber accepts that the genocidal intent of

---

[240] *See* Harding 2013, pp. 247–248 ("The purpose of joint criminal enterprise liability [...] is to capture such crucial organisational actors as serious offenders, and lift their veil of legitimacy by establishing an overarching criminal motivation and dedication. [...] Joint criminal enterprise offences on the other hand comprise directing and facilitating activities which contribute significantly to the eventual commission of the predicate offences".).

[241] *See* Drost 1959, p. 82 ("Culprits participating one way or another in the perpetration of the crime but acting under command of the law or superior orders and therefore claiming to act without intending the destruction of the group as such cannot excuse themselves with the legal plea of not falling under Article II [of the Genocide Convention]. They are to be brought under the sway of the following Article III dealing with the acts punishable under the convention other than acts of genocide proper".).

[242] For my criticism of the knowledge-based approach, *see* Sects. 2.4 and 2.5 *supra*.

[243] Prosecutor v. Karadžić, Transcript, 11 June 2012, p. 28587.

[244] *Ibid.* at 28594.

the physical perpetrators does constitute a legal requirement.[245] Thus, the Chamber begins its factual examination by stating that "[i]n relation to the accused's challenge as to the lack of genocidal intent of the physical perpetrators of the killings in Srebrenica, the Chamber recalls that the specific intent of such perpetrators by its nature is not usually susceptible to direct proof but can be inferred from various factors [...]".[246] In the end, refraining from stating that the physical perpetrators possessed genocidal intent, the Chamber determines that "there is evidence on which, if accepted, a reasonable trier of fact could be satisfied beyond reasonable doubt that genocide [...] was carried out by Bosnian Serb forces in Srebrenica".[247] It is unfortunate, however, that the Trial Chamber too easily treats the physical perpetrators' genocidal intent as if it is a legitimate legal requirement of the crime of genocide. Furthermore, engaging in the risky practice of combining the genocidal intent of physical perpetrators and collective genocidal intent, the Chamber does not hesitate to state that such individual intent "can be inferred from various factors, including the general context of the case, the numerical size of the atrocities committed, the repetition of destructive and discriminatory attacks, or the existence of a plan or policy to commit the underlying offence".[248] On the same issue, the Appeals Chamber's approach is very understandably different from that of the Trial Chamber. It is interesting to see that, in responding to the question whether the genocidal intent of the physical perpetrators is a legal requirement, the Appeals Chamber draws upon the doctrine of JCE. It appears that the Appeals Chamber answers a question of the elements of crime by examining the elements of a mode of liability theory (JCE I). The relevant part of the Appeals Judgment states:

> The Indictment alleges that JCE members, including Karadžić, used others to carry out the crimes forming part of the JCE's common purpose, including members of the Bosnian Serb forces. The Appeals Chamber recalls that members of a JCE can incur liability for crime committed by principal perpetrators who were non-JCE members, provided that it has been established that the crime can be imputed to at least one member of the JCE and that this member—when using the principal perpetrators—acted in accordance with the

---

[245] Similarly, the "Law" part in which the *Kayishema and Ruzindana* Trial Chamber addresses the meaning of "killing" by comparison of the term "*meurtre*" in the French version of the ICTR Statute demonstrates that the phrase "intent to destroy" in the definition of genocide is understood by the Chamber as an individual intent belonging to the very person who physically killed a member of the victim group. The Chamber observes that, since any genocidal conduct of killing "should be considered along with the specific intent of genocide", there is "virtually no difference" between the English term "killing" (which simply means 'causing death') and French term "meurtre" (which means 'deliberate homicide'). Since the matter of intent, recklessness or negligence etc. belongs to the realm of individual *mens rea*, it is safe to assume that the specific intent of genocide mentioned by the Chamber means that of physical perpetrator. *See* Prosecutor v. Kayishema and Ruzindana, Trial Judgment, 21 May 1999, paras 101–104.

[246] Prosecutor v. Karadžić, Transcript, 28 June 2012, p. 28751.

[247] *Ibid.* at 28751–28752.

[248] *Ibid.* at 28751.

common objective. Such a link is established by a showing that the JCE member used the non-JCE member to commit a crime pursuant to the common criminal purpose of the JCE. The Appeals Chamber further recalls that the relevant question in the context of JCE I liability is whether the JCE member used the non-JCE member to commit the *actus reus* of the crime forming part of the common purpose; it is not determinative whether the non-JCE member shared the *mens rea* of the JCE member or that the non-JCE member knew of the existence of the JCE. Therefore, in accordance with the allegations underlying Count 1 of the Indictment, it is the genocidal intent of Karadžić and other alleged JCE members, not the physical perpetrators of the underlying alleged genocidal acts, that is determinative for purposes of JCE I.[249]

This paragraph evidently shows that JCE as a mode of liability has the power to decide the applicable scope of the elements of crimes. Given that genocidal intent is certainly an element of crime, as opposed to an element of mode of liability, in the Appeals Chamber's reasoning above, a theory of modes of liability (JCE) distributes an element of crime (genocidal intent) between JCE members and non-JCE members. In this conceptual scheme, collective genocidal intent satisfied by JCE members and specific underlying acts performed by physical perpetrators (which ultimately satisfy the substantiality requirement) together constitutes *one* crime of genocide.[250] That is to say, in a given situation, there can be only one crime of genocide committed, but not two or more. Thus, in the reasoning of the Appeals Chamber above the notion of genocide is of a generic nature. If the Prosecution pleaded a different mode of liability than JCE, would it possible for the Appeals Chamber to reach a differing answer as to the question of whether the physical perpetrators' genocidal intent is legally required or not? I believe not, because there still exists the inherent logic of JCE within genocide. The logic of JCE within genocide is real, the most significant implication of which is that collective genocidal intent (as a counterpart of 'common purpose/plan' of the logic of JCE) becomes determinative in attributing genocidal liability to individual participants in a genocidal enterprise. And, importantly, such attribution of liability occurs in a top-down vertical manner. In this regard, Thomas Weigend provides an insightful overview of the liability-attribution scheme within JCE:

> If international crime is collective rather than individual, a new approach toward allocating responsibility of individuals may be required. The *ad hoc* international tribunals, by relying on the model of joint criminal enterprise, have chosen to replace the traditional bottom-up analysis of participation in criminal law by a top-down model of responsibility: according to their view, the chain of attribution no longer starts from the palpable act of the man with the gun and moves up the causal links until it (perhaps) reaches the chief strategist of the system, but responsibility focuses on participation in some kind of common enterprise to which all individual criminal acts are linked. The criminal enterprise thus becomes the centerpiece of attribution. If attribution starts from the collective act or the common criminal enterprise, it is not necessary to establish a direct connection between actors in the background and the individuals directly carrying out the offence, but

---

[249] Prosecutor v. Karadžić, Rule 98 *bis* Appeals Judgement, 11 July 2013, para 79.

[250] Concerning the issue of number of crime vis-à-vis the crime of genocide, *see also* Sect. 3.5 *supra*.

it is sufficient to link both to the common enterprise. Clearly, this way of attributing responsibility casts the net more widely than traditional forms of perpetratorship and accessorial liability, and makes for greater flexibility in adjudicating collective crime. This approach also reflects the proximity of international criminal law to international law, which has traditionally limited liability to states and similar collectives.[251]

Although it is true that the net is cast "more widely", the peculiar characteristic of genocide itself being a criminal enterprise narrows down the sphere of principal liability through the objectified analysis of individual genocidal intent that heightens the required level of evidentiary basis concerning individual 'participation/ contribution' and 'rank'. Put otherwise, within the top-down vertical liability attribution scheme of genocidal intent, there exists a self-imposed lower limit of principal liability owing to the objective evidentiary threshold. It was for this very reason of the top-down verticality of genocidal intent that the *Stakić* Appeals Chamber expressed its reservation about the compartmentalized mode of analysis of the genocidal intent element that starts its analysis from the underlying acts of genocide at the 'conduct level' (as opposed to the 'context level').[252] Since the crux of the crime of genocide lies in the collective genocidal intent that exists at the 'context level' apart from any individual's state of mind, it is only when a

---

[251] Weigend 2014, p. 264.

[252] Prosecutor v. Stakić, Appeals Judgment, 22 March 2006, para 55. *See also* Prosecutor v. Karadžić, Rule 98 *bis* Appeals Judgement, 11 July 2013, paras 56 ("The Appeals Chamber recalls that, in the context of assessing evidence of genocidal intent, a compartmentalised mode of analysis may obscure the proper inquiry. Rather than considering separately whether an accused intended to destroy a protected group through each of the relevant genocidal acts, a trial chamber should consider whether all the evidence, taken together, demonstrates a genocidal mental state".).
In direct opposition to the intuition of collective criminality involving core international crimes which projects a top-down vertical individual responsibility scheme as well reflected in the principal liability theories centering around the notion of 'common purpose/plan', *Nizeyimana* is a typical example of the bottom-up analysis of genocidal intent. The genocidal intent element as understood and applied by the *Nizeyimana* Trial Chamber is incident-based, not case-based. That is to say, for the purpose of deciding on genocidal intent, the Chamber examines the relevant facts in each incident respectively. It thus follows that, while in one incident the accused can have genocidal intent, and in another incident it is possible for him not to have that intent. Does a person's intent to destroy a group change from time to time while engaging in almost the same act— i.e., killing members of the group? The *Nizeyimana* Trial Chamber's analysis of genocidal intent always starts from finding genocidal intent of physical perpetrators whose personal identity is unknown. Sometimes, they exist as a large group including soldiers, militiamen and armed civilians. In other occasions, they just form a small group of killers manned at a roadblock. Yet, the Chamber appears to be so confident in proclaiming their genocidal intent saying, "[t]he Chamber has no doubt that the assailants [...] possessed genocidal intent". Prosecutor v. Nizeyimana, Trial Judgment, 19 June 2012, paras 1505, 1513, 1521, 1523 and 1530. The famous *Akayesu* dictum ending with the phrase "even impossible to determine" seems to be unknown to the Trial Chamber in *Nizeyimana*. In any event, this genocidal intent of unidentified physical perpetrators always provides a ground upon which Nizeyimana's individual genocidal intent is to be established. For Claus Kress's criticism of ICJ's bottom-up mode of analysis that starts from inquiries "into the possible genocidal intent of unnamed individual perpetrators", *see* Kress 2007. p. 623.

genocide case is approached from a macro perspective that the attribution of individual genocidal liability is to be executed with self-restraint properly reflecting the spirit of legality, individual culpability and fair labeling. In other words, it is only through the sole governing notion of genocide—i.e., collective genocidal intent—that the complex interaction of various named and unnamed actors within a genocidal enterprise is appropriately accounted for.

References

Agbor AA (2013) Instigation to crimes against humanity: the flawed jurisprudence of the trial and appeals chambers of the International Criminal Tribunal for Rwanda. Brill/Nijhoff, Leiden

Akhavan P (2005) The crime of genocide in the ICTR jurisprudence. J Int Crim Justice 3:989–1006

Ambos K (2007) Joint criminal enterprise and command responsibility. J Int Crim Justice 5:159–183

Ambos K (2009) What does "intent to destroy" in genocide mean? Int Rev Red Cross 91:833–858

Ambos K (2014) Treatise on international criminal law, vol II: the crimes and sentencing. Oxford University Press, Oxford

Bantekas I (2010) International criminal law, 4th edn. Hart Publishing, Oxford

Bassiouni MC (1993) Article 19: genocide. In: Bssiouni MC (ed) Commentaries on the International Law Commission's 1991 draft code of crimes against the peace and security of mankind, vol 11. Nouvelles Études Pénales, pp 233–236

Boas G, Bischoff JL, Reid NL (2008) International criminal law practitioner library, vol II: elements of crimes under international law. Cambridge University Press, Cambridge

Cassese A, Gaeta P, Baig L, Fan M, Gosnell C, Whiting A (2013) Cassese's international criminal law. Oxford University Press, Oxford

Cryer R, Friman H, Robinson D, Wilmshurst E (2010) An introduction to international criminal law and procedure. Cambridge University Press, Cambridge

Cupido M (2014a) Pluralism in theories of liability: joint criminal enterprise versus joint perpetration. In: van Sliedregt E, Vasiliev S (eds) Pluralism in international criminal law. Oxford University Press, Oxford, pp 128–158

Cupido M (2014b) The contextual embedding of genocide: a casuistic analysis of the interplay between law and facts. Melbourne J Int Law 15:1–36

Drost P (1959) The crime of state: genocide. Leyden, Sythoff

Elliott C (2001) French criminal law. Willan Publishing, Cullompton

Fisher Kirsten (2012) Moral accountability and international criminal law: holding agents of atrocity accountable to the world. Routledge, London

Fletcher GP, Ohlin JD (2005) Reclaiming fundamental principles of criminal law in the Darfur case. J Int Crim Justice 3:539–561

Gadirov J (2014) Collective intentions and individual criminal responsibility in international criminal law. In: van Sliedregt E, Vasiliev S (eds) Pluralism in international criminal law. Oxford University Press, Oxford, pp 342–367

Greenawalt AKA (1999) Rethinking genocidal intent: the case for a knowledge-based interpretation. Colum Law Rev 99:2259–2294

Haan V (2005) The development of the concept of joint criminal enterprise at the international criminal tribunal for the former Yugoslavia. Int Crim Law Rev 5:167–201

Hallevy G (2014) Liability for crimes involving artificial intelligence systems. Springer, Heidelberg

Harding C (2013) Criminal enterprise: individuals, organisations and criminal responsibility. Routledge, Oxon

Jain N (2013) Individual responsibility for mass atrocity: in search of a concept of perpetration. Am J Comp Law 61:831–872

Jain N (2014) Perpetrators and accessories in international criminal law: individual modes of responsibility for collective crimes. Hart Publishing, Oxford

Jones JRWD (2003) "Whose intent is it anyway?": genocide and the intent to destroy a group. In: Vohrah LC et al (eds) Mans's inhumanity to man: essays on international law in Honour of Antonio Cassese. Martinus Nijhoff, Leiden, pp 467–480

Jørgensen N (2001) A reappraisal of the abandoned Nuremberg concept of criminal organizations in the context of justice in Rwanda. Crim Law Forum 12:371–406

Kress C (2006) The crime of genocide under international law. Int Crim Law Rev 6:461–502

Kress C (2007) The International Court of Justice and the elements of the crime of genocide. Eur J Int Law 18:619–629

Lemkin R (1947) Genocide as a crime under international law. Am J Int Law 41:145–151

Lemkin R (2008) Axis rule in occupied Europe: laws of occupation, analysis of government, proposals for redress, 2nd edn. The Law Book Exchange Ltd, Clark

May L (2006) State aggression, collective liability, and individual mens rea. In: French PA, Wettstein HK (eds) Shared intentions and collective responsibility, vol 30, pp 309–324 (Midwest Stud. Phil.)

May L (2010) Genocide: a normative account. Cambridge University Press, Cambridge

Mundorff K (2009) Other people's children: a textual and contextual interpretation of the genocide convention, article 2(e). Harv Int Law J 50:61–127

Obote-Odora A (2002) Complicity in genocide as understood through the ICTR experience. Int Crim Law Rev 2:375–408

Ohlin JD (2007) Three conceptual problems with the doctrine of joint criminal enterprise. J Int Crim Justice 5:69–90

Ohlin JD (2011) Joint intentions to commit international crimes. Chicago J Int Law 11:693–753

Ohlin JD (2014) Searching for the hinterman: in praise of subjective theories of imputation. J Int Crim Justice 12:325–343

Osiel M (2009) Making sense of mass atrocity. Cambridge University Press, Cambridge

Sadler BJ (2006) Shared intentions and shared responsibility (French PA, Wettstein HK (eds)). Midwest Stud Phil 30:115–144

Schabas W (2001) Was genocide committed in Bosnia and Herzegovina? first judgments of the International Criminal Tribunal for the former Yugoslavia. Fordham Int Law J 25:23–53

Schabas W (2005) Darfur and the "odious scourge': The Commission of Inquiry's findings on genocide. Leiden J Int Law 18:871–885

Schabas W (2007) State policy as an element of international crimes. J. Crim Law Criminol 98:953–982

Schabas W (2009) Genocide in international law: the crime of crimes. Cambridge University Press, Cambridge

Schabas W (2012) Unimaginable atrocities: justice, politics, and rights at the war crimes tribunals. Oxford University Press, Oxford

Shapira-Ettinger K (2007) The conundrum of mental states: substantive rules and evidence combined. Cardozo Law Rev 28:2577–2596

Stuckenberg CF (2014) Problems of 'subjective imputation' in domestic and international criminal law. J Int Crim Justice 12:311–323

Triffterer O (2001) Genocide, its particular intent to destroy in whole or in part the group as such. Leiden J Int Law 14:399–408

Vajda MM (2015) Ethnic cleansing as genocide—assessing the Croatian genocide case before the ICJ. Int Crim Law Rev 15:147–169

van Haren MK (2006) The report of the international commission of inquiry on Darfur & genocidal intent—a critical analysis. Neth Int Law Rev 53:205–245 van Sliedregt E (2012a) The curious case of international criminal liability. J Int Crim Justice 10:1171–1188

van Sliedregt E (2012b) Individual criminal responsibility in international law. Oxford University Press, Oxford

Verdirame G (2000) The genocide definition in the jurisprudence of the ad hoc tribunals. Int Comp Law Quarterly 49:578–598

Vest H (2007) A structure-based concept of genocidal intent. J Int Crim Justice 5:781–797

Weigend T (2014) Problems of attribution in international criminal law: a German perspective. J Int Crim Justice 12:253–266

Werle G (2007) German jurisprudence on genocidal intent and the European convention for the protection of human rights and fundamental freedoms. In: Nuotio K (ed) Festschrift in honour of Raimo Lahti. University of Helsinki, Helsinki, Faculty of Law, pp 43–60

Zahar A, Sluiter G (2007) International criminal law: a critical introduction. Oxford University Press, Oxford

Chapter 5
Conclusion

Thus far, I have developed a collective theory of genocidal intent. My discussion began with a critique of individualistic approaches to interpreting the genocidal intent element. I criticized the knowledge-based theory mainly in view of its legal implications of attaching principal liability to subordinate actors. I asked whether there still remains room for aiding and abetting liability of genocide in the territory of the knowledge-based approach. In the context of a systematic genocidal campaign, there should be only a few who lacks knowledge of such overall context of violence, which factually overlaps with the destructive consequences to a significant extent. Thus, in terms of crime of genocide, the applicable scope of the knowledge standard is almost limitless.

My second challenge to the knowledge-based analysis relied heavily on the distinctive feature of the two domestic *mens rea* concepts of 'direct intent/purposely' and 'indirect intent/knowingly'. I grasped that the former is always directed toward the 'main effect', while the latter, by definition, corresponds to a 'side-effect'. I then demonstrated that the 'destruction of a group' should always be perceived as a 'main effect' desired by an actor. Yet, the actual practice of *ad hoc* tribunals where genocidal intent has been primarily inferred from the overall context of genocidal campaigns kept me from proclaiming the victory of the purpose-based theory over its knowledge-based counterpart. How can you infer my mind primarily from the general context which is geographically and temporally far exceeds my personal realm? In this context, I entitled the last section of the analysis of individualistic approaches to genocidal intent as 'Complications and Frustrations'. These observations urged us to depart from the individualistic analysis.

Equipped with a lens of collectivist perspective, we embarked on the study of 'collective genocide' against the backdrop of distinguishing 'conduct level' and 'context level'. Subsequently, we learned that, contrary to the slogan of 'crime of *mens rea*', the crime of genocide seen from a collective standpoint claims itself as a 'crime of collective *actus reus*'. Employing the notion of 'collective genocide', we concluded that the destructive consequence of a substantial part of a protected group at the 'context level' is the gist of genocide. In particular, it was anticipated that, in the borderline cases of genocide in respect of which it is not clear whether the substantiality requirement has been met, the 'concrete threat (to the survival of the group)' would feature in the decision on the substantiality requirement. All these crucial features of the crime of genocide were detected at the 'context level', which led us to a conclusion that individual genocidal intent at the 'conduct level' might not as essential as we have thought thus far in constituting the crime of genocide.

Accordingly we turned our focus to the conceptual counterpart of individual genocidal intent—i.e., 'collective genocidal intent' called by various names such as 'genocidal plan/plan of genocide', 'wider plan to destroy', 'wider-ranging intention to destroy', 'overall intent', and so on in the relevant jurisprudence in the *ad hoc* tribunals. We saw that, without collective genocidal intent, there was no individual genocidal intent. We also took note that what the *ad hoc* tribunals inferred from the overall context of violence had not been individual genocidal intent, but its collective counterpart.

In the course of analyzing the notion of collective genocidal intent, we spotted a possibility of conceptual congruence between 'collective genocidal intent' of genocide and 'common purpose/plan' of JCE. A common characteristic of collective criminality was horizontally linking the two substantive theories of genocide and JCE. It was also noted that both theories share a similar vertical structure: the combinations of 'context level' and 'conduct level' for genocide, and the level of 'JCE members' and that of 'non-JCE members' for JCE. Within this horizontal and vertical structure of both theories, we employed the two sets of parallel notions: 'collective genocidal intent' (objective element of genocide) corresponding to 'common purpose/plan' (objective element of JCE) on one hand, and 'individual genocidal intent' (subjective element of genocide) corresponding to 'shared intent' (subjective element of JCE) on the other.

Within this conceptual framework, we detected the inherent logic of JCE within genocide. Under the conceptual force of the logic of JCE, individual genocidal intent was presumed (and thereby watered down) on the basis of objective features of individual participation, contribution and rank, in the same manner as 'shared intent' is presumed under the JCE doctrine. It was only when the evidentiary weight of such objective aspects of an individual actor is strong enough to convince the triers of fact that they proceed to presume individual genocidal intent. In this way, the catchphrase of the 'crime of *mens rea*' proved empty.

At this juncture, the flow of arguments of this dissertation compelled us to make a difficult observation: genocide being a leadership crime. The weight and importance of collective criminality at the 'context level' (reflected in the two essential notions of 'collective genocide' and 'collective genocidal intent') which forcefully operates through the inherent logic of JCE within genocide left no other option. In this context, admitting principal liability for subordinate actors means *unfair* labeling of criminal liability of leadership actors and subordinate actors by grouping them together without proper differentiation. This would result in a deflation of criminal liability of leadership-level actors, while inflating that of subordinates.[1] At the same time, it was emphasized that this does not exonerate subordinate actors: they can still be convicted as aiders and abettors of genocide. A reference to the crime of aggression (generally considered a typical leadership crime) would help us perceive the new picture of genocide as a leadership crime. A little modification of the crime of aggression part of the ICC Elements of Crimes, reflecting the findings of this dissertation would read as follows:

[Elements of Genocide as a Leadership Crime]

1. The perpetrator planned, prepared, initiated or executed a 'collective genocide'.
2. The perpetrator was a person in a position to exercise control over or to direct the political or military action of the State or an organization which committed the 'collective genocide'.
3. The 'collective genocide', in which a substantial part of a protected group has been destroyed in pursuance of a collective genocidal intent to destroy the group, was committed.

---

[1] *See* Chap. 2, footnote 116 *supra* and accompanying text.

Index

A

Akayesu case, 18–22, 29, 36, 53, 64, 81–83, 86–88, 107–113, 118, 120, 121, 136, 150, 156, 165, 175, 182–185, 189–192, 224

Al Bashir case, 9, 18, 19, 46, 65, 104, 135, 138, 139, 146–149, 151–153, 155, 160, 161

Ambos, Kai, 21–23, 28, 29, 31, 32, 34, 35, 38, 44, 45, 47, 52, 56, 57, 59, 64, 65, 104, 146, 181, 193, 196

B

Bassiouni, M. Cherif, 24–26, 46, 75, 187–189, 215

Blagojević and Jokić case, 19, 20, 34, 42, 123, 175, 200, 214, 220

Boas, Gideon, 219

C

Collective criminality, 172, 197, 203, 216, 219, 224

Common purpose (or common plan), 10, 35, 44, 104, 167, 193, 194, 198–203, 205, 207, 209–212, 220, 222–224, 230

Concrete threat to a group, 9, 146–155, 160, 161, 230

Conduct crime, 54, 141–143, 149, 150, 151

Control theory, 34, 35, 38, 40, 41, 104, 204, 205, 219

Criminal enterprise (joint criminal enterprise or JCE), 6–8, 10, 23, 32, 33, 35, 36, 44, 49, 86, 88–90, 104, 125, 159, 166, 167, 173, 174, 178, 186, 193–204, 206–215, 217–224, 230

in a descriptive sense, 195, 196
in a normative sense, 195–197, 199

D

Darfur, International Commission of Inquiry (or Darfur Report), 9, 21, 24, 128, 154, 173, 176, 179–181

Desire in a broad sense, 8, 40, 45, 62, 78–80, 82, 89, 90

Direct intent (purposely; dolus directus; dolus directus in the first degree; purposely), 5, 8, 16, 19, 28, 40, 45, 50–52, 56, 58–64, 66–69, 71–76, 78, 80, 229

Dolus eventualis, 5, 16, 19, 22, 25, 28, 32, 47, 59, 61–64, 71, 77, 80, 145, 190

Drost, Pieter, 135, 221

Dubost, Charles, 102

Duff, R.A., 17, 63, 64, 71–73, 77, 85, 103

F

Fair labeling, principle of, 23, 35, 43, 44, 225

Finnis, John, 52, 60, 61, 73, 75, 77, 78

Fisher, Kirsten, 191, 197

Fletcher, George, 5, 16, 18, 34, 38–41, 60, 64–66, 77, 91, 101, 129, 142, 144, 145, 159, 174, 180, 191, 196, 197

Foresight (of a consequence), 25, 28, 32, 33, 61, 63, 64, 69, 74, 76, 77, 79, 90

G

Gacumbitsi case, 29, 132, 138, 140, 175, 185

Genocide

© T.M.C. ASSER PRESS and the author 2016
S. Kim, *A Collective Theory of Genocidal Intent*, International Criminal Justice Series 7, DOI 10.1007/978-94-6265-123-4